THE WORKS OF
SIR JOHN VANBRUGH

THE COMPLETE WORKS OF
SIR JOHN VANBRUGH

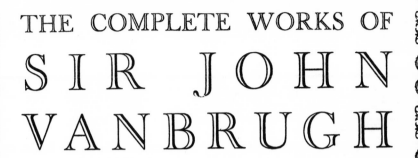

The plays edited by
BONAMY DOBRÉE

The letters edited by
GEOFFREY WEBB

THE THIRD VOLUME *containing*

❡ THE CONFEDERACY ❡ THE MISTAKE

❡ A JOURNEY TO LONDON ❡ THE PROVOK'D HUSBAND

BLOOMSBURY

THE NONESUCH PRESS

16 Great James Street, W.C.

MCMXXVII

AMS PRESS, INC. • NEW YORK • 1967

Reprinted with the permission of
THE BODLEY HEAD LTD.

AMS Press, Inc.
New York, N.Y. 10003
1967

Manufactured in the United States of America

The Contents

THE

CONFEDERACY

A

COMEDY

As it is Acted at the

Queen's Theatre in the

Hay-Market

By Her MAJESTY'S Sworn Servants.

By the Author of *The Relapse, Provok'd Wife,* and *Æsop.*

Source

THIS play is from *Les Bourgeoises à la Mode* of Dancourt, acted in Paris in 1682. It is the fifteenth of that author's pieces. There seems no reason why Vanbrugh should have chosen this play rather than *Le Chevalier à la Mode* or the delightful *Fête de Village*, except the possibility that he may have seen it in Paris.

The translation " follows " the original in Vanbrugh's usual manner, but in this play, after the experiment of *The Country House*, he consistently " improves " upon his original, that is, makes it more realistic and racy of urban life. A few quotations are given below to serve as standards of comparison. As Ward accurately states, " Three scenes in *The Confederacy* belong to Vanbrugh alone: the opening scene of the play, between Mrs. Amlet and Mrs. Cloggit [who is an addition of Vanbrugh's]; the first scene of the third act, between Dick Amlet and his mother; and the second scene of the fifth act, as far as the entrance of the goldsmith." The place is transferred from Paris to London, and the names are changed or Englished, as *Brass* for *Frontin*.

In 1703 Richard Estcourt had produced *The Fair Example; or the Modish Citizens*, which takes a good deal from Dancourt's comedy. *The Fair Example* was, however, printed after *The Confederacy*, to which allusion is made as follows in Estcourt's satirical dedication to Rich:

" Know then, Sir, that you are likely to have Foreign Enemies as well as Domestick, for Monsieur d'Ancour has lately joined in a Confederacy against your House and Interest: It broke out on the 30th of October last, and every Post in *London* and *Westminster* bore News of it. You may remember, most watchful Sir, if these unhappy Troubles have not rendred you incapable, this Piece (for so I must call it in a Dedication) was sent you by me above three Years ago, under this Fair Title of *The Modish Citizens* from *Le Bourgeois Alamode* [sic]. It spoke English enough to be understood upon the Stage, it was (like other works of this kind) acted sometimes, and put by ever since. Now, Sir, this French Refugee being thus entertain'd, and as it were in Articles with you, is gone to t'other House; and tho' you (by Reason of your Calamities) may have slighted it, yet you see one of the most rising Authors of this Age builds very much upon it, and has put it in the Front of this Campaign."

Escourt seems to claim that Rich had a right to translations of *Les Bourgeoises à la Mode* since *The Fair Example* was his. But Vanbrugh owes nothing to Estcourt, whose play is not a translation, but takes certain incidents and characters to weave a quite different plot.

The opening of Dancourt's play may be compared with the parallel passage in Vanbrugh's, namely, Act I from *Enter* Dick.

Le Chevalier.　Hé bien, Frontin! as-tu donné mon billet à Lisette?
Frontin.　J'arrive comme vous, je n'ai encore vu personne; mais j'ai appris en ville une très fâcheuse nouvelle.
Le Chevalier.　Quelle nouvelle? de quoi s'agit-il?
Frontin.　Il faut quitter ce pays-ci.

Le Chevalier. Et la raison?
Frontin. Il s'y forme un orage épouvantable.
Le Chevalier. Comment?
Frontin. On a fait de mauvais rapports à la justice.
Le Chevalier. A la justice! que veux-tu dire?
Frontin. Ce jeune homme a qui vous gagnâtes l'autre jour ces deux mille écus qu'il venoit de toucher pour faire cette compagnie de cavalerie. . . .
Le Chevalier. Hé bien?
Frontin. Il est fâché de les avoir perdus.
Le Chevalier. Tu me dis là une belle nouvelle! Et qui en doute?
Frontin. Ce n'est pas tout; il a eu l'indiscrétion de s'en plaindre.
Le Chevalier. Tant pis pour lui.
Frontin. Tant pis pour vous, car on informe.
Le Chevalier. Que cela ne t'embarrasse point, je m'en tirerai bien d'affaire.
Frontin. Écoutez, vous menez une vie diablement libertine, franchement.
Le Chevalier. Cela commence à me fatiguer, je te l'avoue.
Frontin. Nous sommes furieusement décriés dans Paris.

The following may show Vanbrugh's admirably idiomatic manner:

—Bonjour, Lisette. Ta maîtresse est-elle habillée?
—Oui, mais c'est une grande merveille, et nous n'avons pas coutume d'être si diligentes.
—Eh! sais-tu qu'il est près de midi?

Is your mistress dress'd?
What, already? Is the Fellow drunk?
Why, with Respect to her Looking-Glass, it's almost two.

It cannot be denied that Vanbrugh coarsens. He is innocent of that light, graceful, if slightly metallic quality of the French comedy of the period. He is in some ways nearer Regnard, though he could never have written *Les Folies Amoureuses.* Compare the second scene of the first act, the paragraph " Alas, what signifies beauty and wit . . ." with:

" Non vraiment, ma pauvre Lisette: je n'ose médire personne; je ne puis risquer la moindre petite querelle avec des femmes qui me déplaisent; je suis privée du plaisir de me moquer de mille ridicules. Enfin, Lisette, quand on a de l'esprit, il est bien fâcheux, faute de rang et de naissance, de ne pouvoir le mettre dans tout son jour."

The whole passage from " Why, I dare abuse no body . . ." to ". . . the State I am in. " is a development of the above.

But if Vanbrugh shatters the fragile delicacy of the French he replaces it by a burly volubility, which makes his characters live in the world of flesh and blood rather than in the imaginary, self-contained world of French comedy.

Jasmin. Madame Amelin, votre marchande de modes.
Lisette. C'est de l'argent qu'elle vous demande.
Angelique. Je n'en ai point à lui donner.

Jessamin. Madam, there's the Woman below that sells Paint and Patches, Iron-Bodice, false Teeth, and all sorts of Things to the Ladies; I can't think of her Name.

Flippanta. 'Tis Mrs. *Amlet*, she wants Money.

Clarissa. Well, I han't enough for my self, it's an unreasonable thing she should think I have any for her.

Flippanta. She's a troublesome Jade.

Clarissa. So are all people that come a Dunning.

Sometimes also he introduces some phrases of high comedy which are outside Dancourt's scope. All that passage in Act II where Corinna explains how thinking improves a girl's mind is entirely Vanbrugh's. But then Marianne is innocent, Corinna is not. On the other hand, in the next scene Vanbrugh eliminates Dancourt's comic flavour, for in the French Griffard (Moneytrap) aids Lisette (Flippanta) in describing the horrible thing a husband is, without suspecting that, though married, he could be included in that odious category.

Text

THE text is from the first edition of 1705 (Q), a not very well-printed nor edited text, collated with those in the collected editions of 1719 and 1730. Those of 1751 and 1762 have also been referred to, but throw no light on Q. All variations from Q which have been adopted are noted, besides some divergencies of mild interest which have not been adopted. *The City Wive's Confederacy*, as acted at The Theatres Royal in Drury Lane and Covent Garden, 1779, does not differ except in making certain small cuts, one or two of which are noted. Obvious misprints, of which there are many, such as Hsband for Husband, Ponnd for Pound, have been silently corrected.

Theatrical History

THE *Confederacy* was first acted at Vanbrugh's Theatre in the Haymarket on Tuesday, 30 October, 1705. Genest says it ran for ten days, but this appears to be an error. It was acted on Wednesday, Thursday and Friday of the same week, on Tuesday, 6 November, and repeated on 4 and 26 December. Leigh and Doggett took the parts of Gripe and Moneytrap, and must have contrasted admirably. Leigh was an experienced actor, "of the mercurial kind," who appears to have acted fancifully near exaggeration, but always kept just within bounds. "He had a great variety in his manners, and was famous in very different characters." Doggett, who was naturally of a happy temper, was a comic actor of a rather different, grimmer humour. As Moneytrap he "used to wear an old threadbare black coat, to which he had put new cuffs, pockets, lids and buttons on purpose to make its natural rustiness more conspicuous: the neck was so stuffed as to make him appear round-shouldered and give his head the greater prominency: his square-toed shoes were large enough to buckle over those he wore in common, which made his legs appear smaller than they really were. Booth, not yet at the height of his fame, played Dick, a part which no doubt helped his rapid rise in the popular favour.

Mrs. Barry must have given every atom of comic value to the part of Clarissa by acting it in the manner of an indomitable, wilful woman, determined to carry everything before her by sheer force of personality. "In characters of greatness she had a presence of elevated dignity, her mien and motion superb, and gracefully majestick; her voice full, clear and strong, so that no violence of passion could be too much for her," and if her greatest triumphs were in tragic parts, her manner must have suited her admirably, for though no longer beautiful, she was "alert, easy, genteel." Mrs. Bracegirdle was her maid, and her black-eyed grace, mingled with the impertinence she must have known how to put into her part, no doubt suited her mistress excellently. She was not to remain on the stage much longer, and possibly now only acted to oblige Congreve. Mrs. Porter was much the friend of Mrs. Betterton and Mrs. Bracegirdle.

The play would certainly have been more successful had the acoustics of the theatre been better. It was acted again at that theatre on 12 June, 1706, and on 1 December, with Norris as Moneytrap, Bowen as Gripe. It was not seen again until revived at Drury Lane on 17 and 19 December, 1709, with Clarissa played by Mrs. Knight, a part she kept for some time; twice in January, 1710, and once in June, besides a performance at Greenwich in September, for Spiller's benefit, Powell playing Dick. It was seen again at Drury Lane in 1711, with Doggett in his old part; Corinna Mrs. Santlow: 1712, 1713 more than once each year; and in 1715 it had a run of three days at Lincoln's Inn Fields. Between then and 1739 it was acted at Drury Lane, Lincoln's Inn Fields and Covent Garden just over fifty times, nearly every performance being a separate revival. There were, however, some gaps, namely, between 1715 and 1719, and 1720 and 1725, when it was erroneously advertised as "not acted 7 years." Then Spiller played Moneytrap; Hippesley Gripe; Mrs. Younger Flippanta; and Mrs. Egleton (Mrs. Giffard) Mrs. Amlet.

On 24 April, 1729, Chapman played Brass; Walker Dick; Hippisley Moneytrap; Mrs. Bullock Clarissa; Mrs. Younger Flippanta. Pinkethman took to Gripe in 1732. On 11 March, 1734, it was acted at Drury Lane for the benefit of Mrs. Clive, who played Flippanta. Macklin played Brass; Norris Moneytrap; Mrs. Horton Clarissa, with Mrs. Willis in her original part of Mrs. Amlet. This brilliant cast largely reappeared again in 1738, and in 1739 the play was acted three times, with Macklin and Mrs. Clive in their old parts; but Griffin played Moneytrap; Mrs. Pritchard Araminta; and Mrs. Macklin made her first appearance as Mrs. Amlet.

It was acted once in 1740, four times in 1741, several times at both Covent Garden and Drury Lane in 1742, once for the benefit of Mrs. Clive, who played Clarissa, and at least once every year until 1746, when Foote, a superb mimic, though Dr. Johnson did not think so, made on 3 March at Drury Lane a success as Dick, with Yates as Moneytrap and Peg Woffington as Clarissa. On 18 November, 1743, it was billed at Covent Garden as " not acted 5 years." Hill played Dick; Mrs. Horton Clarissa; Mrs. Vincent Flippanta; Miss Hippisley Corinna. Brass was played by Chapman. He was " much and justly admired in parts of absurd impudence, of bold intrepidity, and pert foppery." He would obviously be a good Brass, for which indeed he was celebrated, as he was for the Fop in *Æsop*.

It continued to be one of the popular, but not very popular, stock plays, though it was acted nearly every year, and often in Ireland. At Drury Lane on 1 October, 1747, there was a revival with a strong cast, Macklin playing Brass; Havard Dick; Yates Moneytrap; Clarissa was played by Mrs. Woffington; Flippanta by Mrs. Clive; Corinna first by Mrs. Green and later by Miss Hippisley. On 27 and 29 October, 1759, it appeared at the same theatre as " not acted 8 years," with King as Brass, Palmer as Dick, Miss Pope, " the perfect gentlewoman as opposed to the fine lady of comedy," in the part of Corinna, with Wilkinson as Mrs. Amlet, though this part was taken by Mrs. Bradshaw when the play was repeated on 9 January. King was a famous Brass:

> Bred up in modest lore,
> Bashful and young he sought Hibernia's shore;
> Hibernia, fam'd, 'bove ev'ry other grace,
> For matchless intrepidity of face.
> From her his Features caught the gen'rous flame,
> And bid defiance to all sense of shame:
> Tutor'd by her all rivals to surpass,
> 'Mongst Drury's sons he comes, and shines in Brass.

Moneytrap was played by Yates, Clarissa by Mrs. Pritchard, Flippanta by Mrs. Clive. Mrs. Davies played Araminta at Drury Lane, and on 8 December, 1769, King and Palmer reappeared in their old parts, but Flippanta was played by Miss Pope and Corinna by Mrs. Abington, who was shortly to add to her fame by creating Lady Teazle. Another brilliant revival took place at this theatre on 9 April, 1778, for the benefit of Miss Pope, who acted Flippanta. King and Palmer were in their old parts, as was Mrs. Abington; Parsons played Moneytrap; Moody Gripe; Mrs. Bulkeley Clarissa; and Mrs. Hopkins Mrs. Amlet. It was revived there on 7 November, 1782, as " not acted 6 years," and continued to be repeated at intervals until the end of the century, a strong cast taking part in it on 24 November, 1796, with Palmer, by now a famous Sir Peter Teazle, who acted it with " consummate art," as Brass, Bannister junior as Dick, both of them having played this part at the Haymarket in 1785, where Parsons had once more appeared as Moneytrap; but on this occasion Suett, who used to alter his characters by the variety of his wigs, took the part. Miss Pope again acted Flippanta and Miss Farren acted Corinna. Bannister " did not go out of himself to take possession of his part, but put it on over his ordinary dress, like a *surtout*, snug, warm and comfortable. He let his personal character appear through; and it was one great charm of his acting." With him on this occasion was associated in the part of Corinna Mrs. Jordan, " the child of Nature, whose voice was a cordial to the heart because it came from it, rich, full, like the luscious juice of the ripe grape. . . . Her person was large, soft, and generous like her soul."

During the last fifteen years of the century it was fairly popular at the Theatre Royal, Haymarket, but it seems to have dropped out of the Covent Garden repertory, where there had, however, been successful performances earlier in the century. On 13 May, 1762, it was billed as " not acted 5 years," when Shuter played Moneytrap and Mrs. Pitt played Mrs. Amlet. They repeated these parts in 1770 with Yates, who was now getting old, as Brass, for the first time only, and Mrs. Bulkeley as Corinna; but on 16 December, 1807, it was revived for two performances at that theatre: " the gay, fluttering, hair-brained Lewis, he that was called ' Gentleman Lewis,' " was Brass, Munden was Moneytrap, Emery was Gripe; Mrs. C. Kemble played Clarissa; Mrs. Mattocks Flippanta; and Miss Morton Corinna. Munden must have been as good a Moneytrap as Doggett: " when you think he has exhausted his battery of looks, in unaccountable warfare with your gravity, suddenly he sprouts out an entirely new set of features, like Hydra. . . . In the grand grotesque of farce, Munden stands out as single and unaccompanied as Hogarth. . . . The gusto of Munden antiquates and ennobles what it touches . . . he stands wondering, amid the commonplace materials of life, like primæval man with the sun and stars about him."

On 12 January, 1810, the Drury Lane Company played *The Confederacy*, with R. Palmer and Melvin as Dick and Brass, Mathews as Gripe, and Dowton as Moneytrap. A contemporary critic wrote: " The greatest living comedian out of the direct pale of gentility, though we by no means insinuate that he is vulgar, appears to us to be Dowton." Hazlitt thought poorly of him, but wrote on the other hand " there were Bob and Jack Palmer, the Brass and Dick of The Confederacy; the one the pattern of an elder, the other of a younger brother." Dowton played Moneytrap again at Drury Lane on 29 May, 1817, with Harley as Brass to the Flippanta of Miss Kelly, " a shrewd, clever, arch, lively girl; tingles all over with suppressed sensibility; licks her lips at mischief, bites her words in two, or lets a sly meaning out of the corner of her eyes."

Beginning with 10 November, 1819, it was acted four times at Covent Garden, with Fawcett as Brass, and Jones as Dick. Emery played Gripe, and Moneytrap was played by W. Farren. He was especially brilliant as " crusty old bachelors, jealous old husbands," etc. " He had no geniality. . . . His face was handsome, with a wonderful hanging underlip, capable of a great variety of expression; he had a penetrating voice, a clear articulation, a singularly expressive laugh." He was a finished artist, and played the old parts in the old manner. Mrs. Faucit played Araminta, Mrs. Davenport an old part of hers, Mrs. Amlet, while Corinna was played by Miss Foote. She was not a great actress, but she was " young, beautiful, intelligent," and a great fuss was made about her. She married the Earl of Harrington. It was replayed at Drury Lane for two performances, the first being on 2 November, 1825, when Mrs. Yates played Clarissa; Miss Kelly Corinna; and Dowton was seen in his old part of Moneytrap. The play then seems to have gone out of the stock repertory, but it is the one play of Vanbrugh's of which we can say that it still holds the stage in this century. It was acted at the Royalty Theatre from 28 November, 1904, and at the Playhouse, Oxford, from 1 March till 6 March, 1926, with Richard Goolden and Alan Napier as Gripe and Moneytrap and Miss Prudence Vanbrugh in the part of Clarissa.

PROLOGUE

Spoken by a Shabby Poet.

YE Gods! What Crime had my poor Father done,
  That you should make a Poet of his Son?
Or is't for some great Services of his,
Y'are pleas'd to Compliment his Boy——with this?
                                    [Shewing his Crown of Laurel.

The Honour, I must needs confess, is great,
If, with his Crown, you'd tell him where to eat.
Tis well——But I have more Complaints—look here!
                                    [Shewing his ragged Coat.

Hark ye: D'ye think this Suit good Winter Wear?
In a Cold Morning; whu——at a Lord's Gate,
How you have let the Porter let me wait?
You'll say, perhaps, you knew I'd get no Harm,
You'd giv'n me Fire enough to keep me Warm.
Ah——
A World of Blessings to that Fire we owe;
Without it I'd ne'er made this Princely Show.
I have a Brother too, now in my Sight,   [Looking behind the scenes.
A busie Man amongst us here to Night.
Your Fire has made him play a Thousand Pranks,
For which, no doubt you've had his daily Thanks;
He'as thank'd you, first, for all his Decent Plays,
Where he so nick'd it, when he Writ for Praise.
Next for his meddling with some Folks in Black,
And bringing Souse——a Priest upon his Back;
For building Houses here t'oblige the Peers,
And fetching all their House about his Ears;
For a new Play, he'as now thought fit to write,
To sooth the Town——which they—will damn to Night.

These Benefits are such, no Man can doubt
But he'll go on, and set your Fancy out,
'Till for Reward of all his Noble Deeds,
At last like other sprightly Folks he speeds:
Has this great Recompence fix'd on his Brow
As fam'd Parnassus; has your Leave to Bow,
And walk about the Streets—Equipp'd——as I am now.

Dramatis Personæ

MEN.

Gripe,
Moneytrap, } Two rich Money Scriveners. { Mr. *Leigh*.
Mr. *Dogget*.
Dick, a Gamester, Son to Mrs. *Amlet*, Mr. *Booth*.
Brass, his Companion, passes for his *Valet de* } Mr. *Pack*.
Chambre.
Clip, a Goldsmith. Mr. *Mimes*.
Jessamin, Foot-boy to *Clarissa*.

WOMEN.

Clarissa, Wife to *Gripe*, an expensive luxurious } Mrs. *Barry*.
Woman, a great Admirer of Quality.
Araminta, Wife to *Moneytrap*, very intimate } Mrs. *Porter*.
with *Clarissa*, of the same Humour.
Corinna, Daughter to *Gripe* by a former Wife,
a good Fortune, young, and kept very close } Mrs. *Bradshaw*.
by her Father.
Flippanta, *Clarissa*'s Maid. Mrs. *Bracegirdle*.
Mrs. *Amlet*, a Seller of all Sorts of private } Mrs. *Willis*.
Affairs to the Ladies.
Mrs. *Cloggit*, her Neighbour. Mrs. *Baker*.

SCENE, in LONDON.

THE
CONFEDERACY

ACT I. SCENE I.

SCENE, *Covent Garden.*

Enter Mrs. Amlet *and Mrs.* Cloggit, *meeting.*

Aml. GOOD Morrow, Neighbour; good Morrow, Neighbour *Cloggit*; How do's all at your House this Morning?

Clog. Thank you kindly, Mrs. *Amlet*, thank you kindly; how do you do I pray?

Aml. At the old Rate, Neighbour, poor and honest; these are hard Times good lack.

Clog. If they are hard with you, what are they with us? You have a good Trade going, all the great Folks in Town help off with your Merchandize.

Aml. Yes, they do help us off with 'em indeed; they buy all.

Clog. And pay?

Aml. For some.

Clog. Well, 'tis a thousand Pities, Mrs. *Amlet*, they are not as ready at one, as they are at t'other: For, not to wrong 'em, they give very good Rates.

Aml. O for that, let us do 'em Justice, Neighbour; they never make two Words upon the Price, all they haggle about is the Day of Payment.

Clog. There's all the Dispute, as you say.

Aml. But that's a wicked one: For my part, Neighbour, I'm just tir'd off my Legs with trotting after 'em; besides it eats out all our Profit. Would you believe it, Mrs. *Cloggit*, I have worn out four Pair of Pattins, with following my old Lady *Youthful*, for One Sett of false Teeth, and but Three Pots of Paint.

Clog. Look you there now.

Aml. If they would but once let me get enough by 'em, to keep a Coach to carry me a Dunning after 'em, there would be some Conscience in it.

Clog. Ay, that were something. But now you talk of Conscience, Mrs. *Amlet*, how do you speed amongst your City Customers?

Aml. My City Customers! Now by my truth, Neighbour, between the

City and the Court (with Reverence be it spoken) there's not a————to chuse. My Ladies in the City, in Times past, were as full of Gold as they were of Religion, and as punctual in their Payments as they were in their Prayers; but since they have set their Minds upon Quality, adieu one, adieu t'other, their Money and their Consciences are gone, Heav'n knows where. There is not a Goldsmith's Wife to be found in Town, but's as hard-hearted as an ancient Judge, and as poor as a towering Dutchess.

Clog. But what the murrain have they to do with Quality, why don't their Husbands make e'm mind their Shops?

Aml. Their Husbands! their husbands say'st thou, woman? Alack, alack, they mind their Husbands, Neighbour, no more than they do a Sermon.

Clog. Good lack a Day, that Women born of sober Parents, should be prone to follow ill Examples: But now we talk of Quality, when did you hear of your son *Richard*, Mrs. *Amlet?* My daughter *Flipp* says she met him t'other Day in a lac'd Coat, with three fine Ladies, his Footman at his Heels, and as gay as a Bridegroom.

Aml. Is it possible? Ah the Rogue! well Neighbour, all's well that ends well; but *Dick* will be hang'd.

Clog. That were Pity.

Aml. Pity indeed; for he's a hopeful young Man to look on; but he leads a Life,——Well——where he has it Heav'n knows; but they say, he pays his Club with the best of 'em. I have seen him but once these Three Months, Neighbour, and then the Varlet wanted Money; but I bid him march, and march he did to some purpose; for in less than an Hour back comes my Gentleman into the House, walks to and fro in the Room, with his Wigg over his Shoulder, his Hat on one Side, whistling a Minuet, and tossing a Purse of Gold from one Hand to t'other, with no more Respect (Heav'n bless us!) than if it had been an Orange. Sirrah, says I, where have you got that? He answers me never a Word, but sets his Arms a kimbo, cocks his saucy Hat in my Face, turns about upon his ungracious Heel, as much as to say Kiss—and I've never set Eye on him since.

Clog. Look you there now; to see what the Youth of this Age are come to!

Aml. See what they will come to, Neighbour. Heav'n shield, I say; but *Dick's* upon the Gallop. Well, I must bid you good Morrow; I'm going where I doubt I shall meet but a sorry Welcome.

Clog. To get in some old Debt, I'll warrant you?

Aml. Neither better nor worse.

Clog. From a Lady of Quality?

Aml. No, she's but a Scrivener's Wife; but she lives as well, and pays as ill, as the stateliest Countess of 'em all. [*Exeunt several ways.*

Enter Brass *solus.*

Brass. Well, surely thro' the World's wide Extent there never appear'd so impudent a Fellow as my School-fellow *Dick*; pass himself upon the Town for a Gentleman, drop into all the beſt Company with an easie Air, as if his natural Element were in the Sphere of Quality; when the Rogue had a Kettle-drum to his Father, who was hang'd for robbing a Church, and has a Pedlar to his Mother, who carries her Shop under her Arm. But here he comes.

Enter Dick.

Dick. Well, *Brass*, what News? Haſt thou given my Letter to *Flippanta?*

Brass. I'm but juſt come; I han't knockt at the Door yet. But I have a damn'd Piece of News for you.

Dick. As how?

Brass. We muſt quit this Country.

Dick. We'll be hang'd firſt.

Brass. So you will if you ſtay.

Dick. Why, what's the matter?

Brass. There's a Storm a coming.

Dick. From whence?

Brass. From the worſt Point in the Compass; the Law.

Dick. The Law! Why what have I to do with the Law?

Brass. Nothing; and therefore it has something to do with you.

Dick. Explain.

Brass. You know you cheated a young Fellow at Picket t'other Day, of the Money he had to raise his Company.

Dick. Well, what then?

Brass. Why, he's sorry he loſt it.

Dick. Who doubts that?

Brass. Ay, but that is not all, he's such a Fool to think of complaining on't.

Dick. Then I muſt be so Wise to ſtop his Mouth.

Brass. How?

Dick. Give him a little back; if that won't do, Strangle him.

Brass. You are very quick in your Methods.

Dick. Men muſt be so that will dispatch Business.

Brass. Hark you, Colonel, your Father dy'd in's Bed?

Dick. He might have done, if he had not been a Fool.

Brass. Why, he robb'd a Church.

Dick. Ay, but he forgot to make sure of the Sexton.

Brass. Are not you a great Rogue?

Dick. Or I should wear worse Cloaths.

Brass. Hark you, I would advise you to change your Life.

Dick. And turn Ballad-Singer.

Brass. Not so neither.

Dick. What then?

Brass. Why, if you can get this young Wench, reform and live honeſt.

Dick. That's the way to be ſtarv'd.

Brass. No, she has Money enough to buy you a good Place, and pay me into the Bargain for helping her to so good a Match. You have but this Throw left to save you, for you are not ignorant, Youngſter, that your Morals begin to be pretty well known about Town; have a care your noble Birth and your honourable Relations are not discover'd too; there needs but that to have you toss'd in a Blanket, for the Entertainment of the firſt Company of Ladies you intrude into; and then, like a dutiful Son, you may daggle about with your Mother, and sell Paint. She's old and weak, and wants some Body to carry her Goods after her. How like a Dog will you look, with a Pair of Plod Shoes, your Hair cropp'd up to your Ears, and a Band-Box under your Arm?

Dick. Why faith, *Brass,* I think thou art in the right on't; I muſt fix my Affairs quickly, or Madam Fortune will be playing some of her Bitch Tricks with me. Therefore I'll tell thee what we'll do; we'll pursue this old Rogue's Daughter heartily; we'll cheat his Family to purpose, and they shall atone for the reſt of Mankind.

Brass. Have at her then, I'll about your Business presently.

Dick. One Kiss——and Success attend thee.   [*Exit Dick.*

Brass. A great Rogue——Well, I say nothing. But when I have got the thing into a good Poſture, he shall Sign and Seal, or I'll have him tumbled out of the House, like a Cheese. Now for *Flippanta.*

                                                    [*He knocks.*

Enter Flippanta.

Flip. Who's that? *Brass!*

Brass. Flippanta!

Flip. What want you, Rogue's Face?

Brass. Is your Miſtress dress'd?

Flip. What, already? Is the Fellow drunk?

Brass. Why, with Respeᵭ to her Looking-Glass, it's almoſt Two.

Flip. What then, Fool?

Brass. Why then it's time for the Miſtress of the House to come down, and look after her Family.

Flip. Prithee don't be an Owl. Those that go to Bed at Night may rise in the Morning; we that go to Bed in the Morning rise in the Afternoon.

Brass. When does she make her Visits then?

Flip. By Candle-light; it helps off a muddy Complexion; we Women hate inquisitive Sunshine: But do you know that my Lady is going to turn good Huswife?

Brass. What, is she going to die?

Flip. Die?

Brass. Why, that's the only way to save Money for her Family.

Flip. No; but she has thought of a Project to save Chair-hire.

Brass. As how?

Flip. Why all the Company she us'd to keep abroad, she now intends shall meet at her own House. Your Master has advis'd her to set up a Basset-Table.

Brass. Nay, if he advis'd her to't, it's right; but has she acquainted her Husband with it yet?

Flip. What to do? When the Company meet he'll see them.

Brass. Nay, that's true, as you say; he'll know it soon enough.

Flip. Well, I must be gone; have you any Business with my Lady?

Brass. Yes; as Ambassador from *Araminta*, I have a Letter for her.

Flip. Give it me.

Brass. Hold,——and as First Minister of State to the Colonel, I have an Affair to Communicate to thee.

Flip. What is't? quick.

Brass. Why———he's in love.

Flip. With what?

Brass. A Woman——and her Money together.

Flip. Who is she?

Brass. Corinna.

Flip. What would he be at?

Brass. At her——if she's at Leisure.

Flip. Which way?

Brass. Honourably——He has order'd me to demand her of thee in Marriage.

Flip. Of me?

Brass. Why, when a Man of Quality has a Mind to a City Fortune, wou'dst have him apply to her Father and Mother?

Flip. No.

Brass. No, so I think: Men of our End of the Town are better bred than to use Ceremony. With a long Perriwig we strike the Lady, with a you know what we soften the Maid, and when the Parson has done his Job, we open the Affair to the Family: Will you slip this Letter into her Prayer-Book, my little Queen? It's a very passionate one——It's seal'd with a Heart and a Dagger; you may see by that what he intends to do with himself.

Flip. Are there any verses in it? If not, I won't touch it.

Brass. Not one word in prose; it's dated in Rhime.   [*She takes it.*

Flip. Well, but—have you brought nothing else?

Brass. Gad forgive me; I'm the forgetfulleſt Dog——I have a Letter for you too——here——'tis in a Purse, but it's in Prose, you won't touch it.

Flip. Yes, hang it, it is not good to be too dainty.

Brass. How useful a Virtue is Humility! Well, Child, we shall have an Answer to Morrow, shan't we?

Flip. I can't promise you that. For our young Gentlewoman is not so often in my way, as she would be. Her Father (who is a Citizen from the Foot to the Forehead of him) lets her seldom Converse with her Mother-in-Law and me, for fear she should learn the Airs of a Woman of Quality. But I'll take the firſt Occasion: See there's my Lady, go in and deliver your Letter to her.   [*Exeunt.*

SCENE [II], *a Parlour.*

Enter Clarissa, *follow'd by* Flippanta *and* Brass.

Clar. No Messages this Morning from any Body, *Flippanta?* Lard, how dull that is? O, there's *Brass:* I did not see thee, *Brass.* What News doſt thou bring?

Brass. Only a Letter from *Araminta,* Madam.

Clar. Give it me——open it for me, *Flippanta,* I am so lazy to Day.
          [*Sitting down.*

Brass. To Flip.] Be sure now you deliver my Maſter's as carefully as I do this.

Flip. Don't trouble thy self, I'm no Novice.

Clar. to *Brass.*] 'Tis well; there needs no Answer, since she'll be here so soon.

Brass. Your Ladyship has no farther Commands then?

Clar. Not at this time, honeſt, *Brass. Flippanta!*   [*Exit* Brass.

Flip. Madam.

Clar. My Husband's in Love.

Flip. In Love?

Clar. With *Araminta.*

Flip. Impossible.

Clar. This Letter from her, is to give me an Account of it.

Flip. Methinks you are not very much alarm'd.

Clar. No: Thou knowſt I'm not much tortur'd with Jealousie.

Flip. Nay, you are much in the right on't, Madam, for Jealousie's a City Passion; 'tis a Thing unknown amongst People of Quality.

Clar. Fey: A Woman must indeed be of a mechanick Mold, who is either troubled or pleas'd with any thing her Husband can do to her. Prithee mention him no more; 'tis the dullest Theme.

Flip. 'Tis splenatick indeed. But when once you open your Basset-Table, I hope that will put him out of your Head.

Clar. Alas, *Flippanta*, I begin to grow weary even of the Thoughts of that too.

Flip. How so?

Clar. Why I have thought on't a Day and a Night already, and Four and Twenty Hours, thou know'st, is enough to make one weary of any Thing.

Flip. Now by my Conscience, you have more Woman in you than all your Sex together: You never know what you would have.

Clar. Thou mistak'st the Thing quite. I always know what I lack, but I am never pleas'd with what I have. The Want of a Thing is perplexing enough, but the Possession of it is intolerable.

Flip. Well, I don't know what you are made of, but other Women would think themselves blest in your Case; handsome, witty, lov'd by every body, and of so happy a Composure, to care a Fig for no body. You have no one Passion, but that of your Pleasures; and you have in me a Servant devoted to all your Desires, let 'em be as extravagant as they will: Yet all this is nothing; you can still be out of Humour.

Clar. Alas, I have but too much Cause.

Flip. Why what have you to complain of?

Clar. Alas, I have more Subjects for Spleen than One: Is it not a most horrible Thing that I should be but a Scrivener's Wife?——Come—— don't flatter me, don't you think Nature design'd me for something, *plus elevée.*

Flip. Nay, that's certain; but on t'other side, methinks you ought to be in some measure content, since you live like a Woman of Quality, tho' you are none.

Clar. O fey; the very Quintessence of it is wanting.

Flip. What's that?

Clar. Why, I dare abuse no body: I'm afraid to affront People, tho' I don't like their Faces; or to ruin their Reputations, tho' they picque me to it, by taking ever so much Pains to preserve 'em: I dare not raise a Lie of a Man, tho' he neglects to make love to me; nor report a Woman to be a Fool, tho' she's handsomer than I am. In short, I dare not so much as bid my Footman kick the People out of Doors, tho' they come to ask me for what I owe 'em.

Flip. All this is very hard indeed.

Clar. Ah, *Flippanta*, the Perquisites of Quality are of an unspeakable Value.

Flip. They are of some Use, I muſt confess; but we muſt not expect to have every Thing. You have Wit and Beauty, and a Fool to your Husband: Come, come madam, that's a good Portion for one.

Clar. Alas, what signifies Beauty and Wit, when one dares neither jilt the Men, nor abuse the Women? 'Tis a sad thing, *Flippanta*, when Wit's confin'd, 'tis worse than the Rising of the Lights; I have been sometimes almoſt choak'd with Scandal, and durſt not cough it up for want of being a Countess.

Flip. Poor Lady!

Clar. O! Liberty is a fine Thing, *Flippanta*; it's a great Help in Conversation to have Leave to say what one will. I have seen a Woman of Quality, who has not had one Grain of Wit, entertain a whole Company the moſt agreeably in the World, only with her Malice. But 'tis in vain to repine, I can't mend my Condition, 'till my Husband dies: so I'll say no more on't, but think of making the moſt of the State I am in.

Flip. That's your beſt way, Madam: And in Order to it, pray consider how you'll get some ready Money to set your Basset-Table a going; for that's necessary.

Clar. Thou say'ſt true; but what Trick I shall play my Husband to get some, I don't know: For my Pretence of losing my Diamond Necklace has put the Man into such a Passion, I'm afraid he won't hear Reason.

Flip. No matter; he begins to think 'tis loſt in earneſt: So I fancy you may venture to sell it, and raise Money that way.

Clar. That can't be, for he has left odious Notes with all the Goldsmiths in Town.

Flip. Well, we muſt pawn it then.

Clar. I'm quite tyr'd with dealing with those Pawnbrokers.

Flip. I'm afraid you'll continue the Trade a great while, for all that.

[*Aside.*

Enter Jessamin.

Jess. Madam, there's the Woman below that sells Paint and Patches, Iron-Bodice, false Teeth, and all sorts of Things to the Ladies; I can't think of her Name.

Flip. 'Tis Mrs. *Amlet*, she wants Money.

Clar. Well, I han't enough for my self, it's an unreasonable thing she should think I have any for her.

Flip. She's a troublesome Jade.

Clar. So are all people that come a Dunning.

Flip. What will you do with her?

Clar. I have juſt now thought on't. She's very rich, that Woman is, *Flippanta*, I'll borrow some Money of her.

Flip. Borrow? sure you jeſt, Madam.

Clar. No, I'm in earneſt; I give thee Commission to do it for me.

Flip. Me?

Clar. Why doſt thou ſtare, and look so ungainly? don't I speak to be understood?

Flip. Yes, I underſtand you well enough; but Mrs. *Amlet*——

Clar. But Mrs. *Amlet* muſt lend me some Money, where shall I have any to pay her else?

Flip. That's true; I never thought of that truly. But here she is.

Enter Mrs. Amlet.

Clar. How d'you do? How d'you do, Mrs. *Amlet?* I han't seen you these Thousand Years, and yet I believe I'm down in your Books.

Aml. O, Madam, I don't come for that, alack.

Flip. Good-morrow, Mrs. *Amlet.*

Aml. Good-morrow, Mrs. *Flippanta.*

Clar. How much am I indebted to you, Mrs. *Amlet?*

Aml. Nay, if your Ladyship desires to see your Bill, I believe I may have it about me.——There Madam, if it ben't too much Fatigue to you to look it over.

Clar. Let me see it, for I hate to be in Debt, where I am oblig'd to pay. [*Aside.*]——*Reads.*] Imprimis, *For bolſtering out the Countess of* Crump's *left Hip.*————O fie, this does not belong to me.

Aml. I beg your Ladyship's Pardon. I miſtook indeed; 'tis a Countess's Bill I have writ out to little purpose. I furnish'd her Two Years ago with Three Pair of Hips, and am not paid for 'em yet. But some are better Cuſtomers than some. There's your Ladyship's Bill, Madam.

Clar. For the Idea of a new invented Commode.————Ay, this may be mine, but 'tis of a prepoſterous Length. Do you think I can waſte Time to read every Article, Mrs. *Amlet?* I'd as lief read a Sermon.

Aml. Alack a Day, there's no need of fatiguing your self at that Rate; caſt an Eye only, if your Honour pleases, upon the Sum Total.

Clar. Total; Fifty Six pound—and odd things.

Flip. But Six and Fifty Pound?

Aml. Nay, another Body would have made it twice as much, but there's a Blessing goes along with a moderate Profit.

Clar. Flippanta, go to my Cashier, let him give you Six and Fifty Pound. Make haſte: Don't you hear me? Six and Fifty Pound. Is it so difficult to be comprehended?

Flip. No, Madam, I, I comprehend Six and Fifty Pound, but——

Clar. But go fetch it then.

Flip. What she means, I don't know; [*Aside.*] but I shall, I suppose, before I bring her the Money. [*Exit* Flip.

Clar. [*Setting her Hair in a Pocket-Glass.*] The Trade you follow gives you a great deal of trouble, Mrs. *Amlet.*

Aml. Alack a Day, a World of Pain, Madam, and yet there's small Profit, as your Honour sees by your Bill.

Clar. Poor Woman! Sometimes you make great Losses, Mrs. *Amlet?*

Aml. I have Two Thousand Pounds owing me, of which I shall never get Ten Shillings.

Clar. Poor Woman! You have a great Charge of Children, Mrs. *Amlet?*

Aml. Only one wicked Rogue, Madam, who I think will break my Heart.

Clar. Poor Woman!

Aml. He'll be hang'd, Madam——that will be the End of him. Where he gets it Heav'n knows, but he's always shaking his Heels with the Ladies, and his Elbows with the Lords. He's as Fine as a Prince, and as Gim as the beſt of 'em; but the ungracious Rogue tells all he comes near that his Mother is dead, and I am but his Nurse.

Clar. Poor Woman!

Aml. Alas, Madam, he's like the reſt of the World; every Body's for appearing to be more than they are, and that ruins all.

Clar. Well, Mrs. *Amlet*, you'll excuse me, I have a little Business, *Flippanta* will bring you your Money presently. Adieu, Mrs. *Amlet.*

[*Exit* Clarissa.

Aml. I return your Honour many Thanks.
[*Sola.*] Ah, there's my good Lady, not so much as read her Bill; if the reſt were like her, I should soon have Money enough to go as Fine as *Dick* himself.

Enter Dick.

Dick. Sure *Flippanta* muſt have given my Letter by this time; [*Aside.*] I long to know how it has been receiv'd.

Aml. Misericord! what do I see?

Dick. Fiends and Hags——the Witch my Mother!

Aml. Nay, 'tis he; ay, my poor *Dick*, what art thou doing here?

Dick. What a Misfortune! [*Aside.*

Aml. Good Lard! how thou art bravely deck'd. But it's all one, I am thy Mother ſtill; and tho' thou art a wicked Child, Nature will speak I love thee ſtill; ah *Dick*, my poor *Dick*. [*Embracing him.*

Dick. Blood and Thunder! will you ruin me? [*Breaking from her.*

Aml. Ah, the blasphemous Rogue, how he swears!

Dick. You deſtroy all my Hopes.

Aml. Will your Mother's Kiss deſtroy you, Varlet? Thou art an ungracious Bird; kneel down, and ask me Blessing, Sirrah.

Dick. Death and Furies!

Aml. Ah, he's a proper young Man, see what a Shape he has; ah, poor Child.   [*Running to Embrace him, he still avoiding her.*

Dick. Oons keep off, the Woman's mad. If any Body comes, my Fortune's Lost.

Aml. What fortune? ha? speak Graceless. Ah *Dick*, thou'lt be hang'd, *Dick.*

Dick. Good dear mother now, don't call me *Dick* here.

Aml. Not call thee *Dick!* Is it not thy Name? What shall I call thee? Mr. *Amlet?* ha! Art not thou a presumptuous Rascal? Hark you, Sirrah, I hear of your Tricks; you disown me for your Mother, and say I'm but your Nurse. Is not this true?

Dick. No, I love you; I respect you; [*taking her hand.*] I am all Duty. But if you discover me here, you ruin the fairest Prospect that Man ever had.

Aml. What Prospect? ha! Come, this is a Lie now.

Dick. No, my honour'd Parent, what I say is true, I'm about a great Fortune. I'll bring you home a Daughter-in-Law, in a Coach and Six Horses, if you'll but be quiet: I can't tell you more now.

Aml. Is it possible?

Dick. 'Tis true, by *Jupiter.*

Aml. My dear Lad——

Dick. For Heaven's sake——

Aml. But tell me, *Dick*——

Dick. I'll follow you home in a Moment, and tell you all.

Aml. What a Shape is there——

Dick. Pray Mother go.

Aml. I must receive some Money here first, which shall go for thy Wedding Dinner.

Dick. Here's some Body coming; S'death, she'll betray me.
                              [*He makes Signs to his Mother.*

Enter Flippanta.

Dick. Good Morrow, dear *Flippanta*; how do all the Ladies within?

Flip. At your Service, Colonel; as far at least as my Interest goes.

Aml. Colonel?—Law you now how *Dick*'s respected.   [*Aside.*

Dick. Waiting for thee, *Flippanta*, I was making Acquaintance with this old Gentlewoman here.

Aml. The pretty Lad; he's as impudent as a Page.   [*Aside.*

Dick. Who is this good Woman, *Flippanta?*

Flip. A Gin of all Trades; an old daggling Cheat, that hobbles about from House to House to Bubble the Ladies of their Money. I have a small Business of your's in my pocket, Colonel.

Dick. An answer to my Letter?

Flip. So quick indeed? No, it's your Letter it self.

Dick. Haſt thou not given it then yet?

Flip. I han't had an Opportunity; but 'twon't be long firſt. Won't you go in and see my Lady?

Dick. Yes, I'll go make her a short Visit. But, dear *Flippanta*, don't forget: My Life and Fortune are in your Hands.

Flip. Ne'er fear, I'll take care of 'em.

Aml. How he traps 'em; let *Dick* alone.   [*Aside.*

Dick. Your Servant, good Madam.   [*To his Mother.*
    [*Exit* Dick.

Aml. Your Honour's moſt devoted.—A pretty, civil, well-bred Gentleman this, Mrs. *Flippanta*. Pray whom may he be?

Flip. A Man of great Note; Colonel *Shapely*.

Aml. Is it possible? I have heard much of him indeed, but never saw him before: One may see Quality in every Limb of him: He's a fine Man truly.

Flip. I think you are in Love with him, Mrs. *Amlet*.

Aml. Alas, those Days are done with me; but if I were as fair as I was once, and had as much Money as some Folks, Colonel *Shapely* should not catch Cold for Want of a Bed-fellow. I love your Men of Rank, they have something in their Air does so diſtinguish 'em from the Rascality.

Flip. People of Quality are fine Things indeed, Mrs. *Amlet*, if they had but a little more Money; but for Want of that, they are forc'd to do Things their great Souls are asham'd of. For Example,—here's my Lady —she owes you but Six and Fifty Pounds——

Aml. Well?

Flip. Well, and she has it not by her to pay you.

Aml. How can that be?

Flip. I don't know; her Cashkeeper's out of Humour, he says he has no Money.

Aml. What a presumptuous piece of Vermin is a Cashkeeper! Tell his Lady he has no Money?—Now, Mrs. *Flippanta*, you may see his Bags are full, by his being so saucy.

Flip. If they are, there's no Help for't; he'll do what he pleases, 'till he comes to make up his yearly Accounts.

Aml. But Madam plays sometimes, so when she has good Fortune, she may pay me out of her Winnings.

Flip. O ne'er think of that, Mrs. *Amlet;* if she had won a Thousand Pounds, she'd rather die in a Gaol, than pay off a Farthing with it: Play-Money, Mrs. *Amlet*, amongſt People of Quality, is a sacred Thing, and n ot to be profan'd. The *Deux.* 'Tis consecrated to their Pleasures, 'twould be Sacrilege to pay their Debts with it.

Aml. Why what shall we do then? For I han't One Penny to buy Bread.

Flip. ——I'll tell you——it juſt now comes in my Head: I know my Lady has a little Occaſion for Money, at this Time; So——if you lend her——a hundred Pound——do you ſee, then ſhe may pay you your Six and Fifty out of it.

Aml. Sure, Mrs. *Flippanta*, you think to make a Fool of me.

Flip. No, the Devil fetch me if I do——You ſhall have a Diamond Necklace in Pawn.

Aml. Oho, a Pawn! That's another Caſe. And when muſt ſhe have this Money?

Flip. In a Quarter of an Hour.

Aml. Say no more. Bring the Necklace to my Houſe, it ſhall be ready for you.

Flip. I'll be with you in a Moment.

Aml. Adieu, Mrs. *Flippanta*.

Flip. Adieu, Mrs. *Amlet*.   [*Exit* Amlet.

Flippanta sola.

So——this ready Money will make us all happy. This Spring will set our Baſſet going, and that's a Wheel will turn Twenty others. My Lady's young and handſome; ſhe'll have a Dozen Intrigues upon her Hands, before ſhe has been Twice at her Prayers. So much the better; the more the Griſt, the richer the Miller. Sure never Wench got into so hopeful a Place: Here's a Fortune to be Sold, a Miſtreſs to be debauch'd, and a Maſter to be ruin'd. If I don't feather my Neſt, and get a good Huſband, I deſerve to die, both a maid and a beggar.

End of the Firſt Aƈt.

ACT II.

SCENE, *Mr.* Gripe's *House.*

Enter Clarissa *and* Dick.

Clar. WHAT in the Name of Dulneſs is the matter with you, Colonel? you are as ſtudious as a crack'd Chymiſt.

Dick. My Head, Madam, is full of your Huſband.

Clar. The worſt Furniture for a Head in the Univerſe.

Dick. I am thinking of his Paſſion for your Friend *Araminta.*

Clar. Paſſion!——Dear Colonel, give it a leſs violent Name.

Enter Brass.

Dick. Well, Sir, what want you?

Brass. The Affair I told you of goes ill. [*To* Dick, *aside.*] There's an action out.

Dick. The Devil there is.

Clar. What News brings *Brass?*

Dick. Before Gad I can't tell, Madam; the Dog will never speak out. My Lord what d'y call him waits, for me at my Lodging: Is not that it?

Brass. Yes, Sir.

Dick. Madam, I ask your Pardon.

Clar. Your Servant, Sir.　　　　　　　　　　　[*Exeunt* Dick *and* Brass.

Jessamin!　　　　　　　　　　　　　　　　　　　　[*She sits down.*:

Enter Jessamin.

Jes. Madam.

Clar. Where's *Corinna?* Call her to me, if her Father han't lock'd her up; I want her Company.

Jes. Madam, her Guitar Master is with her.

Clar. Psha, she's taken up with her impertinent Guitar Man. *Flippanta* stays an Age with that old Fool, Mrs. *Amlet.* And *Araminta*, before she can come abroad, is so long a placing her Cocquet-Patch, that I must be a Year without Company. How insupportable is a Moment's Uneasiness to a Woman of Spirit and Pleasure!

Enter Flippanta.

O, art thou come at last? Prithee, *Flippanta*, learn to move a little quicker, thou know'st how impatient I am.

Flip. Yes, when you expect Money: If you had sent me to buy a Prayer-Book, you'd have thought I had flown.

Clar. Well, hast thou brought me any, after all?

Flip. Yes, I have brought some. There [*giving her a Purse*] the old Hag has struck off her Bill, the rest is in that Purse.

Clar. 'Tis well; but take care, *Flippanta*, my Husband don't suspect any thing of this; 'twould vex him, and I don't love to make him uneasy: So I would spare him these little sort of Troubles, by keeping 'em from his Knowledge.

Flip. See the Tenderness she has for him, and yet he's always complaining of you.

Clar. 'Tis the nature of 'em, *Flippanta*; a Husband is a grouling Animal.

Flip. How exactly you define 'em!

Clar. O! I know 'em, *Flippanta*; tho' I confess my poor Wretch diverts me sometimes with his ill Humours. I wish he wou'd quarrel with me to-day a little, to pass away the time, for I find my self in a violent Spleen.

Flip. Why, if you please to drop your self in his way, six to four but he scolds one Rubbers with you.

Clar. Ay, but thou know'st he's as uncertain as the Wind, and if instead of quarrelling with me, he shou'd chance to be fond, he'd make me as sick as a Dog.

Flip. If he's kind, you must provoke him; if he kisses you, spit in's face.

Clar. Alas! when Men are in the kissing Fit, (like Lap Dogs) they take that for a Favour.

Flip. Nay, then I don't know what you'll do with him.

Clar. I'll e'en do nothing at all with him——*Flippanta*.   [*Yawning.*

Flip. Madam.

Clar. My Hoods and Scarf, and a coach to the door.

Flip. Why, whither are you going?

Clar. I can't tell yet, but I would go spend some Money, since I have it.

Flip. Why, you want nothing that I know of.

Clar. How aukward an Objection now is that, as if a Woman of Education bought things because she wanted 'em. Quality always distinguishes it self; and therefore, as the Mechanick People buy things, because they have occasion for 'em, you see Women of Rank always buy things, because they have not occasion for 'em. Now, there, *Flippanta*, you see the difference between a Woman that has breeding, and one that has none. O ho, here's *Araminta* come at last.

Enter Araminta.

Lard, what a tedious while you have let me expect you, I was afraid you were not well; how d'y do to day?

Aram. As well as a Woman can do, that has not slept all night.

Flip. Methinks, Madam, you are pretty well awake, however.

Aram. O, 'tis not a little thing will make a Woman of my Vigour look drowsy.

Clar. But, prithee, what was't disturb'd you?

Aram. Not your Husband, don't trouble your self; at least, I am not in love with him yet.

Clar. Well remember'd, I had quite forgot that matter. I wish you much joy, you have made a noble Conquest indeed.

Aram. But now I have subdu'd the Country, pray is it worth my keeping? You know the Ground, you have try'd it.

Clar. A barren Soil, Heaven can tell.

Aram. Yet if it were well cultivated, it would produce something, to my knowledge. Do you know 'tis in my Power to ruine this poor thing of yours? His whole Estate is at my Service.

Flip. Cods-fish, strike him, Madam, and let my Lady go your halves.

There's no Sin in plundering a Husband, so his Wife has share of the Booty.

Aram. Whenever she gives me her Orders, I shall be very ready to obey 'em.

Clar. Why, as odd a thing as such a Project may seem, *Araminta*, I believe I shall have a little serious Discourse with you about it. But, prithee, tell me how you have pass'd the night? For I am sure your Mind has been roving upon some pretty thing or other.

Aram. Why, I have been studying all the ways my Brain could produce, to plague my husband.

Clar. No wonder indeed you look so fresh this Morning, after the satisfaction of such pleasing Ideas all Night.

Aram. Why, can a Woman do less than study Mischief, when she has tumbl'd and toss'd herself into a burning Fever, for want of Sleep, and sees a Fellow lie snoring by her, stock-still, in a fine breathing Sweat?

Clar. Now see the difference of Women's Tempers: If my Dear wou'd make but one Nap of his whole Life, and only waken to make his Will, I shou'd be the happiest Wife in the Universe. But we'll discourse more of these matters as we go, for I must make a tour among the Shops.

Aram. I have a Coach waits at the door, we'll talk of 'em as we rattle along.

Clar. The best place in nature, for you know a Hackney-Coach is a natural Enemy to a Husband. [*Exit* Clar. *and* Aram.

Flippanta sola.

What a pretty little pair of amiable Persons are there gone to hold a Council of War together! Poor Birds! What wou'd they do with their time, if the plaguing their Husbands did not help 'em to Employment. Well, if Idleness be the root of all Evil, then Matrimony's good for something, for it sets many a poor Woman to work. But here comes Miss. I hope I shall help her into the Holy State too e'er long. And when she's once there, if she don't play her part as well as the best of 'em, I'm mistaken. Han't I lost the Letter I'm to give her?——No, here 'tis; so, now we shall see how pure Nature will work with her, for Art she knows none yet.

Enter Corinna.

Cor. What does my Mother-in-law want with me, *Flippanta?* They tell me, she was asking for me.

Flip. She's just gone out, so I suppose 'twas no great Business.

Cor. Then I'll go into my Chamber again.

Flip. Nay, hold a little if you please. I have some Business with you my self, of more Concern than what she had to say to you.

Cor. Make haſte then, for you know my Father won't let me keep you Company; he says, you'll spoil me.

Flip. I spoil you? He's an unworthy Man to give you such ill Impressions of a Woman of my Honour.

Cor. Nay, never take it to heart, *Flippanta*, for I don't believe a Word he says. But he does so plague me with his continual Scolding, I'm almoſt weary of my Life.

Flip. Why, what is't he finds Fault with?

Cor. Nay, I don't know, for I never mind him; when he has babbled for two Hours together, methinks I have heard a Mill going, that's all. It does not at all change my Opinion, *Flippanta*, it only makes my Head ach.

Flip. Nay, if you can bear it so, you are not to be pity'd so much as I thought.

Cor. Not pity'd? Why is it not a miserable thing, such a young Creature as I am shou'd be kept in perpetual Solitude, with no other Company but a Parcel of old fumbling Maſters to teach me Geography, Arithmetick, Philosophy, and a Thousand useless Things. Fine Entertainment, indeed, for a young Maid at Sixteen; methinks one's time might be better employ'd.

Flip. Those things will improve your Wit.

Cor. Fiddle faddle, han't I Wit enough already? My Mother-in-law has learn'd none of this Trumpery, and is not she as happy as the Day's long?

Flip. Then you envy her, I find?

Cor. And well I may. Does she not do what she has a mind to, in spite of her Husband's Teeth?

Flip. Look you there now, [*aside*] if she has not already conceiv'd that, as the Supream Blessing of Life.

Cor. I'll tell you what, *Flippanta*, if my Mother-in-law wou'd but ſtand by me a little, and encourage me, and let me keep her Company, I'd rebel againſt my Father to Morrow, and throw all my Books in the Fire. Why, he can't touch a Groat of my Portion; do you know that, *Flippanta?*

Flip. So——I shall spoil her. [*aside*] Pray Heaven the Girl don't debauch me.

Cor. Look you: In short, he may think what he pleases, he may think himself wise; but Thoughts are free, and I may think in my turn. I'm but a Girl, 'tis true, and a Fool too, if you'll believe him; but let him know, a foolish Girl may make a wise Man's Heart ach; so he had as good be quiet——Now it's out——

Flip. Very well, I love to see a young Woman have Spirit, it's a sign she'll come to something.

Cor. Ah, *Flippanta*, if you wou'd but encourage me, you'd find me quite another thing. I'm a devilish Girl in the bottom; I wish you'd but let me make one amongst you.

Flip. That never can be, till you are marry'd. Come, examine your Strength a little. Do you think, you durst venture upon a Husband?

Cor. A Husband! Why a—if you wou'd but encourage me. Come, *Flippanta*, be a true Friend now. I'll give you Advice, when I have got a little more Experience. Do you in your very Conscience and Soul, think I am old enough to be marry'd?

Flip. Old enough! Why you are Sixteen, are you not?

Cor. Sixteen! I am Sixteen, two Months, and odd Days, Woman. I keep an exact Account.

Flip. The Duce you are!

Cor. Why, do you then truly and sincerely think I am old enough?

Flip. I do, upon my Faith, Child.

Cor. Why then to deal as fairly with you, *Flippanta*, as you do with me, I have thought so any time these Three Years.

Flip. Now I find you have more Wit than ever I thought you had, and to shew you what an Opinion I have of your Discretion, I'll shew you a thing I thought to have thrown in the Fire.

Cor. What is it for *Jupiter*'s Sake?

Flip. Something will make your Heart chuck within you.

Cor. My dear *Flippanta*.

Flip. What do you think it is?

Cor. I don't know, nor I don't care, but I'm mad to have it.

Flip. It's a four-corner'd Thing.

Cor. What, like a Cardinal's Cap?

Flip. No, 'tis worth a whole Conclave of 'em. How do you like it?
                                        [*Shewing the Letter.*

Cor. O Lard, a Letter!——Is there ever a Token in it?

Flip. Yes, and a precious one too. There's a handsome young Gentleman's Heart.

Cor. A handsome young Gentleman's Heart!
Nay, then 'tis time to look grave.   [*Aside.*]

Flip. There.

Cor. I shan't touch it.

Flip. What's the matter now?

Cor. I shan't receive it.

Flip. Sure you jest.

Cor. You'll find I don't. I understand my self better, than to take Letters, when I don't know who they are from.

Flip. I am afraid I commended your Wit too soon.

Cor. 'Tis all one, I shan't touch it, unless I know who it comes from.

Flip. Hey-day! open it and you'll see.

Cor. Indeed I shall not.

Flip. Well——then I must return it where I had it.

Cor. That won't serve your turn, Madam. My Father must have an Account of this.

Flip. Sure you are not in earnest?

Cor. You'll find I am.

Flip. So, here's fine Work. This 'tis to deal with Girls before they come to know the Distinction of Sexes.

Cor. Confess who you had it from, and perhaps, for this once, I mayn't tell my Father.

Flip. Why then, since it must out, 'twas the Colonel: But why are you so scrupulous, Madam?

Cor. Because if it had come from any Body else, I wou'd not have given a Farthing for it.   [*Twitching it eagerly out of her Hand.*

Flip. Ah, my dear little Rogue, [*kissing her.*] you frighten'd me out of my Wits.

Cor. Let me read it, let me read it, let me read it, let me read it, I say. Um, um, um, *Cupid*'s, um, um, um, *Darts*, um, um, um, *Beauty*, um, *Charms*, um, um, um, *Angel*, um, *Goddess*, um—[*Kissing the Letter*]—um, um, um, *truest Lover*, hum, um, *Eternal Constancy*, um, um, um, *cruel*, um, um, um, *Racks*, um, um, *Tortures*, um, um, *Fifty Daggers*, um, um, *bleeding Heart*, um, um, *dead Man*.
Very well, a mighty civil Letter, I promise you; not one smutty Word in it: I'll go lock it up in my Comb-box.

Flip. Well——but what does he say to you?

Cor. Not a Word of News, *Flippanta*; 'tis all about Business.

Flip. Does he not tell you he's in Love with you?

Cor. Ay, but he told me that before.

Flip. How so? He never spoke to you.

Cor. He sent me word by his Eyes.

Flip. Did he so? mighty well. I thought you had been to learn that Language.

Cor. O, but you thought wrong, *Flippanta*. What, because I don't go a visiting, and see the World, you think I know nothing. But you shou'd consider, *Flippanta*, that the more one's alone, the more one thinks; and 'tis thinking that improves a Girl. I'll have you to know, when I was younger than I am now, by more than I'll boast of, I thought of Things wou'd have made you stare again.

Flip. Well, since you are so well vers'd in your Business, I suppose I need not inform you, That if you don't write your Gallant an Answer——he'll die.

Cor. Nay, now, *Flippanta*, I confess you tell me something I did not know before. Do you speak in serious Sadness? Are men given to die, if their Miſtresses are sower to 'em?

Flip. Um——I can't say they all die——No, I can't say they all do, but truly, I believe it wou'd go very hard with the Colonel.

Cor. Lard, I wou'd not have my Hands in Blood for Thousands; and therefore *Flippanta*,——if you'll encourage me———

Flip. O, by all means an Answer.

Cor. Well, since you say it then, I'll e'en in and do it, tho' I proteſt to you (leſt you should think me too forward now) he's the only Man that wears a Beard, I'd Ink my Fingers for. May be if I marry him, in a Year or two's Time I mayn't be so nice.   [*Aside.*
    [*Exit* Corinna.

Flippanta sola.

Now Heaven give him Joy; he's like to have a rare Wife o'thee. But where there's Money, a Man has a Plaiſter to his Sore. They have a blessed time on't, who marry for Love. See!—here come's an Example ——*Araminta*'s dread Lord.

Enter Moneytrap.

Mon. Ah, *Flippanta!* How do you do, good *Flippanta?* How do you do?

Flip. Thank you, Sir, well, at your Service.

Mon. And how does the good Family, your Maſter, and your fair Miſtress? Are they at Home?

Flip. Neither of 'em; my Maſter has been gone out these two Hours, and my Lady is juſt gone with your Wife.

Mon. Well, I won't say I have loſt my labour, however, as long as I have met with you, *Flippanta.* For I have wish'd a great while for an Opportunity to talk with you a little. You won't take it amiss, if I should ask you a few Queſtions?

Flip. Provided you leave me to my liberty in my Answers. What's this Cotquean going to pry into now?   [*Aside.*

Mon. Prithee, good *Flippanta*, how do your Maſter and Miſtress live together?

Flip. Live! Why——like Man and Wife, generally out of Humour, quarrel often, seldom agree, complain of one another; and perhaps have both reason. In short, 'tis much as 'tis at your House.

Mon. Good-lack! but whose side are you generally of?

Flip. O' the right side always, my Lady's. And if you'll have me give you my Opinion of these Matters, Sir, I do not think a Husband can ever be in the right.

Mon. Ha!

Flip. Little, peeking, creeping, sneaking, ſtingy, covetous, cowardly, dirty, cuckoldy Things.

Mon. Ha!

Flip. Fit for nothing but Taylors and Dry-Nurses.

Mon. Ha!

Flip. A Dog in a Manger, snarling and biting, to ſtarve Gentlemen with good Stomachs.

Mon. Ha!

Flip. A Centry upon Pleasure, set to be a Plague upon Lovers, and damn poor Women before their time.

Mon. A Husband is indeed——

Flip. Sir, I say, he is nothing——A Beetle without Wings, a Wind-mill without Sails, a Ship in a Calm.

Mon. Ha!

Flip. A Bag without Money——an empty Bottle——dead Small-Beer.

Mon. Ha!

Flip. A Quack without Drugs.

Mon. Ha!

Flip. A Lawyer without Knavery.

Mon. Ha!

Flip. A Courtier without Flattery.

Mon. Ha!

Flip. A King without an Army——or a People with one. Have I drawn him, Sir?

Mon. Why truly, *Flippanta*, I can't deny, but there are some general Lines of Resemblance. But you know there may be Exceptions.

Flip. Hark you, Sir, shall I deal plainly with you? Had I got a Hus-band, I wou'd put him in mind, that he was marry'd as well as I.

For were I the thing call'd a Wife,   [Sings.
    And my Fool grew too fond of his Power,
He shou'd look like an Ass all his Life,
    For a Prank that I'd play him in an Hour.

Tol lol la ra tol lol, &c.—Do you observe that, Sir?

Mon. I do; and think you wou'd be in the right on't. But, prithee, why doſt not give this Advice to thy Miſtress?

Flip. For fear it should go round to your Wife, Sir, for you know they are Play-fellows.

Mon. O, there's no danger of my Wife; she knows I'm none of those Husbands.

Flip. Are you sure she knows that, Sir?

Mon. I'm sure she ought to know it, *Flippanta*, for really I have but four Faults in the World.

Flip. And, pray, what may they be?

Mon. Why, I'm a little slovenly, I shift but once a Week.

Flip. Fough!

Mon. I am sometimes out of Humour.

Flip. Provoking.

Mon. I don't give her so much Money as she'd have.

Flip. Insolent.

Mon. And a——perhaps I mayn't be quite so young as I was.

Flip. The Devil.

Mon. O, but then consider how 'tis on her side, *Flippanta*. She ruines me with washing, Is always out of Humour, Ever wanting Money, And will never be older.

Flip. That laſt Article, I muſt confess, is a little hard upon you.

Mon. Ah, *Flippanta*, did'ſt thou but know the daily Provocations I have, thou'dſt be the firſt to excuse my Faults. But now I think on't——Thou art none of my Friend, thou doſt not love me at all; no, not at all.

Flip. And whither is this little Reproach going to lead us now?

Mon. You have Power over your fair Miſtress, *Flippanta*.

Flip. Sir.

Mon. But what then? you hate me.

Flip. I underſtand you not.

Mon. There's not a Moment's Trouble her naughty Husband gives her, but I feel it too.

Flip. I don't know what you mean.

Mon. If she did but know what part I take in her Sufferings.

Flip. Mighty obscure.

Mon. Well, I'll say no more; but——

Flip. All *Hebrew*.

Mon. If thou wou'dſt but tell her on't.

Flip. Still darker and darker.

Mon. I shou'd not be ungrateful.

Flip. Ah, now I begin to underſtand you.

Mon. *Flippanta*—there's my Purse.

Flip. Say no more; now you explain, indeed——You are in Love?

Mon. Bitterly—and I do swear by all the Gods——

Flip. Hold——Spare 'em for another time, you ſtand in no need of 'em now. A Usurer that parts with his Purse, gives sufficient Proof of his Sincerity.

Mon. I hate my Wife, *Flippanta*.

Flip. That we'll take upon your bare Word.

Mon. She's the Devil, *Flippanta*.

Flip. You like your Neighbour's better.

Mon. Oh!——an angel.

Flip. What Pity it is the Law don't allow trucking!

Mon. If it did, *Flippanta!*

Flip. But since it don't, Sir——keep the Reins upon your Passion: Don't let your Flame rage too high, lest my Lady shou'd be cruel, and it shou'd dry you up to a Mummy.

Mon. 'Tis impossible she can be so barbarous, to let me die. Alas, *Flippanta,* a very small matter wou'd save my Life.

Flip. Then y'are dead——for we Women never grant any thing to a Man who will be satisfy'd with a little.

Mon. Dear *Flippanta,* that was only my Modesty; but since you'll have it out——I am a very Dragon. And so your lady'll find——if ever she thinks fit to be——Now I hope you'll stand my Friend.

Flip. Well, Sir, as far as my Credit goes, it shall be employ'd in your Service.

Mon. My best *Flippanta,*—tell her—I'm all hers—tell her—my Body's hers—tell her—my Soul's hers—and tell her—my Estate's her's. Lard have mercy upon me, how I'm in love!

Flip. Poor Man! what a Sweat he's in! But hark,—I hear my Master, for Heaven's sake compose your self a little, you are in such a Fit, o' my Conscience he'll smell you out.

Mon. Ah, Dear, I'm in such an Emotion, I dare not be seen; put me in this Closet for a Moment.

Flip. Closet, Man! it's too little, your Love wou'd stifle you. Go air your self in the Garden a little, you have need on't, i'faith.

[*She puts him out.*

Flippanta *sola.*

A rare Adventure by my troth. This will be curious News to the Wives. Fortune has now put their Husbands into their hands, and I think they are too sharp to neglect its Favours.

Enter Gripe.

Gripe. O, here's the right hand; the rest of the Body can't be far off. Where's my Wife, Huswife?

Flip. An admirable Question!——Why, she's gone abroad, Sir.

Gripe. Abroad, abroad, abroad already? Why, she uses to be stewing in her Bed three hours after this time, as late as 'tis: What makes her gadding so soon?

Flip. Business, I suppose.

Gripe. Business! she has a pretty Head for Business truly: Oho, let

(35)

her change her way of living, or I'll make her change a light heart for a heavy one.

Flip. And why wou'd you have her change her way of living, Sir? You see it agrees with her. She never look'd better in her life.

Gripe. Don't tell me of her Looks, I have done with her Looks long since. But I'll make her change her life, or——

Flip. Indeed, Sir, you won't.

Gripe. Why, what shall hinder me, Insolence?

Flip. That which hinders most Husbands; Contradiction.

Gripe. Suppose I resolve I won't be contradicted?

Flip. Suppose she resolves you shall?

Gripe. A Wife's Resolution is not good by Law.

Flip. Nor a Husband's by Custom.

Gripe. I tell thee, I will not bear it.

Flip. I tell you, Sir, you will bear it.

Gripe. Oons, I have borne it three Years already.

Flip. By that you see 'tis but giving your mind to it.

Gripe. My Mind to it! Death and the Devil! My Mind to it!

Flip. Look ye, Sir you may swear and damn, and call the Furies to assist you, but till you apply the Remedy to the right place, you'll never cure the Disease. You fancy you have got an extravagant Wife, is't not so?

Gripe. Prithee change me that word Fancy, and it is so.

Flip. Why there's it. Men are strangely troubled with the Vapours of late. You'll wonder now, if I tell you, you have the most reasonable Wife in Town; And that all the Disorders you think you see in her, are only here, here, here, in your own Head.   [*thumping his Forehead.*

Gripe. She is then, in thy Opinion, a reasonable Woman?

Flip. By my Faith I think so.

Gripe. I shall run mad——Name me an Extravagance in the World she is not guilty of.

Flip. Name me an Extravagance in the World she is guilty of.

Gripe. Come then, does not she put the whole House in disorder?

Flip. Not that I know of, for she never comes into it but to sleep.

Gripe. 'Tis very well: Does she employ any one moment of her life in the Government of her Family?

Flip. She is so submissive a Wife, she leaves it entirely to you.

Gripe. Admirable! Does she not spend more Money in Coach-hire, and Chair-hire, than wou'd maintain six Children?

Flip. She's too nice of your Credit to be seen daggling in the Streets.

Gripe. Good. Do I set eye on her sometimes in a Week together?

Flip. That, Sir, is because you are never stirring at the same time; you keep odd Hours; you are always going to bed when she's rising, and rising just when she's coming to bed.

Gripe. Yes truly, Night into Day, and Day into Night, Bawdy-house Play, that's her Trade; but these are Trifles: Has she not loſt her Diamond Necklace? Answer me to that, Trapes.

Flip. Yes; and has sent as many Tears after it, as if it had been her Husband.

Gripe. Ah!——the Pox take her; but enough. 'Tis resolv'd, and I will put a ſtop to the course of her life, or I will put a ſtop to the course of her Blood, and so she shall know the firſt time I meet with her; [*aside*] which tho' we are Man and Wife, and lie under one Roof, 'tis very possible may not be this Fortnight.   [*Exit* Gripe.

Flippanta *sola.*

Nay, thou haſt a blessed time on't, that muſt be confess'd. What a miserable Devil is a Husband! Insupportable to himself, and a Plague to every thing about them. Their Wives do by them, as Children do by Dogs, teaze and provoke 'em, till they make 'em so curs'd, they snarl and bite at every thing that comes in their reach. This Wretch here, is grown perverse to that degree, he's for his Wife's keeping home, and making Hell of his House, so he may be the Devil in it, to torment her. How niggardly soever he is, of all things he possesses, he is willing to purchase her Misery, at the expence of his own Peace. But he'd as good be ſtill, for he'll miss of his Aim. If I know her (which I think, I do) she'll set his Blood in such a Ferment, it shall bubble out at every Pore of him; whilſt her's is so quiet in her Veins, her Pulse shall go like a Pendulum.

ACT III.

SCENE, *Mrs.* Amlet's *House.*

Enter Dick.

WHERE's this old Woman?——A-hey. What the devil? No body at home? Ha! her ſtrong Box!——And the Key in't! 'tis so. Now Fortune be my Friend. What the duce——Not a Penny of Money in Cash!——Nor a Chequer Note!——Nor a Bank-Bill—— [*Searching the ſtrong Box*]——Nor a crooked Stick! Nor a——Mum—— here's something——A Diamond Necklace by all the Gods! Oons the old Woman——Zeſt.

Claps the Necklace in his Pocket, then runs and asks her Blessing.

(37)

Enter Mrs. Amlet.

——Pray Mother, pray to, *&c.*

Aml. Is it possible?——*Dick* upon his humble Knee! Ah my dear Child!——May Heaven be good unto thee.

Dick. I'm come, my dear Mother, to pay my Duty to you, and to ask your Consent to——

Aml. What a Shape is there!

Dick. To ask your Consent, I say, to marry a great Fortune; for what is Riches in this World without a Blessing, and how can there be a Blessing without Respect and Duty to Parents?

Aml. What a Nose he has!

Dick. And therefore it being the Duty of every good Child, not to dispose of himself in Marriage, without the . . . .

Aml. Now the Lord love thee [*kissing him*]——for thou art a goodly young Man: Well *Dick*——And how goes it with the Lady? Are her Eyes open to thy Charms? Does she see what's for her own good? Is she sensible of the Blessings thou haſt in ſtore for her? Ha! is all sure? Haſt thou broke a Piece of Money with her? Speak Bird, do: Don't be modeſt, and hide thy Love from thy Mother, for I'm an indulgent Parent.

Dick. Nothing under Heaven can prevent my good Fortune; but its being discover'd I am your Son——

Aml. Then thou art ſtill asham'd of thy natural Mother. . . . Graceless! Why, I'm no Whore, Sirrah.

Dick. I know you are not——A Whore! Bless us all——

Aml. No; My Reputation's as good as the beſt of 'em; and tho' I'm old, I'm chaſt, you Rascal you.

Dick. Lord, that is not the thing we talk of, Mother, but . . .

Aml. I think as the World goes, they may be proud of marrying their Daughter into a vartuous Family.

Dick. Oons, Vartue is not the Case——

Aml. Where she may have a good Example before her Eyes.

Dick. O Lord! O Lord! O Lord!

Aml. I'm a Woman that don't so much as encourage an Incontinent Look towards me.

Dick. I tell you, 'sdeath I tell you——

Aml. If a Man shou'd make an uncivil Motion to me, I'd spit in his lascivious Face: And all this you may tell 'em, Sirrah.

Dick. Death and Furies! the Woman's out of her——

Aml. Don't you Swear, you Rascal you, don't you Swear; we shall have thee damn'd at laſt, and then I shall be disgrac'd.

Dick. Why then in cold Blood hear me speak to you: I tell you it's a City-Fortune I'm about, she cares not a Fig for your Virtue; she'll hear of nothing but Quality: She has quarrel'd with one of her Friends, for having a better Complexion, and is resolved she'll marry, to take place of her.

Aml. What a Cherry-Lip is there!

Dick. Therefore, good dear Mother now, have a care and don't discover me; for if you do, all's lost.

Aml. Dear, dear, how thy fair Bride will be delighted? Go, get thee gone, go: Go fetch her home, go fetch her home; I'll give her a Sack-Posset, and a Pillow of Down she shall lay her Head upon. Go fetch her home, I say.

Dick. Take care then of the main Chance, my dear Mother, remember, if you discover me——

Aml. Go, fetch her home, I say.

Dick. You promise me then——

Aml. March.

Dick. But swear to me——

Aml. Begone, Sirrah.

Dick. Well, I'll rely upon you—But one Kiss before I go.

[*Kisses her heartily and runs off.*

Aml. Now the Lord love thee; for thou art a comfortable young Man.

[*Exit Mrs.* Amlet.

SCENE [II], Gripe's *House*.

Enter Corinna *and* Flippanta.

Cor. But hark you, *Flippanta*, if you don't think he loves me dearly, don't give him my Letter, after all.

Flip. Let me alone.

Cor. When he has read it, let him give it you again.

Flip. Don't trouble your self.

Cor. And not a word of the Pudding to my Mother-in-law.

Flip. Enough.

Cor. When we come to love one another, to the purpose, she shall know all.

Flip. Ay, then 'twill be time.

Cor. But remember 'tis you make me do all this, now, so if any Mischief comes on't, 'tis you must answer for't.

Flip. I'll be your Security.

Cor. I'm young, and know nothing of the matter; but you have Experience; so it's your business to conduct me safe.

Flip. Poor Innocence!

Cor. But tell me in serious sadness, *Flippanta*, does he love me with the very Soul of him?

Flip. I have told you so a hundred times, and yet you are not satisfy'd.

Cor. But, methinks, I'd fain have him tell me so himself.

Flip. Have patience, and it shall be done.

Cor. Why, Patience is a Virtue; that we must all confess——but, I fancy, the sooner it's done the better, *Flippanta*.

Enter Jessamin.

Jess. Madam, yonder's your Geography-Master waiting for you. [*Exit.*

Cor. Ah! how I am tyr'd with these old fumbling Fellows, *Flippanta*.

Flip. Well, don't let 'em break your Heart, you shall be rid of 'em all e're long.

Cor. Nay, 'tis not the Study I'm so weary of, *Flippanta*, 'tis the odious thing that teaches me. Were the Colonel my Master I fancy I could take pleasure in Learning every thing he cou'd shew me.

Flip. And he can shew you a great deal, I can tell you that. But get you gone in, here's somebody coming, we must not be seen together.

Cor. I will, I will, I will.——O! the dear Colonel. [*Running off.*

Enter Mrs. Amlet.

Flip. O ho, it's Mrs. *Amlet.*——What brings you so soon to us again, Mrs. *Amlet?*

Aml. Ah! my dear Mrs. *Flippanta*, I'm in a furious Fright.

Flip. Why, what's come to you?

Aml. Ah! Mercy on us all,——Madam's Diamond Necklace——

Flip. What of that?

Aml. Are you sure you left it at my House?

Flip. Sure I left it? a very pretty Question truly.

Aml. Nay, don't be angry; say nothing to Madam of it, I beseech you: It will be found again, if it be Heavens good will. At least 'tis, I must bear the loss on't. 'Tis my Rogue of a Son has laid his Bird-lime Fingers on't.

Flip. Your Son, Mrs. *Amlet?* Do you breed your Children up to such Tricks as these then?

Aml. What shall I say to you, Mrs. *Flippanta?* Can I help it? He has been a Rogue from his Cradle, *Dick* has. But he has his Desarts too: And now it comes in my Head, may hap he may have no ill Design in this neither.

Flip. No ill Design, Woman? He's a pretty Fellow if he can steal a Diamond Necklace with a good one.

Aml. You don't know him, Mrs. *Flippanta*, so well as I that bore him. *Dick*'s a Rogue, 'tis true, but——Mum——

Flip. What does the Woman mean?

Aml. Hark you, Mrs. *Flippanta*, is not here a young Gentlewoman in your House, that wants a Husband?

Flip. Why do you ask?

Aml. By way of Conversation only, it does not concern me: but when she marries I may chance to dance at the Wedding. Remember I tell you so; I who am but Mrs. *Amlet.*

Flip. You dance at her Wedding! you!

Aml. Yes, I, I, but don't trouble Madam about her Necklace, perhaps it mayn't go out of the Family. Adieu, Mrs. *Flippanta*.

[*Exit Mrs.* Amlet.

Flip. What—what—what does the Woman mean? Mad! What a Capilotade of a Story's here? The Necklace loſt; and her son *Dick*; and a Fortune to marry; and she shall dance at the Wedding; and——She does not intend, I hope, to propose a Match between her Son *Dick* and *Corinna?* By my Conscience I believe she does. An old Beldame!

Enter Brass.

Brass. Well, Hussy, how ſtand our Affairs? Has Miss writ us an Answer yet? My Maſter's very impatient yonder.

Flip. And why the Duce does he not come himself? What does he send such Idle Fellows as thee of his Errands? Here I had her alone juſt now: He won't have such an opportunity agen this Month, I can tell him that.

Brass. So much the worse for him; 'tis his business.——But now, my dear, let thee and I talk a little of our own: I grow moſt damnably in love with thee; doſt hear that?

Flip. Phu! thou art always timing things wrong; my Head is full, at present, of more important things than Love.

Brass. Then it's full of important things indeed. Doſt want a Privy-Counsellor?

Flip. I want an Assiſtant.

Brass. To do what?

Flip. Mischief.

Brass. I'm thy Man——touch.

Flip. But before I venture to let thee into my Projeƈt, prithee tell me, whether thou find'ſt a natural Disposition to ruine a Husband to oblige his Wife?

Brass. Is she handsome?

Flip. Yes.

Brass. Why then my Disposition's at her Service.

Flip. She's beholding to thee.

Brass. Not she alone neither, therefore don't let her grow vain upon't; for I have three or four Affairs of that kind going at this time.

Flip. Well, go carry this Epiſtle from Miss, to thy Maſter, and when thou com'ſt back, I'll tell thee thy business.

Brass. I'll know it before I go, if you please.

Flip. Thy Maſter waits for an Answer.

Brass. I'd rather he shou'd wait than I.

Flip. Why then, in short, *Araminta*'s Husband is in Love with my Lady.

Brass. Very well, Child, we have a *Rowland* for her *Oliver*: Thy Lady's Husband is in Love with *Araminta*.

Flip. Who told you that, Sirrah?

Brass. 'Tis a Negotiation I am charg'd with, Pert. Did not I tell thee I did business for half the Town? I have managed Maſter *Gripe*'s little Affairs for him these Ten Years, you Slut you.

Flip. Hark thee, *Brass*, the Game's in our hands, if we can but play the Cards.

Brass. Pique and Repique, you Jade you: If the Wives will fall into a good Intelligence.

Flip. Let them alone; I'll answer for 'em they don't slip the Occasion.
——See here they come. They little think what a piece of good News we have for 'em.

Enter Clarissa *and* Araminta.

Clar. *Jessamin*; here, Boy, carry up these things into my Dressing-Room, and break as many of 'em by the way as you can, be sure.——O! art thou there, *Brass*? What news?

Brass. Madam, I only call'd in as I was going by.——But some little Propositions Mrs. *Flippanta* has been ſtarting, have kept me here to offer your Ladyship my humble Service.

Clar. What Propositions?

Brass. She'll acquaint you, Madam.

Aram. Is there any thing new, *Flippanta*?

Flip. Yes, and pretty too.

Clar. That follows of course, but let's have it quick.

Flip. Why, Madam, you have made a Conqueſt.

Clar. Huzzy——But of who? quick.

Flip. Of Mr. *Moneytrap*, that's all.

Aram. My Husband?

Flip. Yes, your Husband, Madam: You thought fit to corrupt ours, so now we are even with you.

Aram. Sure thou art in Jeſt, *Flippanta*.

Flip. Serious as my Devotions.

Brass. And the cross Intrigue, Ladies, is what our Brains have been at work about.

Aram. My dear. [*To* Clarissa.

Clar. My life.

Aram. My angel.

Clar. My soul. [*Hugging one another.*

Aram. The Stars have done this.

Clar. The pretty little Twinklers.

Flip. And what will you do for them now?

Clar. What grateful Creatures ought; shew 'em we don't despise their Favours.

Aram. But is not this a Wager between these two Blockheads?

Clar. I wou'd not give a Shilling to go the Winner's halves.

Aram. Then 'tis the moſt fortunate thing that ever cou'd have happen'd.

Clar. All your laſt Night's Ideas *Araminta*, were Trifles to it.

Aram. *Brass* (my Dear) will be useful to us.

Brass. At your Service, Madam.

Clar. *Flippanta* will be necessary, my Life.

Flip. She waits your Commands, Madam.

Aram. For my part then, I recommend my Husband to thee, *Flippanta,* and make it my earneſt requeſt, thou won't leave him one Half-Crown.

Flip. I'll do all I can to obey you, Madam.

Brass. [*To* Clarissa.] If your Ladyship wou'd give me the same kind Orders for yours.

Clar. O———if thou spar'ſt him, *Brass,* I'm thy Enemy till I die.

Brass. 'Tis enough, Madam, I'll be sure to give you a reasonable Account of him. But how do you intend we shall proceed, Ladies? Muſt we ſtorm the Purse at once, or break Ground in form, and carry it by little and little?

Clar. Storm, dear *Brass,* ſtorm; ever whilſt you live, ſtorm.

Aram. O by all means; muſt it not be so, *Flippanta?*

Flip. In four and twenty Hours, two hundred Pounds apiece, that's my Sentence.

Brass. Very well. But, Ladies, you'll give me leave to put you in mind of some little Expence in Favours, 'twill be necessary you are at, to these honeſt Gentlemen.

Aram. Favours, *Brass?*

Brass. Um . . . a . . . some small Matters, Madam, I doubt muſt be.

Clar. Now that's a vile Article, *Araminta;* for that thing your Husband is so like mine———

Flip. Phu, there's a scruple, indeed. Pray, Madam, don't be so squeamish, tho' the Meat be a little flat, we'll find you savoury Sauce to it.

Clar. This Wench is so mad.

Flip. Why what, in the name of *Lucifer*, is it you have to do, that's so terrible?

Brass. A civil Look only.

Aram. There's no great harm in that.

Flip. An obliging Word.

Clar. That one may afford 'em.

Brass. A little Smile, *à propos.*

Aram. That's but giving one's self an Air.

Flip. Receive a little Letter, perhaps.

Clar. Women of Quality do that from fifty odious Fellows.

Brass. Suffer (may be) a squeeze by the Hand.

Aram. One's so us'd to that one does not feel it.

Flip. Or if a kiss wou'd do't?

Clar. I'd die firſt.

Brass. Indeed, Ladies, I doubt 'twill be necessary to——

Clar. Get their wretched Money, without paying so dear for it.

Flip. Well, juſt as you please for that, my Ladies: But I suppose you'll play upon the square with your Favours, and not pique your selves upon being one more grateful than another.

Brass. And ſtate a fair Account of Receipts and Disbursements.

Aram. That I think shou'd be indeed.

Clar. With all my Heart, and *Brass* shall be our Book-keeper. So get thee to work, Man, as faſt as thou canſt: but not a word of all this to thy Maſter.

Brass. I'll observe my Orders, Madam.   [*Exit* Brass.

Clar. I'll have the pleasure of telling him my self; he'll be violently delighted with it: 'Tis the beſt man in the World, *Araminta*, he'll bring us rare Company to morrow, all sorts of Gameſters; and thou shalt see my Husband will be such a Beaſt to be out of Humour at it.

Aram. The Monſter——But hush, here's my Dear approaching; prithee let's leave him to *Flippanta.*

Flip. Ah, pray do. I'll bring you a good account of him I'll warrant you.

Clar. Dispatch then for the Basset-Tables in haſte.

[*Exit* Clar. *and* Aram.

Flippanta *sola.*

So, now have at him; here he comes: We'll try if we can pillage the Usurer, as he does other Folks.

Enter Moneytrap.

Mon. Well, my pritty *Flippanta*, is thy Miſtriss come home?

Flip. Yes, Sir.

Mon. And where is she, prithee?

Flip. Gone abroad, Sir.

Mon. How doſt mean?

Flip. I mean right, Sir; my lady'll come home and go abroad ten times in an Hour, when she's either in very good Humour, or very bad.

Mon. Good lack! But I'll warrant, in general, 'tis her naughty Husband that makes her House uneasie to her. But haſt thou said a little something to her, Chicken, for an expiring Lover? ha!

Flip. Said——yes, I have said, much good may it do me.

Mon. Well? and how?

Flip. And how?——And how d'you think? you wou'd have me do't, and you have such a way with you, one can refuse you nothing. But I have brought my self into a fine business by it.

Mon. Good lack:——But, I hope, *Flippanta*——

Flip. Yes, your hopes will do much, when I am turn'd out of Doors.

Mon. Was she then terrible angry?

Flip. Oh! had you seen how she flew, when she saw where I was pointing; for you muſt know I went round the Bush, and round the bush, before I came to the matter.

Mon. Nay, 'tis a ticklish Point, that muſt be own'd.

Flip. On my word is it——I mean where a Lady's truly Virtuous, for that's our case you muſt know.

Mon. A very dangerous case indeed.

Flip. But I can tell you one thing——she has an Inclination to you.

Mon. Is it possible?

Flip. Yes, and I told her so at laſt.

Mon. Well, and what did she answer thee?

Flip. Slap——and bid me bring it you for a Token.

[*Giving him a slap on the Face.*

Mon. And you have loſt none on't by the way, with a Pox t'ye. [*Aside.*

Flip. Now this, I think, looks the beſt in the World.

Mon. Yes, but really it feels a little odly.

Flip. Why, you muſt know, Ladies have different ways of expressing their Kindness, according to the Humour they are in: If she had been in a good one, it had been a Kiss; but as long as she sent you something, your Affairs go well.

Mon. Why, truly, I am a little Ignorant in the myſterious Paths of Love, so I muſt be guided by thee: But prithee, take her in a good Humour, next Token she sends me.

Flip. Ah——good Humour?

Mon. What's the matter?

Flip. Poor Lady!

Mon. Ha.

Flip. If I durſt tell you all——

Mon. What then?

Flip. You wou'd not expect to see her in one a good while.

Mon. Why, I pray?

Flip. I must own I did take an unseasonable time to talk of Love Matters to her.

Mon. Why, what's the matter?

Flip. Nothing.

Mon. Nay, prithee tell me.

Flip. I dare not.

Mon. You must indeed.

Flip. Why, when Women are in difficulties, how can they think of Pleasure?

Mon. Why, what Difficulties can she be in?

Flip. Nay, I do but guess after all; for she has that grandeur of Soul, she'd die before she'd tell.

Mon. But what dost thou suspect?

Flip. Why, what should one suspect? where a Husband loves nothing but getting of Money, and a Wife nothing but spending on't.

Mon. So she wants that same then?

Flip. I say no such thing, I know nothing of the Matter; pray make no wrong Interpretation of what I say, my Lady wants nothing that I know of. 'Tis true——she has had ill luck at Cards of late, I believe she has not won once this Month. But what of that?

Mon. Ha?

Flip. 'Tis true, I know her Spirit's that, she'd see her Husband hang'd, before she'd ask him for a Farthing.

Mon. Ha?

Flip. And then I know him again, he'd see her drown'd before he'd give her a Farthing; but that's a help to your Affair you know.

Mon. 'Tis so indeed.

Flip. Ah——well, I'll say nothing; but if she had none of these things to fret her——

Mon. Why really, *Flippanta.*

Flip. I know what you are going to say now; you are going to offer your Service, but 'twon't do; you have a mind to play the Gallant now, but it must not be; you want to be shewing your Liberality, but 'twon't be allow'd; you'll be pressing me to offer it, and she'll be in a rage. We shall have the Devil to do.

Mon. You mistake me, *Flippanta;* I was only going to say——

Flip. Ay, I know what you were going to say well enough; but I tell you it will never do so. If one cou'd find out some way now——ay—— let me see——

Mon. Indeed I hope——

Flip. Pray be quiet——no——but I'm thinking——hum——she'll smoak that tho'——let us consider——If one cou'd find a way to—— 'Tis the niceſt Point in the World to bring about, she'll never touch it, if she knows from whence it comes.

Mon. Shall I try if I can reason her Husband out of twenty Pounds, to make her easie the reſt of her Life?

Flip. Twenty Pound, Man.——why you shall see her set that upon a Card. O——she has a great Soul.——Besides, if her Husband shou'd oblige her, it might, in time, take off her Aversion to him, and by consequence, her Inclination to you. No, no, it muſt never come that way.

Mon. What shall we do then?

Flip. Hold ſtill——I have it. I'll tell you what you shall do.

Mon. Ay.

Flip. You shall make her——a Reſtitution——of two hundred Pounds.

Mon. Ha!——a Reſtitution!

Flip. Yes, yes, 'tis the luckieſt thought in the World, Madam often plays, you know, and Folks who do so, meet now and then with Sharpers. Now, you shall be a Sharper.

Mon. A Sharper?

Flip. Ay, ay, a Sharper; and having cheated her of two hundred Pounds, shall be troubled in Mind, and send it her back agen. You comprehend me?

Mon. Yes, I, I comprehend, but a——won't she suspeƈt if it be so much?

Flip. No, no, the more the better.

Mon. Two hundred Pound?

Flip. Yes, two hundred Pound——Or let me see——so even a Sum may look a little suspicious——ay——let it be two hundred and thirty; that odd thirty will make it look so natural, the Devil won't find it out.

Mon. Ha?

Flip. Pounds too, look I don't know how; Guineas I fancy were better ——ay, Guineas, it shall be Guineas. You are of that Mind, are you not?

Mon. Um——a Guinea, you know, *Flippanta* is——

Flip. A thousand times genteeler, you are certainly in the right on't; it shall be as you say, two hundred and thirty Guineas.

Mon. Ho——well, if it muſt be Guineas, let's see, Two hundred Guineas.

Flip. And thirty; two hundred and thirty. If you, miſtake the sum, you spoil all. So go put 'em in a Purse, while it's fresh in your Head, and send 'em to me with a Penitential Letter, desiring I'll do you the favour to reſtore 'em to her.

Mon. Two hundred and thirty Pounds in a Bag?

Flip. Guineas I say, Guineas.

Mon. Ay, Guineas; 'that's true. But *Flippanta*, if she don't know they come from me, then I give my Money for nothing, you know.

Flip. Phu, leave that to me, I'll manage the Stock for you; I'll make it produce something I'll warrant you.

Mon. Well *Flippanta*, 'tis a great Sum indeed; but I'll go try what I can do for her. You say, two hundred Guineas in a Purse?

Flip. And thirty; if the Man's in his Senses.

Mon. And thirty, 'tis true, I always forget that thirty. [*Exit* Moneytrap.

Flip. So, get thee gone, thou art a rare Fellow, i'faith. *Brass!*——it's thee, is't not?

Enter Brass.

Brass. It is, Huswife. How go matters? I ſtay'd till thy Gentleman was gone. Haſt done any thing towards our common Purse?

Flip. I think I have; he's going to make us a Reſtitution of two or three hundred Pounds.

Brass. A Reſtitution!——good.

Flip. A new way, Sirrah, to make a Lady take a Present without putting her to the Blush.

Brass. 'Tis very well, mighty well indeed. Prithee where's thy Maſter? let me try if I can perswade him to be troubled in Mind too.

Flip. Not so haſty; he's gone into his Closet to prepare himself for a Quarrel I have advis'd him to——with his Wife.

Brass. What to do?

Flip. Why, to make her ſtay at home, now she has resolv'd to do it before-hand. You muſt know, Sirrah, we intend to make a Merit of our Basset-Table, and get a good pretence for the merry Companions we intend to fill his House with.

Brass. Very nicely spun truly, thy Husband will be a happy Man.

Flip. Hold your Tongue you Fool you. See, here comes your Maſter.

Brass. He's welcome.

Enter Dick.

Dick. My dear *Flippanta!* how many thanks have I to pay thee?

Flip. Do you like her ſtyle?

Dick. The kindeſt little Rogue! there's nothing but she gives me leave to hope, I am the happieſt Man the World has in its care.

Flip. Not so happy as you think for neither, perhaps; you have a Rival, Sir, I can tell you that.

Dick. A Rival!

Flip. Yes, and a dangerous one too.

Dick. Who in the name of Terror?

Flip. A devilish Fellow, one Mr. *Amlet.*

Dick. Amlet! I know no such Man.

Flip. You know the Man's Mother tho'; you met her here, and are in her favour, I can tell you. If he worſt you in your Miſtriss, you shall e'en marry her, and disinherit him.

Dick. If I have no other Rival but Mr. *Amlet,* I believe I shan't be diſturb'd in my Amour. But can't I see *Corinna?*

Flip. I don't know, she has always some of her Maſters with her: But I'll go see if she can spare you a moment, and bring you word. [*Exit* Flippanta.

Dick. I wish my old hobbling Mother han't been blabbing something here she shou'd not do.

Brass. Fear nothing, all's safe on that side yet. But, how speaks young Miſtresses epiſtle? soft and tender?

Dick. As Pen can write.

Brass. So you think all goes well there?

Dick. As my Heart can wish.

Brass. You are sure on't?

Dick. Sure on't.

Brass. Why then, Ceremony aside, [*Putting on his Hat.*] You and I muſt have a little talk, Mr. *Amlet.*

Dick. Ah, *Brass,* what art thou going to do? wou't ruine me?

Brass. Look you, *Dick,* few words; you are in a smooth way of making your Fortune, I hope all will rowl on. But how do you intend Matters shall pass 'twixt you and me, in this business?

Dick. Death and Furies! What a time doſt take to talk on't?

Brass. Good Words, or I betray you; they have already heard of one Mr. *Amlet* in the House.

Dick. Here's a Son of a Whore!   [*Aside.*

Brass. In short, look smooth, and be a good Prince, I am your Valet, 'tis true: Your Footman sometimes, which I'm enrag'd at; but you have always had the ascendant, I confess; when we were School-fellows, you made me carry your Books, make your Exercise, own your Rogueries, and sometimes take a Whipping for you: When we were Fellow-Prentices, tho' I was your Senior, you made me open the Shop, clean my Maſter's shoes, cut laſt at Dinner, and eat all the Cruſt. In our sins too, I muſt own you ſtill kept me under; you soar'd up to Adultery with our Miſtriss, while I was at humble Fornication with the Maid. Nay, in our Punishments, you ſtill made good your Poſt; for when once upon a time I was sentenced but to be Whip'd, I cannot deny but you were condemn'd to be Hang'd. So that in all times, I muſt confess, your Inclinations have been greater and nobler than mine. However, I cannot consent that you shou'd at once fix Fortune for Life, and I dwell in my Humilities for the reſt of my Days.

Dick. Hark thee, *Brass,* if I do not moſt nobly by thee, I'm a Dog.

Brass. And when?

Dick. As soon as ever I am Marry'd.

Brass. Ah, the Pox take thee.

Dick. Then you miſtruſt me?

Brass. I do, by my Faith. Look you, Sir, some Folks we miſtruſt, because we don't know 'em: Others we miſtruſt, because we do know 'em. And for one of these Reasons I desire there may be a Bargain before-hand: If not [*Raising his Voice*] look ye, *Dick Amlet*——

Dick. Soft, my dear Friend and Companion. The Dog will ruine me. [*Aside.*] Say, what is't will content thee?

Brass. O ho.

Dick. But how can'ſt thou be such a Barbarian?

Brass. I learnt it at *Algier.*

Dick. Come, make thy *Turkish* demand then.

Brass. You know you gave me a Bank-Bill this Morning to receive for you.

Dick. I did so, of Fifty Pounds, 'tis thine. So, now thou art satisfy'd; all's fixt.

Brass. It is not indeed. There's a Diamond Necklace you rob'd your Mother of e'en now.

Dick. Ah you *Jew.*

Brass. No Words.

Dick. My dear *Brass!*

Brass. I insiſt.

Dick. My old Friend.

Brass. *Dick Amlet* [*Raising his Voice*] I insiſt.

Dick. Ah the Cormorant——Well, 'tis thine. But thou'lt never thrive with't.

Brass. When I find it begins to do me Mischief, I'll give it you again. But I muſt have a Wedding-Suit.

Dick. Well.

Brass. Some good Lace.

Dick. Thou sha't.

Brass. A Stock of Linnen.

Dick. Enough.

Brass. Not yet——a silver Sword.

Dick. Well, thou sha't have that too. Now thou haſt every thing.

Brass. Gad forgive me, I forgot a Ring of Remembrance. I wou'd not forget all these Favours for the World: A sparkling Diamond will be always playing in my Eye, and put me in mind of 'em.

Dick. This unconscionable Rogue! [*Aside.*] Well, I'll bespeak one for thee.

Brass. Brillant.

Dick. It shall. But if the thing don't succeed after all?——

Brass. I'm a Man of Honour, and restore. And so the treaty being finish'd I strike my Flag of Defiance, and fall into my Respects again.

[*Taking off his Hat.*

Enter Flippanta.

Flip. I have made you wait a little, but I cou'd not help it, her Master is but just gone. He has been shewing her Prince *Eugene*'s March into *Italy*.

Dick. Prithee let me come to her, I'll shew her a part of the World he has never shewn her yet.

Flip. So I told her, you must know; and she said, she cou'd like to Travel in good Company; so if you'll slip up those back Stairs you shall try if you can agree upon the Journey.

Dick. My dear *Flippanta!*——

Flip. None of your dear Acknowledgments I beseech you, but up Stairs as hard as you can drive.

Dick. I'm gone. [*Exit* Dick.

Flip. And do you follow him *Jackadandy*, and see he is not surpris'd.

Brass. I thought that was your Post, Mrs. *Useful.* But if you'll come and keep me in Humour, I don't care if I share the Duty with you.

Flip. No words, Sirrah, but follow him, I have somewhat else to do.

Brass. The Jade's so absolute there's no contesting with her. One kiss tho' to keep the Centinel warm. [*Gives her a long Kiss*]——So.

[*Exit* Brass.

Flippanta *sola.*

——A nasty Rogue [*Wiping her mouth*] But, let me see, what have I to do now? 'This *Restitution* will be here quickly, I suppose. In the mean time I'll go know if my Lady's ready for the Quarrel yet. Master, yonder, is so full on't he's ready to burst; but we'll give him vent by and by, with a Witness. [*Exit* Flip.

THE FOURTH ACT.

SCENE Gripe's *House.*

Enter Corinna, Dick, *and* Brass.

Brass. DOn't fear, I'll give you timely notice. [*Goes to the Door.*
Dick. Come, you must consent, you shall consent. How can you leave me thus upon the Wrack? a Man who loves you to that excess that I do.

Cor. Nay, that you love me, Sir, that I'm satisfy'd in, for you have

(51)

sworn you do: And I'm so pleas'd with it, I'd fain have you do so as long as you live, so we muſt never Marry.

Dick. Not marry, my Dear! why what's our Love good for if we don't marry?

Cor. Ah——I'm afraid 'twill be good for little if we do.

Dick. Why do you think so?

Cor. Because I hear my Father and Mother, and my Uncle and Aunt, and *Araminta* and her Husband; and twenty other marry'd Folks, say so from Morning to Night.

Dick. O, that's because they are bad Husbands and bad Wives, but in our Case, there will be a good Husband and a good Wife, and so we shall love for ever.

Cor. Why, there may be something in that truly; and I'm always willing to hear reason, as a reasonable young Woman ought to do. But are you sure, Sir, tho' we are very good now, we shall be so when we come to be better acquainted?

Dick. I can answer for my self, at leaſt.

Cor. I wish you cou'd answer for me too. You see I am a plain Dealer, Sir, I hope you don't like me the worse for it.

Dick. O, by no means, 'tis a sign of admirable Morals; and I hope, since you practice it your self, you'll approve of it in your Lover. In one word, therefore, (for 'tis in vain to mince the matter) my Resolution's fixt, and the World can't ſtagger me, I marry——or I die.

Cor. Indeed, Sir, I have much a-do to believe you, the Disease of Love is seldom so violent.

Dick. Madam, I have two Diseases to end my Miseries, if the firſt don't do't, the latter shall; [*Drawing his Sword*] one's in my Heart, t'other's in my Scabbard.

Cor. Not for a Diadem, [*Catching hold of him*] Ah, put it up, put it up.

Dick. How absolute is your Command! [*Dropping his Sword.*] A word, you see, disarms me.

Cor. What a Power I have over him? [*Aside.*] The wondrous Deeds of Love!——Pray, Sir, let me have no more of these rash doings tho'; perhaps I mayn't be always in the saving Humour——I'm sure if I had let him ſtick himself, I shou'd have been envy'd by all the great Ladies in the Town.   [*Aside.*

Dick. Well, Madam, have I then your Promise? You'll make me the happieſt of Mankind.

Cor. I don't know what to say to you: But I believe I had as good promise, for I find I shall certainly do't.

Dick. Then let us seal the Contract thus.   [*Kisses her.*

Cor. Um——He has almoſt taken away my Breath: He kisses purely.   [*Aside.*

Dick. Hark——somebody comes.   [Brass *peeping in.*
Brass. Gar there, the Enemy——no, hold y'are safe, 'tis *Flippanta.*

Enter Flippanta.

Flip. Come, have you agreed the Matter? If not, you muſt end it another time, for your Father's in Motion, so pray kiss and part.

Cor. That's sweet and sower. [*They kiss.*] Adieu t'ye, Sir.
                                        [*Exit* Dick *and* Cor.

Enter Clarissa.

Clar. Have you told him I'm at home, *Flippanta?*

Flip. Yes, Madam.

Clar. And that I'll see him?

Flip. Yes, that too: But here's News for you; I have juſt now receiv'd the Reſtitution.

Clar. That's killing Pleasure; and how much has he reſtor'd me?

Flip. Two hundred and thirty.

Clar. Wretched Rogue! but retreat, your Maſter's coming to quarrel.

Flip. I'll be within Call, if things run high.   [*Ex.* Flip.

Enter Gripe.

Gripe. Oho——are you there, i'faith? Madam your humble Servant, I'm very glad to see you at home, I thought I shou'd never have had that Honour again.

Clar. Good-morrow, my Dear, how d'ye do? *Flippanta* says you are out of Humour, and that you have a mind to quarrel with me: Is it true, ha?——I have a terrible Pain in my Head, I give you notice on't before hand.

Gripe. And how the Pox shou'd it be otherwise? It's a wonder you are not dead (as a' wou'd you were, [*Aside*) with the Life you lead. Are you not asham'd? and do you not blush to——

Clar. My dear Child, you crack my Brain; soften the harshness of your Voice: Say what thou wou't, but let it be in an agreeable Tone——

Gripe. Tone, Madam? don't tell me of a Tone——

Clar. O——if you will quarrel, do it with Temperance; let it be all in cool Blood, even and smooth, as if you were not mov'd with what you said; and then I'll hear you, as if I were not mov'd with it neither.

Gripe. Had ever Man such need of Patience? Madam, Madam, I muſt tell you, Madam——

Clar. Another Key, or I'll walk off.

Gripe. Don't provoke me.

Clar. Shall you be long, my Dear, in your Remonſtrances?

Gripe. Yes, Madam; and very long.

Clar. If you wou'd quarrel in *abrègèe*, I shou'd have a World of Obligation to you.

Gripe. What I have to say, forsooth, is not to be express'd in *abrègèe*, my Complaints are too numerous.

Clar. Complaints! of what, my Dear? have I ever given you subject of Complaint, my Life?

Gripe. O Pox, my Dear and my Life; I desire none of your *Tendres*.

Clar. How, find fault with my Kindness, and my Expressions of Affection and Respect? the World will guess by this, what the rest of your Complaints may be. I must tell you, I'm scandaliz'd at your Procedure.

Gripe. I must tell you, I am running mad with your's.

Clar. Ah! how insupportable are the Humours of some Husbands, so full of Fancies, and so ungovernable: What have you in the World to disturb you?

Gripe. What have I to disturb me? I have you, Death and the Devil.

Clar. Ay, merciful Heaven! how he Swears! You shou'd never accustom your self to such Words as these; indeed my Dear you shou'd not: Your Mouth's always full of 'em.

Gripe. Blood and Thunder! Madam——

Clar. Ah, he'll fetch the House down: Do you know you make me tremble for you? *Flippanta!* who's there? *Flippanta!*

Gripe. Here's a provoking Devil for you!

Enter Flippanta.

Flip. What in the Name of *Jove*'s the matter? you raise the Neighbourhood.

Clar. Why, here's your Master in a most violent Fuss, and no mortal Soul can tell for what.

Gripe. Not tell for what!

Clar. No, my Life. I have beg'd him to tell me his Griefs, *Flippanta;* and then he swears, good Lord! how he does swear.

Gripe. Ah, you wicked Jade! ah, you wicked Jade!

Clar. Do you hear him *Flippanta?* do you hear him?

Flip. Pray, Sir, let's know a little what puts you in all this Fury?

Clar. Prithee stand near me, *Flippanta*, there's an odd Froth about his Mouth, looks as if his poor Head were going wrong, I'm afraid he'll bite.

Gripe. The wicked Woman, *Flippanta*, the wicked Woman.

Clar. Can any body wonder I shun my own House, when he treats me at this rate in it?

Gripe. At this rate? why in the Devil's Name——

Clar. Do you hear him again?

Flip. Come, a little Moderation, Sir, and try what that will produce.

Gripe. Hang her, 'tis all a pretence to justifie her going abroad.

Clar. A pretence! a pretence! Do you hear how black a Charge he loads me with? Charges me with a pretence? Is this the return for all my down-right open Actions? You know, my Dear, I scorn Pretences: Whene'er I go abroad, it is without pretence.

Gripe. Give me Patience.

Flip. You have a great deal, Sir.

Clar. And yet he's never content, *Flippanta.*

Gripe. What shall I do?

Clar. What a reasonable Man wou'd do; own your self in the wrong, and be quiet: Here's *Flippanta* has Understanding, and I have Moderation; I'm willing to make her Judge of our Differences.

Flip. You do me a great deal of Honour, Madam: but I tell you beforehand, I shall be a little on Master's side.

Gripe. Right; *Flippanta* has sense. Come, let her decide. Have I not reason to be in a Passion? tell me that.

Clar. You must tell her for what, my Life.

Gripe. Why, for the Trade you drive, my Soul.

Flip. Look you, Sir, pray take things right. I know Madam does fret you a little now and then, that's true; but in the Fund, she is the softest, sweetest, gentlest Lady breathing: Let her but live entirely to her own Fancy, and she'll never say a word to you trom Morning to Night.

Gripe. Oons, let her but stay at home, and she shall do what she will. In reason, that is.

Flip. D'ye hear that, Madam? Nay, now I must be on Master's side; you see how he loves you, he desires only your Company: Pray give him that satisfaction, or I must pronounce against you.

Clar. Well, I agree. Thou know'st I don't love to grieve him: Let him be always in good Humour, and I'll be always at home.

Flip. Look you there, Sir, what wou'd you have more?

Gripe. Well, let her keep her Word, and I'll have done quarrelling.

Clar. I must not, however, so far lose the Merit of my Consent, as to let you think I'm weary of going abroad, my Dear; what I do is purely to oblige you; which, that I may be able to perform, without a Relapse, I'll invent what ways I can to make my Prison supportable to me.

Flip. Her Prison! pritty Bird! her Prison! don't that word melt you, Sir?

Gripe. I must confess I did not expect to find her so reasonable.

Flip. O, Sir, soon or late Wives come into good Humour: Husbands must only have a little Patience to wait for it.

Clar. The innocent little Diversions, Dear, that I shall content my self with, will be chiefly Play and Company.

Gripe. O, I'll find you Employment, your Time shan't lie upon your hands; tho' if you have a mind now for such a Companion as a——let me see—*Araminta*, for Example, why I shan't be against her being with you from Morning till Night.

Clar. You can't oblige me more, 'tis the best Woman in the World.

Gripe. Is not she?

Flip. Ah, the old Satyr!   [*aside.*

Gripe. Then we'll have, besides her, may be sometimes——her Husband; and we shall see my Niece that writes Verses, and my Sister *Fidgit*: With her Husband's Brother that's always merry; and his little Cousin, that's to marry the fat Curate; and my Uncle the Apothecary, with his Wife and all his Children. O we shall divert our selves rarely.

Flip. Good.   [*aside.*

Clar. O, for that, my dear Child, I must be plain with you, I'll see none of 'em but *Araminta*, who has the Manners of the Court; for I'll converse with none but Women of Quality.

Gripe. Ay, ay, they shall all have one Quality or other.

Clar. Then, my Dear, to make our home pleasant, we'll have Consorts of Musick sometimes.

Gripe. Musick in my house!

Clar. Yes, my Child, we must have Musick, or the House will be so dull I shall get the Spleen, and be going abroad again.

Flip. Nay, she has so much Complaisance for you, Sir, you can't dispute such things with her.

Gripe. Ay, but if I have Musick——

Clar. Ay, but Sir, I must have Musick——

Flip. Not every Day, Madam don't mean.

Clar. No, bless me, no; but three Consorts a Week: three Days more we'll play after Dinner at *Ombre, Picquet, Basset,* and so forth, and close the Evening with a handsome Supper and a Ball.

Gripe. A Ball?

Clar. Then my Love you know there is but one day more upon our hands, and that shall be the day of Conversation, we'll read Verses, talk of Books, invent Modes, tell Lies, scandalize our Friends, be pert upon Religion; and in short, employ every moment of it in some pretty witty Exercise or other.

Flip. What order you see 'tis she proposes to live in. A most wonderful Regularity.

Gripe. Regularity with a Pox!——   [*aside.*

Clar. And as this kind of Life, so soft, so smooth, so agreeable, must needs invite a vast deal of Company to partake of it, 'twill be necessary to have the decency of a Porter at our Door, you know.

Gripe. A Porter——a Scrivener have a Porter, Madam?

Clar. Positively, a Porter.

Gripe. Why no Scrivener since *Adam* ever had a Porter, Woman!

Clar. You will therefore be renown'd in Story, for having the first, my Life.

Gripe. Flippanta.

Flip. Hang it, Sir, never dispute a Trifle; if you vex her, perhaps she'll insist upon a *Swiss*.   [*Aside to* Gripe.

Gripe. But, Madam——

Clar. But, Sir, a Porter, positively a Porter; without that Treaty null, and I go abroad this Moment.

Flip. Come, Sir, never lose so advantagious a peace for a pitiful Porter.

Gripe. Why, I shall be hooted at, the Boys will throw Stones at my Porter. Besides, where shall I have Money for all this Expence?

Clar. My Dear, who asks you for any? Don't be in a fright, Chicken.

Gripe. Don't be in a fright, Madam. But where I say?——

Flip. Madam plays, Sir, think on that; Women that play have inexhaustible Mines, and Wives who receive least Money from their husbands, are many times those who spend the most.

Clar. So, my Dear, let what *Flippanta* says content you. Go, my Life, trouble your self with nothing, but let me do just as I please, and all will be well. I'm going into my Closet, to consider of some more things to enable me to give you the pleasure of my Company at home, without making it too great a Misery to a yielding Wife.   [*Exit* Clarissa.

Flip. Mirror of Goodness! Pattern to all Wives! well sure, Sir, you are the happiest of all Husbands.

Gripe. Yes——and a miserable Dog for all that too, perhaps.

Flip. Why, what can you ask more, than this matchless Complaisance?

Gripe. I don't know what I can ask, and yet I'm not satisfy'd with what I have neither, the Devil mixes in it all, I think, Complaisant or Perverse, it feels just as't did.

Flip. Why, then your Uneasiness is only a Disease, Sir, perhaps a little Bleeding and Purging wou'd relieve you.

Clar. Flippanta!   [Clarissa *calls within.*

Flip. Madam calls. I come, Madam. Come, be Merry, be Merry, Sir, you have cause, take my Word for't. Poor Devil. [*Aside.*]
                                            [*Exit* Flippanta.

Gripe. I don't know that, I don't know that: But this I do know, that an honest Man, who has marry'd a Jade, whether she's pleas'd to spend her Time at Home or Abroad, had better have liv'd a Batchelor.

Enter Brass.

Brass. O, Sir, I'm mighty glad I have found you.

Gripe. Why, what's the matter, prithee?

Brass. Can no body hear us?

Gripe. No, no, speak quickly.

Brass. You han't seen *Araminta*, since the laſt Letter I carry'd her from you?

Gripe. Not I, I go prudently; I don't press things like your young Firebrand Lovers.

Brass. But seriously, Sir, are you very much in love with her?

Gripe. As mortal Man has been.

Brass. I'm sorry for't.

Gripe. Why so, dear *Brass?*

Brass. If you were never to see her more now? suppose such a thing, d'you think 'twou'd break your Heart?

Gripe. Oh!

Brass. Nay, now I see you love her; wou'd you did not.

Gripe. My dear Friend.

Brass. I'm in your Intereſt deep: you see it.

Gripe. I do: but speak, what miserable Story haſt thou for me?

Brass. I had rather the Devil had, phu——flown away with you quick, than to see you so much in Love, as I perceive you are, since——

Gripe. Since what?——ho.

Brass. Araminta, Sir,——

Gripe. Dead?

Brass. No.

Gripe. How then?

Brass. Worse.

Gripe. Out with't.

Brass. Broke.

Gripe. Broke?

Brass. She is, poor Lady, in a moſt unfortunate situation of Affairs. But I have said too much.

Gripe. No, no, 'tis very sad, but let's hear it.

Brass. Sir, She charg'd me on my Life never to mention it to you, of all Men living.

Gripe. Why, who should'ſt thou tell it to, but to the beſt of her Friends?

Brass. Ay, why there's it now, it's going juſt as I fancy'd. Now will I be hang'd if you are not enough in Love to be engaging in this Matter. But I muſt tell you, Sir, That as much concern as I have, for that moſt excellent, beautiful, agreeable, diſtress'd, unfortunate Lady, I'm too much your Friend and Servant, ever to let it be said, 'twas the means of your being ruin'd for a Woman——by letting you know, she eſteem'd you more than any other Man upon Earth.

Gripe. Ruin'd! what doſt thou mean?

Brass. Mean? why I mean that Women always ruine those that love 'em, that's the Rule.

Gripe. The rule?

Brass. Yes, the Rule; why wou'd you have 'em ruine those that don't? how shall they bring that about?

Gripe. But is there a necessity then, they shou'd ruine somebody?

Brass. Yes, marry is there; how wou'd you have 'em support their Expence else? Why, Sir, you can't conceive now——you can't conceive what *Araminta*'s Privy-Purse requires. Only her Privy-Purse, Sir! Why, what do you imagine now she gave me for the laſt Letter I carry'd her from you? 'Tis true, 'twas from a Man she lik'd, else, perhaps, I had had my Bones broke. But what do you think she gave me?

Gripe. Why, mayhap——a Shilling.

Brass. A Guinea, Sir, a Guinea. You see by that how fond she was on't, by the by. But then, Sir, her Coach-hire, her Chair-hire, her Pin-Money, her Play-Money, her China, and her Charity——wou'd consume Peers: A great Soul, a very great Soul! but what's the end of all this?

Gripe. Ha?

Brass. Why, I'll tell you what the end is——a Nunnery.

Gripe. A Nunnery!

Brass. A Nunnery——In short, she is at laſt reduc'd to that Extremity, and attack'd with such a Battalion of Duns, that rather than tell her Husband, (who you know is such a Dog, he'd let her go if she did) she has e'en determin'd to turn Papiſt, and bid the World adieu for Life.

Gripe. O terrible! a Papiſt?

Brass. Yes, when a handsome Woman has brought her self into Difficulties, the Devil can't help her out of,——To a Nunnery, that's another Rule, Sir.

Gripe. But, but, but, prithee *Brass*, but——

Brass. But all the buts in the World, Sir, won't ſtop her; she's a Woman of a noble Resolution. So, Sir, your humble Servant; I pity her, I pity you, Turtle and Mate; but the Fates will have it so, all's packt up, and I'm now going to call her a Coach; for she resolves to slip off without saying a word; and the next Visit she receives from her Friends, will be through a melancholy Grate, with a Veil inſtead of a Top-knot. [*Going.*

Gripe. It muſt not be, by the Powers it muſt not; she was made for the World, and the World was made for her.

Brass. And yet you see, Sir, how small a share she has on't.

Gripe. Poor Woman! Is there no way to save her?

Brass. Save her! no, how can she be saved? why she owes above five hundred Pound.

Gripe. Oh!

Brass. Five hundred Pound, Sir, she's like to be sav'd indeed.——Not but that I know them in this Town wou'd give me one of the five, if

I wou'd perswade her to accept of t'other four: but she has forbid me mentioning it to any Soul living; and I have disobey'd her only to you; and so——I'll go and call a Coach.

Gripe. Hold——doſt think, my poor *Brass*, one might not order it so, as to compound those Debts for——for——twelve Pence in the pound?

Brass. Sir, d'ye hear?——I have already try'd 'em with ten Shillings, and not a Rogue will prick up his Ear at it. Tho', after all, for three hundred Pounds all in glittering Gold, I cou'd set their Chaps a watering. But where's that to be had with Honour? there's the thing, Sir,——I'll go and call a Coach.

Gripe. Hold, once more: I have a Note in my Closet of two hundred, ay——and fifty, I'll go and give it her my self.

Brass. You will, very genteel truly. Go, slap dash, and offer a Woman of her Scruples Money! bolt in her Face; Why, you might as well offer her a Scorpion, and she'd as soon touch it.

Gripe. Shall I carry it to her Creditors then, and treat with them?

Brass. Ay, that's a rare thought.

Gripe. Is not it, *Brass?*

Brass. Only one little Inconvenience by the way.

Gripe. As how?

Brass. That they are your Wife's Creditors as well as her's; and perhaps it might not be altogether so well, to see you clearing the Debts of your Neighbour's Wife, and leaving those of your own unpaid.

Gripe. Why that's true now.

Brass. I'm wise you see, Sir.

Gripe. Thou art; and I'm but a young Lover: But what shall we do then?

Brass. Why I'm thinking, that if you give me the Note, do you see? and that I promise to give you an account of it——

Gripe. Ay, but look you, *Brass*——

Brass. But look you!——Why what, d'ye think I'm a Pick-pocket? D'ye think I intend to run away with your Note? your paltry Note.

Gripe. I don't say so——I say only that in case——

Brass. Case, Sir! there's no Case but the Case I have put you; and since you heap Cases upon Cases, where there is but three hundred rascally Pounds in the Case——I'll go and call a Coach.

Gripe. Prithee don't be so teſty; come, no more words, follow me to my Closet, and I'll give thee the Money.

Brass. A terrible effort you make indeed; you are so much in Love, your Wits are all upon the Wing, juſt a going; and for three hundred Pounds you put a ſtop to their flight: Sir, your Wits are worth that, or your Wits are worth nothing. Come away.

Gripe. Well, say no more, thou shalt be satisfy'd.   [*Exeunt.*

Enter Dick.

Dick. S't——*Brass!* S't——

Re-enter Brass.

Brass. Well, Sir?

Dick. 'Tis not well, Sir, 'tis very ill, Sir, we shall be all blown up.

Brass. What? with Pride and Plenty?

Dick. No, Sir, with an officious Slut that will spoil all. In short, *Flippanta* has been telling her Miſtriss and *Araminta*, of my Passion for the young Gentlewoman, and truly to oblige me (suppos'd no ill Match by the by,) they are resolv'd to propose it immediately to her Father.

Brass. That's the Devil; we shall come to Papers and Parchments, Joyntures and Settlements, Relations meet on both sides; that's the Devil.

Dick. I intended this very day to propose to *Flippanta*, the carrying her off: And I'm sure the young Houswife wou'd have tuck'd up her Coats and have march'd.

Brass. Ay, with the Body and the Soul of her.

Dick. Why then what damn'd luck is this?

Brass. 'Tis your damn'd Luck, not mine: I have always seen it in your ugly Phiz, in spight of your powder'd Periwig——Pox take ye——he'll be hang'd at laſt: Why don't you try to get her off yet?

Dick. I have no Money you dog, you know you have ſtript me of every Penny.

Brass. Come, damn it. I'll venture one Cargo more upon your rotten bottom: But if ever I see one glance of your hempen Fortune agen, I'm off of your Partnership for ever——I shall never thrive with him.

Dick. An impudent Rogue, but he's in possession of my Eſtate, so I muſt bear with him.   [*Aside.*

Brass. Well, come, I'll raise a hundred Pounds for your use, upon my Wife's Jewels here; [*Pulling out the necklace.*] her necklace shall Pawn for't.

Dick. Remember tho' that if things fail, I'm to have the Necklace again; you know you agreed to that.

Brass. Yes, and if I make it good, you'll be the better for't, if not, I shall; so you see where the Cause will pinch.

Dick. Why, you barbarous Dog, you won't offer to——

Brass. No words now; about your business march. Go ſtay for me at the next Tavern: I'll go to *Flippanta*, and try what I can do for you.

Dick. Well I'll go, but don't think to——O Pox, Sir—— [*Exit* Dick.

Brass solus.

Brass. Will you be gone? A pretty Title you'd have to sue me upon truly. If I shou'd have a mind to ſtand upon the Defensive, as perhaps I may, I have done the Rascal Service enough to lull my Conscience upon't

I'm sure: But 'tis time enough for that. Let me see——First I ll go to *Flippanta*, and put a ſtop to this Family way of Matchmaking, then sell our Necklace for what ready Money 'twill produce; and by this time to Morrow I hope we shall be in Possession of——t'other Jewel here; a precious Jewel, as she's set in Gold: I believe for the Stone it self we may part with't again to a Friend———for a Teſter.   [*Exit*.

The End of the Fourth Act.

THE FIFTH ACT.

SCENE *Gripe*'s House.

Enter Brass *and* Flippanta.

Brass. WELL, you agree I'm in the right, don't you?
   Flip. I don't know, if your Maſter has the Eſtate he talks of, why not do't all above-board? Well, tho' I am not much of his Mind, I'm much in his Intereſt, and will therefore endeavour to serve him in his own way.
   Brass. That's kindly said, my Child, and I believe I shall reward thee one of these Days, with as pretty a Fellow to thy Husband for't, as——
   Flip. Hold your prating, Jackadandy, and leave me to my business.
   Brass. I obey—adieu [*Kisses her.*]   [*Exit* Brass.
   Flip. Rascal.

Enter Corinna.

Cor. Ah, *Flippanta*, I'm ready to sink down, my Legs tremble under me, my dear *Flippy*.
   Flip. And what's the Affair?
   Cor. My Father's there within, with my Mother and *Araminta*; I never saw him in so good a Humour in my Life.
   Flip. And is that it that frightens you so?
   Cor. Ah, *Flippanta*, they are juſt going to speak to him, about my marrying the Colonel.
   Flip. Are they so? so much the worse; they're too haſty.
   Cor. O no, not a Bit: I slipt out on purpose, you muſt know, to give 'em an opportunity, wou'd 'twere done already.
   Flip. I tell you no; get you in again immediately, and prevent it.
   Cor. My Dear, Dear, I am not able; I never was in such a way before.
   Flip. Never in a way to be marry'd before, ha? is not that it?

Cor. Ah, Lord, if I'm thus before I come to't, *Flippanta*, what shall I be upon the very spot? Do but feel with what a thumpaty thump it goes.

[*Putting her Hand to her Heart.*

Flip. Nay it does make a filthy buſtle, that's the truth on't, Child. But I believe I ſhall make it leap another way, when I tell you, I'm cruelly afraid your Father won't consent, after all.

Cor. Why, he won't be the Death o'me, will he?

Flip. I don't know, old Folks are cruel; but we'll have a Trick for him. *Brass* and I have been consulting upon the Matter, and agreed upon a surer way of doing it in spight of his Teeth.

Cor. Ay, marry Sir, that were something.

Flip. But then he muſt not know a word of any thing towards it.

Cor. No, no.

Flip. So, get you in immediately.

Cor. One, two, three and away. [*Running off.*

Flip. And prevent your Mother's speaking on't.

Cor. But is t'other way sure, *Flippanta?*

Flip. Fear nothing, 'twill only depend upon you.

Cor. Nay then———O ho, ho, ho, how pure that is. [*Exit* Corinna.

Flippanta *sola.*

Poor Child! we may do what we will with her, as far as marrying her goes: when that's over 'tis possible she mayn't prove altogether so traƈtable. But who's here? my Sharper, I think: Yes.

Enter Moneytrap.

Mon. Well, my beſt Friend, how go Matters? has the Reſtitution been receiv'd, ha? Was she pleas'd with it?

Flip. Yes, truly, that is, she was pleas'd to see there was so honeſt a Man in this immoral Age.

Mon. Well, but a————does she know that 'twas I that————

Flip. Why, you muſt know I begun to give her a little sort of a hint, and————and so————why, and so she begun to put on a sort of a severe, haughty, reserv'd, angry, forgiving Air, but soft. Here she comes: You'll see how you ſtand with her presently: but don't be afraid. Courage.

Mon. He, hem.

Enter Clarissa.

'Tis no small piece of good Fortune, Madam, to find you at home: I have often endeavour'd it in vain.

Clar. 'Twas then unknown to me, for if I cou'd often receive the Visits of so good a Friend at home, I shou'd be more reasonably blam'd for being so much abroad.

Mon. Madam, you make me——

Clar. You are the Man of the World whose Company I think is most to be desir'd. I don't Complement you when I tell you so, I assure you.

Mon. Alas, Madam, your poor humble Servant——

Clar. My poor humble Servant however (with all the esteem I have for him) stands suspected with me for a vile Trick, I doubt he has play'd me, which if I could prove upon him, I'm afraid I should punish him very severely.

Mon. I hope, Madam, you'll believe I am not capable of——

Clar. Look you, look you, you are capable of whatever you please, you have a great deal of Wit, and know how to give a nice and gallant turn to every thing; but if you will have me continue your Friend, you must leave me in some uncertainty in this Matter.

Mon. Madam, I do then protest to you——

Clar. Come protest nothing about it, I am but too penetrating, as you may perceive; but we sometimes shut our Eyes, rather than break with our Friends; for a thorough knowledge of the truth of this business, wou'd make me very seriously angry.

Mon. 'Tis very certain, Madam, that——

Clar. Come, say no more on't I beseech you, for I'm in a good deal of heat while I but think on't; if you'll walk in, I'll follow you presently.

Mon. Your Goodness, Madam, is——

Flip. War Horse,   [*Aside to* Moneytrap.
No fine Speeches, you'll spoil all.

Mon. Thou art a most incomparable Person.

Flip. Nay, it goes rarely, but get you in, and I'll say a little something to my Lady for you, while she's warm.

Mon. But S't, *Flippanta*, how long dost think she may hold out?

Flip. Phu, not a Twelvemonth.

Mon. Boo.

Flip. Away, I say.   [*Pushing him out.*

Clar. Is he gone? What a Wretch it is? he never was quite such a Beast before.

Flip. Poor Mortal, his Money's finely laid out truly.

Clar. I suppose there may have been much such another Scene within between *Araminta* and my Dear: But I left him so insupportably brisk, 'tis impossible he can have parted with any Money: I'm afraid *Brass* has not succeeded as thou hast done, *Flippanta?*

Flip. By my Faith but he has, and better too; he presents his humble Duty to *Araminta*, and has sent her——this.   [*Shewing the note.*

Clar. A Bill for my Love for two hundred and fifty Pounds. The Monster! he wou'd not part with ten to save his lawful Wife from everlasting Torment.

Flip. Never complain of his Avarice, Madam, as long as you have his Money.

Clar. But is not he a Beast, *Flippanta?* methinks the Restitution look'd better by half.

Flip. Madam, the Man's Beast enough, that's certain; but which way will you go to receive his beastly Money; for I must not appear with his Note.

Clar. That's true; why send for Mrs. *Amlet;* that's a mighty useful Woman, that Mrs. *Amlet.*

Flip. Marry is she; we shou'd have been basely puzled how to dispose of the Necklace without her, 'twou'd have been dangerous offering it to Sale.

Clar. It wou'd so, for I know your Master has been laying out for't amongst the Goldsmiths. But I stay here too long, I must in and Coquet it a little more to my Lover, *Araminta* will get Ground on me else.

[*Exit* Clarissa.

Flip. And I'll go send for Mrs. *Amlet.*   [*Exit* Flip.

SCENE *Opens.*

Araminta, Corinna, Gripe, *and* Moneytrap *at a Tea-Table,*
very gay and laughing.

Clarissa *comes in to 'em.*

Omnes. Ha! ha! ha! ha!

Mon. Mighty well, O mighty well indeed!

Clar. Save you, save you good Folks, you are all in rare Humour methinks.

Gripe. Why, what shou'd we be otherwise for, Madam?

Clar. Nay, I don't know, not I, my Dear, but I han't had the happiness of seeing you since our Honey-Moon was over, I think.

Gripe. Why to tell you the truth, my Dear, 'tis the Joy of seeing you at home; [*Kisses her.*] You see what Charms you have, when you are pleas'd to make use of 'em.

Aram. Very gallant truly.

Clar. Nay, and what's more, you must know, he's never to be otherwise henceforwards; we have come to an Agreement about it.

Mon. Why, here's my Love and I have been upon just such another Treaty too.

Aram. Well, sure there's some very peaceful Star Rules at present. Pray Heaven continue its Reign.

(65)

Mon. Pray do you continue its Reign, you ladies; for 'tis all in your Power. [*Learing at* Clarissa.

Gripe. My Neighbour *Moneytrap* says true, at least I'll confess frankly [*Ogling* Araminta.] 'tis in one Lady's Power to make me the best humour'd Man on Earth.

Mon. And I'll answer for another, that has the same over me. [*Ogling* Clarissa.

Clar. 'Tis mighty fine, Gentlemen, mighty civil Husbands indeed.

Gripe. Nay, what I say's true, and so true, that all Quarrels being now at an end, I am willing, if you please, to dispense with all that fine Company we talk'd of to-day, be content with the friendly Conversation of our two good Neighbours here, and spend all my toying Hours alone with my sweet Wife.

Mon. Why, truly, I think now, if these good Women pleas'd, we might make up the prettiest little neighbourly Company, between our two Families, and set a defiance to all the impertinent People in the world.

Clar. The Rascals. [*Aside.*

Aram. Indeed, I doubt you'd soon grow weary if we grew fond.

Gripe. Never, never, for our Wives have Wit, Neighbour, and that seldom palls.

Clar. And our Husbands have Generosity, *Araminta*, and that seldom palls.

Gripe. So, that's a wipe for me now, because I did not give her a New-Year's Gift last time; but be good and I'll think of some Tea-Cups for you, next Year.

Mon. And perhaps I mayn't forget a Fan, or as good a thing——hum, Hussy?

Clar. Well, upon these Encouragements, *Araminta*, we'll try how good we can be.

Gripe. Well, this goes most rarely: poor *Moneytrap*, he little thinks what makes his Wife so easie in his Company. [*Aside.*

Mon. I can but pity poor Neighbour *Gripe*, Lard, Lard, what a Fool does his Wife and I make of him? [*Aside.*

Clar. Are not these two wretched Rogues, *Araminta?* [*Aside to* Araminta.

Aram. They are indeed. [*Aside to* Clarissa.

Enter Jessamin.

Jess. Sir, Here's Mr. *Clip* the Goldsmith desires to speak with you.

Gripe. Cods so, perhaps some News of your Necklace, my Dear.

Clar. That would be News indeed.

Gripe. Let him come in.

Enter Mr. Clip.

Gripe. Mr. *Clip*, your Servant, I'm glad to see you: How do you do?

Clip. At your Service, Sir, very well. Your Servant, Madam *Gripe.*

Clar. Horrid Fellow!   [*Aside.*

Gripe. Well, Mr. *Clip*, no News yet of my Wife's Necklace?

Clip. If you please to let me speak with you in the next Room, I have something to say to you.

Gripe. Ay, with all my Heart. Shut the Door after us. [*They come forward, and the Scene shuts behind them.*] Well, any News?

Clip. Look you, Sir, here's a Necklace brought me to sell, at least very like that you describ'd to me.

Gripe. Let's see't——*Victoria!* the very same. Ah my dear Mr. *Clip* ——[*Kisses him.*] But who brought it you? you shou'd have seiz'd him.

Clip. 'Twas a young Fellow that I know: I can't tell whether he may be guilty, tho' its like enough. But he has only left it me now, to shew a Brother of our Trade, and will call upon me again presently.

Gripe. Wheedle him hither, dear Mr. *Clip.* Here's my Neighbour *Moneytrap* in the House, he's a Justice, and will commit him presently.

Clip. 'Tis enough.

Enter Brass.

Gripe. O, my friend *Brass!*

Brass. Hold, Sir, I think that's a Gentleman I'm looking for. Mr. *Clip*, O your servant: What, are you acquainted here? I have just been at your Shop.

Clip. I only stept here to shew Mr. *Gripe* the Necklace you left.

Brass. Why, Sir, do you understand jewels? [*To Gripe.*] I thought you had dealt only in Gold. But I smoak the Matter; hark you,——a word in your Ear——you are going to play the Gallant again, and make a Purchase on't for *Araminta*; ha, ha?

Gripe. Where had you the Necklace?

Brass. Look you, don't trouble your self about that; it's in Commission with me, and I can help you to a Penniworth on't.

Gripe. A Penniworth on't, Villain?   [*Strikes at him.*

Brass. Villain! a hey, a hey: Is't you or me, Mr. *Clip*, he's pleas'd to Complement?

Clip. What do you think on't, Sir?

Brass. Think on't? now the Devil fetch me if I know what to think on't.

Gripe. You'll sell a Penniworth, Rogue! of a thing you have stol'n from me.

Brass. Stol'n! pray, Sir———what Wine have you drank to-day? It has a very merry effect upon you.

Gripe. You Villain! either give me an account how you ſtole it, or——

Brass. Oho, Sir, if you please, don't carry your Jeſt too far, I don't underſtand hard words, I give you warning on't: if you han't a mind to buy the Necklace, you may let it alone, I know how to dispose on't, what a Pox!——

Gripe. O, you shan't have that trouble, Sir. Dear Mr. *Clip*, you may leave the Necklace here. I'll call at your Shop, and thank you for your Care.

Clip. Sir, your humble Servant. [*Going.*

Brass. O ho, Mr. *Clip*, if you please, Sir, this won't do, [*Stopping him.*] I don't underſtand Raillery in such matters.

Clip. I leave it with Mr. *Gripe*, do you and he dispute it. [*Exit* Clip.

Brass. Ay, but 'tis from you, by your leave, Sir, that I expeƈt it.
[*Going after him.*

Gripe. You expeƈt, you Rogue, to make your escape, do you? But I have other Accounts besides this, to make up with you. To be sure the Dog has cheated me of two hundred and fifty Pound. Come, Villian, give me an Account of——

Brass. Account of!——Sir, give me an Account of my Necklace, or I'll make such a Noise in your House I'll raise the Devil in't.

Gripe. Well said, Courage.

Brass. Blood and Thunder give it me, or——

Gripe. Come, hush, be wise, and I'll make no noise of this Affair.

Brass. You'll make no Noise! But I'll make a Noise, and a damn'd Noise too. O, don't think to——

Gripe. I tell thee I will not hang thee.

Brass. But I tell you I will hang you, if you don't give me my Necklace, I will, rot me.

Gripe. Speak softly, be wise, how came it thine? who gave it thee?

Brass. A Gentleman, a Friend of mine.

Gripe. What's his name?

Brass. His name!——I'm in such a Passion I have forgot it.

Gripe. Ah, brazen Rogue——thou haſt ſtole it from my Wife; 'tis the same she loſt six Weeks ago.

Brass. This has not been in *England* a Month.

Gripe. You are a Son of a Whore.

Brass. Give me my Necklace.

Gripe. Give me my two hundred and fifty Pound Note.

Brass. Yet I offer Peace: One word without Passion: The case ſtands thus, Either I'm out of my Wits, or you are out of yours: Now 'tis plain I am not out of my wits, *Ergo*——

Gripe. My Bill, hang Dog, or I'll ſtrangle thee. [*They ſtruggle.*

Brass. Murder, Murder.

Enter Clarissa, Araminta, Corinna, Flippanta, *and* Moneytrap.

Flip. What's the matter? What's the matter here?

Gripe. I'll matter him.

Clar. Who makes thee cry out thus, poor *Brass?*

Brass. Why, your Husband, Madam, he's in his Altitudes here.

Gripe. Robber.

Brass. Here, he has cheated me of a Diamond Necklace.

Cor. Who, Papa? ah dear me.

Clar. Prithee what's the meaning of this great Immotion, my Dear?

Gripe. The meaning is that———I'm quite out of Breath———this Son of a Whore has got your Necklace, that's all.

Clar. My Necklace!

Gripe. That Birdlime there——ſtole it.

Clar. Impossible!

Brass. Madam, you see Maſter's a little———touch'd, that's all. Twenty Ounces of Blood let loose, wou'd set all right again.

Gripe. Here, call a Conſtable presently. Neighbour *Moneytrap*, you'll commit him.

Brass. D'ye hear? d'ye year? See how wild he looks? how his Eyes Rowl in his head: tie him down, or he'll do some Mischief or other.

Gripe. Let me come at him.

Clar. Hold,——prithee, my Dear, reduce things to a little Temperance, and let us coolly into the secret of this disagreeable Rupture.

Gripe. Well then, without Passion: Why, you muſt know, (but I'll have him hang'd) you muſt know that he came to Mr. *Clip*, to Mr. *Clip* the Dog did——with a Necklace to sell; so Mr. *Clip* having notice before that, (can you deny this, Sirrah?) that you had loſt yours, brings it to me. Look at it here, do you know it again? Ah, you traytor.　　　[*To* Brass.

Brass. He makes me mad, here's an appearance of something now to the Company, and yet nothing in't in the bottom.

Enter Conſtable.

Clar. Flippanta. [*Aside to* Flippanta, *shewing the necklace*].

Flip. 'Tis it Faith, here's some Myſtery in this, we muſt look about us.

Clar. The safeſt way is point blank to disown the Necklace.

Flip. Right, ſtick to that.

Gripe. Well, Madam, do you know your old Acquaintance, ha?

Clar. Why, truly, my Dear, tho' (as you may all imagine) I shou'd be very glad to recover so valuable a thing as my Necklace, yet I muſt be juſt to all the World, this Necklace is not mine.

Brass. Huzza——here Conſtable, do your Duty, Mr. Juſtice, I demand my Necklace, and satisfaction of him.

Gripe. I'll die before I part with it, I'll keep it, and have him hang'd.

Clar. But be a little Calm, my Dear, do my Bird, and then thou'lt be able to judge rightly of things.

Gripe. O good lack, O good lack.

Clar. No, but don't give way to Fury and Interest both, either of 'em are Passions strong enough to lead a wise Man out of the way. The Necklace not being really mine, give it the Man again, and come drink a Dish of Tea.

Brass. Ay, Madam says right.

Gripe. Oons, if you, with your addle Head, don't know your own Jewels, I with my solid one do. And if I part with it, may Famine be my Portion.

Clar. But don't swear and curse thy self at this fearful rate, don't my Dove: Be temperate in your Words, and just in all your Actions, 'twill bring a Blessing upon you and your Family.

Gripe. Bring Thunder and Lightning upon me and my Family, if I part with my Necklace.

Clar. Why, you'll have the Lightning burn your House about your Ears, my Dear, if you go on in these Practices.

Mon. A most excellent Woman this. [*Aside.*

Enter Mrs. Amlet.

Gripe. I'll keep my Necklace.

Brass. Will you so? then here comes one has a Title to it if I han't; let *Dick* bring himself off with her as he can. Mrs. *Amlet*, you are come in very good time, you lost a Necklace t'other Day, and who do you think has got it?

Aml. Marry that I know not, I wish I did.

Brass. Why then here's Mr. *Gripe* has it, and swears 'tis his Wife's.

Gripe. And so I do, Sirrah——look here, Mistriss, do you pretend this is yours?

Aml. Not for the round World I wou'd not say it; I only kept it, to do Madam a small courtesie, that's all.

Clar. Ah, *Flippanta*, all will out now. [*Aside to* Flip.

Gripe. Courtesie! what courtesie?

Aml. A little Money only that Madam had present need of, please to pay me that and I demand no more.

Brass. So here's fresh Game, I have started a new Hare, I find. [*Aside.*

Gripe. How, forsooth, is this true? [*To* Clarissa.

Clar. You are in a Humour at present, Love, to believe any thing, so I won't take the pains to contradict it.

Brass. This damn'd Necklace will spoil all our Affairs, this is *Dick*'s luck again. [*Aside.*

Gripe. Are you not asham'd of these ways? Do you see how you are expos'd before your best Friends here? don't you blush at it?

Clar. I do blush, my Dear, but 'tis for you, that here it shou'd appear to the World, you keep me so bare of Money, I'm forc'd to pawn my Jewels.

Gripe. Impudent Houswife!   [*Raising his Hand to strike her.*

Clar. Softly Chicken, you might have prevented all this, by giving me the two hundred and fifty Pound you sent to *Araminta* e'en now.

Brass. You see, Sir, I deliver'd your Note: How I have been abus'd to-day?

Gripe. I'm betray'd——Jades on both sides, I see that.   [*Aside.*

Mon. But, Madam, Madam, is this true I hear? Have you taken a Present of two hundred and fifty Pound? Pray what were you to return for these Pounds, Madam, ha?

Aram. Nothing, my Dear, I only took 'em to reimburse you of about the same Sum you sent to *Clarissa.*

Mon. Hum, hum, hum.

Gripe. How, Gentlewoman, did you receive Money from him?

Clar. O, my Dear, 'twas only in Jest, I knew you'd give it again to his Wife.

Aml. But amongst all this *Tintamar*, I don't hear a word of my hundred Pounds. Is it Madam will pay me, or Master?

Gripe. I pay? the Devil shall pay.

Clar. Look you, my Dear, Malice apart, pay Mrs. *Amlet* her Money, and I'll forgive you the Wrong, you intended my Bed with *Araminta:* Am not I a good Wife now?

Gripe. I burst with Rage, and will get rid of this Noose, tho' I tuck myself up in another.

Mon. Nay, pray, e'en tuck me up with you.   [*Exit* Mon. *and* Gripe.

Clar. & Aram. B'ye Dearies.

Enter Dick.

Cor. Look, look, *Flippanta*, here's the Colonel come at last.

Dick. Ladies, I ask your pardon, I have stay'd so long, but———

Aml. Ah Rogues Face, have I got thee? old good for nought, Sirrah, Sirrah, do you think to amuse me with your Marriages, and your great Fortunes? Thou hast play'd me a rare prank, by my Conscience. Why you ungracious Rascal, what do you think will be the end of all this? Now Heaven forgive me, but I have a great Mind to hang thee for't.

Cor. She talks to him very familiarly, *Flippanta*.

Flip. So methinks, by my Faith.

Brass. Now the Rogue's Star is making an end of him.   [*Aside.*

Dick. What shall I do with her? [*Aside.*

Aml. Do but look at him, my Dames, he has the Countenance of a Cherubim, but he's a Rogue in his Heart.

Clar. What is the meaning of all this, Mrs. *Amlet?*

Aml. The meaning, good lack. Why this all to be powder'd Rascal here, is my Son an't please you; ha, Graceless? Now I'll make you own your Mother, Vermine.

Clar. What, the Colonel your Son?

Aml. 'Tis *Dick,* Madam, that Rogue *Dick,* I have so often told you of, with Tears trickling down my old Cheeks.

Aram. The Woman's mad, it can never be.

Aml. Speak Rogue, am I not thy Mother? ha? Did I not bring thee forth? say then.

Dick. What will you have me say? you had a mind to ruine me, and you have done't; wou'd you do any more?

Clar. Then, Sir, you are Son to good Mrs. *Amlet?*

Aram. And have had the Assurance to put upon us all this while?

Flip. And the Confidence to think of Marrying *Corinna?*

Brass. And the Impudence to hire me for your Servant, who am as well born as your self.

Clar. Indeed I think he shou'd be Corrected.

Aram. Indeed I think he deserves to be Cudgell'd.

Flip. Indeed I think he might be Pumpt.

Brass. Indeed I think he will be Hang'd.

Aml. Good lack a day, good lack a day, there's no need to be so smart upon him neither: If he is not a Gentleman, he's a Gentleman's fellow. Come hither, *Dick,* they shan't run thee down neither, Cock up thy Hat *Dick,* and tell 'em, tho' Mrs. *Amlet* is thy Mother, she can make thee amends, with 10000 good Pounds to buy thee some Lands, and build thee a House in the midst on't.

Omnes. How!

Clar. Ten thousand Pounds, Mrs. *Amlet?*

Aml. Yes Forsooth; tho' I shou'd lose the hundred you pawn'd your Necklace for. Tell 'em of that, *Dick.*

Cor. Look you, *Flippanta,* I can hold no longer, and I hate to see the young Man abus'd. And so, Sir, if you please, I'm your Friend and Servant, and what's mine is yours, and when our Estates are put together, I don't doubt but we shall do as well as the best of 'em.

Dick. Say'st thou so, my little Queen? Why then if dear Mother will give us her Blessing, the Parson shall give us a Tack. We'll get her a score of Grand-children, and a merry House we'll make her.

[*They kneel to Mrs.* Amlet.

Aml. Ah——ha, ha, ha, the pretty pair, the pretty Pair, rise my chickens, rise, rise and Face the proudest of 'em. And if Madam does not deign to give her Consent, a Fig for her *Dick*——Why how now?

Clar. Pray, Mrs. *Amlet,* don't be in a Passion, the Girl is my Husband's Girl, and if you can have his Consent, upon my word you shall have mine, for any thing that belongs to him.

Flip. Then all's Peace again, but we have been more Lucky than Wise.

Aram. And I suppose, for us, *Clarissa,* we are to go on with our Dears, as we us'd to do.

Clar. Just in the same Tract, for this late Treaty of Agreement with 'em, was so unnatural, you see it could not hold. But 'tis just as well with us, as if it had. Well, 'tis a strange Fate, good Folks. But while you live, every thing gets well out of a Broil, but a Husband.

FINIS.

EPILOGUE

Spoke by Mrs. BARRY.

I'VE heard wise Men in Politicks lay down,
   What Feats by little England might be done,
Were all agreed, and all would act as One.
Ye Wives a useful Hint from this might take,
The heavy, old, despotick Kingdom shake,
And make your Matrimonial Monsieurs quake.
Our Heads are feeble, and we're cramp'd by Laws;
Our Hands are weak, and not too strong our Cause:
Yet would those Heads and Hands, such as they are,
In firm Confed'racy resolve on War,
You'd find your Tyrants——what I've found my Dear.
What only Two united can produce
You've seen to Night, a Sample for your Use;
Single, we found we nothing could obtain;
We join our Force—and we subdu'd our Men.
Believe me, (my dear Sex) they are not Brave;
Try each your Man, you'll quickly find your Slave.
I know they'll make Campaigns, risk Blood and Life;
But this is a more terrifying Strife;
They'll stand a Shot, who'll tremble at a Wife.
Beat then your Drums, and your shrill Trumpets sound,
Let all your Visits of your Feats resound:
And Deeds of War in Cups of Tea go round:
The Stars are with you, Fate is in your Hand,
In Twelve Months Time you've vanquish'd half the Land;
Be Wise, and keep 'em under good Command.
This Year will to your Glory long be known,
And deathless Ballads hand your Triumphs down;
Your late Atchievements ever will remain,
For tho' you cannot boast of many Slain,
Your Pris'ners shew, you've made a brave Campaign.

THE

MISTAKE

A

COMEDY

As it is Acted at the

QUEEN'S THEATRE in the

Hay-Market.

By Her MAJESTY's Sworn Servants.

By the Author of *The Provok'd Wife*, &c.

Source

THE *Mi take* is a translation of *Le Dépit Amoureux* of Molière, which was first acted at Béziers in 1654 for the Prince de Conti, and in December, 1658, at the Théâtre du Petit-Bourbon. The names are so considerably altered, owing to Vanbrugh laying the scene in Spain, that the French *Dramatis Personæ* is here given.

Éraste, amant de Lucile.	Béjart aîné.
Albert, père de Lucile et d'Ascagne.	Molière.
Gros-René, valet d'Éraste.	Duparc.
Valère, fils de Polidore.	Béjart.
Lucile, fille d'Albert.	Mlle. de Brie.
Marinette, suivante de Lucile.	Madeleine Béjart.
Polidore, père de Valère.	
Frosine, confidente d'Ascagne.	
Ascagne, fille d'Albert, déguisée en homme.	
Mascarille, valet de Valère.	
Métaphraste, pédant.	Du Croisy.
La Rapière, bretteur.	De Brie.

This is one of the earliest of Molière's comedies, full of the influence of the *Commedia dell' Arte* and of the author's natural graces. Vanbrugh followed it closely, scene by scene, taking fewer liberties than he did with Boursault or Dancourt, but it was not in him to reproduce that humane pessimism already apparent in Molière's work. Owing to the difference in phrasing, it becomes a different work under his hands. Some passages of Molière are here quoted for comparison, and a few important variations are mentioned in the notes.

This is the speech of Métaphraste at the conclusion of Act II. All the rough and tumble towards the end of that act are Vanbrugh's.

> D'où vient fort à propos cette sentence expresse
> D'un philosophe : parle, afin qu'on te connoisse.
> Doncques si de parler le pouvoir m'est ôté,
> Pour moi, j'aime autant perdre aussi l'humanité,
> Et changer mon essence en celle d'une bête.
> Me voilà pour huit jours avec un mal de tête.
> Oh, que les grands parleurs par moi sont détestés.
> Mais quoi ! Si les savans ne sont pas écoutés,
> Si l'on veut que toujours ils aient la bouche close,
> Il faut donc renverser l'ordre de chaque chose.

Que les poules dans peu dévorent les renards;
Que les jeunes enfans remontrent aux vieillards;
Qu'à poursuivre les loups les agnelets s'ébattent;
Qu'un fou fasse les loix, que les femmes combattent;
Que par les criminels les juges soient jugés,
Et par les écoliers les maîtres fustigés;
Que le malade au sain présente le remède;
Que le lièvre craintif . . .

The following is from Act IV, Scene iii:

Éraste. . . . Mais enfin, il n'importe; et puisque votre haine
Chasse un cœur tant de fois que l'amour vous ramène,
C'est la dernière ici des importunités
Que vous aurez jamais de mes vœux rebutés.
 Lucile. Vous pouvez faire aux miens la grace toute entière
Monsieur, et m'épargner encor cette dernière.
 Éraste. Hé bien, Madame, hé bien, ils seront satisfaits.
Je romps avecque vous, et j'y romps pour jamais,
Puisque vous le voulez. Que je perde la vie
Lorsque de vous parler je reprendrai l'envie.
 Lucile. Tant mieux; c'est m'obliger.
 Éraste. Non, non, n'ayez pas peur
Que je fausse parole; eussé-je un foible cœur
Jusques à n'en pouvoir effacer votre image,
Croyez que vous n'aurez jamais cet avantage
De me voir revenir.
 Lucile. Ce seroit bien en vain.
 Éraste. Moi-même de cent coups je percerois mon sein,
Si j'avois jamais fait cette bassesse insigne
De vous revoir après ce traitement indigne.
 Lucile. Soit; n'en parlons donc plus.
 Éraste. Oui, oui, n'en parlons plus;
Et, pour trancher ici tous propos superflus,
Et vous donner, ingrate, une preuve certaine
Que je veux, sans retour, sortir de votre chaîne,
Je ne veux rien garder, qui puisse retracer
Ce que de mon esprit il me faut effacer.
Voici votre portrait; il présente à la vue
Cent charmes merveilleux dont vous êtes pourvue,
Mais il cache sous eux cent défauts aussi grands,
Et c'est un imposteur enfin que je vous rends.
 Gros-René. Bon.
 Lucile. Et moi, pour vous suivre au dessein de tout rendre,
Voilà le diamant que vous m'avez fait prendre.
 Marinette. Fort bien.
 Éraste. Il est à vous encor ce brasselet.
 Lucile. Et cette agate à vous, qu'on fit mettre en cachet.

SOURCE

Éraste (lit).　*Vous m'aimez d'un amour extrême,*
　　　　　　　Éraste, et de mon cœur voulez être éclairci;
　　　　　　　Si je n'aime Éraste de même,
　　　　　　　Au moins aimai-je fort qu' Éraste m'aime ainsi.　Lucile.

Vous m'assuriez par là d'agréer mon service;
C'est une fausseté digne de ce supplice.
　　　　　　(Il déchire la lettre.)
Lucile (lit).　*J'ignore le destin de mon amour ardente,*
　　　　　　Et jusqu' à quand je souffrirai:
　　　　　　Mais je sais, ô beauté charmante!
　　　　　　Que toujours je vous aimerai.　Éraste.

Voilà qui m'assurait à jamais de vos feux:
Et la main, et la lettre, ont menti toutes deux.
　　　　　　(Elle déchire la lettre.)
Gros-René.　Poussez.
Éraste.　　　　　Elle est de vous.　Suffit, même fortune.
Marinette (à Lucille).　Ferme.
Lucile.　　　　　　J'aurois regret d'en épargner aucune.
Gros-René (à Éraste).　N'ayez pas le dernier.
Marinette (à Lucille).　　　　Tenez bon jusqu'au bout.
Lucile.　Enfin voilà le reste.
Éraste.　　　　　Et, grace au ciel, c'est tout.
Je sois exterminé, si je ne tiens parole.
　Lucile.　Me confonde le ciel, si la mienne est frivole!
Éraste.　Adieu donc.
Lucile.　　　　　Adieu donc.
Marinette (à Lucille).　　　　Voilà qui va des mieux.
Gros-René (à Éraste).　Vous triomphez.
Marinette (à Lucille).　　　　Allons, ôtez-vous de ses yeux.
Gros-René (à Éraste).　Retirez-vous après cet effort de courage.
Marinette (à Lucille).　Qu' attendez-vous encor?
Gros-René (à Éraste).　　　　Que faut-il d'avantage?
　Éraste.　Ah! Lucile, Lucile, un cœur comme le mien
Se fera regretter, et je le sais fort bien.
　Lucile.　Eraste, Éraste, un cœur comme est fait le vôtre,
Se peut facilement réparer par un autre.
　Éraste.　Non, non, cherchez par-tout, vous n'en aurez jamais
De si passioné pour vous, je vous promets.
Je ne dis pas cela pour vous rendre attendrie;
J'aurois tort d'en former encore quelqu' envie.
Mes plus ardens respects n'ont pu vous obliger,
Vous avez voulu rompre; il n'y faut plus songer:
Mais personne, après moi, quoi qu'on vous fasse entendre,
N'aura jamais pour vous de passion si tendre.

　　Molière's play is drawn partly from the *Interresse di Nicolo Secchi*, at least as far
as regards the part of Ascagne, and partly, according to Riccoboni, from an old piece

Sdegni Amorosi. The scene just quoted is entirely original, and is indeed typically Molièresque. Monsieur Bret, the editor of 1778, wrote: " On a remarqué que ces scènes de dépit, toujours sûres du succès, sont une imitation de l'Ode d'Horace, *Donec gratus eram,* et Molière est le premier qui ait fait passer ce tableau charmant sous nos yeux; on l'a beaucoup imité depuis, et c'est aujourd'hui ce qu'on appelle un *lieu commun.*" The Ode is Lib. III, ix.

Text

THE text is from the first edition of 1706, quarto. Since the play was not reprinted till very much later in the century as a separate piece, it has been collated with the copy in the first collected edition of 1719. One or two obvious misprints, such as "lanthon" for "lanthorn," have been silently corrected where 1719 gives authority.

Theatrical History

THE *Mistake* was first acted at Vanbrugh's own theatre in the Haymarket, and during his management, on Thursday, 27 December, 1705, to be repeated on the 31st, and on 1 and 2 January, 1706. Genest says it ran nine nights, Ward six, but only a fifth performance can be traced, namely, on 25 March. Betterton, " the Phœnix of the Stage," played Don Alvarez, while Booth played Don Carlos, a part which must have suited him very well. His description would agree with that of many a *jeune premier* of to-day. " He was of a Form altogether Graceful, accompanied with an Air that gave the highest Dignity to all his Gestures. His Face had a manly Sweetness; and his features were so happily turn'd, as to be able to express the roughest Passions, without losing any thing of the Agreeableness of his Countenance. His Voice had great Strength in it, and a Tone uncommonly musical. His articulation was so exceedingly distinct and clear, that he could be heard to the farthest Part of the Theatre, even in a Whisper." Doggett, " a little, lively man," was his servant. " He was the most original . . . of all his contemporaries. He borrow'd from none of them; his manner was all his own. . . . He could be extremely ridiculous, without stepping into the least impropriety to make him so. His great success was in characters of lower life, which he improv'd, from the delight he took, in his observations of that kind, in the real world." Mrs. Bowman, Betterton's adopted child, played Leonora, but we miss the star names from the ladies' parts, unless we except Mrs. Porter.

Though tolerably well liked, it was not popular enough to become a stock play, and was not acted again until 1710, when it was put on three times at Drury Lane and twice at Pinkethman's theatre at Greenwich. At first it was rarely revived, lying dormant until 1715, when Lincoln's Inn Fields put it on at the beginning and end of the year. It then rested until 1726, when it entered upon an era of prosperity, being acted twice that year at Lincoln's Inn Fields, five times the next year, three times in 1728, twice in 1729, no fewer than six times in 1730, and six times in 1731.

At the first of these performances Ryan played Don Carlos; Spiller, an excellent young actor, who could magically change his appearance, Lopez; Walker Lorenzo; and Boheme Don Alvarez. The part of Sancho was taken by Hippisley, who made up for a poor appearance by putting a deal of thought into his parts. Mrs. Bullock played Camillo, and Mrs. Younger Leonora. In the 1729 productions Milward took over Alvarez and Chapman Lopez. In 1732 it was acted twice at the same theatre, where on 15 March Mrs. Hallam played Isabella. Genest says that on 15 May it was acted at Drury Lane with Wilks, probably as Pedro, possibly his last time of acting, as he died that year. But on that day it was acted at Lincoln's Inn Fields. (*Daily Journal.*) In December, 1733, it was acted at Goodman's Fields on two occasions, and then became part of the Covent Garden repertory, though it appeared again twice at Goodman's Fields early in 1734, making four times for that season at that theatre. After that, with the exception of 1736, it was acted at least once every year at Covent Garden until 1745. In the revival of 1738, which took place on 31 January, Ryan and Hippisley were still in their old parts of Don Carlos and Sancho, but Lopez was played by Chapman, Alvarez by Bridgewater, while Mrs. Horton played Leonora and Mrs. Kilby Jacinta.

It came back to Drury Lane on 13 March, 1755, being described as "not acted 30 years," meaning at that theatre, though even so it was an inaccuracy. It was a superb cast: Garrick played Don Carlos; Palmer Lorenzo; Mrs. Pritchard, for whose benefit it was, played Leonora; and Mrs. Clive Jacinta, all stars of the first order. "This excellent comedy," Genest remarks, "was never so well acted before, and in all probability never will be again." It was repeated with almost the same cast on 20 March, 1760, for Mrs. Clive's benefit, the main change being that King played Sancho, an admirable part for him, which had previously been played by Woodward. It was repeated on 10 April for the benefit of Fleetwood, the manager, who acted Don Felix, and on 20 March, 1762, for Mrs. Pritchard, with Garrick and Mrs. Clive in their old parts.

Beginning on 24 February, it was revived again at the same theatre in 1764 for three nights, with Holland, a somewhat erratic actor, who was at his best when imitating Garrick, as Don Carlos. On 31 October, 1765, Mrs. Palmer played Leonora. Though not a very good actress, she could on occasion, as in Juliet, show "great softness, good sense and feeling." "She was rather low, but her figure was extremely elegant, and her deportment particularly genteel." She left the stage in 1768.

Covent Garden advertised the play as "not acted 14 years," at that theatre of course, when it was revived there on 6 February, 1766. Smith played Don Carlos; Shuter Sancho; and Woodward Lopez. Woodward had naturally a very regular and composed face, apparently adapted to serious parts, "but the moment he spoke on the stage, a certain ludicrous air laid hold of his features, and every muscle of his face ranged itself on the side of levity." Camillo was played by Miss Macklin, and Jacinta by Miss Pitt, this being her first appearance as an actress.

The last revival of The Mistake as such appears to have been that at Drury Lane on 15 February, 1772, when Garrick acted Don Felix. But as Lover's Quarrels, an adaptation attributed to King, the actor, it was played at Covent Garden on 11 February, 1790. King himself played Sancho and Ryder Lopez; Farren played Lorenzo; Mrs. Pope Leonora; and Miss Chapman Camillo. The evening, which was for King's benefit, included Sheep Shearing, or Florizel and Perdita, and concluded with Bon Ton. This version was acted, at any rate once again, in 1794.

PROLOGUE

Written by Mr. Steele.

Spoken by Mr. *Booth.*

OUR *Author's Wit and Raillery to-Night*
 Perhaps might please, but that your Stage-Delight
No more is in your Minds, but Ears and Sight;
With Audiences compos'd of Belles and Beaux,
The first Dramatick Rule is, Have good Cloathes.
To charm the gay Spectator's gentle Breast,
In Lace and Feather Tragedy's express'd,
And Heroes die unpity'd, if ill dress'd.

 The other Style you full as well advance;
If 'tis a Comedy, you ask,——Who dance?
For oh! what dire Convulsions have of late
Torn and distracted each Dramatick State,
On this great Question, Which House first should sell
The New French Steps, imported by Ruel?
Desbarques *can't rise so high, we must agree,*
They've half a Foot in Height more Wit than we.
But tho' the Genius of our learned Age
Thinks fit to Dance and Sing, quite off the Stage,
True Action, Comick Mirth, and Tragick Rage;
Yet, as your Taste now stands, our Author draws
Some Hopes of your Indulgence and Applause.
For that great End this Edifice he made,
Where humble Swain at Lady's Feet is laid;
Where the pleas'd Nymph her conquer'd Lover spies,
Then to Glass Pillars turns her conscious Eyes,
And points a-new each Charm, for which he dies.

 The Muse, before nor Terrible nor Great,
Enjoys by him this awful gilded Seat:
By him Theatrick Angels mount more high,
And Mimick Thunders shake a broader Sky.

PROLOGUE

Thus all must own, our Author has done more
For your Delight, than ever Bard before.
His Thoughts are still to raise your Pleasures fill'd;
To Write, Translate, to Blazon, or to Build.
Then take him in the Lump, nor nicely pry
Into small Faults, that 'scape a busie Eye;
But kindly, Sirs, consider, he to-Day
Finds you the House, the Actors, and the Play:
So, tho' we Stage-Mechanick Rules omit,
You must allow it in a Whole-Sale Wit.

Dramatis Personæ

MEN.

Don *Alvarez*, Father to *Leonora*.	Mr. *Betterton*.
Don *Felix*, Father to *Lorenzo*.	Mr. *Bright*.
Don *Carlos*, in Love with *Leonora*.	Mr. *Booth*.
Don *Lorenzo*, in Love with *Leonora*.	Mr. *Husbands*.
Metaphrastus, Tutor to *Camillo*.	Mr. *Freeman*.
Sancho, Servant to Don *Carlos*.	Mr. *Dogget*.
Lopez, Servant to Don *Lorenzo*.	Mr. *Pack*.
A Bravo.	

WOMEN.

Leonora, Daughter to Don *Alvarez*.	Mrs. *Bowman*.
Camillo, suppos'd Son to Don *Alvarez*.	Mrs. *Harcourt*.
Isabella, her Friend.	Mrs. *Porter*.
Jacinta, Servant to *Leonora*.	Mrs. *Baker*.

THE

MISTAKE

ACT I. SCENE I.

SCENE, *the Street*.

Enter Don Carlos *and* Sancho.

Don Car. I Tell thee, I am not satisfy'd, I'm in Love enough to be suspicious of every body.

San. And yet methinks, Sir, you should leave me out.

Don Car. It may be so; I can't tell; but I'm not at ease. If they don't make a Knave, at least they'll make a Fool of thee.

San. I don't believe a Word on't: But good faith, Master, your Love makes somewhat of you; I don't know what 'tis; but methinks when you suspect me, you don't seem a Man of half those Parts I us'd to take you for. Look in my Face, 'tis round and comely, not One hollow Line of a Villain in it: Men of my Fabrick don't use to be suspected for Knaves, and when you take us for Fools, we never take you for wise Men. For my part, in this present Case, I take my self to be mighty deep. A Stander by, Sir, sees more than a Gamester. You are pleas'd to be jealous of your poor Mistress without a Cause, she uses you but too well, in my humble Opinion; she sees you, and talks with you, 'till I am quite tired on't sometimes; and your Rival that you are so scar'd about, forces a Visit upon her, about once in a Fortnight.

Don Car. Alas, thou art ignorant in these Affairs, he that's the civilly'st receiv'd is often the least car'd for: Women appear warm to one, to hide a Flame for another. *Lorenzo* in short appears too compos'd of late to be a rejected Lover, and the Indifference he shews upon the Favours I seem to receive from her, poisons the Pleasure I else should taste in 'em, and keeps me on a perpetual Rack. No—I would fain see some of his jealous Transports, have him fire at the Sight o' me, contradict me whenever I speak, affront me wherever he meets me, challenge me, fight me——

San. ——Run you through the Guts.

Don Car. But he's too calm, his Heart's too much at Ease, to leave me mine at Rest.

San. But, Sir, you forget that there are two Ways for our Hearts to get at Ease; when our Mistresses come to be very fond of us, or we—not to care a Fig for them. Now suppose, upon the Rebukes you know he has had, it should chance to be the latter.

Don Car. Again thy Ignorance appears: Alas, a Lover who has broke his Chain will shun the Tyrant that enslav'd him, Indifference never is his Lot, he loves or hates for ever; and if his Mistress prove another's Prize, he cannot calmly see her in his Arms.

San. For my part, Master, I'm not so great a Philosopher as you be, nor (thank my Stars) so bitter a Lover, but what I see,——that I generally believe; and when *Jacinta* tells me she loves me dearly, I have good Thoughts enough of my Person never to doubt the Truth on't. See, here the Baggage comes.

Enter Jacinta *with a Letter.*

Hist, *Jacinta,* my Dear.

Jacin. Who's that? Blunderbuss? Where's your Master?

San. Hard by.   *[Shewing him.*

Jacin. O Sir, I'm glad I have found you at last; I believe I have travell'd five Miles after you, and could neither find you at home, nor in the Walks, nor at Church, nor at the Opera, nor——

San. Nor any where else, where he was not to be found; if you had look'd for him where he was, 'twas Ten to One but you had met with him.

Jacin. I had, Jackadandy?

Don Car. But prithee what's the Matter? Who sent you after me?

Jacin. One who's never well but when she sees you, I think; 'twas my Lady.

Don Car. Dear *Jacinta,* I fain would flatter my self, but am not able; the Blessing's too great to be my Lot: Yet 'tis not well to trifle with me; how short soe'er I am in other Merit, the Tenderness I have for *Leonora* claims something from her Generosity. I should not be deluded.

Jacin. And why do you think you are? methinks she's pretty well above-board with you, what must be done more to satisfie you?

San. Why, *Lorenzo* must hang himself, and then we are content.

Jacin. How? *Lorenzo?*

San. If less will do, he'll tell you.

Jacin. Why you are not mad, Sir, are you? Jealous of him! Pray which Way may this have got into your Head? I took you for a Man of Sense before.——Is this your Doings, Log?   *[To* Sancho.

San. No forsooth, Pert, I'm not much given to Suspicion, as you can tell, Mrs. Forward.——If I were, I might find more Cause, I guess, than your Mistress has given our Master here. But I have so many pretty

Thoughts of my own Person, Houswife, more than I have of yours, that I stand in dread of no Man.

Jacin. That's the Way to prosper, however so far I'll confess the Truth to thee, at least if that don't do, nothing else will. Men are mighty simple in Love-Matters, Sir: When you suspect a Woman's falling off, you fall a plaguing her to bring her on again, attack her with Reason, and a sour Face; udslife, Sir, attack her with a Fiddle, double your good Humour, ——give her a Ball,——powder your Perriwig at her,——let her cheat you at Cards a little, and I'll warrant all's right again. But to come upon a poor Woman with the gloomy Face of Jealousie, before she gives the least Occasion for't, is to set a complaisant Rival in too favourable a Light. Sir, Sir, I must tell you, I have seen those have ow'd their Success to nothing else.

Don Car. Say no more; I have been to blame, but there shall be no more on't.

Jacin. I should punish you but justly however for what's past, if I carry'd back what I have brought you; but I'm good-natur'd, so here 'tis; open it, and see how wrong you tim'd your Jealousie.

Don Car. reads.] *If you love me with that Tenderness you have made me long believe you do, this Letter will be welcome; 'tis to tell you, you have Leave to plead a Daughter's Weakness to a Father's Indulgence; and if you prevail with him to lay his Commands upon me, you shall be as happy as my Obedience to 'em can make you.*

Leonora.

Then I shall be what Man was never yet; [*Kissing the Letter.*] Ten Thousand Blessings on thee for thy News, I could adore thee as a Deity.

[*Embracing* Jacin.

San. True Flesh and Blood, every Inch of her, for all that.

Don Car. reads again.] *And if you prevail with him to lay his Commands upon me, you shall be as happy as my Obedience to 'em can make you.*

O happy, happy *Carlos:* But what shall I say to thee for this welcome Message? [*To* Jacin.] Alas! I want Words—But let this speak for me, and this, and this, and——   [*Giving her his Ring, Watch and Purse*

San. Hold, Sir; pray leave a little Something for our Board-Wages. You can't carry 'em all, I believe: [*To* Jacinta.] Shall I ease thee of this?

[*Offering to take the Purse.*

Jacin. No; but you may carry—That, Sirrah.

[*Giving him a Box o'th' Ear.*

San. The Jade's grown Purse-proud already.

Don Car. Well, dear *Jacinta,* say something to your charming Mistress, that I am not able to say my self: But, above all, excuse my late unpardonable Folly, and offer her my Life to expiate my Crime.

Jacin. The best Plea for Pardon will be never to repeat the Fault.

Don Car. If that will do, 'tis seal'd for ever.

Jacin. Enough. But I must be gone; Success attend you with the old Gentleman. Good by t'ye, Sir.　　　　　　　　　　　　[*Ex.* Jacin.

Don Car. Eternal Blessings follow thee.

San. I think she has taken 'em all with her; the Jade has got her Apron full.

Don Car. Is not that *Lorenzo* coming this way?

San. Yes, 'tis he; for my part now I pity the poor Gentleman.

Enter Don Lorenzo.

Don Car. I'll let him see at last I can be chearful too. Your Servant, *Don Lorenzo;* how do you do this Morning?

Don Lor. I thank you, *Don Carlos*, perfectly well, both in Body and in Mind.

Don Car. What? Cur'd of your Love then?

Don Lor. No, nor I hope I never shall. May I ask you how 'tis with yours?

Don Car. Encreasing every Hour; we are very constant both.

Don Lor. I find so much Delight in being so, I hope I never shall be otherwise.

Don Car. Those Joys I am well acquainted with, but should lose 'em soon were I to meet a cool Reception.

Don Lor. That's ev'ry generous Lover's Case, no doubt; an Angel could not Fire my Heart, but with an equal Flame.

Don Car. And yet you said you still lov'd *Leonora*.

Don Lor. And yet I said I lov'd her.

Don Car. Does she then return you——?

Don Lor. Ev'ry thing my Passion can require.

Don Car. Its Wants are small, I find.

Don Lor. Extended as the Heav'ns.

Don Car. I pity you.

Don Lor. He must be a Deity that does so.

Don Car. Yet I'm a Mortal, and once more can pity you. Alas *Lorenzo*, 'tis a poor Cordial to an aching Heart, to have the Tongue alone anounce it happy; besides, 'tis mean; you should be more a Man.

Don Lor. I find I have made you an unhappy one, so can forgive the Boilings of your Spleen.

Don Car. This seeming Calmness might have the Effect your Vanity proposes by it; had I not a Testimony of her Love would (should I shew it) sink you to the Center.

Don Lor. Yet still I'm calm as ever.

Don Car. Nay, then have at your Peace. Read that, and end the Farce. [*Gives him* Leonora's *Letter.*

Don Lor. reads.] I have read it.

Don Car. And know the Hand?

Don Lor. 'Tis *Leonora*'s I have often seen it.

Don Car. I hope you then at last are satisfy'd.

Don Lor. I am, [*Smiling.*] Good-morrow *Carlos.*   [*Ex.* Don Lor.

San. Sure he's mad, Master.

Don Car. Mad, say'st thou?

San. And yet birlady, that was a sort of a dry, sober Smile at going off.

Don Car. A very sober one. Had he shewn me such a Letter, I had put on another Countenance.

San. Ay a' my Conscience had you.

Don Car. Here's Mystery in this——I like it not.

San. I see his Man and Confident there, *Lopez.* Shall I draw him on a *Scotch* Pair of Boots, Master, and make him tell all?

Don Car. Some Questions I must ask him; call him hither.

San. Hem, *Lopez*, hem.

Enter Lopez.

Lop. Who calls?

San. I, and my Master.

Lop. I can't stay.

San. You can indeed, Sir.   [*Laying hold on him.*

Don Car. Whither in such haste, honest *Lopez*; what? upon some Love Errand?

Lop. Sir, your Servant; I ask your Pardon, but I was going——

Don Car. I guess where; but you need not be shy of me any more, thy Master and I are no longer Rivals, I have yielded up the Cause; the Lady will have it so, so I submit.

Lop. Is it possible, Sir? Shall I then live to see my Master and you Friends again?

San. Yes; and what's better: Thou and I shall be Friends too. There will be no more fear of Christian Blood-shed, I give thee up *Jacinta*; she's a slippery Houswife, so Master and I are going to match our selves elsewhere.

Lop. But is it possible, Sir, your Honour should be in earnest? I'm afraid you are pleas'd to be merry with your poor humble Servant.

Don Car. I'm not at present much Dispos'd to Mirth, my Indifference in this Matter is not so thoroughly form'd; but my Reason has so far master'd my Passion, to shew me 'tis in vain to pursue a Woman whose Heart already is anothers. 'Tis what I have so plainly seen of late, I have rouz'd my Resolution to my Aid, and broke my Chains for ever.

Lop. Well, Sir, to be plain with you, this is the joyfull'st News I have heard this long time, for I always knew you to be a mighty honest Gentleman, and good Faith it often went to the Heart o' me to see you so abus'd. Dear, dear, have I often said to my self (when they have had a private Meeting just after you have been gone.)——

Don Car. Ha?

San. Hold, Master, don't kill him yet.   [*To* Don Car. *aside.*

Lop. I say I have said to my self, What wicked Things are Women, and what pity it is they should be suffer'd in a Christian Country; what a Shame they should be allow'd to play Will in the Wisp with Men of Honour, and lead 'em through Thorns and Briers, and Rocks and rugged Ways, 'till their Hearts are torn in Pieces, like an old Coat in a Fox Chace? I say, I have said to my self——

Don Car. Thou hast said enough to thy self, but say a little more to me: Where were these secret Meetings thou talk'st of?

Lop. In sundry Places, and by divers Ways; sometimes in the Cellar, sometimes in the Garret, sometimes in the Court, sometimes in the Gutter; but the Place where the Kiss of Kisses was given was——

Don Car. In Hell.

Lop. Sir?

Don Car. Speak, Fury; what dost thou mean by the Kiss of Kisses?

Lop. The Kiss of Peace, Sir; the Kiss of Union; the Kiss of Consummation.

Don Car. Thou ly'st, Villain.

Lop. I don't know but I may, Sir,——What the Devil's the Matter now?   [*Aside.*

Don Car. There's not one Word of Truth in all thy cursed Tongue has utter'd.

Lop. No, Sir, I—I—believe there is not.

Don Car. Why then did'st thou say it, Wretch?

Lop. O—only in Jest, Sir.

Don Car. I am not in a jesting Condition.

Lop. Nor I—at present, Sir.

Don Car. Speak then the Truth, as thou wou'dst do it at the Hour of Death.

Lop. Yes, at the Gallows, and be turn'd off as soon as I've done. [*Aside.*

Don Car. What's that you murmur?

Lop. Nothing but a short Prayer.

Don Car. I am distracted, and fright the Wretch from telling me what I am upon the Rack to know. [*Aside.*] Forgive me, *Lopez,* I am to blame to speak thus harshly to thee: Let this obtain thy Pardon. [*Gives him Mony.*] Thou see'st I am disturb'd.

Lop. Yes, Sir, I see I have been led into a Snare; I have said too much.

Don Car. And yet thou muſt say more; nothing can lessen my Torment, but a farther Knowledge of what causes my Misery. Speak then! Have I any thing to hope?

Lop. Nothing; but that you may be a happier Batchelour, than my Maſter may probably be a Married Man.

Don Car. Married, say'ſt thou?

Lop. I did, Sir; and I believe he'll say so too in a Twelve-month.

Don Car. O Torment!——But give me more on't: When, How, to Who, Where?

Lop. Yeſterday, to *Leonora*, by the Parson, in the Pantry.

Don Car. Look to't, if this be false, thy Life shall pay the Torment thou haſt given me: Begone!

Lop. With the Body and the Soul o'me.   [*Exit* Lopez.

San. Base News, Maſter.

Don Car. Now my insulting Rival's Smile speaks out; O cursed, cursed Woman.

Enter Jacinta.

Jacin. I'm come in haſte to tell you, Sir, that as soon as the Moon's up, my Lady'll give you a Meeting in the Close Walk by the back Door of the Garden; she thinks she has something to propose to you, will certainly get her Father's Consent to marry you.

Don Car. Paſt Sufferance; this Aggravation is not to be borne; go, thank her—with my Curses: Fly—and let 'em blaſt her, while their Venom's ſtrong.   [*Exit* Don Car.

Jacin. ——Won't thou explain? What's this Storm for?

San. And dar'ſt thou ask me Queſtions, smooth-fac'd Iniquity, Crocodile of *Nile*, Syren of the Rocks? Go, carry back the too gentle Answer thou haſt receiv'd; only let me add with the Poet,

We are no Fools, Trollop, my Maſter nor me:
And thy Miſtress may go——to the Devil, with thee.

          [*Exit* Sancho.

Jacinta *sola.*

Am I awake?——I fancy not; A very idle Dream this. Well: I'll go talk in my Sleep to my Lady about it; and when I awake, we'll try what Interpretation we can make on't.   [*Exit.*

End of the Firſt Act.

ACT II.   SCENE I.

Enter Camillo *and* Isabella.

Isab. HOW can you doubt my Secrecy? Have you not Proofs of it?
Cam. Nay, I am determin'd to truſt you; but are we safe here? Can no body over-hear us?

Isab. Safer much than in a Room: No body can come within hearing, before we see 'em.

Cam. And yet how hard 'tis for me to break Silence?

Isab. Your Secret sure muſt be of great Importance.

Cam. You may be sure it is, when I confess, 'tis with Regret I own it ev'n to you, and were it possible you shou'd not know it.

Isab. 'Tis frankly own'd indeed; but 'tis not kind, perhaps not prudent, after what you know I already am acquainted with. Have I not been bred up with you? And am I ignorant of a Secret, which were it known——

Cam. Wou'd be my Ruin, I confess it wou'd. I own you know why both my Birth and Sex are thus disguis'd; you know how I was taken from my Cradle, to secure the Eſtate, which had else been loſt by Young *Camillo*'s Death: But which is now safe in my suppos'd Father's Hands, by my passing for his Son; and 'tis because you know all this, I have resolv'd to open farther Wonders to you: But before I say any more, you muſt resolve one Doubt which often gives me great Diſturbance; Whether *Don Alvarez* ever was himself privy to the Myſtery which has disguis'd my Sex, and made me pass for his Son?

Isab. What you ask me, is a Thing has often perplex'd my Thoughts, as well as yours, nor cou'd my Mother ever resolve the Doubt. You know, when that young Child, *Camillo* dy'd, in whom was wrap'd up so much Expeĉtation, from the great Eſtate his Uncle's Will (even before he came into the World) had left him; his Mother made a Secret of his Death to her Husband *Alvarez*, and readily fell in with a Proposal made her, to take you, (who then were juſt *Camillo*'s Age) and bring you up in his Room. You have heard how you were then at Nurse with my Mother, and how your own was privy and consenting to the Plot; but *Don Alvarez* was never let into it by 'em.

Cam. Don't you then think it probable, his Wife might after tell him?

Isab. 'Twas ever thought, nothing but a Death-bed Repentance cou'd draw it from her to any One: And that was prevented, by the suddeness of her Exit to t'other World; which did not give her even Time to call Heav'n's Mercy on her. And yet, now I have said all this, I own the Correspondence and Friendship I observe he holds with your real Mother, gives me some Suspicion, and the Presents he often makes her (which People seldom do for nothing) confirm it. But since this is all I can say to you on that Point, pray let us come to the Secret, which you have made me impatient to hear.

Cam. Know then, that tho' *Cupid* is blind, he is not to be deceiv'd; I can hide my Sex from the World, but not from him; his Dart has found the Way through the manly Garb I wear, to pierce a Virgin's tender Heart. ——I Love————

Isab. How?

Cam. Nay, be'nt surpriz'd at that, I have other Wonders for you.

Isab. Quick, let me hear 'em.

Cam. I love *Lorenzo*.

Isab. *Lorenzo!* Most nicely hit. The very Man from whom your Imposture keeps this vast Estate; and who on the first Knowledge of your being a Woman wou'd enter into Possession of it. This is indeed a Wonder.

Cam. Then wonder farther still, I am his Wife.

Isab. Ha! His Wife?

Cam. His Wife, *Isabella*; and yet thou hast not all my Wonders, I am his Wife, without his Knowledge; he does not even know I am a Woman.

Isab. Madam, your humble Servant, if you please to go on, I won't interrupt you, indeed I won't.

Cam. Then hear how these strange Things have past: *Lorenzo*, bound unregarded in my Sister's Chains, seem'd in my Eyes a Conquest worth her Care. Nor cou'd I see him treated with Contempt, without growing warm in his Interest: I blam'd *Leonora*, for not being touch'd with his Merit; I blam'd her so long, 'till I grew touch'd with it my self. And the Reasons I urg'd, to vanquish her Heart, insensibly made a Conquest of my own: 'Twas thus, my Friend, I fell. What was next to be done, my Passion pointed out; my Heart I felt was warm'd to a noble Enterprise, I gave it way, and boldly on it led me. *Leonora*'s Name and Voice, in the dark Shades of Night, I borrow'd to engage the Object of my Wishes. I met him, *Isabella*, and so deceiv'd him; he cannot blame me sure, for much I blest him. But to finish this strange Story: In short I own'd I long had lov'd, but finding my Father most adverse to my Desires, I at last had forc'd my self to this secret Correspondence; I urg'd the Mischiefs wou'd attend the knowledge on't, I urg'd 'em so he thought 'em full of Weight, so yielded to observe what Rules I gave him; they were, To pass the Day with cold Indifference, to avoid even Signs or Looks of Intimacy, but gather for the still, the secret Night, a Flood of Love to recompence the Losses of the Day. I will not trouble you with Lovers Cares, nor what Contrivances we form'd to bring this Toying to a solid Bliss. Know only, When three Nights we thus had pass'd, the fourth it was agreed shou'd make us one for ever; each kept their Promise, and last Night has join'd us.

Isab. Indeed your Talents pass my poor Extent; you serious Ladies are well form'd for Business: What wretched work a poor Coquet had made on't? But still there's that remains will try your Skill, you have your Man, but——

Cam. Lovers think no farther, the Object of that Passion possesses all Desire; however I have open'd to you my wondrous Situation, if you can advise me in my Difficulties to come, you will. But see——my Husband.

Enter Don Lorenzo.

Don Lor. You look as if you were busie, pray tell me if I interrupt you? I'll retire.

Cam. No, no, you have a Right to interrupt us, since you were the Subject of our Discourse.

Don Lor. Was I?

Cam. You were: Nay I'll tell you how you entertain'd us too.

Don Lor. Perhaps I had as good avoid hearing that.

Cam. You need not fear, it was not to your Disadvantage; I was commending you, and saying, if I had been a Woman I had been in danger, nay I think I said I shou'd infallibly have been in Love with you.

Don Lor. While such an If is in the way you run no great Risque in declaring, but you'd be finely catch'd now shou'd some wonderful Transformation give me a Claim to your Heart.

Cam. Not sorry for't at all, for I ne'er expect to find a Mistress please me half so well as you wou'd do, if I were yours.

Don Lor. Since you are so well inclin'd to me in your Wishes, Sir, I suppose (as the Fates have ordain'd it) you wou'd have some pleasure in helping me to a Mistress, since you can't be mine your self.

Cam. Indeed I shou'd not.

Don Lor. Then my Obligation is but small to you.

Cam. Why, wou'd you have a Woman that is in Love with you her self, employ her Interest to help you to another?

Don Lor. No, but you being no Woman might.

Cam. Sir, 'tis as a Woman I say what I do, and I suppose my self a Woman, when I design all these Favours to you. Therefore out of that Supposition, I have no other good Intentions to you than you may expect, from any one that says, he's——Sir, your humble Servant.

Don Lor. So unless Heav'n is pleas'd to work a Miracle, and from a sturdy young Fellow, make you a kind-hearted young Lady, I'm to get little by your good Opinion of me.

Cam. Yes; there is one Means yet left, (on this Side a Miracle) that wou'd perhaps engage me, if with an honest Oath you cou'd declare, Were

I Woman I might dispute your Heart, even with the first of my pretending Sex.

Don Lor. Then solemnly and honestly I swear, That had you been a Woman, and I the Master of the World, I think I shou'd have laid it at your Feet.

Cam. Then honestly and solemnly I swear, henceforwards all your Interest shall be mine.

Don Lor. I have a Secret to impart to you will quickly try your Friendship.

Cam. I have a Secret to unfold to you, will put you even to a fiery Trial.

Don Lor. What do you mean, *Camillo?*

Cam. I mean that I love, where I never durst yet own it, yet where 'tis in your Power to make me the happiest of——

Don Lor. Explain, *Camillo;* and be assur'd, if your Happiness is in my Power, 'tis in your own?

Cam. Alas! you promise me, you know not what.

Don Lor. I promise nothing, but what I will perform; name the Person.

Cam. 'Tis one who's very near to you.

Don Lor. If 'tis my Sister, why all this Pain in bringing forth the Secret?

Cam. Alas! It is your——

Don Lor. Speak!

Cam. I cannot yet: Farewel.

Don Lor. Hold! Pray speak it now.

Cam. I must not: But when you tell me your Secret, you shall know mine.

Don Lor. Mine is not in my Power, without the Consent of another.

Cam. Get that Consent, and then we'll try who best will keep their Oaths.

Don Lor. I am Content.

Cam. And I: Adieu.

Don Lor. Farewel.   [*Exit* Don Lorenzo.

Enter Leonora *and* Jacinta.

Leon. 'Tis enough: I will Revenge my self this Way; if it does but torment him, I shall be content to find no other Pleasure in it. Brother, you'll wonder at my Change; after all my ill Usage of *Lorenzo,* I am determin'd to be his Wife.

Cam. How, Sister? So sudden a Turn? This Inequality of Temper indeed is not commendable.

Leon. Your Change, Brother, is much more justly surprising; you hitherto have pleaded for him strongly, accus'd me of Blindness, Cruelty and Pride; and now I yield to your Reasons, and resolve in his Favour, you blame my Compliance, and appear against his Interest.

Cam. I quit his Service, for what's dearer to me, yours: I have learn'd from sure Intelligence, the Attack he made on you was but a Feint, and that his Heart is in another's Chain; I wou'd not therefore see you so expos'd, to offer up your self to one who must refuse you.

Leon. If that be all, leave me my Honour to take care of; I am no Stranger to his Wishes, he won't refuse me, Brother, nor I hope will you, to tell him of my Resolution; if you do, this Moment with my own Tongue (through all a Virgin's Blushes) I'll own to him I am determin'd in his Favour.——You pause as if you'd let the Task lie on me.

Cam. Neither on you, nor me; I have a Reason you are yet a Stranger to: Know then, there is a Virgin, young and tender, whose Peace and Happiness so much are mine I cannot see her Miserable; she loves him with that Torrent of Desire, that were the World resign'd her in his stead she'd still be wretched; I will not picque you to a Female Strife, by saying you have not Charms to tear him from her, but I would move you to a Female Softness, by telling you, her Death wou'd wait your Conquest: What I have more to plead, is as a Brother, I hope that gives me some small Interest in you; whate'er it is, you see how I'd employ it.

Leon. You ne'er cou'd put it to a harder Service. I beg a little Time to think: Pray leave me to my self a while.

Cam. I shall; I only ask that you wou'd think, and then you won't refuse me. [*Exit* Camillo.

Jacin. Indeed, Madam, I'm of your Brother's Mind, tho' for another Cause; but sure 'tis worth thinking twice on for your own sake: You are too Violent.

Leon. A slighted Woman knows no Bounds. Vengeance is all the Cordial she can have, so snatches at the nearest. Ungrateful Wretch! to use me with such Insolence.

Jacin. You see me as much enrag'd at it, as you are your self, yet my Brain is roving after the Cause, for something there must be; never Letter was receiv'd by Man, with more Passion and Transport; I was almost as charming a Goddess as your self, only for bringing it. Yet, when in a Moment after I come with a Message worth a dozen on't, never was Witch so handled; something must have pass'd between one and t'other, that's sure.

Leon. Nothing cou'd pass worth my enquiring after, since nothing cou'd happen that can excuse his Usage of me; he had a Letter under my Hand which own'd him Master of my Heart; and 'till I contradicted it with my Mouth, he ought not to doubt the Truth on't.

Jacin. Nay I confess, Madam, I han't a Word to say for him, I'm afraid he's but a Rogue at Bottom, as well as my Shameless that attends him; we are bit by my Troth, and haply well enough serv'd, for list'ning to the glib Tongues of the Rascals: But be comforted, Madam; they'll fall into the Hands of some foul Sluts or other, before they dye, that will set our Account even with 'em.

Leon. Well: Let him laugh; let him glory in what he has done: He shall see I have a Spirit can use him as I ought.

Jacin. And let one Thing be your Comfort by the way Madam, that in spight of all your dear Affections to him, you have had the Grace to keep him at Arms end. You han't thank'd me for't; but good Faith 'twas well I did not stir out of the Chamber that fond Night. For there are Times the stoutest of us are in Danger, the Rascals wheedle so.

Leon. In short, my very Soul is fir'd with this Treatment; and if ever that perfidious Monster should relent, tho' he shou'd crawl like a poor Worm beneath my Feet, nay plunge a Dagger in his Heart, to bleed for Pardon; I charge thee strictly, charge thee on thy Life, thou do not urge a Look to melt me toward him, but strongly buoy me up in brave Resentment; and if thou see'st (which Heav'ns avert) a Glance of Weakness in me, rouse to my Memory the vile Wrongs I've borne, and blazon 'em with Skill in all their glaring Colours.

Jacin. Madam, never doubt me; I'm charg'd to the Mouth with Fury. and if ever I meet that Fat Traytor of mine, such a Volley will I pour about his Ears——Now Heav'n prevent all hasty Vows; but in the Humour I am, methinks I'd carry my Maiden-Head to my cold Grave with me, before I'd let it simper at the Rascal. But soft; here comes your Father.

Enter Don Alvarez.

Don Alv. Leonora, I'd have you retire a little, and send your Brother's Tutor to me, *Metaphrastus.*   [*Exit* Leo. *and* Ja.

Solus.

I'll try if I can discover, by his Tutor, what 'tis that seems so much to work his Brain of late, for something more than common there plainly does appear, yet nothing sure that can disturb his Soul, like what I have to torture mine on his Account. Sure nothing in this World is worth a troubled Mind: What Racks has Avarice stretch'd me on; I wanted nothing, kind Heav'n had given me a plenteous Lot, and seated me in great Abundance; why then approve I of this Imposture? What have I gain'd by it? Wealth and Misery; I have barter'd peaceful Days for restless Nights; a wretched Bargain! and he that Merchandizes thus, must be undone at last.

Enter Metaphrastus.

Metaph. Mandatum tuum, curo diligenter.

Don Alv. Master, I had a Mind to ask you——

Metaph. The Title, Master, comes from *Magis* and *Ter*, which is as much as to say, *Thrice worthy.*

Don Alv. I never heard so much before, but it may be true for ought I know: But, Master,——

Metaph. Go on.

Don Alv. Why so I will if you'll let me, but don't interrupt me then.

Metaph. Enough, proceed.

Don Alv. Why then, Master, for the Third time, my Son *Camillo* gives me much uneasiness of late; you know I love him, and have many careful Thoughts about him.

Metaph. 'Tis true. *Filio non potest præferri, nisi Filius.*

Don Alv. Master, when one has Business to talk on, these Scholastick Expressions are not of use; I believe you a great Latinist; possibly you may understand *Greek;* those who recommended you to me said so, and I am willing it should be true: But the thing I want to discourse you about at present, does not properly give you an Occasion to display your Learning. Besides, to tell you Truth, 'twill at all times be lost upon me; my Father was a wise Man, but he taught me nothing beyond common Sense; I know but one Tongue in the World, which luckily being understood by you as well as me, I fancy whatever Thoughts we have to Communicate to one another, may reasonably be convey'd in that, without having Recourse to the Language of *Julius Cæsar.*

Metaph. You are wrong, but may proceed.

Don Alv. I thank you: What is the matter I do not know, but tho' it is of the utmost Consequence to me to marry my Son, what Match soever I propose to him, he still finds some Pretence or other to decline it.

Metaph. He is, perhaps, of the Humour of a Brother of *Marcus Tullius,* who——

Don Alv. Dear Master, leave the *Greeks,* and the *Latins,* and the *Scotch,* and the *Welsh,* and let me go on in my Business; what have those People to do with my Son's Marriage?

Metaph. Again you are wrong; but go on.

Don Alv. I say then, that I have strong Apprehensions from his refusing all my Proposals, that he may have some secret Inclination of his own; and to confirm me in this Fear, I yesterday observ'd him (without his knowing it) in a Corner of the Grove, where no Body comes——

Metaph. A Place out of the way, you would say; a Place of Retreat.

Don Alv. Why, the Corner of the Grove, where no Body comes, is a Place of Retreat; is it not?

Metaph. In *Latin, Secessus.*

Don Alv. Ha?

Metaph. As *Virgil* has it, *Est in Secessu Locus.*

Don Alv. How could *Virgil* have it, when I tell you no Soul was there but he and I.

Metaph. Virgil is a famous Author, I quote his Saying as a Phrase more proper to the Occasion than that you use, and not as one who was in the Wood with you.

Don Alv. And I tell you, I hope to be as famous as any *Virgil* of 'em all, when I have been dead as long, and have no need of a better Phrase than my own to tell you my Meaning.

Metaph. You ought however to make Choice of the Words most us'd by the best Authors. *Tu vivendo bonos*, as they say, *Scribendo sequare peritos*.

Don Alv. Again?——

Metaph. 'Tis *Quintilian's* own Precept.

Don Alv. Oons——

Metaph. And he has something very learned upon it, that may be of Service to you to hear.

Don Alv. You Son of a Whore, will you hear me speak?

Metaph. What may be the Occasion of this unmanly Passion? What is it you would have with me?

Don Alv. What you might have known an Hour ago, if you had pleas'd.

Metaph. You would then have me hold my Peace——I shall.

Don Alv. You will do very well.

Metaph. You see I do well; go on.

Don Alv. Why then, to begin once again, I say my Son *Camillo*——

Metaph. Proceed; I shan't interrupt you.

Don Alv. I say, my Son *Camillo*——

Metaph. What is it you say of your Son *Camillo*?

Don Alv. That he has got a Dog of a Tutor, whose Brains I'll beat out, if he won't hear me speak.

Metaph. That Dog is a Philosopher, contemns Passion, and yet will hear you.

Don Alv. I don't believe a Word on't, but I'll try once again; I have a Mind to know from you whether you have observ'd any thing in my Son.——

Metaph. Nothing that is like his Father. Go on.

Don Alv. Have a care.

Metaph. I do not interrupt you; but you are long in coming to a Conclusion.

Don Alv. Why thou hast not let me begin yet.

Metaph. And yet it is high time to have made an end.

Don Alv. Dost thou know thy Danger? I have not——thus much Patience left.   [*Shewing the End of his Finger.*

Metaph. Mine is already consum'd. I do not use to be thus treated; my Profession is to teach, and not to hear, yet I have harken'd like a School-Boy, and am not heard, altho' a Master.

Don Alv. Get out of the Room.

Metaph. I will not. If the Mouth of a Wise Man be shut, he is, as it were, a Fool; for who shall know his Understanding; therefore a certain Philosopher said well, Speak, that thou may'ſt be known; great Talkers, without Knowledge, are as the Winds that whiſtle; but they who have Learning should speak aloud. If this be not permitted, we may expeĉt to see the whole Order of Nature o'erthrown; Hens devour Foxes, and Lambs deſtroy Wolves, Nurses Suck Children, and Children give Suck; Generals mend Stockings, and Chambermaids take Towns; we may expeĉt, I say——

Don Alv. That, and that, and that, and——

> [*Strikes him, and kicks him; then follows him off with a Bell at his Ear.*

Metaph. O Tempora! O Mores!

End of the Second Aĉt.

ACT III.   SCENE I.

SCENE, *the Street.*

Enter Lopez.

Lop. SOmetimes Fortune seconds a bold Design, and when Folly has brought us into a Trap, Impudence brings us out on't. I have been caught by this hot-headed Lover here, and have told like a Puppy what I shall be beaten for like a Dog. Come! Courage, my dear *Lopez;* Fire will fetch out Fire: Thou haſt told one Body thy Maſter's Secret, e'en tell it to half a Dozen more, and try how that will thrive; go tell it to the Two old Dons, the Lovers Fathers. The Thing's done, and can't be retriev'd; perhaps they'll lay their two ancient Heads together, club a Pennyworth of Wisdom a-piece, and with great Penetration at laſt find out, that 'tis beſt to submit, where 'tis not in their Power to do otherwise. This being resolv'd, there's no Time to be loſt.

> [*Knocks at* Don Alvarez's *Door.*

Don Alv. Who knocks?   [*Within.*
Lop. Lopez.
Don Alv. What doſt want?   [*Looking out.*
Lop. To bid you good Morrow, Sir.
Don Alv. Well, good Morrow to thee again.   [*Retires.*
Lop. What a——I think he does not care for my Company.

> [*Knocks again.*

Don Alv. Who knocks?

Lop. Lopez.

Don Alv. What wouldſt have? [*Looking out.*

Lop. My old Maſter, Sir, gives his Service to you, and desires to know how you do.

Don Alv. How I do? Why, well; how should I do? Service to him again. [*Retires.*

Lop. Sir.

Don Alv. returning.] What the deux wouldſt thou have with me? with thy good Morrows, and thy Services.

Lop. This Man does not underſtand good Breeding, I find. [*Aside.*] Why Sir, my Maſter has some very earneſt Business with you.

Don Alv. Business? About what? What Business can he have with me?

Lop. I don't know truly; but 'tis some very important Matter: He has juſt now (as I hear) discover'd some great Secret, which he muſt needs talk with you about.

Don Alv. Ha? a Secret, say'ſt thou?

Lop. Yes; and bid me bring him word, if you were at home, he'd be with you presently. Sir, your humble Servant. [*Exit* Lopez.

Don Alvarez *solus.*

A Secret; and muſt speak with me about it! Heav'ns, how I tremble! What can this Message mean? I have very little Acquaintance with him, what Business can he have with me? An important Secret 'twas, he said, and that he had juſt discover'd it. Alas, I have in the World but One, if it be that,—I'm loſt; an eternal Blot muſt fix upon me. How unfortunate am I, that I have not follow'd the honeſt Councils of my Heart, which have often urg'd me to set my Conscience at Ease, by rendring to him the Eſtate that is his due, and which by a foul Impoſture I keep from him: But 'tis now too late; my Villainy is out, and I shall not only be forc'd with Shame to reſtore him what is his, but shall be perhaps condemn'd to make him Reparation with my own. O terrible View!

Enter Don Felix.

Don Felix. My Son to go and marry her, without her Father's Knowledge? this can never end well. I don't know what to do, he'll conclude I was privy to it, and his Power and Intereſt are so great at Court he may with ease contrive my Ruin: I tremble at his sending to speak with me. ——Mercy on me, there he is. [*Aside.*

Don Alv. Ah! Shield me, kind Heav'n! There's *Don Felix* come: How I am ſtruck with the Sight of him! O the Torment of a guilty Mind! [*Aside.*

Don Felix. What shall I say to soften him?   [*Aside.*

Don Alv. How shall I look him in the Face?   [*Aside.*

Don Felix. 'Tis impossible he can forgive it.   [*Aside.*

Don Alv. To be sure he'll expose me to the whole World.   [*Aside.*

Don Felix. I see his Countenance change.   [*Aside.*

Don Alv. With what Contempt he looks upon me!   [*Aside.*

Don Felix. I see, *Don Alvarez*, by the Disorder of your Face, you are but too well inform'd of what brings me here.

Don Alv. 'Tis true.

Don Felix. The News may well surprize you, 'tis what I have been far from apprehending.

Don Alv. Wrong, very wrong indeed.

Don Felix. The Action is certainly to the last Point to be condemn'd, and I think no body should pretend to excuse the Guilty.

Don Alv. They are not to be excus'd; tho' Heav'n may have Mercy.

Don Felix. That's what I hope you will consider.

Don Alv. We should act as Christians.

Don Felix. Most certainly.

Don Alv. Let Mercy then prevail.

Don Felix. It is indeed of heav'nly Birth.

Don Alv. Generous *Don Felix*.

Don Felix. Too indulgent *Alvarez*.

Don Alv. I thank you on my Knee.

Don Felix. 'Tis I ought to have been there first.   [*They kneel.*

Don Alv. Is it then possible we are Friends?

Don Felix. Embrace me to confirm it.   [*They embrace.*

Don Alv. Thou best of Men.

Don Felix. Unlook'd for Bounty.

Don Alv. Did you know the Torment [*rising.*] this unhappy Action has given me,——

Don Felix. 'Tis impossible it could do otherwise; nor has my Trouble been less.

Don Alv. But let my Misfortune be kept secret.

Don Felix. Most willingly; my Advantage is sufficient by it, without the Vanity of making it publick to the World.

Don Alv. Incomparable Goodness! That I should thus have wrong'd a Man so worthy! [*Aside.*] My Honour then is safe?

Don Felix. For ever, even for ever let it be a Secret, I am content.

Don Alv. Noble Gentleman. [*Aside.*] As to what Advantages ought to accrue to you by it, it shall be all to your entire Satisfaction.

Don Felix. Wonderful Bounty! [*Aside.*] As to that, *Don Alvarez*, I leave it entirely to you, and shall be content with whatever you think reasonable.

Don Alv. I thank you, from my Soul I muſt, you know I muſt. This muſt be an Angel, not a Man.   [*Aside.*

Don Felix. The Thanks lye on my Side, *Alvarez*, for this unexpected Generoſity; but may all Faults be forgot, and Heav'n ever proſper you.

Don Alv. The ſame Prayer, I, with a double Fervour, offer up for you.

Don Felix. Let us then once more embrace, and be Forgiveness ſeal'd for ever.

Don Alv. Agreed; thou beſt of Men, agreed.   [*They embrace.*

Don Felix. This Thing then being thus happily terminated, let me own to you, *Don Alvarez*, I was in extream Apprehenſions of your utmoſt Reſentment on this Occaſion, for I could not doubt but you had form'd more happy Views, in the Diſpoſal of so fair a Daughter as *Leonora*, than my poor Son's inferior Fortune, e'er can anſwer; but ſince they are join'd, and that——

Don Alv. Ha?

Don Felix. Nay, 'tis very likely to diſcourſe of it may not be very pleaſing to you, tho' your Chriſtianity and natural Goodness have prevail'd on you so generouſly to forgive it. But to do Juſtice to *Leonora*, and ſkreen her from your too harsh Opinion in this unlucky Action, 'twas that cunning wicked Creature that attends her, who by unuſual Arts wrought her to this Breach of Duty, for her own Inclinations were diſpos'd to all the Modeſty and Reſignation a Father could ask from a Daughter; my Son I can't excuſe, but ſince your Bounty does so, I hope you'll quite forget the Fault of the less guilty *Leonora*.

Don Alv. What a Miſtake have I lain under here! And from a groundless Apprehenſion of one Misfortune, find my ſelf in the Certainty of another.   [*Aside.*

Don Felix. He looks diſturb'd; what can this mean?   [*Aside.*

Don Alv. My Daughter marry'd to his Son?——Confuſion. But I find my ſelf in such unruly Agitation, ſomething wrong may happen if I continue with him; I'll therefore leave him.   [*Aside.*

Don Felix. You ſeem thoughtful, Sir, I hope there's no——

Don Alv. A ſudden Diſorder I am ſeiz'd with; you'll pardon me, I muſt retire.   [*Exit* Don Alvarez.

Don Felix *solus.*

I don't like this:——He went oddly off.——I doubt he finds this Bounty difficult to go thorough with. His natural Reſentment is making an Attack upon his acquir'd Generoſity: Pray Heav'n it ben't too ſtrong for't. The Misfortune is a great one, and can't but touch him nearly. It was not natural to be so calm: I wiſh it don't yet drive him to my Ruin. But here comes this young hot-brain'd Coxcomb, who with his Midnight Amours has been the Cauſe of all this Miſchief to me.

Enter Don Lorenzo.

So, Sir, are you come to receive my Thanks for your noble Exploit? You
think you have done bravely now, ungracious Off-spring, to bring perpetual Troubles on me. Muſt there never pass a Day, but I muſt drink
some bitter Potion or other of your Preparation for me?

Don Lor. I am amaz'd, Sir; pray what have I done to deserve your
Anger?

Don Felix. Nothing; no manner of Thing in the World; nor never do.
I am an old teſty Fellow, and am always scolding, and finding Fault for
nothing; complaining that I have got a Coxcomb of a Son that makes me
weary of my Life, fancying he perverts the Order of Nature, turning Day
into Night, and Night into Day; getting Whims in my Brain, that he con-
sumes his Life in Idleness, unless he rouses now and then to do some noble
Stroke of Mischief; and having an impertinent Dream at this time, that
he has been making the Fortune of the Family, by an under-hand Marriage
with the Daughter of a Man who will crush us all to Powder for it. Ah—
ungracious Wretch; to bring an old Man into all this Trouble: The Pain
thou gav'ſt thy Mother to bring thee into the World, and the Plague thou
haſt given me to keep thee here, make the Getting thee (tho' 'twas in our
Hony-Moon) a bitter Remembrance to us both.   [*Exit* Don Felix.

Don Lorenzo *solus.*

So——all's out——Here's a noble Storm arising, and I'm at Sea in a
Cock-boat. But which way could this Business reach him? By this Traitor
Lopez; it muſt be so; it could be no other Way; for only he, and the
Prieſt that marry'd us, know of it. The Villain will never confess tho',
I muſt try a little Address with him, and conceal my Anger. O, here
he comes.

Enter Lopez.

Don Lor. Lopez.

Lop. Do you call, Sir?

Don Lor. I find all's discover'd to my Father; the Secret's out; he
knows my Marriage?

Lop. He knows your Marriage? How the Peſt should that happen?
Sir, 'tis impossible; that's all.

Don Lor. I tell thee 'tis true; he knows every Particular of it.

Lop. He does?——Why then, Sir, all I can say is, That Satan and he
are better acquainted than the Devil and a good Chriſtian ought to be.

Don Lor. Which Way he has discover'd it I can't tell, nor am I much
concern'd to know, since beyond all my Expeĉtations, I find him perfeĉtly

easie at it, and ready to excuse my Fault with better Reasons than I can find to do it my self.

Lop. Say you so?——I'm very glad to hear that, then all's safe. [*Aside.*

Don Lor. 'Tis unexpected good Fortune; but it could never proceed purely from his own Temper, there must have been Pains taken with him to bring him to this Calm: I'm sure I owe much to the Bounty of some Friend or other; I wish I knew where my Obligation lay, that I might acknowledge it as I ought.

Lop. Are you thereabouts, I-faith: Then Sharp's the Word; I-gad I'll own the Thing, and receive his Bounty for't. [*Aside.*] Why, Sir,——not that I pretend to make a Merit o'the Matter, for alas, I am but your poor Hireling, and therefore bound in Duty to render you all the Service I can.——But——'tis I have don't.

Don Lor. What hast thou done?

Lop. What no Man else could have done; the Job, Sir; told him the Secret, and then talk'd him into a Liking on't.

Don Lor. 'Tis impossible; thou dost not tell me true.

Lop. Sir, I scorn to reap any thing from another Man's Labours, but if this poor piece of Service carries any Merit with it, you now know where to reward it.

Don Lor. Thou art not serious.

Lop. I am; or may Hunger be my Mess-mate.

Don Lor. And may Famine be mine, if I don't reward thee for't, as thou deserv'st.——Dead.   [*Making a Pass at him.*

Lop. Have a Care there. [*Leaping on one side.*] What do you mean, Sir? I bar all Surprize.

Don Lor. Traitor, is this the fruit of the Trust I plac'd in thee—— Villain?   [*Making another Thrust at him.*

Lop. Take heed, Sir; you'll do one a Mischief before y'are aware.

Don Lor. What Recompence canst thou make me, Wretch, for this Piece of Treachery? Thy sordid Blood can't expiate the Thousandth—— But I'll have it however.   [*Thrusts again.*

Lop. Look you there again: Pray Sir, be quiet; is the Devil in you? 'Tis bad jesting with edg'd Tools. I-gad that last Push was within an Inch o' me. I don't know what you make all this Bustle about, but I'm sure I've done all for the best, and I believe 'twill prove for the best too at last, if you'll have but a little Patience. But if Gentlemen will be in their Airs in a Moment——Why, what the deux——I'm sure I have been as eloquent as *Cicero* in your Behalf; and I don't doubt to good Purpose too, if you'll give Things time to work. But nothing but foul Language, and naked Swords about the House, sa, sa; run you through, you Dog: Why no body can do Business at this Rate.

Don Lor. And suppose your Project fail, and I'm ruin'd by't, Sir.

Lop. Why, 'twill be time enough to kill me then, Sir; won't it? What should you do it for now? Besides, I an't ready, I'm not prepar'd, I might be undone by't.

Don Lor. But what will *Leonora* say to her Marriage being known, Wretch?

Lop. Why may be she'll draw—her Sword too. [*Shewing his Tongue.*] but all shall be well with you both, if you will but let me alone.

Don Lor. Peace; here's her Father.

Lop. That's well: We shall see how Things go presently.

Enter Don Alvarez.

Don Alv. The more I recover from the Disorder this Discourse has put me in, the more strange the whole Adventure appears to me. *Leonora* maintains there is not a Word of Truth in what I have heard; that she knows nothing of Marriage: And indeed she tells me this with such a naked Air of Sincerity, that for my part I believe her. What then must be their Project? Some villainous Intention, to be sure; tho' which Way, I yet am ignorant. But here's the Bridegroom; I'll accost him.——I am told, Sir, you take upon you to scandalize my Daughter, and tell idle Tales of what can never happen.

Lop. Now methinks, Sir, if you treated your Son-in-Law with a little more Civility, things might go just as well in the main.

Don Alv. What means this insolent Fellow by my Son-in-Law? I suppose 'tis you, Villain, are the Author of this impudent Story.

Lop. You seem angry, Sir,——perhaps without Cause.

Don Alv. Cause, Traitor! Is a Cause wanting where a Daughter's defam'd, and a Noble Family scandaliz'd?

Lop. There he is; let him answer you.

Don Alv. I should be glad he'd answer me; why, if he had any Desires to my Daughter, he did not make his Approaches like a Man of Honour.

Lop. Yes; and so have had the Doors bolted against him, like a House-Breaker.   [*Aside.*

Don Lor. Sir, to justifie my Proceeding, I have little to say, but to excuse it I have much, if any Allowance may be made to a Passion, which in your Youth you have your self been sway'd by; I love your Daughter to that excess——

Don Alv. You would undo her for a Night's Lodging.

Don Lor. Undo her, Sir?——

Don Alv. Yes, that's the Word; you knew it was against her Interest to marry you, therefore you endeavour'd to win her to't in private; you knew her Friends would make a better Bargain for her, therefore you kept your Designs from their Knowledge, and yet you love her to that excess——

Don Lor. I'd readily lay down my Life to serve her.

Don Alv. Could you readily lay down Fifty Thousand Piftoles to serve her, your excessive Love would come with better Credentials; an Offer of Life is very proper for the Attack of a Counterscarp, but a Thousand Ducats will sooner carry a Lady's Heart; you are a young Man, but will learn this when you are older.

Lop. But since things have succeeded better this once, Sir, and that my Mafter will prove a moft incomparable good Husband, (for that he'll do, I'll answer for him) and that 'tis too late to recall what's already done, Sir,——

Don Alv. What's done, Villain?

Lop. Sir, I mean, that since my Mafter and my Lady are marry'd, and——

Don Alv. Thou ly'ft; they are not marry'd.

Lop. Sir!——I say, that since they are marry'd, and that they love each other so passing dearly, indeed I fancy that——

Don Alv. Why, this Impudence is beyond all bearing: Sir, do you put your Rascal upon this?

Don Lor. Sir, I am in a Wood; I don't know what it is you mean.

Don Alv. And I am in a Plain, Sir, and think I may be underftood; Do you pretend you are marry'd to my Daughter?

Don Lor. Sir, 'tis my Happiness on one side, as it is my Misfortune on another.

Don Alv. And you do think this idle Projeft can succeed; you do believe your affirming you are marry'd to her will induce both her and me to consent it shall be so?

Lop. Sir, I see you make my Mafter almoft out of his Wits to hear you talk so; but I, who am but a Stander by now, as I was at the Wedding, have mine about me, and desire to know, Whether you think this Projeft can succeed? Do you believe your affirming they are not marry'd, will induce both him and I to give up the Lady? One short Queftion to bring this Matter to an Issue, Why do you think they are not marry'd?

Don Alv. Because she utterly renounces it.

Lop. And so she will her Religion, if you attack it with that dreadful Face. D'ye hear, Sir? the poor Lady is in Love heartily, and I wish all poor Ladies that are so, would dispose of themselves so well as she has done; but you scare her out of her Senses; bring her here into the Room, speak gently to her, tell her you know the thing is done, that you have it from a Man of Honour, Me. That may be you wish it had been otherwise, but are a Chriftian, and profess Mercy, and therefore have resolv'd to pardon her: Say this, and I fhall appear a Man of Reputation, and have Satisfaction made me.

Don Alv. Or an impudent Rogue, and have all your Bones broke.

Lop. Content.

Don Alv. Agreed. *Leonora*; who's there? call *Leonora.*

Lop. All will go rarely, Sir; we shall have shot the Gulf in a Moment.
[*Aside to* Don Lorenzo.

Enter Leonora.

Don Alv. Come hither, *Leonora.*

Lop. So, now we shall see.

Don Alv. I call'd you to answer for your self; here's a ſtrong Claim upon you; if there be any thing in the pretended Title conceal it no farther, it muſt be known at laſt, it may as well be so now. Nothing is so uneasie as Uncertainty, I would therefore be gladly freed from it; if you have done what I am told you have, 'tis a great Fault indeed; but as I fear 'twill carry much of its Punishment along with it, I shall rather reduce my Resentment into mourning your Misfortune, than suffer it to add to your Affliction, therefore speak the Truth.

Lop. Well, this is fair Play; now I speak, Sir; You see, fair Lady, the Goodness of a tender Father, nothing need therefore hinder you from owning a moſt loving Husband. We had like to have been altogether by the Ears about this Business, and Pails of Blood were ready to run about the House, but, thank Heav'n, the Sun shines out again, and one Word from your sweet Mouth makes fair Weather for ever. My Maſter has been forc'd to own your Marriage, he begs you'll do so too.

Leon. What does this impudent Rascal mean?

Lop. Ha!——Madam!

Leon. Sir, I should be very glad to know, (*To* Don Lorenzo] what can have been th' Occasion of this wild Report; sure you cannot be your self a Party in it?

Lop. He, he——

Don Lor. Forgive me, dear *Leonora*, I know you had ſtrong Reasons for the Secret being longer kept; but 'tis not my Fault, our Marriage is disclos'd.

Leon. Our Marriage, Sir!——

Don Lor. 'Tis known, my Dear, tho' much againſt my Will; but since it is so, 'twould be in vain for us to deny it longer.

Leon. Then, Sir, I am your Wife? I fell in Love with you, and marry'd you without my Father's Knowledge?

Don Lor. I dare not be so vain to think 'twas Love; I humbly am content to owe the Blessing to your Generosity; you saw the Pains I suffer'd for your sake, and in Compassion eas'd 'em.

Leon. I did, Sir? Sure this exceeds all Human Impudence.

Lop. Truly, I think it does. She'd make an incomparable Aĉtress.
[*Aside.*

Don Lor. I begin to be surpriz'd, Madam, at your carrying this thing so far; you see there's no Occasion for it, and for the Discovery, I have already told you 'twas not my Fault.

Lop. My Master's? no, 'twas I did it: Why what a Bustle's here? I knew things would go well, and so they do, if Folks would let 'em. But if Ladies will be in their Merriments, when Gentlemen are upon serious Business, why what a deux can one say to 'em.

Leon. I see this Fellow is to be an Evidence in your Plot; where you hope to drive it is hard to guess: For if any thing can exceed its Impudence; it is its Folly. A Noble Stratagem indeed, to win a Lady by; I cou'd be diverted with it, but that I see a Face of Villainy requires a rougher Treatment: I cou'd almost methinks forget my Sex, and be my own Avenger.

Don Lor. Madam; I am surpriz'd beyond all——

Lop. Pray Sir, let me come to her; you are so surpriz'd, you'll make nothing on't: She wants a little snubbing. Look you, Madam; I have seen many a pleasant Humour amongst Ladies, but you out-cut 'em all. Here's Contradiction with a Vengeance; you han't been Marry'd eight and forty Hours, and you are Slap——at your Husband's Beard already: Why, do you consider who he is?——Who this Gentleman is?——And what he can do——by Law? Why, he can Lock you up——Knock you down——tye you Neck and Heels.——

Don Lor. Forbear, you Insolent Villain you.   [*Offering to Strike him.*

Leon. That;—for what's past however.   [*Giving him a Box o'th' Ear.*

Lop. I think—she gave me a Box o'th' Ear; ha!   [*Exit* Leonora. Sir, will you suffer your old Servants to be us'd thus by new Comers? It's a shame, a meer shame: Sir, will you take a poor Dog's Advice for once. She denies she's Marry'd to you: Take her at her Word; you have seen some of her Humours,——let her go.

Don Alv. Well, Gentlemen; thus far you see I have heard all with Patience; have you Content? Or how much farther do you design to go with this Bus'ness?

Lop. Why truly Sir, I think we are near at a stand.

Don Alv. 'Tis time, you Villain you.

Lop. Why and I am a Villain now, if every Word I've spoke, be not as true as—as the Gazette: And your Daughter's no better than a—a—a whimsical young Woman, for making Disputes among Gentlemen. And if every Body had their Deserts; she'd have a good——I won't speak it out to enflame Reckonings; but let her go, Master.

Don Alv. Sir, I don't think it well, to spend any more Words with your Impudent and Villainous Servant, here.

Lop. Thank you Sir. But I'd let her go.

Don Alv. Nor have I more to say to you, than this: That you must not think, so daring an Affront to my Family can go long unresented: Farewel.
                                                    [*Exit* Don Alvarez.

Don Lor. Well Sir, what have you to say for your self now?

Lop. Why Sir, I have only to say, that I am a very unfortunate——Middle-ag'd Man; and that I believe all the Stars upon Heav'n and Earth have been concern'd in my Destiny. Children now unborn, will hereafter sing my Downfall, in mournful Lines, and Notes of doleful Tune: I am at present troubled in Mind; Despair around me, signified in appearing Gibbets, with a great Bundle of Dog Whips, by Way of Preparation.

> I therefore will go seek some Mountains high,
> If high enough some Mountain may be found,
> With distant Valley, dreadfully profound,
> And from the horrid Cliff——Look calmly all around:
> Farewel.   *[Aside.*

Don Lor. No, Sirrah: I'll see your wretched End my self; die here, Villain;   *[Drawing his Sword.*

Lop. I can't Sir, if any Body looks upon me.

Don Lor. Away, you trifling Wretch; but think not to escape, for thou shalt have thy Recompence.   *[Exit Don Lorenzo.*

Solus.

Lop. Why what a Mischeivous Jade is this, to make such an Uproar in a Family the first Day of her Marriage? Why my Master won't so much as get a Hony-Moon out of her; I-Gad I'd let her go. If she be thus in her soft and tender Youth, she'll be rare Company at Threescore: Well; he may do as he pleases, but were she my Dear I'd let go——Such a Foot at her Tail, I'd make the Truth bounce out at her Mouth, like a Pellet out of a Pot-gun.   *[Exit.*

End of the Third Act.

ACT IV.   SCENE I.

Enter Camillo *and* Isabella.

Isab. 'TIS an unlucky Accident indeed.

Cam. Ah! *Isabella*; Fate has now determin'd my Undoing. This Thing can ne'er end here, *Leonora* and *Lorenzo* must soon come to some Explanation; the Dispute is too Monstrous to pass over, without further Enquiry, which must discover all; and what will be the Consequence I tremble at; for whether *Don Alvarez* knows of the Imposture, or whether he is deceiv'd with the rest of the World, when once it breaks out, and that the Consequence is the Loss of that great Wealth he now enjoys by it, What muſt become of me? All Paternal Affeĉtions then muſt cease; and regarding me as an unhappy Inſtrument in the Trouble which will then o'er load him, he will return me to my humble Birth, and then I'm loſt for ever. For what, alas! will the deceiv'd *Lorenzo* say? A Wife with neither Fortune, Birth nor Beauty; inſtead of one moſt plenteously endow'd with all. Oh Heav'ns! What a Sea of Misery I have before me.

Isab. Indeed you reason right, but these Refleĉtions are ill-tim'd; why did you not employ 'em sooner?

Cam. Because I lov'd.

Isab. And don't you do so now?

Cam. I do, and therefore 'tis I make these cruel juſt Refleĉtions.

Isab. So that Love, I find, can do any thing.

Cam. Indeed it can: Its Powers are wondrous great; its Pains no Tongue can tell, its Bliss no Heart conceive, Crowns cannot recompence its Torments, Heav'n scarce supply its Joys. My Stake is of this value: O counsel me how I shall save it.

Isab. Alas, that Council's much beyond my Wisdom's Force, I see no Way to help you.

Cam. And yet 'tis sure there's one.

Isab. What?

Cam. Death.

Isab. There possibly may be another; I have a Thought this moment ——perhaps there's nothing in't; yet a small Passage comes to my Remembrance that I regarded little when it happen'd——I'll go and search for one may be of Service. But hold; I see *Don Carlos:* He'll but diſturb us now, let us avoid him.   [*Exeunt* Camillo *and* Isabella.

Enter Don Carlos *and* Sancho.

Don Car. Repuls'd again? This is not to be borne. What tho' this Villain's Story be a Falsehood; was I to blame to harken to it? This Usage cannot be supported: How was it she treated thee?

San. Never was Ambassador worse receiv'd: Madam, my Maſter asks Ten Thousand Pardons, and humbly begs one Moment's Interview:—— Begone, you Rascal you. Madam, what Answer shall I give my Maſter? ——Tell him he's a Villain. Indeed, fair Lady, I think this is haſty Treatment.—Here, my Footmen, toss me this Fellow out at the Window; and away she went to her Devotions.

Don Car. Did you see *Jacinta?*

San. Yes; she saluted me with half-a-score Rogues and Rascals too. I think our Deſtinies are much alike, Sir: And o' my Conscience, a couple of scurvy Jades we are hamper'd with.

(113)

Don Car. Ungrateful Woman, to receive with such Contempt so quick a Return of a Heart so justly alarm'd.

San. Ha, a, a.

Don Car. What, no Allowance to be made to the first Transports of a Lover's Fury? when rouz'd by so dreadful an Appearance? As just as my Suspicions were, have I long suffer'd 'em to Arraign her?

San. No.

Don Car. Have I waited for Oaths or Imprecations to clear her?

San. No.

Don Car. Nay even now: Is not the whole World still in suspence about her? whilst I alone conclude her Innocent.

San. 'Tis very true.

Don Car. She might, methinks, through this profound Respect, observe a Flame another wou'd have cherish'd; she might support me against groundless Fears, and save me from a Rival's Tyranny; she might release me from these cruel Racks; and wou'd no doubt, if she cou'd love as I do.

San. Ha! ha! ha!

Don Car. But since she don't, what do I whining here? Curse on the base Humilities of Love.

San. Right.

Don Car. Let Children kiss the Rod that fleas 'em, let Dogs lye down and lick the Shooe that spurns 'em.

San. Ay.

Don Car. I am a Man, by Nature meant for Power; the Scepter's given us to wield, and we betray our Trust, whene'er we meanly lay it at a Woman's Feet.

San. True, we are Men; boo————Come, Master, let us both be in a Passion; here's my Scepter. [*Shewing a Cudgel.*] Subject *Jacinta*, look about you. Sir, was you ever in *Muscovy?* the Women there love the Men dearly, why? because,——[*Shaking his Stick.*] there's your Love-powder, for you. Ah, Sir, were we but Wise and Stout, what work shou'd we make with 'em: But this humble Love-making spoils 'em all. A rare way indeed to bring Matters about with 'em; we are persuading 'em all Day they are Angels and Goddesses, in order to use 'em at Night like human Creatures; we are like to succeed truly.

Don Car. For my part, I never yet cou'd bear a Slight from any Thing, nor will I now. There's but one Way however to resent it from a Woman; and that's to drive her bravely from your Heart, and place a worthier in her vacant Throne.

San. Now with Submission to my Betters, I have another way, Sir; I'll drive my Tyrant from my Heart, and place my self in her Throne. Yes: I will be Lord of my own Tenement, and keep my Houshold in Order. Wou'd you wou'd do so too, Master; for look you, I have been Servitor in a Colledge at *Salamancha*, and read Philosophy with the Doctors; where I found that a Woman in all Times has been observ'd to be an Animal hard to understand, and much inclin'd to Mischief. Now, as an Animal is always an Animal, and a Captain always a Captain, so a Woman is always a Woman: Whence it is that a certain *Greek* says, Her Head is like a Bank of Sand; or as another, A solid Rock; or according to a Third, A Dark Lanthorn. Pray Sir, observe; for this is close Reasoning; and so, as the Head is the Head of the Body; and that the Body without a Head, is like a Head without a Tail; and that where there is neither Head nor Tail 'tis a very strange Body: So I say a Woman is by Comparison; do you see; (for nothing explains things like Comparisons) I say by Comparison, as *Aristotle* has often said before me, one may compare her to the raging Sea; for as the Sea, when the Wind rises, knits its Brows like an angry Bull, and that Waves mount upon Rocks, and Rocks mount upon Waves; that Porpusses leap like Trouts, and Whales skip about like Gudgeons; that Ships rowl like Beer-Barrels, and Mariners pray like Saints; just so I say a Woman——A Woman, I say, just so, when her Reason is Shipwrack'd upon her Passion, and the Hulk of her Understanding lies thumping against the Rock of her Fury; then it is I say, that by certain Immotions, which——um—cause, as one may suppose, a sort of Convulsive,—yes——Hurricanious—um—Like in short; a Woman, is like the Devil, Sir.

Don Car. Admirably reason'd indeed, *Sancho*.

San. Pretty well, I thank Heav'n; but here come the Crocodiles, to weep us into Mercy.

Enter Leonora *and* Jacinta.

Master, let us shew our selves Men, and leave their briny Tears to wash their dirty Faces.

Don Car. It is not in the Power of Charms to move me.

San. Nor me, I hope; and yet I fear those Eyes will look out sharp, to snap up such a Prize.   [*Pointing to* Jacinta.

Jacin. He's coming to us, Madam, to beg Pardon; but sure you'll never grant it him?

Leon. If I do, may Heav'n never grant me mine.

Jacin. That's brave.

Don Car. You look, Madam, upon me, as if you thought I came to trouble you with my usual Importunities; I'll ease you of that Pain by telling you, my Bus'ness now is calmly to assure you, but I assure it you with Heav'n and Hell for seconds, for may the Joys of one fly from me, whilst the Pains of t'other overtake me, if all your Charms display'd e'er shake my Resolution; I'll never see you more.

San. Bon.

Leon. You are a Man of that nice Honour, Sir, I know you'll keep your Word; I expected this Assurance from you, and came this way only to thank you for't.

Jacin. Very well.

Don Car. You did, imperious Dame, you did: How base is Woman's Pride? How wretched are the Ingredients it is form'd of. If you saw Cause for just Disdain, why did you not at first repulse me? Why lead a Slave in Chains, that cou'd not grace your Triumphs? If I am thus to be contemn'd, think on the Favours you have done the Wretch, and hide your Face for ever.

San. Well argu'd.

Leon. I own you have hit the only Fault the World can charge me with; the Favours I have done to you, I am indeed asham'd of; but since Women have their Frailties, you'll allow me mine.

Don Car. 'Tis well; extreamly well, Madam. I'm happy however, you at last speak frankly, I thank you for it; from my Soul I thank you; but don't expect me groveling at your Feet again; don't! for if I do——

Leon. You will be treated as you deserve; trod upon.

Don Car. Give me Patience;——but I don't want it; I am calm: Madam, farewel; be happy if you can; by Heav'ns I wish you so, but never spread your Net for me again; for if you do——

Leon. You'll be running into it.

Don Car. Rather run headlong into Fire and Flames; rather be torn with Pincers Bit from Bit; rather be broil'd, like Martyrs upon Gridirons ——But I am wrong; this sounds like Passion, and Heav'n can tell I am not angry: Madam, I think we have no farther Business together; your most humble Servant.

Leon. Farewel t'ye, Sir.

Don Car. Come along. [*To* Sancho.

[*Goes to the Scene, and returns.*

Yet once more before I go, (lest you should doubt my Resolution) may I starve, perish, rot, be blasted, dead, damn'd, or any other thing that Men or Gods can think of, if on any Occasion whatever, Civil or Military, Pleasure or Business, Love or Hate, or any other Accident of Life, I, from this Moment, change one Word or Look with you.

[*Going off* Sancho *claps him on the Back.*

Leon. Content: Come away, *Jacinta.*

Don Carlos *returns.*

Don Car. Yet one Word, Madam, if you please; I have a little thing here belongs to you, a foolish Bawble I once was fond of.

[*Twitching her Picture from his Breast.*

Will you accept a Trifle from your Servant?

Leon. Willingly, Sir; I have a Bawble too I think you have some Claim to; you'll wear it for my sake.

[Breaks a Bracelet from her Arm, and gives it him.

Don Car. Most thankfully; this too I should restore you, it once was yours.——— *[Giving her a Table-book.*

By your Favour, Madam,———there is a Line or two in it, I think you did me once the Honour to Write with your own fair Hand. Here it is.

[Reads.

> *You love me,* Carlos, *and would know*
> *The secret Movements of my Heart:*
> *Whether I give you mine or no,*
> *With yours, methinks, I'd never, never part.*

Thus you have encourag'd me, and thus you have deceiv'd me.

San. Very true.

Leon. I have some faithful Lines too; I think I can produce 'em.

[Pulls out a Table-book; reads, and then gives it him.

> *How long soe'er, to sigh in vain,*
> *My Destiny may prove*
> *My Fate (in spight of your Disdain,)*
> *Will let me glory in your Chain,*
> *And give me leave eternally to Love.*

There, Sir, take your Poetry again, *[Throwing it at his Feet.* 'tis not much the worse for my wearing; 'twill serve again upon a fresh Occasion.

Jacin. Well done.

Don Car. I believe I can return the Present, Madam, with—a Pocketful of your Prose.———There. *[Throwing a handful of Letters at her Feet.*

Leon. Jacinta, give me his Letters. There, Sir, not to be behind Hand with you.

[Takes a handful of his Letters out of a Box, and throws 'em in his Face.

Jacin. And there, and there, and there, Sir.

*[*Jacinta *throws the rest at him.*

San. 'Cods my Life, we want Ammunition; but for a shift———There, and there, you saucy Slut, you.

*[*Sancho *pulls a Pack of dirty Cards out of his Pocket, and throws 'em at her; then they close; he pulls off her Head-cloaths, and she his Wigg, and then part, running she to her Mistress, he to his Master.*

Jacin. I think, Madam, we have clearly the better on't.

Leon. For a Proof, I resolve to keep the Field.

Jacin. Have a care he don't rally, and beat you yet tho'; pray walk off.

Leon. Fear nothing.

San. How the Armies stand and gaze at one another after the Battel! What think you, Sir, of shewing your self a great General, by making an honourable Retreat?

Don Car. I scorn it: Oh *Leonora! Leonora!* A Heart like mine should not be treated thus.

Leon. Carlos, Carlos, I have not deserv'd this Usage.

Don Car. Barbarous *Leonora;* but 'tis useless to reproach you; she that is capable of what you have done, is form'd too cruel ever to repent of it. Go on then, Tyrant; make your Bliss compleat; torment me still; for still, alas, I love enough to be tormented.

Leon. Ah *Carlos!* little do you know the tender Movements of that thing you name; the Heart, where Love presides, admits no Thought against the Honour of its Ruler.

Don Car. 'Tis not to call that Honour into doubt, if conscious of our own Unworthiness, we interpret every Frown to our Destruction.

Leon. When Jealousie proceeds from such humble Apprehensions, it shews it self with more Respect than yours has done.

Don Car. And where a Heart is guiltless, it easily forgives a greater Crime.

Leon. Forgiveness is not now in our Debate; if both have been in Fault, 'tis fit that both should suffer for it; our Separation will do Justice on us.

Don Car. But since we are our selves the Judges of our Crimes, what if we should inflict a gentler Punishment?

Leon. 'Twould but encourage us to Sin again.

Don Car. And if it should?——

Leon. 'Twould give a Fresh Occasion for the pleasing Exercise of Mercy.

Don Car. Right; and so we act the Part of Earth and Heav'n together, of Men and Gods, and taste of both their Pleasures.

Leon. The Banquet's too inviting to refuse it.

Don Car. Then thus let us fall on, and feed upon't for ever.

              [*Carries her off, embracing her, and kissing her Hand.*

Leon. Ah Woman! foolish, foolish Woman!

San. Very foolish indeed.

Jacin. But don't expect I'll follow her Example.

San. You would, Mopsie, if I'd let you.

Jacin. I'd sooner tear my Eyes out; ah——that she had had a little of my Spirit in her.

San. I believe I shall find thou hast a great deal of her Flesh, my Charmer; but 'twon't do; I am all Rock, hard Rock, very Marble.

Jacin. A very Pumice-stone, you Rascal, you, if one would try thee; but to prevent thy Humilities, and shew thee all Submission would be vain; to convince thee thou hast nothing but Misery and Despair before thee, here———take back thy paultry Thimble, and be in my Debt, for the Shirts I have made thee with it.

San. Nay, if y'are at that Sport, Mistress, I believe I shall lose nothing by the Balance of the Presents. There, take thy Tobacco-stopper, and stop thy———

Jacin. Here———take thy Satin Pincushion, with thy curious half hundred of Pins in't, thou mad'st such a Vapouring about yesterday: Tell 'em carefully, there is not one wanting.

San. There's thy Ivory-hafted Knife again, whet it well; 'tis so blunt 'twill cut nothing but Love.

Jacin. And there's thy pretty Pocket-Sissars thou hast honour'd me with, they'll cut off a Leg or an Arm, Heav'n bless 'em.

San. Here's the enchanted Handkerchief you were pleas'd to endear with your precious Blood, when the Violence of your Love at Dinner t'other Day made you cut your Fingers.———There.

[Blows his Nose in't, and gives it her.

Jacin. The Rascal so provokes me, I won't even keep his paltry Garters from him. D'you see these? You pitiful beggarly Scoundrel you:——— There, take 'em, there.

[She takes her Garters off, and slaps 'em about his Face.

San. I have but one thing more of thine, *[Shewing his Cudgel.]* I own 'tis the top of all thy Presents, and might be useful to me; but that thou may'st have nothing to upbraid me with, e'en take it again with the rest of 'em. *[Lifting it up to strike her, she leaps about his Neck.*

Jacin. Ah, cruel *Sancho:*———Now beat me, *Sancho,* do.

San. Rather, like *Indian* Beggars, beat my precious self.

[Throws away his Stick, and embraces her.

Rather let Infants Blood about the Streets,
Rather let all the Wine about the Cellar,
Rather let———Oh *Jacinta*———thou hast o'ercome.
How foolish are the great Resolves of Man!
Resolves, which we neither would keep, nor can.
When those bright Eyes in Kindness please to shine,
Their Goodness I must needs return, with mine:
Bless my *Jacinta* in her *Sancho's* Arms;———

Jacin. And I my *Sancho* with *Jacinta's* Charms. *[Exeunt.*

End of the Fourth Act.

ACT V. SCENE I.

SCENE, *the Street.*

Enter Lopez.

AS soon as it is Night, says my Master to me, tho' it cost me my Life, I'll enter *Leonora*'s Lodgings; therefore make haste, *Lopez*, prepare every thing necessary, Three Pair of Pocket-Pistols, Two wide-mouth'd Blunderbusses, some Six Ells of Sword-Blade, and a Couple of dark Lanthorns. When my Master said this to me, Sir, said I to my Master, (that is, I would have said it, if I had not been in such a Fright I could say nothing; however I'll say it to him now, and shall probably have a quiet Hearing;) Look you, Sir, by dint of Reason I intend to confound you: You are resolv'd, you say, to get into *Leonora*'s Lodgings, tho' the Devil stand in the Door-way?——Yes, *Lopez*, that's my Resolution.——Very well; and what do you intend to do when you are there?——Why, what an injur'd Man should do; make her sensible of——Make her sensible of a Pudding; Don't you see she's a Jade? She'll raise the House about your Ears, arm the whole Family, set the great Dog at you.——Were there Legions of Devils to repulse me, in such a Cause I could disperse 'em all.——Why then you have no Occasion for Help, Sir, you may leave me at home to lay the Cloth.——No; thou art my ancient Friend, my Fellow-Traveller, and to reward thy faithful Services, this Night thou shalt partake my Danger and my Glory.——Sir, I have got Glory enough under you already, to content any reasonable Servant for his Life.——Thy Modesty makes me willing to double my Bounty; this Night may bring eternal Honour to thee and thy Family.——Eternal Honour, Sir, is too much in Conscience for a Serving-Man; besides, Ambition has been many a great Soul's Undoing.——I doubt thou art afraid, my *Lopez*; thou shalt be arm'd with Back with Breast and Head-piece.——They will encumber me in my Retreat.——Retreat, my Hero! Thou never shalt retreat.——Then by my Troth I'll never go, Sir.—— But here he comes.

Enter Don Lorenzo.

Don Lor. Will it never be Night? Sure 'tis the longest Day the Sun e'er travell'd.

Lop. Would 'twere as long as those in *Greenland*, Sir, that you might spin out your Life t'other half Year. I don't like these nightly Projects; a Man can't see what he does: We shall have some scurvy Mistake or other happen: A Brace of Bullets blunder through your Head in the Dark perhaps, and spoil all your Intrigue.

Don Lor. Away, you trembling Wretch, away.

Lop. Nay, Sir, what I say is purely for your Safety; for as to my self
——Uds-death, I no more value the losing a Quart of Blood, than I do
drinking a Quart of Wine. Besides, my Veins are too full; my Physician
advis'd me but yesterday to let go Twenty Ounces for my Health. So
you see, Sir, there's nothing of that in the Case.

Don Lor. Then let me hear no other Objections; for 'till I see *Leonora*
I must lye upon the Rack, I cannot bear her Resentment, and will pacifie
her this Night, or not live to see to Morrow.

Lop. Well, Sir, since you are so determin'd, I shan't be impertinent
with any farther Advice; but I think you have laid your Design to——
[*He coughs.*] (I have got such a Cold to Day) to get in privately, have
you not?

Don Lor. Yes; and have taken care to be introduc'd as far as her
Chamber-door, with all Secrecy.

Lop. [*He Coughs.*]—This unlucky Cough. I had rather have had a
Feaver at another time. Sir, I shou'd be sorry to do you more Harm than
Good upon this Occasion: If this Cough shou'd come upon me in the
midst of the Action,   [*Coughs.*
and give the Alarm to the Family, I shou'd not forgive my self as long
as I liv'd.

Don Lor. I have greater Ventures than that, to take my Chance for,
and can't dispence with your Attendance, Sir.

Lop. This 'tis to be a good Servant, and make one's self necessary.

Enter Toledo.

Tol. Sir,——I am glad I have found you. I am a Man of Honour,
you know; and do always profess losing my Life upon a handsome Occasion: Sir, I come to offer you my Service. I am inform'd from unquestion-
able Hands, that *Don Carlos* is enrag'd against you, to a dangerous Degree;
and that old *Alvarez* has given positive Directions, to break the Legs and
Arms of your Servant *Lopez.*

Lop. Look you there now; I thought what 'twou'd come to; what do
they meddle with me for? What have I to do in my Master's Amours?
The old Don's got out of his Senses I think; have I Married his Daughter?

Don Lor. Fear nothing, we'll take care o'thee.——Sir, I thank you for
the Favour of your Intelligence, 'tis nothing however but what I expected,
and am provided for.

Tol. Sir, I wou'd advise you to provide your self with good Friends.
I desire the Honour to keep your back-Hand my self.

Lop. 'Tis very kind indeed: Pray Sir, have you ne'er a Servant with
you, cou'd hold a Racket for me too?

Tol. I have two Friends, fit to head two Armies. And yet——A Word in your Ear, they shan't coſt you above a Ducat a-piece.

Lop. Take 'em by all Means, Sir; you were never offer'd a better penny-worth in your Life.

Tol. Ah Sir,——little *Diego*——you have heard of him; he'd have been worth a Legion upon this Occasion: You know, I suppose, how they have serv'd him?——They have hang'd him: But he made a Noble Execution: They clapp'd the Rack and the Prieſt to him at once; but cou'd neither get a Word of Confession nor a Groan of Repentance: He dy'd mighty well truly.

Don Lor. Such a Man is indeed much to be Regretted: As for the reſt of your Escort, Captain, I thank you for 'em; but shall not use 'em.

Tol. I'm sorry for't Sir, because I think you go in very great Danger; I'm much afraid your Rival won't give you fair Play.

Lop. If he do's I'll be hang'd. He's a damn'd Passionate Fellow, and cares not what Mischief he does.

Don Lor. I shall give him a very good Opportunity; for I'll have no other Guards about me but you Sir. So come along.

Lop. Why Sir, this is the Sin of Presumption; setting Heav'n a Defiance; making Jack-pudding of a Blunderbuss.

Don Lor. No more, but follow. Hold! Turn this Way; I see *Camillo* there. I wou'd avoid him, 'till I see what Part he takes in this odd **Affair** of his Siſter's. For I wou'd not have the Quarrel fix'd with him, if it be possible to avoid it. [*Exit* Don Lorenzo.

Lop. Sir——Captain *Toledo*, One Word if you please, Sir; I'm mighty sorry to see my Maſter won't accept of your friendly Offer: Look ye; I'm not very Rich, but as far as the Expence of a Dollar went, if you'd be so kind to take a little Care of me, it shou'd be at your Service.

Tol. Let me see?——A Dollar you say?——But suppose I'm wounded?

Lop. Why you shall be put to no extraordinary Charge upon that: I have been Prentice to a Barber, and will be your Surgeon my self.

Tol. 'Tis too cheap in Conscience; but my Land Eſtate is so ill paid this War Time——

Lop. That a little Induſtry may be commendable: So say no more; that Matter's fix'd. [*Exeunt* Lop. *and* Tol.

Enter Camillo.

How miserable a Perplexity have I brought my self into? Yet why do I complain? Since with all the dreadful Torture I endure, I can't repent of one wild Step I've made. O Love: What Tempeſts can'ſt thou raise, what Storms can'ſt thou asswage? To all thy Cruelties I am resign'd: Long Years, through Seas of Torment, I'm content to rowl, so thou wilt guide me to the happy Port of my *Lorenzo*'s Arms, and bless me there with one calm Day at laſt.

Enter Isabella.

What News, dear *Isabella?* Methinks there's something chearful in your Looks may give a trembling Lover Hopes. If you have Comfort for me speak, for I indeed have need of it.

Isab. Were your Wants yet still greater than they are, I bring a plentiful Supply.

Cam. O Heav'ns! Is't possible?

Isab. New Mysteries are out, and if you can find Charms to wean *Lorenzo* from your Sister, no other Obstacle is in your way to all you wish.

Cam. Kind Messenger from Heav'n, speak on.

Isab. Know then, that you are Daughter to *Alvarez.*

Cam. How? Daughter to *Alvarez?*

Isab. You are: The Truth this Moment's come to Light. And 'till this Moment, he, altho' your Father, was a Stranger to it. Nay; did not even know you were a Woman. In short: The great Estate which has occasion'd these uncommon Accidents, was left but on Condition of a Son; great Hopes of one there was, when you destroy'd 'em, and to your Parents came a most unwelcome Guest; to repair the Disappointment you were exchang'd for that young *Camillo;* who few Months after dy'd. Your Father then was absent, but your Mother quick in Contrivance, bold in Execution, during that Infant's Sickness, had resolv'd his Death shou'd not deprive her Family of those Advantages his Life had given it, so order'd things with such Dexterity, that once again there past a Change between you; of this (for Reasons yet unknown to me) she made a Secret to her Husband, and took such wise Precautions, that 'till this Hour 'twas so to all the World, except the Person from whom I now have heard it.

Cam. This News indeed affords a View of no unhappy Termination. Yet there are Difficulties still may be of fatal Hindrance.

Isab. None, except that one I just now nam'd to you; for to remove the rest, know, I have already unfolded all both to *Alvarez* and *Don Felix.*

Cam. And how have they receiv'd it?

Isab. To your Wishes both. As for *Lorenzo*, he is yet a Stranger to all has past; and the two old Fathers desire he may some Moments longer continue so. They have agreed to be a little Merry with the Heats he is in, and engage you in a Family Quarrel with him.

Cam. I doubt, *Isabella*, I shall act that Part but faintly.

Isab. No matter, you'll make amends for it in the Scene of Reconciliation.

Cam. Pray Heav'n it be my Lot to act it with him.

Isab. Here comes *Don Felix*, to wish you Joy.

Enter Don Felix.

(123)

Don Felix. Come near, my Daughter, and with extended Arms of great Affection let me receive thee.   [*Kisses her.*
Thou art a dainty Wench, good faith thou art, and 'tis a mettl'd Action thou haſt done; if *Lorenzo* don't like thee the better for't, 'Cods my Life, he's a pitiful Fellow, and I shan't believe the bony old Man had the getting of him.

Cam. I'm so encourag'd by your Forgiveness, Sir, methinks I have some flattering Hopes of his.

Don Felix. Of his? I-gad and he had beſt, I believe he'll meet with his Match if he don't. What do'ſt think of trying his Courage a little, by way of a Joak or so?

Isab. I was juſt telling her your Design, Sir.

Don Felix. Why I'm in a mighty witty Way upon this whimsical Occasion. But I see him coming. You muſt not appear yet; go your way in to the reſt of the People there, and I'll inform him what a Squable he has work'd himself into here.   [*Exeunt* Camillo *and* Isabella.

Enter Don Lorenzo *and* Lopez.

Lop. Pray, Sir, don't be so obſtinate now, don't affront Heav'n at this rate: I had a Vision laſt Night about this Business on purpose to forewarn you; I Dreamt of Goose Eggs, a blunt Knife and the Snuff of a Candle; I'm sure there's Mischief towards.

Don Lor. You Cowardly Rascal, hold your Tongue.

Don Felix. Lorenzo, come hither my Boy, I was juſt going to send for thee. The Honour of our Ancient Family lies in thy Hands; there is a Combat preparing, thou muſt fight, my Son.

Lop. Look you there now, did not I tell you? O, Dreams are wondrous things; I never knew that Snuff of a Candle fail yet.

Don Lor. Sir, I do not doubt but *Carlos* seeks my Life, I hope he'll do it fairly.

Lop. Fairly, do you hear, fairly? Give me leave to tell you, Sir, Folks are not fit to be truſted with Lives, that don't know how to look better after 'em. Sir, you gave it him; I hope you'll make him take a little more care on't.

Don Felix. My care shall be to make him do as a Man of Honour ought to do.

Lop. What, will you let him fight then? Let your own Flesh and Blood fight?

Don Felix. In a good Cause, as this is.

Lop. O, *Monſtrum Horrendum!* Now I have that Humanity about me, that if a Man but talks to me of Fighting I shiver at the Name on't.

Don Lor. What you do on this Occasion, Sir, is worthy of you: And had I been wanting to you, in my due Regards before, this noble Action wou'd have ſtamp'd that Impreſſion, which a grateful Son ought to have for so Generous a Father.

Lop. Very Generous truly; gives him leave to be run through the Guts, for his Poſterity to brag on a Hundred Years hence.   [*Aside.*

Don Lor. I think, Sir, as things now ſtand, it won't be right for me to wait for *Carlos*'s Call: I'll, if you please, prevent him.

Lop. Ay, pray, Sir, do prevent him by all means; 'tis better made up, as you say, a Thousand times.

Don Felix. Hold your Tongue, you impertinent Jackanapes, I will have him fight, and fight like a Fury too; if he don't he'll be worſted, I can tell him that. For know, Son, your Antagoniſt is not the Person you name, it is an Enemy of twice his Force.

Lop. O dear, O dear, O dear, and will no Body keep 'em asunder?

Don Lor. No Body shall keep us asunder, if once I know the Man I have to deal with.

Don Felix. Thy Man then is——*Camillo*.

Don Lor. Camillo!

Don Felix. 'Tis he; he'll suffer no Body to decide this Quarrel but himself.

Lop. Then there are no Seconds, Sir.

Don Felix. None.

Lop. He's a Brave Man.

Don Felix. No, he says no Bodys Blood shall be spilt on this Occasion, but theirs who have a Title to it.

Lop. I believe he'll scarce have a Law Suit upon the Claim.

Don Felix. In short, he accuses thee of a shameful Falshood, in pretending his Siſter *Leonora* was thy Wife; and has upon it prevail'd with his Father, as thou has done with thine, to let the Debate be ended by the Sword 'twixt him and thee.

Lop. And pray, Sir, with Submiſſion, one short Queſtion if you please; What may the gentle *Leonora* say of this Business?

Don Felix. She approves of the Combat, and Marries *Carlos*.

Lop. Why God-a-mercy.

Don Lor. Is it poſſible? sure she's a Devil not a Woman.

Lop. I-cod, Sir, a Devil and a Woman both, I think.

Don Felix. Well, thou sha't have Satisfaction of some of 'em. Here they all come.

Enter Don Alvarez, Leonora, Don Carlos, Sancho *and*
Jacinta.

Don Alv. Well, *Don Felix*; have you prepar'd your Son? for Mine, he's ready to engage.

Don Lor. And so is his. My Wrongs prepare me for a Thousand

Combats. My Hand has hitherto been held, by the Regard I've had to every thing of Kin to *Leonora;* but since the monſtrous Part she acts has driven her from my Heart, I call for Reparation from her Family.

Don Alv. You'll have it, Sir; *Camillo* will attend you inſtantly.

Lop. O lack, O lack; will no Body do a little something to prevent Bloodshed? Why, Madam, have you no Pity, no Bowels? [*To* Leonora.] Stand and see one of your Husbands ſtoter'd before your Face? 'Tis an arrant Shame.

Leon. If Widowhood be my Fate, I muſt bear it as I can.

Lop. Why did you ever hear the like?

Don Lor. Talk to her no more. Her monſtrous Impudence is no other-wise to be reply'd to, than by a Dagger in her Brother's Heart.

Leon. Yonder he's coming to receive it. But have a care, brave Sir, he does not place it in another's.

Don Lor. It is not in his Power. He has a rotten Cause upon his Sword; I'm sorry he's engag'd in't; but since he is, he muſt take his Fate. For you, my Bravo, expect me in your Turn.   [*To* Don Carlos.

Don Car. You'll find *Camillo*, Sir, will set your Hand out.

Don Lor. A beardless Boy. You might have match'd me better, Sir: But Prudence is a Virtue.

Don Felix. Nay, Son, I wou'd not have thee despise thy Adversary neither; thou'lt find *Camillo* will put thee hardly to't.

Don Lor. I wish we were come to the Trial. Why do's he not appear?

Jacin. Now do I hate to hear People brag thus. Sir, with my Lady's leave, I'll hold a Ducat he disarms you.   [*They laugh.*

Don Lor. Why, what?——I think I'm sported with. Take heed, I warn you all; I am not to be trifled with.

Enter Camillo *and* Isabella.

Leon. You sha'nt, Sir; here's one will be in earneſt with you.

Don Lor. He's welcome: Tho' I had rather have drawn my Sword againſt another. I'm sorry, *Camillo*, we shou'd meet, on such bad Terms as these; yet more sorry your Siſter shou'd be the wicked Cause on't; but since nothing will serve her but the Blood either of a Husband or Brother, she shall be glutted with't. Draw!

Lop. Ah Lard, ah Lard, ah Lard.

Don Lor. And yet, before I take this Inſtrument of Death into my fatal Hand, hear me, *Camillo*; hear, *Alvarez;* all! I imprecate the utmoſt Powers of Heav'n, to shower upon my Head the deadlieſt of its Wrath I ask; that all Hell's Torments may unite, to round my Soul with our eternal Anguish, if Wicked *Leonora* ben't my Wife.

Omnes. O Lord, O Lord, O Lord.

(126)

Leon. Why then, may all those Curses pass him by, and wrap me in their everlasting Pains, if ever once I had a fleeting Thought of making him my Husband.

Lop. O Lord, O Lord, O Lord.

Leon. Nay more: To strike him Dumb at once, and shew what Men with honest Looks can practice; Know, He's Married to another.

Don Alv. and *Don Felix.* How?

Leon. The Truth of this is known to some are here.

Jacin. Nay, 'tis certainly so.

Isab. 'Tis to a Friend of mine.

Don Car. I know the Person.

Don Lor. 'Tis false, and thou art a Villain for thy Testimony.

Cam. Then let me speak; What they aver is true, and I my self was in Disguise a Witness of its doing.

Don Lor. Death and Confusion! He a Villain too! Have at thy Heart.
                              [*He draws.*

Lop. Ah!——I can't bear the Sight on't.

Cam. Put up that furious Thing, there's no Business for't.

Don Lor. There's Business for a Dagger, Stripling; 'tis that shou'd be thy Recompence.

Cam. Why then, to shew thee. Naked to the World, and close thy Mouth for ever,——I am, my self thy Wife.——

Don Lor. What does the Dog mean?

Cam. To fall upon the Earth, and sue for Mercy.
                      [*Kneels and lets her Perriwig fall off.*

Don Lor. A Woman?——

Lop. I-Cod, and a pretty one too; you Waggs you.

Don Lor. I'm all Amazement. Rise, *Camillo*, (if I am still to call you by that Name) and let me hear the Wonders you have for me.

Isab. That part her Modesty will ask from me: I'm to inform you then, That this Disguise hides other Mysteries, besides a Woman; a large and fair Estate was cover'd by't, which with the Lady now will be resign'd you. 'Tis true, in Justice it was yours before; but 'tis the God of Love has done you Right. To him you owe this strange Discovery, through him you are to know, the true *Camillo*'s dead, and that this fair Adventurer is Daughter to *Alvarez.*

Don Lor. Incredible! But go on; let me hear more.

Don Felix. She'll tell thee the rest her self, the next dark Night she meets thee in the Garden.

Don Lor. Ha!——Was it *Camillo* then, that I——

Isab. It was *Camillo* who there made you happy: And who has Virtue, Beauty, Wit and Love——enough to make you so, while Life shall last you.

Don Lor. The Proof she gives me of her Love, deserves a large Acknowledgment indeed. Forgive me therefore, *Leonora*, if what I owe this Goodness and these Charms, I with my utmoſt Care, my Life, my Soul, endeavour to repay.

Cam. Is it then possible you can forgive me?

Don Lor. Indeed I can; few Crimes have such a Claim to Mercy; but join with me then, dear *Camillo*, (for ſtill I know you by no other Name) join with me to obtain your Father's Pardon; yours, *Leonora*, too, I muſt Implore: And yours, my Friend, for now we may be such. (*To* Don Carlos.] Of all I ask Forgiveness. And since there is so a fair Cause of all my wild Miſtakes, I hope, I by her Intereſt shall obtain it.

Don Alv. You have a Claim to mine, *Lorenzo*, I wish I had so ſtrong a one to yours; but if by future Services (though I lay down my Life amongſt 'em) I may blot out of your Remembrance a Fault (I cannot name) I then shall leave the World in Peace.

Don Lor. In Peace then, Sir, enjoy it; for from this very Hour, what e'er is paſt, with me, is gone for ever. Your Daughter is too fair a Mediatrix to be refus'd his Pardon, to whom she owes the Charms she pleads with for it.

> From this good Day, then let all Discord cease;
> Let those to come be Harmony and Peace,
> Henceforth let all our diff'rent Int'reſts join,
> Let Fathers, Lovers, Friends, let all combine,
> To make each others Days as bleſt as she will mine.

EPILOGUE

Written by Mr. *Motteux*.

I'M thinking, now good Husbands are so few,
   To get one like my Friend, what I must do.
Camillo *ventur'd hard*; yet at the worst,
She stole Love's Hony-Moon; and try'd her Lover first.
Many poor Damsels, if they dar'd to tell,
Have done as much, but have not scap'd so well.
'Tis well the Scene's in Spain; thus in the Dark,
I shou'd be loath to trust a London Spark.
Some Accident might, for a private Reason,
Silence a Female, all this Acting Season.
Hard Fate of Woman! Any one wou'd vex,
To think what Odds, you Men have, of our Sex.
Restraint and Customs share our Inclination,
You Men can try; and run o'er half the Nation.
We dare not, even to avoid Reproach,
When y'are at Whites, Peep out of Hackney-Coach;
Nor with a Friend at Night, our Fame regarding,
With Glass drawn up, Drive about Covent-Garden.
If poor Town-Ladies steal in here, you Rail,
Tho' like Chaste Nuns, their Modest Looks they Veil;
With this decorum, they can hardly gain
To be thought Virtuous, even in Drury-Lane.
Tho' this you'll not allow, yet sure you may
A Plot to Snap you, in an honest Way.
In Love-Affairs, one scarce would spare a Brother:
All cheat; and Married Folks may keep a Pother,   }
But look as if they cheated one another.
You may pretend, our Sex dissembles most,
But of your Truth none have much Cause to boast:
You Promise bravely; but for all your Storming,
We find y'are not so Valiant at Performing.
   Then sure Camillo's Conduct you'll approve:
Wou'd you not do as much for one you love?
Wedlock's but a blind Bargain at the best,
You venture more, sometimes, to be not half so blest.
All, soon or late, that dang'rous Venture make,
And some of you may make a worse Mistake.

FINIS.

A

JOURNEY

TO

LONDON

BEING

Part of a Comedy

Written by the Late

Sir *John Vanbrugh*, Knt.

And Printed after his own Copy:

Which (since his Decease) has been made an

Intire Play,

By Mr. CIBBER

And call'd, *The* Provok'd Husband &c,

Text

THE text is from the first edition of 1728, collated with that of 1730 and the first collected edition of 1730. Cibber seems to have taken great care over the first edition, in contrast with his edition of *The Provok'd Husband*, which is a horrid production.

Dramatis Personæ

MEN.

Sir *Francis Headpiece*, a Country Gentleman.
Lord *Loverule*.
Sir *Charles*.
Uncle *Richard*, Uncle to Sir *Francis*.
Squire *Humphry*, Son to Sir *Francis*.
Colonel *Courtly*.
John Moody, Servant to Sir *Francis*.
James, Servant to Uncle *Richard*.

WOMEN.

Lady *Headpiece*.
Miss *Betty*, her Daughter.
Lady *Arabella*, Wife to Lord *Loverule*.
Clarinda, a young unmarried Lady.
Mrs. *Motherly*, one that lets Lodgings.
Martilla, her Neice.

A

JOURNEY *to* LONDON

ACT I. SCENE I.

SCENE, *Uncle* Richard's *House.*

Uncle Richard *solus.*

WHAT prudent Cares does this deep foreseeing Nation take, for the Support of its worshipful Families! In order to which, and that they may not fail to be always Significant and useful in their Country, it is a settled Foundation-Point that every Child that is born, shall be a Beggar——Except one; and that he——shall be a Fool.

My Grandfather was bred a Fool, as the Country report: my Father was a Fool,———as my mother us'd to say; my Brother was a Fool, to my own Knowledge, tho' a Great Justice of the Peace; and he has left a Son, that will make his Son a Fool, or I am mistaken.

The Lad is now fourteen years old, and but just out of his Psalter. As to his honour'd Father, my much esteemed nephew, Here I have him.
[*Shewing a letter.*

In this profound Epistle (which I have just now receiv'd) there is the Top and Bottom of him. Forty years and two is the Age of him; in which it is computed by his Butler, his own person has drank two and thirty Ton of Ale. The rest of his Time has been employ'd in persecuting all the poor four-legg'd Creatures round, that wou'd but run away fast enough from him, to give him the high-mettled pleasure of running after them.

In this noble Employ, he has broke his right Arm, his left Leg, and both his Collar-bones——Once he broke his Neck, but that did him no harm; a nimble Hedge-leaper, a Brother of the Stirrup that was by, whipt off his Horse and mended it.

His Estate being left him with two Joyntures, and three weighty Mortgages upon it; He, to make all easy, and pay his Brother's and Sister's Portions, marry'd a profuse young Housewife for Love, with never a Penny of Money. Having done all this, like his brave Ancestors, for the Support of the Family, he now finds Children and Interest-Money make such a bawling about his Ears, that he has taken the friendly Advice of his Neighbour, the good Lord *Courtlove*, to run his Estate two thousand Pounds more in debt, that he may retrieve his Affairs by being a Parliament-Man, and bringing his Wife to *London* to play off a hundred Pounds at Dice with Ladies of Quality, before breakfast.

But let me read this Wiseacre's Letter, once over again.

Most Honoured Uncle,

I *Do not doubt but you have much rejoyced at my Success, in my Election; It has cost me some Money, I own: but what of all that! I am a Parliament-Man, and that will set all to rights. I have lived in the Country all my Days, 'tis true; but what then! I have made Speeches at the Sessions, and in the Vestry too, and can Elsewhere perhaps, as well as some others that do; and I have a Noble Friend hard by, who has let me into some small Knowledge of what's what at* Westminster. *And so, that I may be always at hand to serve my Country, I have consulted with my Wife, about taking a house at* London, *and bringing her and my Family up to Town; which, her Opinion is, will be the rightest Thing in the World.*

My Wife's Opinion about bringing her to *London?* I'll read no more of thee——Beast. [*Strikes the letter down with his stick.*

Enter James *hastily.*

James. Sir, Sir, do you hear the News? they are all a coming.
Unc. Rich. Ay Sirrah, I hear it, with a Pox to it.
James. Sir, here's *John Moody* arriv'd already; he's stumping about the Streets in his dirty Boots, and asking every Man he meets, if they can tell where he may have a good Lodging for a Parliament-Man, 'till he can hire such a House as becomes him; he tells them his Lady and all the Family are coming too, and that they are so nobly attended, they care not a Fig for any Body.

Sir, they have added two Cart-Horses to the four old Geldings, because my Lady will have it said, she came to Town in her Coach and Six, and (ha, ha,) heavy *George* the Plowman rides Postilion.

Unc. Rich. Very well; the Journey begins as it shou'd do——*James.*
James. Sir.
Unc. Rich. Dost know whether they bring all the Children with them?
James. Only 'Squire *Humphry*, and Miss *Betty*, Sir; the other Six are put to board at Half a Crown a week a Head, with *Joan Growse*, at *Smoke-dunghil* Farm.

Unc. Rich. The Lord have Mercy upon all good Folks, what Work will these People make? dost know when they'll be here?
James. *John* says, Sir, they'd have been here last Night, but that the

old wheezy-belly Horse tir'd, and the two fore-wheels came crash down at once in *Wagonrut*-Lane. Sir, they were cruelly loaden, as I understand; my Lady herself, he says, laid on four Mail-Trunks, besides the great Deal-box, which fat *Tom* sate upon behind.

Unc. Rich. Soh!

James. Then within the Coach there was Sir *Francis*, my Lady, and the great fat Lap-dog, 'Squire *Humphry*, Miss *Betty*, my Lady's Maid Mrs. *Handy*, and *Doll Tripe* the Cook; but she puked with sitting backward, so they mounted her into the Coach-box.

Unc. Rich. Very well.

James. Then Sir, for fear of a Famine, before they shou'd get to the Baiting-place, there was such Baskets of Plumbcake, Dutch-Gingerbread, Cheshire-Cheese, Naples-Biscuits, Maccaroons, Neats-Tongues, and cold boyl'd Beef——and in case of Sickness, such Bottles of Usquebaugh, Black-cherry Brandy, Cinamon-water, Sack, Tent, and Strong beer, as made the old Coach crack again.

Unc. Rich. Well said!

James. And for Defence of this Good Cheer, and my Lady's little Pearl Necklace, there was the Family Basket-hilt Sword, the great Turkish Cimiter, the old Blunderbuss, a good Bag of Bullets, and a great Horn of Gunpowder.

Unc. Rich. Admirable!

James. Then for Band-boxes, they were so bepiled up, to Sir *Francis*'s Nose, that he cou'd only peep out at a chance Hole with one Eye, as if he were viewing the Country thro' a Perspective-Glass.

But Sir, if you please, I'll go look after *John Moody* a little for fear of Accidents; for he never was in *London* before, you know, but one Week, and then he was kidnapp'd into a House of ill Repute, where he exchang'd all his Money and Cloaths for a————um. So I'll go look after him, Sir.   [*Exit.*

Unc. Rich. Nay, I don't doubt but this wise Expedition will be attended with more Adventures than one.————

This noble Head, and Supporter of his Family, will, as an honest Country Gentleman, get Credit enough amongst the Tradesmen, to run so far in debt in one Session, as will make him just fit for a Goal, when he's dropt at the next Election.

He will make Speeches in the House, to shew the Government of what Importance he can be to them, by which they will see, he can be of no Importance at all; and he will find in time, that he stands valued at (if he votes right) being sometimes————invited to Dinner.

Then his Wife (who has ten times more of a Jade about her than she yet knows of) will so improve in this rich Soil, she will, in one Month, learn every Vice the finest Lady in the Town can teach her.

She will be extremely courteous to the Fops who make Love to her in jest, and she will be extremely grateful to those who do it in earnest.

She will visit all Ladies that will let her into their Houses, and she will run in Debt to all the Shop-keepers that will let her into their Books.

In short, before her Husband has got five Pound by a Speech at *Westminster*, she will have lost five hundred at Cards and Dice in the Parish of St. *James's*.

Wife and Family to *London* with a Pox! [*Going off.*

[SCENE II. *A Room in Mrs.* Motherly's *House.*]

Enter James *and* John Moody.

James. Dear *John Moody*, I am so glad to see you in *London* once more.

John Moody. And I you, dear Mr. *James:* Give me a kiss——Why that's friendly

James. I wish they had been so, *John*, that you met with when you were here before.

John Moody. Ah————Murrain upon all Rogues and Whores, I say; but I am grown so cunning now, the Deel himself can't handle me. I have made a notable Bargain for these Lodgings here, we are to pay but five Pounds a Week, and have all the House to ourselves.

James. Where are the people that belong to it to be then?

John Moody. O! there's only the Gentlewoman, her two Maids, and a Cousin, a very pretty Civil young Woman truly, and the Maids are the merriest Griggs——

James. Have a Care, *John*.

John Moody. O, fear nothing, we did so play together last Night.

James. Hush, here comes my Master.

Enter Uncle Richard.

Unc. Rich. What! *John* has taken these Lodgings has he?

James. Yes Sir, he has taken 'em.

Unc. Rich. Oh *John!* how dost do, honest *John?* I am glad to see thee with all my Heart.

John Moody. I humbly thank your Worship. I'm staut still, and a faithful awd Servant to th' Family. Heav'n prosper aw that belong to't.

Unc. Rich. What, they are all upon the Road?

John Moody. As mony as the awd Coach wou'd hauld, Sir: the Lord send 'em well to tawn.

Unc. Rich. And well out on't again, *John*, ha!

John Moody. Ah Sir! you are a wise Man, so am I: Home's home,, I say. I wish we get any Good here. I's sure we ha' got little upo' the Road. Some Mischief or other, aw the day long. Slap goes one thing, crack goes another; my Lady cries out for driving faſt; the awd Cattle are for going slow; *Roger* whips, they ſtand ſtill and kick; nothing but a sort of a Contradiction aw the Journey long. My Lady wou'd gladly have been here laſt Night Sir, tho' there was no Lodgings got; but her Ladyship said, she did naw care for that, she'd lye in the Inn where the Horses ſtood, as long as it was in *London.*

Unc. Rich. These Ladies, these Ladies, *John*———

John Moody. Ah Sir, I have seen a little of 'em, tho' not so much as my Betters. Your Worship is naw marry'd yet?

Unc. Rich. No, *John*, no; I am an old Batchelor ſtill.

John Moody. Heav'ns bless you and preserve you, Sir.

Unc. Rich. I think you have loſt your Good-woman, *John?*

John Moody. No Sir, that I have not; *Bridget* ſticks to me ſtill, Sir, she was for coming to *London* too, but, no, says I, there may be Mischief enough done without you.

Unc. Rich. Why that was bravely spoken, *John*, and like a Man.

John Moody. Sir, were my Meaſter but hafe the Mon that I am, Gadswookers———tho' he'll speak ſtautly too sometimes, but then he conno hawd it; no, he conno hawd it.

Enter Maid.

Maid. Mr. *Moody*, Mr. *Moody*, here's the Coach come.

John Moody. Already? no sure.

Maid. Yes, yes, it's at the Door, they are getting out; my Miſtress is run to receive 'em.

John Moody. And so will I, as in Duty bound.   [*Exeunt* John *and Maid.*

Unc. Rich. And I will ſtay here, not being in Duty bound to do the Honours of this House.

Enter Sir Francis, *Lady,* 'Squire Humphry, *Mrs.* Betty,
Mrs. Handy, Doll Tripe, John Moody, *and*
Mrs. Motherly.

Lady Head. Do you hear, *Moody*, let all the Things be firſt laid down here, and then carry'd where they'll be us'd.

John Moody. They shall, an't please your Ladyship.

Lady Head. What, my uncle *Richard* here to receive us! this is kind indeed: Sir, I am extremely glad to see you.

Unc. Rich. Neice, your servant.   [*Salutes her.*
I am extremely sorry to see you, in the worſt Place I know in the World for a good Woman to grow better in.

Nephew, I am your Servant too; but I don't know how to bid you welcome.

Fran. I am sorry for that, Sir.

Unc. Rich. Nay, 'tis for your own sake: I'm not concern'd.

Sir Fran. I hope, Uncle, I shall give you such weighty Reasons for what I have done, as shall convince you I'm a prudent Man.

Unc. Rich. That wilt thou never convince me of, whilſt thou shalt live.   [*Aside.*

Sir Fran. Here *Humphry*, come up to your Uncle——Sir, this is your Godson.

Squire Humph. Honour'd Uncle and Godfather, I crave leave to ask your Blessing.   [*Kneels.*

Unc. Rich. Thou art a Numscull I see already.   [*Aside.*
There thou haſt it.   [*Puts his hand on his head.*
And if it will do thee any good, may it be, to make thee, at leaſt, as wise a man as thy father.

Lady Head. Miss *Betty*, don't you see your Uncle?

Unc. Rich. And for thee, my Dear, may'ſt thou be, at leaſt, as good a Woman as thy Mother.

Miss Betty. I wish I may ever be so handsome, Sir.

Unc. Rich. Ha! Miss Pert! now that's a Thought that seems to have been hatcht in the Girl on this side *Highgate*.   [*Aside.*

Sir Fran. Her Tongue is a little nimble, Sir.

Lady Head. That's only from her Country Education, Sir *Francis*, she has been kept there too long; I therefore brought her to *London*, Sir, to learn more Reserve and Modeſty.

Unc. Rich. O! the beſt Place in the World for it. Every Woman she meets, will teach her something of it.

There's the good Gentlewoman of the House, looks like a knowing Person, ev'n she perhaps will be so good to read her a Lesson, now and then, upon that Subjeƈt.

An errant Bawd, or I have no Skill in Phisiognomy.   [*Aside.*

Mrs. Moth. Alas, Sir, Miss won't ſtand long in need of my poor Inſtructions; if she does, they'll be always at her Service.

Lady Head. Very obliging, indeed, Mrs. *Motherly*.

Sir Fran. Very kind and civil truly; I believe we are got into a mighty good House here.

Unc. Rich. For good Business, very probable.   [*Aside.*
Well, neice, your Servant for to-night; you have a great deal of Affairs upon your Hands here, so I won't hinder you.

Lady Head. I believe, Sir, I shan't have much less every day, while I ſtay in this Town, of one sort or other.

Unc. Rich. Why, 'tis a Town of much Aƈtion indeed.

Miss Betty. And my Mother did not come to it to be idle, Sir.

Unc. Rich. Nor you neither, I dare say, young Mistress.

Miss Betty. I hope not, Sir.

Unc. Rich. Um! Miss Mettle.   [*Going, Sir* Francis *following him.*
Where are you going, Nephew?

Sir Fran. Only to attend you to the Door, Sir.

Unc. Rich. Phu! no Ceremony with me; you'll find I shall use none
with you, or your Family.   [*Exit.*

Sir Fran. I must do as you command me, Sir.

Miss Betty. This Uncle *Richard*, Papa, seems but a crusty sort of an old
Fellow.

Sir Fran. He is a little odd, Child, but you must be very civil to him,
for he has a great deal of Money, and no body knows who he may give it to.

Lady Head. Phu, A fig for his Money; you have so many Projects of
late about Money, since you are a Parliament-Man, we must make ourselves Slaves to his testy Humours, seven Years perhaps, in hopes to be
his Heirs; and then he'll be just old enough to marry his Maid. But
pray let us take care of our Things here: are they all brought in yet?

Mrs. Han. Almost, my Lady, there are only some of the Band-boxes
behind, and a few odd things.

Lady Head. Let 'em be fetcht in presently.

Mrs. Han. They are here; come, bring the things in: is there all yet?

Serv. All but the great Basket of Apples, and the Goose Pye.

Enter Cook-maid.

Cook. Ah my Lady! we're aw undone, the Goose Pye's gwon.

All. Gone?

Sir Fran. The Goose Pye gone? how?

Cook. Why Sir, I had got it fast under my Arm to bring it in, but being
almost dark, up comes two of these thin starv'd *London* Rogues, one gives
me a great Kick o' the——here; [*Laying her Hand upon her Backside*]
While t'other hungry Varlet twitcht the dear Pye out of my Hands, and
away they run dawn Street like two Greyhounds. I cry'd out Fire! but
heavy *George*, and fat *Tom* are after 'em with a Vengeance; they'll sawce
their Jackets for 'em, I'll warrant 'em.

Enter George *with a bloody Face, and* Tom.

So, have you catcht 'em?

Geo. Catcht 'em! the Gallows catch 'em for me. I had naw run hafe
the length of our Bearn, before somewhat fetcht me such a wherry a-cross
the Shins, that dawn came I flop o' my Feace all along in the Channel,
and thought I shou'd ne're ha' gotten up again; but *Tom* has skaward
after them, and cry'd Murder as he'd been stuck.

Tom. Yes, and ſtrait upo' that, swap comes somewhat across my Fore-head, with such a Force, that dawn came I, like an Ox.

Squire Humph. So, the poor Pye's quite gone then.

Tom. Gone, young Meaſter? yeaten I believe by this time. These I suppose are what they call Sharpers in this Country.

Squire Humph. It was a rare good Pye.

Cook. As e'er these Hands put Pepper to.

Lady Head. Pray Mrs. *Motherly*, do they make a Practice of these things often here?

Mrs. Moth. Madam, they'll twitch a Rump of Beef out of a boiling Copper; and for a Silver Tankard, they make no more Conscience of that, than if it were a *Tunbridge* Sugar-box.

Sir Fran. I wish the Coach and Horses, *George*, were safe got to the Inn. Do you and *Roger* take special Care that no body runs away with them, as you go thither.

Geo. I believe Sir, aur Cattle woant yeasily be run away with to-night; but wee'ſt take beſt care we con of them, Poor Sauls! [*Exit.*

Sir Fran. Do so, pray now.

Squire Humph. Feather, I had rather they had run away with heavy *George* than the Goose Pye, a slice of it before Supper to-night would have been pure.

Lady Head. This Boy is always thinking of his Belly.

Sir Fran. But, my Dear, you may allow him to be a little hungry after a Journey.

Lady Head. Pray, good Sir *Francis*, he has been conſtantly eating in the Coach, and out of the Coach, above seven Hours this Day. I wish my poor Girl cou'd eat a quarter as much.

Miss Betty. Mama, I cou'd eat a good deal more than I do, but then I shou'd grow fat mayhap, like him, and spoil my Shape.

Lady Head. Mrs. *Motherly*, will you be so kind to tell them where they shall carry the Things.

Mrs. Moth. Madam, I'll do the beſt I can: I doubt our Closets will scarce hold 'em all, but we have Garrets and Cellars, which, with the help of hiring a Store-room, I hope may do.

Sir, will you be so good to help my Maids a little in carrying away the Things? [*To* Tom.

Tom. With all my Heart, Forsooth, if I con but see my way; but these Whoresons have awmoſt knockt my Eyen awt. [*They carry off the Things.*

Mrs. Moth. Will your Ladyship please to refresh your self with a Diſh of Tea, after your Fatigue? I think I have pretty good.

Lady Head. If you please, Mrs. *Motherly.*

Squire Humph. Would not a good Tankard of Strong Beer, Nutmeg, and Sugar, do better, Feather, with a Toaſt and some Cheese?

Sir Fran. I think it wou'd, Son: here, *John Moody*, get us a Tankard of good hearty Stuff presently.

John Moody. Sir, here's *Norfolk-nog* to be had next door.

Squire Humph. That's best of all, Feather; but make haste with it, *John*.
[*Exit* Moody.

Lady Head. Well, I wonder, Sir *Francis*, you will encourage that Lad to swill his Guts thus with such beastly, lubberly liquor; if it were *Burgundy*, or *Champain*, something might be said for't; they'd, perhaps, give him some Wit and Spirit; but such heavy, muddy Stuff as this will make him quite stupid.

Sir Fran. Why you know, my Dear! I have drank good Ale, and Strong Beer these thirty Years, and by your Permission I don't know, that I want Wit.

Miss Betty. But you might have more, Papa, if you'd have been govern'd by my Mother.

Enter John Moody *with a Tankard, etc.*

Sir Fran. Daughter, he that is govern'd by his Wife, has no Wit at all.

Miss Betty. Then I hope I shall marry a Fool, Father, for I shall love to govern dearly.

Sir Fran. Here *Humphry*, here's to thee.   [*Drinks.*
You are too pert, Child, it don't do well in a young Woman.

Lady Head. Pray, Sir *Francis*, don't Snub her, she has a fine growing Spirit, and if you check her so, you'll make her as dull as her Brother there.

Squire Humph. Indeed Mother, I think my Sister is too forward.
[*after drinking a long Draught.*

Miss Betty. You? you think I'm too forward? what have you to do to think, Brother Heavy? you are too fat to think of any thing but your Belly.

Lady Head. Well said, Miss; he's none of your Master, tho' he's your elder Brother.

Enter George.

Geo. Sir, I have no good Opinion of this Tawne, it's made up of Mischief, I think.

Sir Fran. Why, what's the matter now?

Geo. I'se tell your Worship; before we were gotten to the Street end, a great Lugger-headed Cart, with Wheels as thick as a good Brick Wall, layd hawld of the Coach, and has pood it aw to Bits: An this be *London*, wa'd we were all weel i' th' Country again.

Miss Betty. What have you to do, Sir, to wish us all in the Country again, Lubber? I hope we shan't go in the Country again these seven Years, Mama, let twenty Coaches be pull'd to pieces.

Sir Fran. Hold your tongue, *Betty*.

Was *Roger* in no fault in this?

Geo. No Sir, nor I neither. Are you not asham'd, says *Roger* to the Carter, to do such an unkind thing to Strangers? No, says he, you Bumkin.

Sir, he did the thing on very Purpose, and so the Folks said that stood by; but they said your Worship need na be concern'd, for you might have a Law-Suit with him when you pleas'd, that wou'd not cost you above a hundred Pounds, and mayhap you might get the better of him.

Sir Fran. I'll try what I can do with him, I'gad, I'll make such——

Squire Humph. Feather, have him before the Parliament.

Sir Fran. And so I will: I'll make him know who I am. Where does he live?

Geo. I believe in *London*, Sir.

Sir Fran. What's the Villain's name?

Geo. I think I heard Somebody call him *Dick*.

Sir Fran. Where did he go?

Geo. Sir, he went Home.

Sir Fran. Where's that?

Geo. By my Troth I do naw knaw. I heard him say he had nothing more to do with us to-night, and so he'd go Home and smoke a Pipe.

Lady Head. Come, Sir *Francis*, don't put yourself in a Heat; Accidents will happen to People in travelling Abroad to see the World. Eat your Supper heartily, go to Bed, sleep quietly, and to-morrow see if you can buy a handsome second-hand Coach for present Use, bespeak a new one, and then all's easy. [*Exeunt.*

Enter Col. Courtly.

Col. Who's that, *Deborah?*

Deb. At your Service, Sir.

Col. What, do you keep open House here? I found the Street Door as wide as it cou'd gape.

Deb. Sir, we are all in a Bustle, we have Lodgers come in to-night, the House full.

Col. Where's your Mistress?

Deb. Prodigious busy with her Company, but I'll tell Mrs. *Martilla* you are here, I believe she'll come to you. [*Exit.*

Col. That will do as well.

Poor *Martilla!* she's a very good Girl, and I have lov'd her a great while, I think; six months it is, since like a merciless Highwayman, I made her deliver all she had about her; she begg'd hard, poor Thing, I'd leave her one small Bawble. Had I let her keep it, I believe she had still kept me. Cou'd Women but refuse their ravenous Lovers, that one dear destructive Moment, how long might they reign over them!

But for a Bane to both their Joys and ours, when they have indulg'd us with such Favours, as make us adore them, they are not able to refuse us that one, which puts an end to our Devotion.

Enter Martilla.

Col. Martilla, how doſt thou do, my Child?

Mart. As well as a losing Gameſter can.

Col. Why, what have you loſt?

Mar. I have loſt you.

Col. How came you to lose me?

Mart. By losing my self.

Col. We can be friends ſtill.

Mart. Dull ones.

Col. Useful ones perhaps. Shall I help thee to a good Husband?

Mart. Not if I were rich enough to live without one.

Col. I'm sorry I am not rich enough to make thee so; but we won't talk of melancholly things. Who are these Folks your Aunt has got in her House?

Mart. One Sir *Francis Headpiece* and his Lady, with a Son and Daughter.

Col. Headpiece! Cotso, I know 'em a little. I met with 'em at a Race in the Country two Years since; a sort of Blockhead, is not he?

Mart. So they say.

Col. His Wife seem'd a mettled Gentlewoman, if she had had but a fair Field to range in.

Mart. That she won't want now, for they ſtay in Town the whole Winter.

Col. Oh that will do, to shew all her Parts in.

Enter Mrs. Motherly.

How do you do, my old Acquaintance?

Mrs. Moth. At your Service you know always, Colonel.

Col. I hear you have got good Company in the House.

Mrs. Moth. I hope it will prove so; he's a Parliament Man only Colonel, you know there's some danger in that.

Col. O, never fear, he'll pay his Landlady, tho' he don't pay his Butcher.

Mrs. Moth. His Wife's a clever Woman.

Col. So she is.

Mrs. Moth. How do you know?

Col. I have seen her in the Country, and begin to think I'll visit her in Town.

Mrs. Moth. You begin to look like a Rogue.

Col. What, your wicked Fancies are ſtirring already?

Mrs. Moth. Yours are, or I'm miſtaken. But——I'll have none of your Pranks play'd upon her.

Col. Why, she's no Girl, she can defend her self.

Mrs. Moth. But what if she won't?

Col. Why then she can blame neither you nor me.

Mrs. Moth. You'll never be quiet till you get my Windows broke; but I must go and attend my Lodgers, so good Night.

Col. Do so, and give my Service to my Lady, and tell her, if she'll give me Leave, I'll do my self the Honour to-morrow to come and tender my Services to her, as long as she stays in Town.

If it ben't too long. [*Aside.*

Mrs. Moth. I'll tell her what a Devil you are, and advise her to have a care of you. [*Exit.*

Col. Do, that will make her every time she sees me think of what I'd be at.

Dear *Martilla*, good Night; I know you won't be my Hindrance; I'll do you as good a Turn some time or other. Well, I am so glad, you don't love me too much.

Mart. When that's our Fate, as too too oft we prove,
How bitterly we pay the past Delights of Love.

ACT II. SCENE I.

SCENE, *Lord* Loverule's *House.*

Enter Lord Loverule, *and Lady* Arabella. *He following her.*

Lady Arabella.

WELL, look you, my Lord, I can bear it no longer; nothing still but about my Faults, my Faults! an agreeable Subject truly!

Lord Love. But Madam, if you won't hear of your Faults, how is it likely you shou'd ever mend 'em?

Lady Ara. Why I don't intend to mend 'em. I can't mend 'em, I have told you so a hundred times; you know I have try'd to do it, over and over, and it hurts me so, I can't bear it. Why, don't you know, my Lord, that whenever (just to please you only) I have gone about to wean my self from a Fault (one of my Faults I mean that I love dearly) han't it put me so out of Humour, you cou'd scarce endure the House with me?

Lord Love. Look you, my Dear, it is very true, that in weaning one's self from——

Lady Ara. Weaning? why ay, don't you see, that ev'n in weaning poor

Children from the Nurse, it's almost the Death of 'em? and don't you see your true Religious People, when they go about to wean themselves, and have solemn Days of Fasting and Praying, on purpose to help them, does it not so disorder them, there's no coming near 'em; are they not as cross as the Devil? and then they don't do the Business neither; for next Day their Faults are just where they were the Day before.

Lord Love. But Madam, can you think it a Reasonable thing, to be abroad till Two a Clock in the Morning, when you know I go to Bed at Eleven?

Lady Ara. And can you think it a Wise thing (to talk your own way now) to go to Bed at Eleven, when you know I am likely to disturb you by coming there at Three?

Lord Love. Well, the manner of Women's living of late is insupportable, and some way or other——

Lady Ara. It's to be mended, I suppose——Pray, my Lord, one Word of fair Argument: You complain of my late Hours; I of your early ones; so far we are even, you'll allow: but which gives us the best Figure in the Eye of the polite World? my Two a Clock speaks Life, Activity, Spirit, and Vigour; your Eleven has a Dull, Drowsy, Stupid, good-for-nothing Sound with it. It savours much of a Mechanick, who must get to Bed betimes, that he may rise early to open his Shop. Faugh!

Lord Love. I thought to go to Bed early and rise so, was ever esteem'd a right Practice for all People.

Lady Ara. Beasts do it.

Lord Love. Fy, fy, Madam, fy; but 'tis not your ill Hours alone disturb me; but the ill Company who occasion those ill Hours.

Lady Ara. And pray what ill Company may those be?

Lord Love. Why, Women that lose their Money, and Men that win it: especially when 'tis to be paid, out of their Husband's estate; or if that fail, and the Creditor be a little pressing, the Lady will perhaps be oblig'd to try, if the Gentleman instead of gold will accept of a Trinket.

Lady Ara. My Lord, you grow scurrilous, and you'll make me hate you. I'll have you to know I keep Company with the politest People in the Town, and the Assemblies I frequent are full of such.

Lord Love. So are the Churches now and then.

Lady Ara. My Friends frequent them often, as well as the Assemblies.

Lord Love. They wou'd do it oftener, if a Groom of the Chamber there were allow'd to furnish Cards and Dice to the Company.

Lady Ara. You'd make a Woman mad.

Lord Love. You'd make a Man a Fool.

Lady Ara. If Heav'n has made you otherwise, that won't be in my Power.

Lord Love. I'll try if I can prevent your making me a Beggar at least.

Lady Ara. A Beggar! Crœsus! I'm out of Patience—I won't come home 'till four to-morrow Morning.

Lord Love. I'll order the Doors to be lock'd at Twelve.

Lady Ara. Then I won't come home till to-morrow Night.

Lord Love. Then you shall never come home again, Madam.   [*Exit.*

Lady Ara. There he has knock'd me down: My Father upon our Marriage said, Wives were come to that pass, he did not think it fit they shou'd be trusted with Pin-money, and so wou'd not let this Man settle one Penny upon his poor Wife, to serve her at a dead Lift for separate Maintenance.

Enter Clarinda.

Clar. Good-morrow, Madam; how do you do to-day? you seem to be in a little fluster.

Lady Ara. My Lord has been in one, and as I am the most complaisant poor Creature in the World, I put myself into one too, purely to be suitable Company to him.

Clar. You are prodigious good; but surely it must be mighty agreeable when a Man and his Wife can give themselves the same turn of Conversation.

Lady Ara. O, the prettiest Thing in the World.

Clar. But yet, tho' I believe there's no Life so happy as a marry'd one, in the main; yet I fancy, where two People are so very much together, they must often be in want of something to talk upon.

Lady Ara. Clarinda, you are the most mistaken in the world; marry'd People have things to talk of, Child, that never enter into the Imagination of others. Why now, here's my Lord and I, we han't been marry'd above two short Years you know, and we have already eight or ten Things constantly in Bank, that whenever we want Company, we can talk of any one of them for two Hours together, and the Subject never the flatter. It will be as fresh next Day, if we have occasion for it, as it was the first Day it entertain'd us.

Clar. Why that must be wonderful pretty.

Lady Ara. O there's no Life like it. This very Day now for Example, my Lord and I, after a pretty cheerful *tête à tête* Dinner, sat down by the Fire-side, in an idle, indolent, pick-tooth Way for a while, as if we had not thought of one another's being in the Room. At last (stretching himself, and yawning twice) My Dear, says he, you came home very late last Night. 'Twas but Two in the Morning, says I. I was in bed (yawning) by Eleven, says he. So you are every Night, says I. Well, says he, I am amazed, how you can sit up so late. How can you be amazed, says I, at a Thing that happens so often? Upon which, we enter'd into Conversation. And tho' this is a Point has entertain'd us above fifty times already, we always find so many pretty new Things to say upon't, that I believe in my Soul it will laſt as long as we live.

Clar. But in such sort of Family Dialogues (tho' extreamly well for passing of Time) don't there now and then enter some little witty sort of Bitterness?

Lady Ara. O yes; which don't do amiss at all; a little something that's sharp, moderates the extream Sweetness of matrimonial Society, which wou'd else perhaps be cloying. Tho' to tell you the truth, *Clarinda*, I think we squeezed a little too much Lemon into it, this Bout; for it grew so sour at laſt, that I think I almoſt told him he was a Fool; and he talkt something odly of turning me out of Doors.

Clar. O, but have a care of that.

Lady Ara. Why, to be serious, *Clarinda*, what wou'd you have a Woman do in my Case? There is no one Thing he can do in this World to please me——Except giving me Money; and that he is grown weary of; and I at the same time (partly by Nature, and partly perhaps by keeping the beſt Company) do with my Soul love almoſt every Thing that he hates; I doat upon Assemblies, adore Masquerades, my Heart bounds at a Ball; I love Play to diſtraction, Cards enchant me, and Dice—put me out of my little Wits—Dear, dear Hazard, what Music there is in the Rattle of the Dice, compared to a sleepy Opera! Do you ever play at Hazard, *Clarinda?*

Clar. Never; I don't think it sits well upon Women; it's very masculine, and has too much of a Rake; you see how it makes the Men swear and curse. Sure it muſt incline the Women to do the same too, if they durſt give way to it.

Lady Ara. So it does; but hitherto, for a little Decency, we keep it in; and when in spite of our Teeth, an Oath gets into our Mouths, we swallow it.

Clar. That's enough to burſt you; but in time perhaps you'll let 'em fly as they do.

Lady Ara. Why 'tis probable we may, for the Pleasure of all polite Women's Lives now, you know, is founded upon entire Liberty to do what they will. But shall I tell you what happen'd t'other Night? Having loſt all my Money but ten melancholy Guineas, and throwing out for them, what do you think slipt from me?

Clar. An Oath?

Lady Ara. Gud soons!

Clar. O Lord! O Lord! did not it frighten you out of your Wits?

Lady Ara. *Clarinda*, I thought a Gun had gone off.—But I forget, you are a Prude, and design to live soberly.

Clar. Why 'tis true; both my Nature and my Education, do in a good degree incline me that Way.

Lady Ara. Well, surely to be sober is to be terribly dull: You will marry, won't you?

Clar. I can't tell but I may.

Lady Ara. And you'll live in Town?

Clar. Half the Year, I shou'd like it very well.

Lady Ara. And you wou'd live in *London* half a Year, to be sober in it?

Clar. Yes.

Lady Ara. Why can't you as well go and be sober in the Country?

Clar. So I wou'd t'other half Year.

Lady Ara. And pray what pretty Scheme of Life wou'd you form now, for your Summer and Winter sober Entertainments?

Clar. A Scheme that, I think, might very well content us.

Lady Ara. Let's hear it.

Clar. I cou'd in Summer, pass my Time very agreeably, in riding soberly, in walking soberly, in sitting under a Tree soberly, in Gardening soberly, in reading soberly, in hearing a little Musick soberly, in conversing with some agreeable Friends soberly, in working soberly, in managing my Family and Children (if I had any) soberly, and possibly by these means I might induce my Husband to be as sober as my self.

Lady Ara. Well, *Clarinda*, thou art a most contemptible Creature. But let's have the sober Town Scheme too, for I am charm'd with the Country one.

Clar. You shall, and I'll try to stick to my Sobriety there too.

Lady Ara. If you do, you'll make me sick of you. But let's hear it however.

Clar. I would entertain my self in observing the new Fashions soberly, I would please my self in new Cloaths soberly, I would divert my self with agreeable Friends at Home and Abroad soberly. I would play at Quadrille soberly, I would go to Court soberly, I would go to some Plays soberly, I would go to Operas soberly, and I think I cou'd go once, or, if I lik'd my Company, twice to a Masquerade soberly.

Lady Ara. If it had not been for that last Piece of Sobriety, I was going to call for some Surfeit-water.

Clar. Why don't you think, that with the further Aid of breakfasting, dining, supping, and sleeping (not to say a word of Devotion) the four and twenty Hours might rowl over, in a tolerable manner?

Lady Ara. How I detest that Word, Tolerable! And so will a Country Relation of ours, that's newly come to Town, or I'm mistaken.

Clar. Who is that?

Lady Ara. Even my dear Lady *Headpiece.*

Clar. Is she come?

Lady Ara. Yes, her Sort of a tolerable Husband has gotten to be chosen

Parliament-Man at some simple Town or other, upon which she has persuaded him to bring her and her Folks up to *London*.

Clar. That's Good; I think she was never here before.

Lady Ara. Not since she was nine years old; but she has had an outragious Mind to it ever since she was marry'd.

Clar. Then she'll make the moſt of it I suppose, now she is come.

Lady Ara. Depend upon that.

Clar. We muſt go and visit her.

Lady Ara. By all means; and may be you'll have a Mind to offer her your Tolerable Scheme for her *London* Diversion this Winter; if you do, Miſtress, I'll shew her mine too, and you shall see, she'll so despise you and adore me, that if I do but chirrup to her, she'll hop after me like a tame Sparrow, the Town round. But there's your Admirer I see coming in, I'll oblige him, and leave you to receive Part of his Visit, while I ſtep up to write a Letter. Besides, to tell you the Truth, I don't like him half so well as I us'd to do: he falls off of late from being the Company he was, in our way. In short, I think he's growing to be a little like my Lord. [*Exit.*

Enter Sir Charles.

Sir Charles. Madam, your Servant; they told me Lady *Arabella* was here.

Clar. She's only ſtept up to write a Letter, she'll come down presently.

Sir Charles. Why, does she write Letters? I thought she had never Time for't: pray how may she have dispos'd of the reſt of the Day?

Clar. A good deal as usual; she has Visits to make 'till six; she's then engag'd to the Play; from that 'till Court-time, she's to be at cards at Mrs. *Idle's*; after the Drawing-room, she takes a short Supper with Lady *Hazard*, and from thence they go together to the Assembly.

Sir Charles. And are you to do all this with her?

Clar. The Visits and the Play, no more.

Sir Charles. And how can you forbear all the reſt?

Clar. 'Tis easy to forbear, what we are not very fond of.

Sir Charles. I han't found it so. I have paſt much of my Life in this hurry of the Ladies, yet was never so pleas'd, as when I was at quiet without 'em.

Clar. What then induc'd you to be with 'em?

Sir Charles. Idleness, and the Fashion.

Clar. No Miſtresses in the case?

Sir Charles. To speak honeſtly, yes. When one is in a Toy-shop, there was no forbearing the Bawbles; so I was perpetually engaging with some Coquet or other, whom I cou'd love perhaps juſt enough, to put it into her Power to plague me.

Clar. Which Power I suppose she sometimes made use of.

Sir Charles. The Amours of a Coquet, Madam, generally mean nothing farther; I look upon them and Prudes to be Nusances much alike, tho' they seem very different; the first are always disturbing the Men, and the latter always abusing the Women.

Clar. And all I think is to establish the Character of being virtuous.

Sir Charles. That is, being chaste they mean, for they know no other Virtue; therefore indulge themselves in every Thing else that's vicious; they (against Nature) keep their Chastity, only because they find more Pleasure in doing Mischief with it, than they shou'd have in parting with it. But, Madam, if both these Characters are so odious, how highly to be valued is that Woman, who can attain all they aim at, without the Aid of the Folly or Vice of either!

Enter Lady Arabella.

Lady Ara. Your Servant, Sir. I won't ask your Pardon for leaving you alone a little with a Lady that I know shares so much of your good Opinion.

Sir Charles. I wish, Madam, she cou'd think my good Opinion of Value enough, to afford me a small Part in hers.

Lady Ara. I believe, Sir, every Woman who knows she has a place in a fine Gentleman's good Opinion, will be glad to give him one in hers, if she can. But however you two may stand in one another's, you must take another Time, if you desire to talk farther about it, or we shan't have enough to make our Visits in; and so your Servant, Sir. Come, *Clarinda.*

Sir Charles. I'll stay and make my Lord a Visit, if you will give me leave.

Lady Ara. You have my Leave, Sir, tho' you were a Lady.

[*Exit with* Clar.

Enter Lord Loverule.

Lord Love. Sir *Charles*, your Servant; what, have the Ladies left you?

Sir Charles. Yes, and the ladies in general I hope will leave me too.

Lord Love. Why so?

Sir Charles. That I mayn't be put to the ill Manners of leaving them first.

Lord Love. Do you then already find your Gallantry inclining to an Ebb?

Sir Charles. 'Tis not that I am yet old enough to justify my self in an idle Retreat, but I have got, I think, a sort of Surfeit on me, that lessens much the Force of female Charms.

Lord Love. Have you then been so glutted with their Favours?

Sir Charles. Not with their Favours, but with their Service; it is un-merciful. I once thought my self a tolerable Time-killer; I drank, I play'd, I intrigu'd, and yet I had Hours enow for reasonable Uses; but he that will lift himself a Lady's Man of Mettle now, she'll work him so at Cards and Dice, she won't afford him time enough to play with her at any thing else, tho' she her self should have a tolerable good Mind to it.

Lord Love. And so the disorderly Lives they lead, make you incline to a Reform of your own.

Sir Charles. 'Tis true; for bad Examples (if they are but bad enough) give us as useful Reflections as good ones do.

Lord Love. 'Tis pity any Thing that's bad, shou'd come from Women.

Sir Charles. 'Tis so indeed, and there was a happy time, when both you and I thought there never cou'd.

Lord Love. Our early first Conceptions of them, I well remember, were that they never cou'd be vicious, nor never cou'd be old.

Sir Charles. We thought so then; the beauteous Form we saw them cast in seem'd design'd a Habitation for no Vice, nor no Decay; all I had conceiv'd of Angels, I conceiv'd of them; true, tender, gentle, modest, generous, constant, I thought was writ in every Feature; and in my Devotions, Heav'n, how did I adore thee, that Blessings like them shou'd be the Portion of such poor inferior Creatures, as I took my self and all Men else (compar'd with them) to be—but where's that Adoration now?

Lord Love. 'Tis with such fond young Fools as you and I were then.

Sir Charles. And with such it ever will be.

Lord Love. Ever. The Pleasure is so great, in believing Women to be, what we wish them; that nothing but a long and sharp Experience can ever make us think them otherwise. That Experience, Friend, both you and I have had; but yours has been at other Men's Expence; mine—— at my own.

Sir Charles. Perhaps you'd wonder, shou'd you find me dispos'd to run the Risque of that Experience too.

Lord Love. I shou'd, indeed.

Sir Charles. And yet 'tis possible I may; I know at least, I still have so much of my early Folly left, to think, there's yet one Woman fit to make a Wife of: How far such a one can answer the Charms of a Mistress; marry'd Men are silent in, so pass——for that, I'd take my Chance; but cou'd she make a Home easy to her Partner, by letting him find there a cheerful Companion, an agreeable Intimate, a useful Assistant, a faithful Friend, and (in its Time perhaps) a tender Mother, such change of Life, from what I lead, seems not unwise to think of.

Lord Love. Not unwise to purchase, if to be had for Millions; but——

Sir Charles. But what?

Lord Love. If the reverse of this shou'd chance to be the bitter Disappointment, what wou'd the Life be then?

Sir Charles. A damn'd one.

Lord Love. And what Relief?

Sir Charles. A short one; leave it, and return to that you left, if you can't find a better.

Lord Love. He says right—that's the Remedy, and a juſt one——for if I sell my Liberty for Gold, and I am fouly paid in Brass, shall I be held to keep the Bargain?   [*Aside.*

Sir Charles. What are you thinking of?

Lord Love. Of what you have said.

Sir Charles. And was it well said?

Lord Love. I begin to think it might.

Sir Charles. Think on, 'twill give you Ease——the Man who has courage enough to part with a Wife, need not much dread the having one; and he that has not ought to tremble at being a Husband——But perhaps I have said too much; you'll pardon however the Freedom of an old Friend, because you know I am so; so your Servant.   [*Exit.*

Lord Love. Charles, farewel, I can take nothing as ill meant that comes from you.

Nor ought my Wife to think I mean amiss to her; if I convince her I'll endure no longer that she should thus expose her self and me: No doubt 'twill grieve her sorely. Physick's a loathsome Thing, till we find it gives us Health, and then we are thankful to those who made us take it. Perhaps she may do so by me, if she does 'tis well; if not, and she resolves to make the House ring with Reprisals; I believe (tho' the Misfortune's great) he'll make a better Figure in the World, who keeps an ill Wife out of Doors, than he that keeps her within.

ACT III. SCENE I.

Enter Lady Headpiece *and Mrs.* Motherly.

Lady Head. SO, you are acquainted with Lady *Arabella,* I find.

Mrs. Moth. Oh Madam, I have had the Honour to know her Ladyship almoſt from a Child, and a charming Woman she has made.

Lady Head. I like her prodigiously; I had some Acquaintance with her in the Country two years ago; but she's quite another Woman here.

Mrs. Moth. Ah Madam, two Years keeping Company with the polite People of the Town will do Wonders in the Improvement of a Lady, so she has it but about her.

Lady Head. Now 'tis my Misfortune, Mrs. *Motherly*, to come late to School.

Mrs. Moth. Oh! don't be discouraged at that, Madam, the Quickness of your Ladyship's Parts will easily recover your Loss of a little Time.

Lady Head. O! You flatter me! But I'll endeavour by Industry and Application to make it up; such Parts as I have shall not lye idle. My Lady *Arabella* has been so good, to offer me already her Introduction, to those Assemblies, where a Woman may soonest learn to make herself valuable to every Body.

Mrs. Moth. But her Husband.   *[Aside.*

Her Ladyship, Madam, can indeed, better than any Body, introduce you, where every Thing, that accomplishes a fine Lady, is practised, to the last Perfection; Madam, she her self is at the very Tip Top of it——'tis pity, poor Lady, she shou'd meet with any Discouragements.

Lady Head. Discouragements! from whence pray?

Mrs. Moth. From Home sometimes——my Lord a——

Lady Head. What does he do?

Mrs. Moth. But one shou'd not talk of People of Qualities Family-Concerns.

Lady Head. O, no matter, Mrs. *Motherly*, as long as it goes no farther. My Lord, you were saying——

Mrs. Moth. Why, my Lord, Madam, is a little humoursome, they say.

Lady Head. Humoursome?

Mrs. Moth. Yes, they say he's humoursome.

Lady Head. As how, pray?

Mrs. Moth. Why, if my poor Lady perhaps does but stay out at Night, may be four or five Hours after he's in Bed, he'll be cross.

Lady Head. What, for such a thing as that?

Mrs. Moth. Yes, he'll be cross; and then, if she happens, it may be, to be unfortunate at Play, and lose a great deal of Money, more than she has to pay, then Madam——he'll snub.

Lady Head. Out upon him, snub such a Woman as she is? I can tell you, Mrs. *Motherly*, I that am but a Country Lady, should Sir *Francis* take upon him to snub me, in *London*, he'd raise a Spirit wou'd make his Hair stand an end.

Mrs. Moth. Really Madam, that's the only way to deal with 'em.

Enter Miss Betty.

And here comes pretty Miss *Betty*, that I believe will never be made a Fool of, when she's marry'd.

Miss Betty. No, by my Troth won't I. What, are you talking of my being marry'd, Mother?

Lady Head. No, Miss; Mrs. *Motherly* was only saying what a good Wife you wou'd make, when you were so.

Miss Betty. The sooner it's try'd, Mother, the sooner it will be known. Lord, here's the Colonel, Madam!

Enter Colonel.

Lady Head. Colonel, your Servant.

Miss Betty. Your Servant, Colonel.

Col. Ladies, your moſt obedient——I hope, Madam, the Town Air continues to agree with you?

Lady Head. Mighty well, Sir.

Miss Betty. Oh prodigious well, Sir. We have bought a new Coach, and an Ocean of new Cloaths, and we are to go to the Play to-night, and to-morrow we go to the Opera, and next Night we go to the Assembly, and then the next Night after, we——

Lady Head. Softly, Miss. . . . Do you go to the Play to-night, Colonel?

Col. I did not design it, Madam; but now I find there is to be such good Company, I'll do my self the Honour (if you'll give me leave, Ladies) to come and lead you to your Coach.

Lady Head. It's extreamly obliging.

Miss Betty. It is indeed mighty well-bred.

Lord Colonel, what a difference there is, between your way and our Country Companions; one of them wou'd have said, What, you are aw gooing to the Playhouse then? Yes, says we, won't you come and lead us out? No, by good Feggins, says he, ye ma' e'en ta' Care o' your sells, y'are awd enough; and so he'd ha' gone to get drunk at the Tavern againſt we came Home to Supper.

Mrs. Moth. Ha, ha, ha! well, sure Madam, your Ladyship is the hap- pieſt Mother in the World to have such a charming Companion to your Daughter.

Col. The prettieſt Creature upon Earth!

Miss Betty. D'ye hear that, Mother? Well, he's a fine Gentleman really, and I think a Man of admirable Sense.

Lady Head. Softly Miss, he'll hear you.

Miss Betty. If he does, Madam, he'll think I say true, and he'll like me never the worse for that, I hope.

Where's your Neice *Martilla*, Mrs. *Motherly?* Mama, won't you carry *Martilla* to the Play with us?

Lady Head. With all my Heart, Child.

Col. She's a very pretty civil sort of Woman, Madam, and Miss will be very happy in having such a Companion in the House with her.

Miss Betty. So I shall indeed, Sir, and I love her dearly already, we are growing very great together.

Lady Head. But what's become of your Brother, Child? I han't seen him these two Hours, where is he?

Miss Betty. Indeed, Mother, I don't know where he is; I saw him a-sleep about half an Hour ago by the Kitchen Fire.

Col. Must not he go to the Play too?

Lady Head. Yes, I think he shou'd go, tho' he'll be weary on't, before it's half done.

Miss Betty. Weary? yes, and then he'll sit, and yawn, and stretch like a Greyhound by the Fire-side, 'till he does some nasty thing or other, that they'll turn him out of the House, so it's better to leave him at Home.

Mrs. Moth. O, that were pity, Miss. Plays will enliven him——see, here he comes, and my Neice with him.

Enter Squire Humphry *and* Martilla.

Col. Your Servant, Sir; you come in good time, the Ladies are all going to the Play, and wanted you to help Gallant them.

Squire Humph. And so 'twill be Nine a Clock, before one shall get ony Supper.

Miss Betty. Supper! why your Dinner is not out of your Mouth yet, at least 'tis all about the Brims of it. See how greasy his Chops is, Mother.

Lady Head. Nay, if he han't a Mind to go, he need not. You may stay here 'till your Father comes home from the Parliament House, and then you may eat a broil'd Bone together.

Miss Betty. Yes, and drink a Tankard of Strong Beer together, and then he may tell you all he has been doing in the Parliament House, and you may tell him all you have been thinking of when you were asleep, in the Kitchen; and then if you'll put it all down in Writing, when we come from the Play, I'll read it to the Company.

Squire Humph. Sister, I don't like your Joking, and you are not a well-behav'd young Woman; and altho' my Mother encourages you, my Thoughts are, you are not too big to be whipt.

Miss Betty. How, sirrah?

Squire Humph. There's a civil young Gentlewoman stands there, is worth a hundred of you. And I believe she'll be Marry'd before you.

Miss Betty. Cots my Life, I have a good Mind to pull your Eyes out.

Lady Head. Hold, Miss, hold, don't be in such a Passion neither.

Miss Betty. Mama, it is not that I am angry at any thing he says to commend *Martilla*, for I wish she were to be marry'd to-morrow, that I might have a Dance at her Wedding; but what need he abuse me for?

I wish the Lout had Mettle enough to be in Love with her, she'd make pure Sport with him. [*Aside.*

Does your Heaviness find any Inclinations moving towards the Lady you admire?——speak! are you in Love with her?

Squire Humph. I am in Love with no Body; and if any Body be in Love with me, mayhap they had as good be quiet.

Miss Betty. Hold your Tongue, I'm quite sick of you. Come, *Martilla*, you are to go to the Play with us.

Mart. Am I, Miss? I am ready to wait upon you.

Lady Head. I believe it's time we shou'd be going; Colonel, is not it?

Col. Yes, Madam, I believe it is.

Lady Head. Come, then; who is there?

Enter Servant.

Is the Coach at the Door?

Serv. It has been there this hafe Haur, so please your Ladyship.

Miss Betty. And are all the People in the Street gazing at it, *Tom?*

Serv. That are they, Madam; and *Roger* has drank so much of his own Beveridge, that he's e'en as it were gotten a little drunk.

Lady Head. Not so drunk, I hope, but that he can drive us?

Serv. Yes, yes, Madam, he drives best when he's a little upish. When *Roger*'s Head turns, raund go the Wheels, i'faith.

Miss Betty. Never fear, Mama, as long as it's to the Play-house, there's no Danger.

Lady Head. Well, Daughter, since you are so couragious, it shan't be said I make any Difficulty; and if the Colonel is so gallant, to have a Mind to share our Danger, we have room for him, if he pleases.

Col. Madam, you do me a great deal of Honour, and I'm sure you give me a great deal of Pleasure.

Miss Betty. Come, dear Mama, away we go.

[*Exeunt all but* Squire, Martilla, *and Mrs*. Motherly.

Squire Humph. I did not think you wou'd have gone. [*To* Martilla.

Mart. O, I love a Play dearly. [*Exit.*

Mrs. Moth. I wonder, Squire, that you wou'd not go to the Play with 'em.

Squire Humph. What needed *Martilla* have gone? they were enow without her.

Mrs. Moth. O, she was glad to go to divert her self; and besides, my Lady desir'd her to go with them.

Squire Humph. And so I am left alone.

Mrs. Moth. Why, shou'd you have car'd for her Company?

Squire Humph. Rather than none.

Mrs. Moth. On my Conscience, he's ready to cry; this is Matter to think of; but here comes Sir *Francis*. [*Aside.*

Enter Sir Francis.

How do you do, Sir? I'm afraid these late Parliament Hours won't agree with you.

Sir Fran. Indeed, I like them not, Mrs. *Motherly;* if they wou'd dine at twelve a Clock, as we do in the Country, a Man might be able to drink a reasonable Bottle between that and Supper-time.

Mrs. Moth. That wou'd be much better indeed, Sir *Francis.*

Sir Fran. But then when we consider that what we undergo, is in being busy for the Good of our Country,————O, the Good of our Country is, above all Things; what a Noble and Glorious Thing it is Mrs. *Motherly,* that *England* can boast of five hundred zealous Gentlemen, all in one Room, all of one Mind, upon a fair Occasion, to go all together by the Ears for the Good of their Country————*Humphry,* perhaps you'll be a Senator in time, as your Father is now; and when you are, remember your Country; Spare nothing for the Good of your Country; and when you come Home, at the end of the Sessions, you will find your self so ador'd, that your Country will come and dine with you every Day in the Week.

O, here's my uncle *Richard.*

Enter Uncle Richard.

Mrs. Moth. I think, Sir, I had best get you a Mouthful of something to stay your Stomach 'till Supper.   *[Exit.*

Sir Fran. With all my Heart, for I'm almost famisht.

Squire Humph. And so shall I before my Mother comes from the Play-house, so I'll go and get a butter'd Toast.   *[Exit.*

Sir Fran. Uncle, I hope you are well.

Unc. Rich. Nephew, if I had been Sick, I would not have come abroad; I suppose you are well, for I sent this Morning, and was inform'd you went out early; was it to make your Court to some of the Great Men?

Sir Fran. Yes Uncle, I was advis'd to lose no time, so I went to one Great Man, whom I have never seen before.

Unc. Rich. And who had you got to introduce you?

Sir Fran. No body; I remember'd I had heard a wise Man say, My Son, be bold; so I introduc'd my self.

Unc. Rich. As how, I pray?

Sir Fran. Why thus, Uncle; Please your Lordship, says I, I am Sir *Francis Headpiece* of *Headpiece-Hall,* and Member of Parliament for the Ancient Borough of *Gobble-Guiney.* Sir, your humble Servant, says my Lord, tho' I have not the Honour to know your Person, I have heard you are a very honest Gentleman, and I am very glad your Borough has made choice of so Worthy a Representative; have you any Service to Command me? Those last Words, Uncle, gave me great Encouragement; and tho' I know you have not any very great Opinion of my Parts, I believe you won't say I mist it now.

Unc. Rich. I hope I shall have no Cause.

Sir Fran. My Lord, says I, I did not design to say any thing to your

Lordship to-day, about Business; but since your Lordship is so kind and free, as to bid me speak if I have any Service to Command you, I will.

Unc. Rich. So.

Sir Fran. I have, says I, my Lord, a good Eſtate, but it's a little aut at Elbows, and as I desire to serve my King as well as my Country, I shall be very willing to accept of a Place at Court.

Unc. Rich. This was bold indeed.

Sir Fran. I'cod, I shot him flying, Uncle; another Man wou'd have been a Month before he durſt have open'd his Mauth about a Place. But you shall hear. Sir *Francis*, says my Lord, what sort of a Place may you have turn'd your Thoughts upon? My Lord, says I, Beggars muſt not be chusers; but some Place about a thousand a Year, I believe, might do pretty weel to begin with. Sir *Francis*, says he, I shall be glad to serve you in any thing I can; and in saying these Words he gave me a Squeeze by the Hand, as much as to say, I'll do your Business. And so he turn'd to a Lord that was there, who lookt as if he came for a Place too.

Unc. Rich. And so your Fortune's made.

Sir Fran. Don't you think so, Uncle?

Unc. Rich. Yes, for juſt so mine was made————twenty Years ago.

Sir Fran. Why, I never knew you had a Place, Uncle.

Unc. Rich. Nor I neither upon my Faith, Nephew: but you have been down at the House since you made your Court, have not you?

Sir Fran. O yes; I wou'd not negleﬆ the House, for ever so much.

Unc. Rich. And what might they have done there To-day, I pray?

Sir Fran. Why truly, Uncle, I cannot well tell what they did, but I'll tell you what I did. I happen'd to make a little sort of a Miſtake.

Unc. Rich. How was that?

Sir Fran. Why you muſt know, Uncle, they were all got into a sort of a hodge-podge Argument for the Good of the Nation, which I did not well underſtand; however, I was convinc'd, and so resolv'd to Vote aright, according to my Conscience; but they made such a puzling Business on't, when they put the Queſtion, as they call it, that, I believe, I cry'd Ay, when I should have cry'd No; for a sort of a *Jacobite* that sate next me, took me by the Hand, and said, Sir, You are a Man of Honour, and a true *Englishman*, and I shou'd be glad to be better acquainted with you, and so he pull'd me along with the Crowd into the Lobby with him, when, I believe I shou'd have ſtay'd where I was.

Unc. Rich. And so, if you had not quite made your Fortune before, you have clencht it now.

Ah, thou Head of the *Headpieces!*   [*Aside.*
How now, what's the Matter here?

Enter Lady Headpiece, *&c. in disorder, some dirty, some lame, some bloody.*

Sir Fran. Mercy on us! they are all kill'd.

Miss Betty. Not for a thousand Pounds; but we have been all down in the Dirt together.

Lady Head. We have had a sad Piece of work on't, Sir *Francis*, over-turn'd in the Channel, as we were going to the Playhouse.

Miss Betty. Over and over, Papa; had it been coming from the Play-house I shou'd not have car'd a Farthing.

Sir Fran. But Child you are hurt, your Face is all bloody.

Miss Betty. O Sir, my new Gown is all dirty.

Lady Head. The new Coach is all spoil'd.

Miss Betty. The Glasses are all to bits.

Lady Head. *Roger* has put out his Arm.

Miss Betty. Wou'd he had put out his Neck, for making us lose the Play.

Squire Humph. Poor *Martilla* has scratch'd her little Finger.

Lady Head. And here's the Poor Colonel; no body asks what he has done. I hope, Sir, you have got no harm?

Col. Only a little wounded with some Pins I met with about your Ladyship.

Lady Head. I am sorry any thing about me should do you harm.

Col. If it does, Madam, you have that about you, if you please, will be my Cure. I hope your Ladyship feels nothing amiss?

Lady Head. Nothing at all, tho' we did rowl about together ſtrangely.

Col. We did indeed. I'm sure we rowl'd so, that my poor Hands were got once————I don't know where they were got. But her Ladyship I see will pass by Slips. [*Aside.*

Sir Fran. It wou'd have been pity the Colonel shou'd have receiv'd any Damage in his Services to the Ladies; he is the moſt complaisant Man to e'm, uncle; always ready when they have occasion for him.

Unc. Rich. Then I believe, Nephew, they'll never let him want Business.

Sir Fran. O, but they shou'd not ride the free Horse to death neither. Come Colonel, you'll ſtay and drink a Bottle, and eat a little Supper with us, after your Misfortune?

Col. Sir, since I have been prevented from attending the Ladies to the Play, I shall be very proud to obey their Commands here at home.

Sir Fran. A prodigious civil Gentleman, Uncle; and yet as bold as *Alexander* upon Occasion.

Unc. Rich. Upon a Lady's Occasion.

Sir Fran. Ha, ha, you're a Wag, Uncle; but I believe he'd ſtorm any thing.

Unc. Rich. Then I believe your Citadel may be in Danger. [*Aside.*

Sir Fran. Uncle, won't you break your Rule for once, and sup from Home?

Unc. Rich. The Company will excuse me, Nephew, they'll be freer without me; so good Night to them and you.

Lady Head. Good Night to you, Sir, since you won't ſtay. Come Colonel.

Unc. Rich. Methinks this facetious Colonel is got upon a pretty, familiar, easy foot already with the Family of the *Headpieces*——hum. [*Aside. Exit.*

Sir Fran. Come, my Lady, let's all in, and pass the Evening cheerfully. And, d'ye hear, Wife——a Word in your Ear——I have got a Promise of a Place at Court, of a thousand a Year, he, hem.

ACT IV.   SCENE I.

Enter Lady Arabella, *as juſt up, walking pensively to her Toilet, follow'd by* Truſty.

Lady Ara. WELL, sure never Woman had such Luck——these devilish Dice!——Sit up all Night; lose all one's Money, and then——how like a Hag I look.

[*Sits at her toilet, turning her purse inside out.*

Not a Guinea——worth less by a hundred Pounds than I was by one a clock this Morning——and then——I was worth nothing——what is to be done, *Truſty?*

Trus. I wish I were wise enough to tell you, Madam: but if there comes in any good Company to Breakfaſt with your Ladyship, perhaps you may have a Run of better Fortune.

Lady Ara. But I han't a Guinea to try my Fortune——let me see—— who was that impertinent Man, that was so sawcy laſt Week about Money, that I was forc'd to promise, once more, he shou'd have what I ow'd him this Morning?

Trus. O, I remember, Madam; it was your old mercer *Short-yard*, that you turn'd off a Year ago, because he would truſt you no longer.

Lady Ara. That's true; and I think I bid the Steward keep thirty Guineas out of some Money he was paying me, to ſtop his odious Mouth.

Trus. Your Ladyship did so.

Lady Ara. Pr'ythee, *Truſty*, run and see whether the Wretch has got the Money yet; if not, tell the Steward, I have occasion for it my self; run quickly. [Truſty *runs to the door.*

Trus. Ah, Madam, he's juſt paying it away now, in the Hall.

Lady Ara. Stop him! quick, quick, dear *Truſty.*

Trus. Hem, hem, Mr. *Moneybag*, a Word with you quickly.

(162)

Mon. [*within*] I'll come presently.

Trus. Presently won't do, you muſt come this Moment.

Mon. I'm but juſt paying a little Money.

Trus. Cods my life, paying Money, is the Man diſtracted? Come here, I tell you, to my Lady this Moment, quick.

[Moneybag *comes to the Door with a Purse in's Hand.*

My Lady says you muſt not pay the Money to-day, there's a Miſtake in the Account, which she muſt examine; and she's afraid too there was a false Guinea or two left in the Purse, which might disgrace her. [*Twitches the purse from him.*] But she's too busy to look for 'em juſt now, so you muſt bid Mr. What-d'ye-call-'em come another time.

There they are, Madam. [*Gives her the money.*

The poor things were so near gone, they made me tremble; I fancy your Ladyship will give me one of those false Guineas for good Luck.

[*Takes a guinea.*

Thank you, Madam.

Lady Ara. Why, I did not bid you take it.

Trus. No, but your Ladyship lookt as if you were juſt going to bid me, so I took it to save your Ladyship the Trouble of Speaking.

Lady Ara. Well, for once——but hark——I think I hear the Man making a Noise yonder.

Trus. Nay, I don't expect he'll go out of the House quietly. I'll liſten.

[*Goes to the door.*

Lady Ara. Do.

Trus. He's in a bitter Passion with poor *Moneybag*; I believe he'll beat him——Lord, how he swears!

Lady Ara. And a sober Citizen too! that's a Shame.

Trus. He says, he will speak with you, Madam, tho' the Devil held your Door——Lord! he's coming hither full drive, but I'll lock him out.

Lady Ara. No Matter, let him come: I'll reason with him.

Trus. But he's a sawcy Fellow for all that.

Enter Short-yard.

What wou'd you have, Sir?

Short. I wou'd have my Due, Miſtress.

Trus. That wou'd be——to be well cudgel'd, Maſter, for coming so familiarly, where you shou'd not come.

Lady Ara. Do you think you do well, Sir, to intrude into my Dressing-room?

Short. Madam, I sold my Goods to you in your Dressing-room, I don't know why I mayn't ask for my Money there.

Lady Ara. You are very short, Sir.

Short. Your Ladyship won't complain of my Patience being so?

Lady Ara. I complain of nothing, that ought not to be complain'd of; but I hate ill Manners.

Short. So do I, Madam,——but this is the Seventeenth time I have been order'd to come, with good Manners, for my Money, to no Purpose.

Lady Ara. Your Money, Man! Is that the Matter? Why it has lain in the Steward's Hands this Week for you.

Short. Madam, you yourself appointed me to come this very Morning for it.

Lady Ara. But why did you come so late then?

Short. So late! I came soon enough, I thought.

Lady Ara. That thinking wrong, makes us liable to a world of Disappointments; if you had thought of coming one Minute sooner, you had had your Money.

Short. Gad bless me, Madam; I had the Money as I thought, I'm sure it was telling out, and I was writing a Receipt for't.

Trus. Why there you thought wrong again, Master.

Lady Ara. Yes, for you shou'd never think of writing a Receipt 'till the Money is in your Pocket.

Short. Why I did think 'twas in my Pocket.

Trus. Look you, thinking again! Indeed Mr. *Short-yard*, you make so many Blunders, 'tis impossible but you must suffer by it, in your Way of Trade. I'm sorry for you, and you'll be undone.

Short. And well I may, when I sell my Goods to People that won't pay me for 'em, 'till the Interest of my Money eats out all my Profit: I sold them so cheap, because I thought I shou'd be paid the next Day.

Trus. Why, there again! there's another of your Thoughts; paid the next day, and you han't been paid this Twelvemonth, you see.

Short. Oons, I han't been paid at all, Mistress.

Lady Ara. Well, Tradesmen are strange unreasonable Creatures, refuse to sell People any more Things, and then quarrel with 'em because they don't pay for those they have had already.

Now what can you say to that, Mr. *Short-yard?*

Short. Say! Why——'Sdeath, Madam, I don't know what you talk of, I don't understand your Argument.

Lady Ara. Why what do you understand, Man?

Short. Why I understand that I have had above a Hundred Pounds due to me, a Year ago; that I came, by Appointment just now to receive it; that it prov'd at last to be but Thirty instead of a Hundred and Ten; and that while the Steward was telling ev'n that out, and I was writing the Receipt, comes Mrs. *Pop* here, and the Money was gone. But I'll be banter'd no longer if there's law in *England*. Say no more, *Short-yard*.

[*Exit.*

Trus. What a Passion the poor Devil's in?

Lady Ara. Why truly one can't deny but he has some present Cause for a little ill Humour; but when one has Things of so much greater Consequence on foot, one can't trouble ones self about making such Creatures easy; so call for Breakfaſt, *Truſty*, and set the Hazard-Table ready; if there comes no Company I'll play a little by my self.

Enter Lord Loverule.

Lord Love. Pray what Offence, Madam, have you given to a Man I met with juſt now as I came in?

Lady Ara. People who are apt to take Offence, do it for small Matters, you know.

Lord Love. I shall be glad to find this so; but he says you have owd him above a Hundred Pounds this Twelvemonth; that he has been here forty Times by Appointment for it, to no Purpose; and that coming here this Morning upon positive Assurance from your self, he was trickt out of the Money, while he was writing a Receipt for it, and sent away without a Farthing.

Lady Ara. Lord, how these Shop-keepers will lye!

Lord Love. What then is the Business? For some Ground the Man muſt have to be in such a Passion.

Lady Ara. I believe you'll rather wonder to see me so calm, when I tell you, he had the Insolence to intrude into my very Dressing-room here, with a Story without a Head or Tail; you know, *Truſty*, we cou'd not underſtand one Word he said, but when he swore——Good Lord! how the Wretch did swear!

Trus. I never heard the like, for my Part.

Lord Love. And all this for nothing?

Lady Ara. So it prov'd, my Lord, for he got nothing by it.

Lord Love. His Swearing I suppose was for his Money, Madam. Who can blame him?

Lady Ara. If he swore for Money he shou'd be put in the Pillory.

Lord Love. Madam, I won't be banter'd, nor sued by this Man for your Extravagancies: Do you owe him the Money or not?

Lady Ara. He says I do, but such Fellows will say any thing.

Lord Love. Provoking!   [*Aside.*
Did not I desire an Account from you, of all your Debts, but six Months since, and give you Money to clear them?

Lady Ara. My Lord, you can't imagine how Accounts make my Head ake.

Lord Love. That won't do: The Steward gave you two Hundred Pounds besides, but laſt Week; where's that?

Lady Ara. Gone.

Lord Love. Gone! Where?

Lady Ara. Half the Town over I believe by this time.

Lord Love. Madam, Madam, this can be endur'd no longer, and before a Month passes expect to find me——

Lady Ara. Hiſt my Lord, here's Company.

Enter Captain Toupee.

Captain *Toupee*, your Servant: what, no Body with you? do you come quite alone?

Capt. 'Slife, I thought to find Company enough here.
My Lord, your Servant.
What a duce, you look as if you had been up all Night. I'm sure I was in Bed but three Hours; I wou'd you'd give me some Coffee.

Lady Ara. Some Coffee there; Tea too, and Chocolate.

Capt. [*Singing a Minuet and dancing*] Well, what a ſtrange Fellow am I to be thus brisk, after losing all my Money laſt Night——but upon my Soul you look sadly.

Lady Ara. No Matter for that, if you'll let me win a little of your Money this Morning.

Capt. What, with that Face? Go, go wash it, go wash it, and put on some handsome things; you lookt a good likely Woman laſt Night; I wou'd not much have car'd if you had run five hundred Pounds in my Debt; but if I play with you this Morning, I'gad I'd advise you to win, for I won't take your personal Security at present for a Guinea.

Lord Love. To what a nauseous Freedom do Women of Quality of late admit these trifling Fops? and there's a Morning Exercise will give 'em Claim to greater Freedoms ſtill.   [*Points to the Hazard Table.*
Some course muſt be taken.   [*Exit.*

Capt. What, is my Lord gone? he lookt methought as if he did not delight much in my Company. Well, Peace and Plenty attend him for your Ladyship's Sake, and those——who have now and then the Honour to win a hundred Pounds of you.   [*Goes to the Table singing, and throws.*

Lady Ara. [*Twitching the Box from him*] What, do you intend to win all the Money upon the Table. . . . Seven's the Main. . . . Set me a Million, *Toupee.*

Capt. I set you two, my Queen. . . . Six to Seven.

Lady Ara. Six . . . the World's my own.

Both. Ha, ha, ha.

Lady Ara. O that my Lord had but Spirit enough about him, to let me play for a thousand Pounds a-night——But here comes Country Company——

Enter Lady Headpiece, *Miss* Betty, *Mrs.* Motherly, *and* Colonel Courtly.

Your Servant, Madam, Good-morrow to you.

Lady Head. And to you, Madam. We are come to Breakfaſt with you. Lord, are you got to those pretty Things already?   *[Points to the Dice.*

Lady Ara. You see we are not such idle Folks in Town as you Country Ladies take us to be; we are no sooner out of our Beds, but we are at our Work.

Miss Betty. Will dear Lady *Arabella* give us leave, Mother, to do a Stitch or two with her?   *[Takes the Box and throws.*

Capt. The pretty lively Thing!

Lady Ara. With all her Heart; what says your Mama?

Lady Head. She says, she don't love to sit with her Hands before her, when other People's are employ'd.

Capt. And this is the prettieſt little sociable Work, Men and Women can all do together at it.

Lady Head. Colonel, you are one with us, are you not?

Lady Ara. O, I'll answer for him, he'll be out at nothing.

Capt. In a facetious way; he is the politeſt Person; he will lose his Money to the Ladies so Civilly, and will win theirs with so much good Breeding; and he will be so Modeſt to 'em before Company, and so Impudent to 'em in a dark Corner. . . . Ha! Colonel!

Lady Head. So I found him, I'm sure, laſt Night——Mercy on me, an Ounce of Virtue less than I had, and Sir *Francis* had been undone.

Capt. Colonel, I smoke you.

Col. And a fine Character you give the Ladies of me, to help me.

Capt. I give 'em juſt the Character of you they like, modeſt and brave. Come Ladies, to Business; look to your Money, every Woman her Hand upon her Purse.

Miss Betty. Here's mine, Captain.

Capt. O the little soft Velvet one . . . and it's as full . . . Come Lady *Blowse,* rattle your Dice, and away with 'em.

Lady Ara. Six . . . at all . . . Five to Six . . . Five . . . Eight . . . at all again . . . Nine to Eight . . . Nine. . . .

Enter Sir Francis, *and ſtands gazing at 'em.*

Seven's the Main . . . at all for Ever.   *[Throws out.*

Miss Betty. Now Mama, let's see what you can do.

   [Lady Head. *takes the Box.*

Lady Head. Well, I'll warrant you, Daughter——

Miss Betty. If you do, I'll follow a good Example.

Lady Head. Eight's the Main . . . don't spare me Gentlemen, I fear you not . . . have at you all . . . Seven to Eight . . . Seven.

Capt. Eight, Lady Eight——Five Pounds if you please.

Lady Ara. Three, Kinswoman.

Col. Two, Madam.

Miss Betty. And one for Miss, Mama . . . and now let's see what I can do. [*Aside.*] If I shou'd win enough this Morning to buy me another new Gown—O bless me! there they go——Seven . . . come Captain, set me boldly, I want to be at a Handful.

Capt. There's Two for you, Miss.

Miss Bett. I'll at 'em, tho' I dye for't.

Sir Fran. Ah my poor Child, take Care.　　　　[*Runs to stop the Throw.*

Miss Betty. There.

Capt. Out . . . twenty Pounds, young Lady.

Sir Fran. False Dice, Sir.

Capt. False Dice, Sir? I scorn your Words . . . twenty Pounds, Madam.

Miss Betty. Undone, undone!

Sir Fran. She shan't pay you a Farthing, Sir; I won't have Miss cheated.

Capt. Cheated, Sir?

Lady Head. What do you mean, Sir *Francis*, to disturb the Company, and abuse the Gentleman thus?

Sir Fran. I mean to be in a Passion.

Lady Head. And why will you be in a Passion, Sir *Francis?*

Sir Fran. Because I came here to Breakfast with my Lady there, before I went down to the House, expecting to find my Family set round a civil Table with her, upon some Plumb Cake, hot Roles, and a cup of Strong Beer; instead of which, I find these good Women staying their Stomachs with a Box and Dice, and that Man there, with the strange Perriwig, making a good hearty Meal upon my Wife and Daughter.——

Cætera desunt.

The Provok'd Husband;

OR,

A Journey to LONDON.

A

COMEDY.

as it is Acted at the

THEATRE - ROYAL,

By

His MAJESTY's Servants.

Written by the
Late Sir John Vanbrugh
and Mr. Cibber.

——*Vivit Tanquam Vicina Mariti.*   Juv. Sat. VI.

Text

THE text is from the first edition of 1728. This seems to be an edition slubbered up to appear at about the same time as the play. Several passages which appear in the 1729 edition are wanting, whether through carelessness, or that Cibber put them in during rehearsal after the manuscript had gone to press, it is impossible to say: from his preface one might suppose that the contrary had taken place. As some of these are essential to the proper understanding of the play when acted, they have been incorporated in this text, but marked in square brackets. In this case the text is from 1729, with which, and the collected edition of 1730, the original has been collated. The passages in inverted commas are those marked in the Dublin edition of 1804 as omitted from representations at the Theatre Royal. The songs, of which the first lines only are given in 1728, are printed in full at the end of the play in other London editions, except in that of 1804, where they are printed in the text, but marked to be omitted. They are not printed in the Dublin editions of 1728. In 1729 they are printed at the end with the music, an example which is followed here.

Theatrical History

THE *Provok'd Husband* was first acted at Drury Lane on Wednesday, 10 January, 1728. Of the old Vanbrugh players there was Cibber as Sir Francis and Wilks as Lord Townly. Mrs. Oldfield's brilliant performance is described in the Preface, and she was supported by Mrs. Porter, an old and favoured servant of the public, "unparalleled in the vehemence of rage," as Lady Grace. The Mrs. Cibber, who acted Jenny, was not the famous actress we find performing in Vanbrugh's plays later, but Cibber's daughter, not his daughter-in-law.

The production was attended by a curious circumstance. Some ten years previously Colley Cibber had incurred the enmity of High Tories and Jacobites by writing *The Non-Juror*, a version of *Tartufe*. These formed a clique, and determined to damn the play. The story told by the author of *A Companion to the Play-house*, and confirmed by Davies, runs: "Such is the Power of Prejudice and Personal Pique in biassing the judgment, that Mr. *Cibber's* Enemies, ignorant of what Share he had in the writing of the Piece, bestowed the highest Applause on the Part which related to Lord *Townly's* Provocations from his Wife, which was most *Cibber's*, at the same Time that they condemned and opposed the *Journey to London* Part, which was almost entirely *Vanbrugh's*, for no other apparent Reason but that they imagined it to be Mr. *Cibber's*."

Their attack was followed up by "swinging criticism" in the papers. "But," Cibber relates gleefully, "this damn'd play was, notwithstanding, acted twenty-eight nights together (Genest says twenty-seven), and left off, at a receipt of upwards of a hundred and forty pounds; which happen'd to be more, than in fifty years before, could be said of any one play whatsoever."

It was certainly amazingly popular. It was acted four times at Drury Lane in the Spring of 1729, once for Mrs. Thurmond's benefit, and ran intermittently throughout 1730 at Goodman's Fields, being played there twelve times, as well as being revived twice at Drury Lane and twice put on at the Little Theatre in the Haymarket. Up till 1749 it appeared no fewer than two hundred and ten times at Drury Lane, Lincoln's Inn Fields, Goodman's Fields, The Haymarket, and Covent Garden. Note will only be made of some of the more interesting revivals: hardly a great theatrical name will be absent.

At Drury Lane on 11 April, 1730, Miss Raftor (Kitty Clive) played Miss Jenny to the Lady Townly of Mrs. Oldfield, and the old and the new stars met. It then dropped out there for eighteen months, till 1 November, 1731, when Mrs. Heron played Lady Townly. She played it again for her benefit at Drury Lane on 29 March, 1733, with Cibber as Sir Francis and Kitty Clive once more as Jenny.

It went to Lincoln's Inn Fields for the first time on 2 November, 1731, where Lacy Ryan acted Lord Townly with "great ease and freedom"; Quin played Manly, and Hippisley Sir Francis. Mrs. Younger, who "excelled in comic parts," played Lady Townly. It was acted five times, Ryan taking his benefit on 23 March, 1732. In that year Delane (like Powell, too fond of the bottle) acted Manly at Goodman's Fields, and the year after Mrs. Bullock acted Lady Townly at Lincoln's Inn Fields.

On 18 November, 1733, it was acted at the Haymarket for the benefit of John Dennis, who was now very old and quite blind. Pope so far forgot his old spleen as to write a prologue, but it was somewhat equivocal, and Warburton refrained from reprinting it. On 23 March, 1734, it was played for Miller's benefit, with him acting the restored part of John Moody, which had been cut at previous performances. Mrs. Clive played Jenny, and Mrs. Heron returned to the part of Lady Townly, which Mrs. Horton had acted for her benefit earlier in the month. In the autumn, however, Mrs. Horton played the part again at Covent Garden to the Lord Townly of Bridgewater. In 1735 it was acted at Covent Garden on 19 March for the benefit of Ryan, who had been attacked by a footpad and so seriously injured in the face that it was thought he would never act again. In the summer season it was played at Lincoln's Inn Fields by a mixed company from both theatres, Sir Francis Wronghead being played by Mrs. Clarke.

Macklin appeared in the play in 1737, playing Townly to the Lady Townly of Mrs. Furnival; and on 11 January, 1738, George Ann Bellamy played Lady Grace, with Ryan, now long recovered from his wound, playing Townly; Hippisley Sir Francis; and Bridgewater his favourite part of Manly. It was acted in 1740 at Drury Lane for the benefit of Shepherd, who did not act, and at Goodman's Fields later in the year by Mr. and Mrs. Giffard as Lord and Lady Townly, Yates as Squire Richard, and Miss Hippisley as Miss Jenny. At the end of the same season (23 April, 1741) it was acted for the benefit of Laguerre, who was a prisoner of the King's Bench.

The year 1744 brought some fresh actors into the play. At Covent Garden, on 19 March, T. Sheridan acted Lord Townly: his first appearance on the English stage had been less than a fortnight before as Hamlet. On 21 September, at the same theatre, Ryan again acted Lord Townly to the Lady Townly of Mrs. Pritchard. It was said of her that "her talents in comedy are general," though, according to Dr. Johnson, she "in common life was a vulgar ideot, but when she appeared on the stage was inspired by gentility and understanding." She succeeded to the part of Millamant when Peg Woffington gave it up. In that year but in the previous season, namely, 12 March, Garrick played Townly at Drury Lane to the Lady Townly of Peg Woffington, "perhaps the most beautiful woman who ever appeared on the stage," and was "easy and elegant" in the part. This was their first appearance in these characters, and the play was for Mrs. Woffington's benefit. It was acted four times that month, the third time being for the benefit of T. Cibber, who played Manly. At Drury Lane, on 16 March, 1745, Mrs. Cibber played Lady Townly for the first time, and for her benefit. Churchill praised her highly in tragedy:

> Nobly disdainful of each slavish art,
> She makes her first attack upon the heart:
> Pleas'd with the summons, it receives her laws,
> And all is silence, sympathy, applause.

> But when, by fond ambition drawn aside,
> Giddy with praise, and puff'd with female pride,
> She quits the tragic scene, and, in pretence
> To comic merit, breaks down Nature's fence;
> I scarcely can believe my ears or eyes,
> Or find out Cibber through the dark disguise.

Thus on 2 January, 1747, we find Peg Woffington back again as Lady Townly at Drury Lane. Shuter was a noted Squire Richard at this period, and at these performances—it was acted seven times successively—Lord Townly was played by Barry, "noble and commanding," since he was very tall, of whom Murphy wrote:

> Harmonious Barry! with what varied art,
> His grief, rage, tenderness, assailed the heart. . . .

but Churchill:

> What man, like Barry, with such pains, can err
> In elocution, action, character.

though he was a "most pleasing" lover on the stage. He played the part again eighteen months later at the same theatre, when Mrs. Clive played Lady Wronghead for the first time to the Sir Francis of Yates. Blakes (Let critics, with a supercilious air, Decry thy various merit) was Squire Richard; Mrs. Pritchard played Lady Townly; and Miss Jenny Mrs. Green (Miss Hippisley that was). A month or so later, 3 November, Ryan played Lord Townly; Peg Woffington Lady Townly; and Delane Manly, at Covent Garden. In 1752, 7 January, Drury Lane, Yates played Sir Francis; Shuter Squire Richard; Mrs. Pritchard Lady Townly; Ross, "a misfortune which we often meet," played Townly, while Count Basset was played by Blakes. At this period Sparkes used to play Manly. "He was superiour to any other performer, tho' his figure and voice were both unfavourable to him for such a part—in the scenes with Sir Francis, he threw out his insinuations with such forcible meaning, that while the spectators laughed *at* one, they could not avoid smiling *with* the other."

1754, 28 October, Covent Garden. T. Sheridan and Peg Woffington, the former "as yet unsettled in the rank of fame."

1757, 2 April, Drury Lane. Garrick once more as Lord Townly, the first time for ten years; and Miss Macklin, of whom Wilkes said: "in some scenes of Lady Townly she has shown that courtly elegance which has long been wanting on our stage." This performance was for her benefit, while on the 14th it was played for Yates' benefit with Yates as Sir Francis and Mrs. Yates as Lady Townly.

1760, 19 June, Drury Lane. H. Palmer Count Basset; Miss Pope Miss Jenny. Havard played Townly and Mrs. Yates Lady Townly.

1764, 3 March, Drury Lane. Powell, who in this part had "sensibility and ease, but wanted much of the nobleman," Townly; Yates Sir Francis; and in their old parts, Miss Pope and Mrs. Yates:

> Might figure give a title unto fame,
> What rival should with Yates dispute the claim?
> But through the regions of that beauteous face
> We no variety of passions trace.

Although she was said to be "the Queen of English Tragedy between Mrs. Cibber and Mrs. Siddons." Mrs. Palmer played the part in May, and the play was seen at Covent Garden in the same season with Ross and Shuter.

1769, 29 November, Covent Garden. Smith, "the genteel, the airy and the smart," and Mrs. Yates. In 1772 Quick played Moody at Liverpool.

1774, 11 November, Drury Lane. Smith and Mrs. Yates in their old part;

Packer Manly; Mrs. Davies Miss Jenny. It was played the next day at Covent Garden with Mr. and Mrs. Barry as Lord and Lady Townly, with Shuter and Mrs. Pitt in the cast. It was performed later with Mrs. Bulkeley as Lady Townly, and had been played at Bath earlier in the year.

1778, 21 August, Haymarket. For the benefit of Parsons, who acted Sir Francis, with Digges, who had played the part there in the previous year, Lord Townly, and Miss Elizabeth Farren Lady Townly. Palmer played the part of Moody one night only, and Mrs. Hitchcock played Lady Grace. Digges was the original Young Norval in *Douglas:* Miss Farren had only been on the stage a year and this was her first triumph. "No person," Colman said, "ever has more successfully performed the elegant levities of Lady Townly upon the stage." Hazlitt speaks of her "fine-lady airs and graces, with that elegant turn of the head, and motion of her face, and tripping of her tongue." She left the stage in 1797 to marry the Earl of Derby.

1790, 17 December, Covent Garden. Holman and Mrs. Esten. She often used to recite Collins' *Ode on the Passions* at the end of a performance. Farren played Manly and Quick Moody.

1796, 22 November, Drury Lane. J. P. Kemble and Miss Farren in her old rôle. Kemble was best in characters "which consisted in the development of some one solitary sentiment or exclusive passion." "The distinguishing excellence of his acting may be summed up in one word—*intensity.*" The next year it was acted at Covent Garden by Pope and Miss Wallis. On 23 February, 1799, Mrs. Siddons played Lady Townly at Bath; she never ventured the part in London.

J. P. Kemble appeared in the part again at Covent Garden on 5 October, 1803, with Miss Brunton, who made her debut as Lady Townly. "No actress in the prescriptive line of genteel comedy had so much entranced the town." Her person was so "tall, lovely and commanding" that the Earl of Craven chose her for his Countess. It was acted again the next year with "the delightful old croaker" Suett in the part of Moody; and on 13 March, 1810, Elliston, the favourite of Charles Lamb, played Lord Townly at Bath. "To descant upon his merit as a Comedian would be superfluous."

On 22 November, 1816, J. P. Kemble played the part once more at Covent Garden, with Eliza O'Neill as Lady Townly. She was stronger in tragedy than in comedy, but her gestures were always "just, simple and expressive." In 1819 Charles Kemble took over the part of Lord Townly from his elder brother, who was about to retire from the stage, and played it at Covent Garden on 19 September, for one performance only, with Miss Foote as Lady Grace. He played it again at the same theatre on 11 May, 1821, with Miss Dance as Lady Townly. Fawcett played Sir Francis; Harriet Faucit Lady Grace; Emery, unsurpassed in rustic characters, played John Moody; and Miss Foote transferred to the part of Jenny. It was acted seven times.

1821, 5 July, Haymarket. Mrs. Chatterley (Louisa Simeon), a famous Kate Hardcastle and Lady Teazle, played Lady Townly to the Lord Townly of Conway, who had not been seen in London for five years; but he was so handled by the critics that he swore he would leave the stage. He was on the whole a good actor, and in 1824 accepted an engagement in New York. The play was produced by Terry.

At the end of that decade the play had a new run of popularity. Drury Lane once more seized it, and produced it on 21 March, 1829, Young playing Lord Townly;

Miss Phillips Lady Townly; W. Farren Sir Francis, with Mrs. Faucit in her old part of Lady Grace. It was acted seven times, so Covent Garden once more took it over on 6 October, with Charles Kemble and Fawcett in their old parts, Abbott as Manly, while Lady Townly was played by Ellen Tree (Mrs. Kean), whose singing so delighted Hazlitt. This was her first appearance. Miss Faucit said that she had at this time " much beauty and fascination." Though not a great actress, being at her best in tender parts (" she was essentially womanly in her art "), " she had genuine humour and provocative mirth." She was fond of playing Romeo to Fanny Kemble's Juliet.

On 1 November, 1830, at Covent Garden, Charles Kemble once more played Lord Townly, this time with his fascinating daughter Fanny, who was " so attractive that she enabled the proprietors of Covent Garden to pay off a debt of £13,000." " The puffs on her in the papers were extravagant." The next year, however, Ellen Tree resumed the part of Lady Townly, Warde playing Townly. He revived it at the Haymarket on 13 September, 1835, playing it with Miss Taylor; but on 15 October of the same year Ellen Tree, perhaps jealous of her part, played it at Drury Lane with Macready, who no doubt gave one of his finely intellectual performances.

The next year, at Covent Garden, 26 March, Charles Kemble once more took up the rôle, this time with Helen Faucit, the daughter of Harriett, who, though only nineteen, was so highly applauded that she was earning £30 a week. She became Macready's leading lady, and married Sir Theodore Martin. Browning wrote of her:

> " Genius " is a common story!
> Few guess that the spirit's glory
> They hail nightly, is the sweetest,
> Fairest, gentlest and completest
> Shakespeare's-lady, ever poet
> Longed for: few guess this: I know it.

She died in 1898. Macready last acted Townly to her Lady Townly at Drury Lane on 19 May, 1842.

On 20 November, 1855, Henry Howe acted it at the Haymarket with Charlotte Cushman, whom Macready had discovered in America, and who had come over in 1844. Her first " retirement " had taken place three years earlier. She had great power of moving audiences with her extraordinary intensity of manner. She resembled Macready—

> the walk on the toes,
> The eloquent, short, intellectual nose,
> The bend of the knee, the slight sneer of the lip,
> The frown on the forehead, the hand on the hip.
> In the chin, in the voice, 'tis the same to a tittle,
> Miss Cushman is Mr. Macready in little.

Phelps played Lord Townly in his theatre at Sadler's Wells on 22 September, 1858, with Mrs. Charles Young, widow of the famous tragedian. The part must have suited Phelps excellently, as he was most successful " in such characters of comedy as called for dry humour." This appears to have been its last revival, unless we include a reading Miss Adelaide Neilson gave of selections of the play on 26 May, 1870, at the Charing Cross Theatre (afterwards Toole's). However, one may say that the play held the stage as a popular favourite for some one hundred and fifty years.

TO THE
QUEEN

May it please your Majesty

THE *English* THEATRE throws itself with this Play, at Your
MAJESTY's Feet, for Favour and Support.

As their Publick Diversions are a strong Indication of the Genius of
a People; the following Scenes are an Attempt to Establish such as are
fit to Entertain the Minds of a sensible Nation; and to wipe off that
Aspersion of Barbarity, which the *Virtuosi* among our Neighbours have
sometimes thrown upon our Taste.

The *Provok'd Husband*, is, at least, an Instance, that any *English* Comedy
may, to an unusual number of Days, bring many Thousands of His
Majesty's good Subjects together, to their Emolument and Delight, with
Innocence. And however little Share of that Merit my unequal Pen may
pretend to, yet I hope the just Admirers of Sir *John Vanbrugh* will allow
I have, at worst, been a careful Guardian of his Orphan Muse, by leading
it into Your Majesty's Royal Protection.

The Design of this Play being chiefly to expose, and reform the licentious Irregularities that, too often, break in upon the Peace and Happiness
of the Married State; Where could so hazardous and unpopular an
Undertaking be secure, but in the Protection of a PRINCESS, whose
Exemplary Conjugal Virtues have given such Illustrious Proof, of what
sublime Felicity that holy State is capable?

And though a Crown is no certain Title to Content; yet to the Honour
of that Institution be it said, the Royal Harmony of Hearts that now
enchants us from the Throne, is a Reproach to the frequent Disquiet of
those many insensible Subjects about it, who (from His Majesty's Paternal
Care of His People) have more Leisure to be Happy: And 'tis our
QUEEN's peculiar Glory, that we often see Her as Eminently rais'd above
her Circle, in private Happiness, as in Dignity.

Yet Heaven, MADAM, that has placed You on such Height, to be the
more conspicuous Pattern of your Sex, had still left your Happiness
Imperfect, had it not given those inestimable Treasures of your Mind,
and Person, to the only Prince on Earth, that could have deserv'd them:
A Crown receiv'd from Any, but the Happy Monarch's Hand, who
invested You with This, which You now adorn, had only seem'd the
Work of *Fortune*: But *Thus* bestow'd, the World acknowledges it the Due
Reward of PROVIDENCE, for One You once so gloriously Refus'd.

(177)

But as the Fame of such elevated Virtue has lifted the Plain Addresses of a whole Nation into Eloquence, the best repeated Eulogiums on that Theme, are but Intrusions on your Majesty's greater Pleasure of secretly deserving them. I therefore beg leave to subscribe my self,

May it please Your MAJESTY,

Your Majesty's most Devoted,

Most Obedient, and

Most Humble Servant,

COLLEY CIBBER.

TO THE
READER

HAVING taken upon me, in the Prologue to this Play, to give the Auditors some short Account of that Part of it which Sir *John Vanbrugh* left unfinish'd, and not thinking it adviseable, in that place, to limit their Judgment by so high a Commendation, as I thought it deserv'd; I have therefore, for the Satisfaction of the Curious, printed the whole of what he wrote, separately, under the Single Title he gave it of *A Journey to London*, without presuming to alter a line: which the Booksellers will sell, with, or without the *Provok'd Husband*.

Yet when I own, that in my last Conversation with him, (which chiefly turn'd upon what he had done towards a Comedy) he excus'd his not shewing it me, 'till he had review'd it, confessing the Scenes were yet undigested, too long, and irregular, particularly in the Lower Characters, I have but one Excuse for publishing, what he never design'd should come into the World, as it then was, *viz.* I had no other way of taking those many Faults to myself, which may be justly found in my presuming to finish it.

However, a Judicious Reader will find in his Original Papers, that the Characters are strongly drawn, new, spirited, and natural, taken from sensible Observations on high and lower Life, and from a just Indignation at the Follies in fashion. All I could gather from him of what he intended in the *Catastrophe*, was, that the Conduct of his Imaginary Fine Lady had so provok'd him, that he designed actually to have made her Husband turn her out of his Doors. But when his Performance came, after his Decease, to my Hands, I thought such violent Measures, however just they might be in real Life, were too severe for Comedy, and would want the proper Surprize, which is due to the End of a Play. Therefore with much ado (and 'twas as much as I could do, with Probability) I preserv'd the Lady's Chastity, that the Sense of her Errors might make a Reconciliation not Impracticable; And I hope the Mitigation of her Sentence has been, since, justified, by its Success.

My Inclination to preserve as much as possible of Sir *John*, I soon saw had drawn the Whole into an unusual Length; the Reader will therefore find here a Scene or two of the Lower Humour that were left out, after the first Day's Presentation.

The Favour the Town has shewn to the higher Characters in this Play, is a Proof, that their Taste is not wholly vitiated, by the barbarous

Entertainments that have been so expensively set off to corrupt it: But, while the Repetition of the best old Plays is apt to give Satiety, and good new Ones are so scarce a Commodity, we must not wonder, that the poor Actors are sometimes forced to trade in Trash for a Livelihood.

I cannot yet take leave of the Reader, without endeavouring to do Justice to those Principal Actors, who have so evidently contributed to the Support of this Comedy: And I wish I could separate the Praises due to them from the secret Vanity of an Author: For all I can say will still insinuate, that they cou'd not have so highly excell'd, unless the Skill of the Writer had given them proper Occasion. However, as I had rather appear vain, than unthankful, I will venture to say of Mr. *Wilks*, that in the last Act, I never saw any Passion take so natural a Possession of an Actor, or any Actor take so tender a Possession of his Auditors. . . . Mr. *Mills*, too, is confess'd by every Body, to have surpriz'd them, by so far excelling himself. . . . But there is no doing Right to Mrs. *Oldfield*, without putting People in mind of what others, of great Merit, have wanted to come near her. . . . 'Tis not enough to say, she *Here Out-did* her usual *Out-doing*. I might therefore justly leave her to the constant Admiration of those Spectators, who have the Pleasure of living while She is an Actress. But as this is not the only Time She has been the Life of what I have given the Publick, so perhaps my saying a little more of so memorable an Actress, may give this Play a chance to be read, when the People of this Age shall be Ancestors. . . . May it therefore give Emulation to a Succession of our Successors of the stage, to know, That to the ending of the year 1727, a Cotemporary Comedian relates, that Mrs. *Oldfield* was, then, in her highest Excellence of Action, happy in all the rearly-found Requisites, that meet in one Person to compleat them for the Stage. . . . She was in Stature just rising to that Height, where the *Graceful* can only begin to shew it self; of a lively Aspect and a Command in her Mein, that like the principal Figure in the finest Paintings, first seizes, and longest delights the Eye of the Spectator. Her Voice was sweet, strong, piercing, and melodious: her Pronunciation voluble, distinct, and musical; and her Emphasis always placed where the Spirit of the Sense, in her Periods, only demanded it. If She delighted more in the Higher Comick than in the Tragick Strain, 'twas because the last is too often written in a lofty Disregard of Nature. But in Characters of modern practis'd Life, she found occasions to add the particular Air and Manner which distinguish'd the different Humours she presented. Whereas in Tragedy, the Manner of Speaking varies, as little as the blank verse it is written in. . . . She had one peculiar Happiness from Nature, she look'd and maintain'd the *Agreeable* at a time when other Fine Women only raise Admirers by their Understanding——The Spectator was always as much informed by her Eyes, as her Elocution; for the Look is the only Proof that an Actor

DEDICATION

rightly conceives what he utters, there being scarce an Instance, where the Eyes do their Part, that the Elocution is known to be faulty. The qualities she had *acquired* were the *Genteel* and the *Elegant*. The one in her Air, and the other in her Dress, never had her Equal on the Stage; and the Ornaments she herself provided, (particularly in this Play) seem'd in all respects the *Paraphernalia* of a Woman of Quality. And of that Sort were the Characters she chiefly excell'd in; but her natural good Sense and lively Turn of Conversation made her Way so easy to Ladies of the highest Rank, that it is a less Wonder, if on the Stage she sometimes *was*, what might have become the finest Woman in real Life, to have supported.

Theatre-Royal,
Jan. 27,
172⅞.

C. CIBBER.

PROLOGUE

Spoken by Mr. *Wilks*.

THIS *Play took Birth from Principles of Truth,*
    To make Amends for Errors past, of Youth.
A Bard, that's now no more, in riper Days,
Conscious review'd the Licence of his Plays:
And though Applause his wanton Muse had fir'd,
Himself condemn'd what sensual Minds admir'd.
At length, he own'd, that Plays should let you see
Not only, What you Are, but Ought to be:
Though Vice was natural, t'was never meant
The Stage should shew it, but for Punishment!
Warm with that Thought, his Muse once more took Flame,
Resolv'd to bring licentious Life to Shame.
Such was the Piece his latest Pen design'd,
But left no Traces of his Plan behind.
Luxuriant Scenes unprun'd, or half contriv'd;
Yet, through the Mass, his Native Fire surviv'd:
Rough, as rich Oar, in Mines the Treasure lay,
Yet still 'twas Rich, and forms at length a Play.
In which the bold compiler boasts no merit,
But that his Pains have sav'd your Scenes of Spirit.
Not Scenes, that would a noisy Joy impart,
But such as hush the Mind, and warm the Heart.
From Praise of Hands no sure account he draws,
But fixt Attention is sincere Applause:
    If then (for hard, you'll own the Task) his Art
Can to those Embrion-Scenes new Life impart,
The Living proudly would exclude his Lays,
And to the Buried Bard resign the Praise.

Dramatis Personæ

Lord *Townly*, of a Regular Life. — Mr. *Wilks*.

Lady *Townly*, Immoderate in her Pursuits of Pleasures. ⎫ Mrs. *Oldfield*.

Lady *Grace*, Sister to Lord *Townly*, of Exemplary Virtue. ⎫ Mrs. *Porter*.

Mr. *Manly*, Her Admirer. — Mr. *Mills*, sen.

Sir *Francis Wronghead*, A Country Gentleman. — Mr. *Cibber*, sen.

Lady *Wronghead*, ⎫ Wife; inclin'd to be a fine Lady. ⎫ Mrs. *Thurmond*.

Squire *Richard*, ⎱ his ⎰ Son; a meer Whelp. — Young *Wetherelt.*

Miss *Jenny*, Daughter; Pert, and Forward. ⎫ Mrs. *Cibber*.

John Moody, Servant; an Honest Clown. ⎫ Mr. *Miller*.

Count *Basset*, A Gamester. — Mr. *Bridgwater*.

Mrs. *Motherly*, One that letts Lodgings. — Mrs. *Moore*.

Myrtilla, her Neice, seduc'd by the Count. — Mrs. *Grace*.

Mrs. *Trusty*, Lady *Townly*'s Woman. — Mrs. *Mills*.

Masqueraders, Constable, Servants, &c.
The SCENE *Lord* Townly's *House, and sometimes Sir* Francis's *Lodgings.*

THE

PROVOK'D HUSBAND

Or, *A JOURNEY to* LONDON.

ACT I.   SCENE I.

SCENE, *Lord* Townly's *Apartment.*

Lord Townly, *solus.*

WHY did I marry?——Was it not evident, my plain, rational Scheme of Life was impracticable, with a Woman of so different a way of Thinking?——Is there one Article of it, that she has not broke in upon?——Yes,——let me do her Justice——her Reputation—— That——I have no Reason to believe is in Question——but then how long her profligate Course of Pleasures may make her able to keep it—— is a shocking Question! and her Presumption While she keeps it——insupportable! for on the Pride of that single Virtue she seems to lay it down, as a fundamental Point, that the free Indulgence of every other Vice, this fertile Town affords, is the Birth-right Prerogative of a Woman of Quality——Amazing! that a Creature so warm in the pursuit of her Pleasures, should never cast one Thought towards her Happiness—— Thus, while she admits no Lover, she thinks it a greater Merit still, in her Chastity, not to care for her Husband; and while she herself is solacing in one continual Round of Cards and good Company, he, poor Wretch! is left, at large, to take care of his own Contentment——'Tis time, indeed, some Care were taken, and speedily there shall be——Yet let me not be rash——Perhaps this Disappointment of my Heart may make me too Impatient; and some Tempers, when reproach'd, grow more untractable. —Here she comes——Let me be calm a while.

Enter Lady Townly.

Going out so soon after Dinner, Madam?
    Lady Town. Lard, my Lord! what can I, possibly, do at Home?
    Lord Town. What does my Sister, Lady *Grace*, do at Home?

(185)

Lady Town. Why, that is to me Amazing! Have you ever any Pleasure at Home?

Lord Town. It might be in your Power, Madam, I confess, to make it a little more Comfortable to me.

Lady Town. Comfortable! and so, my good Lord, you would really have a Woman of my Rank and Spirit ſtay at Home to Comfort her Husband! Lord! what Notions of Life some Men have!

Lord Town. Don't you think, Madam, some Ladies Notions are full as Extravagant?

Lady Town. Yes, my Lord, when the Tame Doves live coop'd within the Penn of your Precepts, I do think 'em Prodigious indeed!

Lord Town. And when they fly wild about this Town, Madam, pray what muſt the World think of 'em then?

Lady Town. Oh! this World is not so ill-bred, as to quarrel with any Woman, for liking it.

Lord Town. Nor am I, Madam, a Husband so well bred, as to bear my Wife's being so fond of it; in short, the Life you lead, Madam——

Lady Town. Is, to me, the pleasanteſt Life in the World.

Lord Town. I should not dispute your Taſte, Madam, if a Woman had a Right to please no Body but her self.

Lady Town. Why, whom would you have her please?

Lord Town. Sometimes, her Husband.

Lady Town. And don't you think a Husband under the same Obligation?

Lord Town. Certainly.

Lady Town. Why then we are agreed, my Lord—For if I never go abroad 'till I am weary of being at home——which you know is the Case ——is it not equally reasonable, not to come home till one's a weary of being abroad?

Lord Town. If this be your Rule of Life, Madam, 'tis time to ask you one serious Queſtion?

Lady Town. Don't let it be long a coming then——for I am in haſte.

Lord Town. Madam, when I am serious, I expeċt a serious Answer.

Lady Town. Before I know the queſtion?

Lord Town. Psha——have I Power, Madam, to make you serious, by Intreaty?

Lady Town. You have.

Lord Town. And you promise to answer me sincerely?

Lady Town. Sincerely.

Lord Town. Now then recolleċt your Thoughts, and tell me seriously, Why you married Me?

Lady Town. You insiſt upon Truth, you say?

Lord Town. I think I have a Right to it.

Lady Town. Why then, my Lord, to give you, at once, a Proof of my Obedience, and Sincerity——I think——I married——to take off that Restraint, that lay upon my Pleasures, while I was a single Woman.

Lord Town. How, Madam! is any Woman under less Restraint after Marriage, than before it?

Lady Town. O my Lord! my Lord! they are quite different Creatures! Wives have infinite Liberties in Life, that would be terrible in an unmarried Woman to take.

Lord Town. Name One.

Lady Town. Fifty, if you please——to begin then, in the Morning—— A married Woman may have Men at her Toilet, invite them to Dinner, appoint them a Party, in a Stage Box at the Play; Ingross the Conversation there, call 'em by their Christian Names; talk lowder than the Players;——From thence jaunt into the City——take a Frolicksome supper at an *India*-House——perhaps in her *Gayeté de Cœur* toast a pretty Fellow——Then clatter again to this End of the Town, break with the Morning, into an Assembly, croud to the Hazard Table, throw a familiar Levant upon some sharp lurching Man of Quality, and if he demands his Money, turn it off with a loud Laugh, and cry——you'll owe it him, to vex him! ha! ha!

Lord Town. Prodigious!   *[Aside.*

Lady Town. These now, my Lord, are some few of the many modish Amusements, that distinguish the Privilege of a Wife, from that of a single Woman.

Lord Town. Death! Madam, what Law has made these Liberties less scandalous in any Wife, than in an unmarried Woman?

Lady Town. Why, the strongest Law in the World, Custom——Custom Time out of Mind, my Lord.

Lord Town. Custom, Madam, is the Law of Fools: But it shall never govern Me.

Lady Town. Nay then, my Lord, 'tis time for me to observe the Laws of Prudence.

Lord Town. I wish I could see an Instance of it.

Lady Town. You shall have one this Moment, my Lord: For I think, when a Man begins to lose his Temper at Home; if a Woman has any Prudence, why——she'll go abroad 'till he comes to himself again.

                                          [Going.

Lord Town. Hold, Madam—I am amaz'd you are not more uneasy at the Life we lead! You don't want Sense; and yet seem void of all Humanity: For with a blush I say it, I think, I have not wanted Love.

Lady Town. Oh! don't say that, my Lord, if you suppose I have my Senses.

Lord Town. What is it I have done to you? what can you complain of?

Lady Town. Oh! nothing in the least: 'Tis true, you have heard me say I have owed my Lord *Lurcher* an Hundred Pounds these three Weeks ——but what then——a Husband is not liable to his Wife's Debts of Honour, you know,——and if a silly Woman will be uneasy about Money she can't be sued for, what's that to him? as long as he loves her, to be sure she can have nothing to complain of.

Lord Town. By Heav'n, if my whole Fortune thrown into your Lap, could make you delight in the chearful Duties of a Wife, I should think myself a Gainer by the Purchase.

Lady Town. That is, my Lord, I might receive your whole Estate, provided you were sure I would not spend a Shilling of it.

Lord Town. No, Madam; were I Master of your Heart, your Pleasures would be mine; but different, as they are, I'll feed even your Follies, to deserve it——Perhaps, you may have some other trifling Debts of Honour Abroad that keep you out of Humour at Home——at least it shall not be my fault, if I have not more of your Company——There, there's a Bill of Five Hundred,——and now, Madam——

Lady Town. And now, my Lord, down to the Ground I thank you—— Now am I convinced, were I weak enough to love this Man, I should never get a single Guinea from him.   [*Aside.*

Lord Town. If it be no offence, Madam——

Lady Town. Say what you please, my Lord; I am in that Harmony of Spirits, it is impossible to put me out of Humour.

Lord Town. How long, in Reason then, do you think that Sum ought to last you?

Lady Town. Oh, my dear, dear Lord! now you have spoil'd all again! How is it possible I should answer for an Event, that so utterly depends upon Fortune? But to shew you, that I am more inclin'd to get Money, than to throw it away——I have a strong Prepossession, that with this five hundred, I shall win five thousand.

Lord Town. Madam, if you were to win ten thousand, it would be no Satisfaction to me.

Lady Town. O! the Churl! ten thousand! what! not so much as wish I might win ten thousand!——Ten thousand! O! the charming Sum! what infinite pretty things might a Woman of Spirit do, with ten thousand Guineas! O' my conscience, if she were a Woman of true spirit—she— she might lose 'em all again!

Lord Town. And I had rather it should be so, Madam; provided I could be sure, that were the last you would lose.

Lady Town. Well, my Lord, to let you see I design to play all the good House-wife I can; I am now going to a Party at *Quadrille*, only to piddle with a little of it, at poor two Guineas a Fish, with the Dutchess of *Quiteright.*   [*Exit Lady* Townly.

Lord Town. Insensible Creature! neither Reproaches, or Indulgence, Kindness, or Severity, can wake her to the least Reflection! Continual Licence has lull'd her into such a Lethargy of Care, that she speaks of her Excesses with the same easy Confidence, as if they were so many Virtues. What a turn has her Head taken!——But how to cure it—— I am afraid the Physick must be strong, that reaches her——Lenitives, I see, are to no purpose——take my Friends Opinion——*Manly* will speak freely——my Sister with Tenderness to both sides. They know my Case ——I'll talk with 'em.

Enter a Servant.

Serv. Mr. *Manly*, my Lord, has sent to know, if your Lordship was at home.

Lord Town. They did not deny me?

Serv. No, my Lord.

Lord Town. Very well; step up to my Sister, and say, I desire to speak with her.

Serv. Lady *Grace* is here, my Lord.   [*Exit Serv.*

Enter Lady Grace.

Lord Town. So, Lady fair; what pretty Weapon have you been killing your Time with!

Lady Grace. A huge folio that has almost kill'd me—I think I have half read my Eyes out.

Lord Town. O! you should not pore so much just after Dinner, Child.

Lady Grace. That's true, but any Body's Thoughts are better than always one's own, you know.

Lord Town. Who's there?

Enter Servant.

Leave word at the Door, I am at home, to no Body but Mr. *Manly*.

Lady Grace. And why is He excepted, pray My Lord?

Lord Town. I hope, Madam, you have no Objection to his Company?

Lady Grace. Your particular Orders, upon my being here, look, indeed, as if you thought I had not.

Lord Town. And your Ladyship's Inquiry into the Reason of those Orders, shews, at least, it was not a Matter indifferent to you!

Lady Grace. Lord! you make the oddest Constructions, Brother!

Lord Town. Look you, my grave Lady *Grace*——in one serious Word ——I wish you had him.

Lady Grace. I can't help that.

Lord Town. Ha! you can't help it! ha! ha! The flat Simplicity of that Reply was admirable!

Lady Grace. Pooh! you teize one, Brother!

Lord Town. Come I beg Pardon, Child——this is not a Point, I grant you, to trifle upon; therefore, I hope you'll give me leave to be serious.

Lady Grace. If you desire it, Brother; though upon my Word, as to Mr. *Manly*'s having any serious Thoughts of me,——I know nothing of it.

Lord Town. Well———there's nothing Wrong, in your making a Doubt of it——But in short, I find, by his Conversation of late, that he has been looking round the World for a Wife; and, if you were to look round the World for a Husband, he's the first Man I would give to you.

Lady Grace. Then, whenever he makes me any Offer, Brother, I will certainly tell you of it.

Lord Town. O! that's the last Thing he'll do: he'll never make you an Offer, 'till he's pretty sure it won't be refus'd.

Lady Grace. Now you make me curious. Pray! did he ever make any Offer of that kind to you?

Lord Town. Not directly: but that imports nothing: he is a Man too well acquainted with the Female World, to be brought into a high Opinion of any one Woman, without some well-examin'd Proof of her Merit: Yet I have Reason to believe, that your good Sense, your turn of Mind, and your way of Life, have brought him to so favourable a one of you, that a few Days will reduce him to talk plainly to me: which as yet (notwithstanding our Friendship) I have neither declin'd nor encourag'd him to.

Lady Grace. I am mighty glad we are so near, in our way of thinking: for, to tell you the Truth, he is much upon the same Terms with me: You know he has a satyrical Turn; but never lashes any Folly, without giving due Encomiums to its opposite Virtue: and upon such Occasions, he is sometimes particular, in turning his Compliments upon Me, which I don't receive, with any Reserve, lest he should imagine I take them to my self.

Lord Town. You are right, Child: When a Man of Merit makes his Addresses; good Sense may give him an Answer, without Scorn, or Coquetry.

Lady Grace. Hush! he's here——

Enter Mr. Manly.

Man. My Lord! your most obedient.

Lord Town. Dear *Manly!* yours——I was thinking to send to you.

Man. Then, I am glad I am here, my Lord———Lady *Grace*, I kiss your Hands!——What, only you two! How many Visits may a Man make, before he falls into such unfashionable company? A Brother and Sister soberly sitting at home, when the whole Town is a gadding! I question if there is so particular a *Tête à Tête*, again, in the whole parish· of St. *James*'s.

Lady Grace. Fy! fy! Mr. *Manly;* how censorious you are!

Man. I had not made the Reflection, Madam, but that I saw you an Exception to it—Where's my lady?

Lord Town. That I believe is impossible to guess.

Man. Then I won't try, my Lord——

Lord Town. But, 'tis probable I may hear of her, by that time I have been four or five hours in Bed.

Man. Now, if that were my Case, I believe I should———But I beg Pardon, my Lord.

Lord Town. Indeed, Sir, you shall not: You will oblige me, if you speak out; for it was upon this Head, I wanted to see you.

Man. Why then, my Lord, since you oblige me to proceed,——If that were my Case——I believe I should certainly sleep in another House.

Lady Grace. How do you mean?

Man. Only a compliment, Madam.

Lady Grace. A compliment!

Man. Yes, Madam, in rather turning myself out of doors than her.

Lady Grace. Don't you think, that would be going too far?

Man. I don't know but it might, Madam; for, in strict justice, I think she ought rather to go, than I.

Lady Grace. This is new Doctrine, Mr. *Manly*.

Man. As old, Madam, as *Love, Honour,* and *Obey!* When a Woman will stop at nothing that's wrong, why should a Man ballance any thing, that's right?

Lady Grace. Bless me! but this is fomenting things——

Man. Fomentations, Madam, are sometimes necessary to dispel Tumours; tho' I don't directly advise my Lord to do this——This is only what, upon the same Provocation, I would do my self.

Lady Grace. Ay! ay! You would do! Batchelors' Wives, indeed, are finely govern'd.

Man. If the married Mens' were as well——I am apt to think we should not see so many mutual Plagues taking the Air, in separate Coaches!

Lady Grace. Well! but suppose it was your own Case; would you part with a Wife, because she now and then stays out, in the best Company?

Lord Town. Well said, Lady *Grace!* come, stand up for the Privilege of your Sex! This is like to be a warm Debate! I shall edify.

Man. Madam, I think a Wife, after Midnight, has no Occasion to be in better Company than her Husband's; and that frequent unreasonable Hours make the best Company——the worst Company she can fall into.

Lady Grace. But, if People of Condition are to keep company with one another; how is it possible to be done, unless one conforms to their Hours?

Man. I can't find, that any Woman's good Breeding obliges her to conform to other People's Vices.

Lord Town. I doubt, Child, here we are got a little on the wrong side of the Question.

Lady Grace. Why so, my Lord? I can't think the Case so bad, as Mr. *Manly* states it——People of Quality are not tyed down to the Rules of those, who have their Fortunes to make.

Man. No People, Madam, are above being tyed down to some Rules, that have Fortunes to lose.

Lady Grace. Pooh! I'm sure, if you were to take my side of the Argument, you would be able to say something more for it.

Lord Town. Well, what say you to that, *Manly?*

Man. Why, 'troth! my Lord, I have something to say.

Lady Grace. Ay! that I should be glad to hear now!

Lord Town. Out with it!

Man. Then, in one word, this, my Lord, I have often thought, that the Mis-conduct of my Lady has, in a great measure, been owing to your Lordship's Treatment of her.

Lady Grace. Bless me!

Lord Town. My Treatment!

Man. Ay my Lord, you so idoliz'd her before Marriage, that you even indulg'd her, like a Mistress, after it: in short, you continued the Lover, when you should have taken up the Husband.

Lady Grace. O frightful! this is worse than t'other! can a Husband love a Wife too well!

Man. As easily, Madam, as a Wife may love her Husband too little.

Lord Town. So! you too are never like to agree, I find.

Lady Grace. Don't be positive, Brother;——I am afraid we are both of a Mind already. [*Aside.*] And do you, at this rate, ever intend to be married, Mr. *Manly?*

Man. Never, Madam; 'till I can meet with a woman that likes my Doctrine.

Lady Grace. 'Tis pity but your Mistress should hear it.

Man. Pity me, Madam, when I marry the Woman that won't hear it.

Lady Grace. I think, at least, he can't say, that's me.   [*Aside.*

Man. And so, my Lord, by giving her more Power than was needful, she has none where she wants it; having such entire Possession of you, she is not Mistress of her self! And, Mercy on us! how many fine Womens Heads have been turn'd upon the same Occasion!

Lord Town. O *Manly!* 'tis too true! there's the Source of my Disquiet! she knows, and has abus'd her Power! Nay, I am still so weak (with shame I speak it) 'tis not an Hour ago, that in the midst of my Impatience—— I gave her another Bill for five Hundred, to throw away.

Man. Well——my Lord! to let you see, I am sometimes upon the side of Good-nature, I won't absolutely blame you; for the greater your Indulgence, the more you have to reproach her with.

Lady Grace. Ay, Mr. *Manly!* here now, I begin to come in with you: who knows, my Lord, you may have a good Account of your Kindness!

Man. That, I am afraid, we had not best depend upon: But since you have had so much Patience, my Lord, even go on with it a day or two more! and upon her Ladyship's next Sally, be a little rounder in your Expostulation; if that don't work—drop her some cool Hints of a determin'd Reformation, and leave her——to breakfast upon 'em.

Lord Town. You are perfectly right! how valuable is a Friend, in our Anxiety!

Man. Therefore to divert that, my Lord, I beg, for the present, we may call another Cause.

Lady Grace. Ay! for Goodness sake let's have done with this.

Lord Town. With all my Heart.

Lady Grace. Have you no News abroad, Mr. *Manly?*

Man. *A propos*——I have some, Madam; and, I believe, my Lord, as extraordinary in its kind——

Lord Town. Pray, let's have it.

Man. Do you know that your Country Neighbour, and my Wise Kinsman Sir *Francis Wronghead*, is coming to Town with his whole Family?

Lord Town. The Fool! what can be his Business here?

Man. Oh! of the last Importance, I'll assure you——No less than the Business of the Nation.

Lord Town. Explain!

Man. He has carried his Election————against Sir *John Worthland*.

Lord Town. The Duce! what! for——for——

Man. The famous Borough of *Guzzledown!*

Lord Town. A proper Representative, indeed.

Lady Grace. Pray, Mr. *Manly*, don't I know him?

Man. You have din'd with him, Madam, when I was last down with my Lord, at *Bellmont*.

Lady Grace. Was not that he, that got a little merry before Dinner, and overset the Tea-table, in making his Compliments to my Lady?

Man. The same.

Lady Grace. Pray what are his Circumstances? I know but very little of him.

Man. Then he is worth your knowing, I can tell you, Madam. His estate, if clear, I believe, might be a good two thousand Pound a Year: Though as it was left him, saddled with two Joyntures, and two weighty Mortgages upon it, there is no saying what it is——But that he might be sure never to mend it, he married a profuse, young Hussy, for Love, without ever a penny of Money! Thus having, like his brave Ancestors, provided Heirs for the Family (for his Dove breeds like a tame Pidgeon) he now finds Children and Interest-money make such a bawling about his Ears, that, at last, he has taken the friendly Advice of his Kinsman, the good Lord *Danglecourt*, to run his estate two thousand Pound more in Debt, to put the whole Management of what's left into *Paul Pillage's* Hands, that he may be at leisure himself to retrieve his Affairs by being a Parliament Man.

Lord Town. A most admirable Scheme, indeed!

Man. And with this politick Prospect, he's now upon his Journey to *London*——

Lord Town. What can it end in?

Man. Pooh! a Journey into the Country again.

Lord Town. And do you think he'll stir, 'till his Money's gone? or at least 'till the Session is over?

Man. If my Intelligence is right, my Lord, he won't sit long enough to give his Vote for a Turnpike.

Lord Town. How so?

Man. O! a bitter Business! he had scarce a Vote, in the whole Town, beside the Returning Officer: Sir *John* will certainly have it heard at the Bar of the House, and send him about his Business again.

Lord Town. Then he has made a fine Business of it indeed!

Man. Which, as far as my little Interest will go, shall be done, in as few Days as possible.

Lady Grace. But why would you ruin the poor Gentleman's fortune, Mr. *Manly?*

Man. No, Madam, I would only spoil his Project, to save his Fortune.

Lady Grace. How are you concern'd enough, to do either?

Man. Why,—I have some Obligations to the Family, Madam: I enjoy at this time a pretty Estate, which Sir *Francis* was Heir at Law to: but ——by his being a Booby, the last Will of an obstinate old Uncle gave it to me.

Enter a Servant.

Serv. [*to Manly.*] Sir, here's one of your Servants from your House, desires to speak with you.

Man. Will you give him leave to come in, my Lord?

Lord Town. Sir——the Ceremony's of your own making.

Enter Manly's *Servant.*

Man. Well, *James!* what's the matter now?

James. Sir, here's *John Moody's* just come to Town; he says Sir *Francis*, and all the Family, will be here to-night, and is in a great Hurry to speak with you.

Man. Where is he?

James. At our House, Sir: He has been gaping and ſtumping about the Streets, in his dirty Boots, and asking every one he meets, if they can tell him, where he may have a good Lodging for a Parliament-Man, 'till he can hire a handsome whole House, fit for all his Family, for the Winter.

Man. I am afraid, my Lord, I muſt wait upon Mr. *Moody.*

Lord Town. Pr'ythee! let's have him here: He will divert us.

Man. O my Lord! he's such a Cub! Not but he's so near Common Sense, that he passes for a Wit in the Family.

Lady Grace. I beg of all Things, we may have him: I am in love with Nature, let her Dress be never so homely!

Man. Then desire him to come hither, *James.*   [*Exit* James.

Lady Grace. Pray what may be Mr. *Moody's* poſt?

Man. O! his *Maître d' Hôtel,* his Butler, his Bailiff, his Hind, his Huntsman; and sometimes——his Companion.

Lord Town. It runs in my Head, that the Moment this Knight has set him down, in the House, he will get up, to give them the earlieſt Proof, of what Importance he is to the Publick, in his own County.

Man. Yes, and when they have heard him, he will find, that his utmoſt Importance ſtands valued at——sometimes being invited to Dinner.

Lady Grace. And her Ladyship, I suppose, will make as considerable a Figure, in her Sphere too.

Man. That you may depend upon: For (if I don't miſtake) she has ten times more of the Jade in her, than she yet knows of: And she will so improve in this rich Soil, in a Month, that she will visit all the Ladies, that will let her into their Houses: And run in Debt to all the Shop-keepers, that will let her into their Books: In short, before her Important Spouse has made five Pounds, by his Eloquence, at *Weſtminſter;* she will have loſt five hundred at Dice, and *Quadrille,* in the parish of St. *James's.*

Lord Town. So that, by that time he is declared unduly Elected, a Swarm of Duns will be ready for their Money; and his Worship——will be ready for a Jayl.

Man. Yes, yes, that I reckon will close the Account of this hopeful Journey to *London*——But see here comes the Fore-horse of the Team!

Enter John Moody.

Oh! Honeſt *John!*

John Moody. Ad's waunds, and heart! Meaſter *Manly!* I'm glad I ha' fun ye. Lawd! lawd! give me a Buss! Why that's friendly naw! Flesh! I thought we should never ha' got hither! Well! and how d'ye do Meaſter?

——Good lack! I beg Pardon for my Bawldness——I did not see, 'at his Honor was here.

Lord Town. Mr. *Moody*, your Servant: I am glad to see you in *London*. I hope all the good Family is well.

John Moody. Thanks be prais'd your Honour, they are all in pretty good Heart; thof' we have had a power of Crosses up'oth' Road.

Lady Grace. I hope my Lady has had no Hurt, Mr. *Moody*.

John Moody. Noa, and please your Ladyship, she was never in better Humour: There's Money enough stirring now.

Man. What has been the matter, *John?*

John Moody. Why we came up, in such a Hurry, you mun think, that our Tackle was not so tight as it should be.

Man. Come, tell us all——Pray how do they travel?

John Moody. Why, i'th' awld Coach, Measter; and 'cause my Lady loves to do things handsome, to be sure, she would have a couple of Cart-Horses clapt to th' four old Geldings, that Neighbours might see she went up to *London* in her Coach and Six! And so *Giles Joulter* the Plowman rides Postilion!

Man. Very well! the Journey sets out as it should do. [*Aside*] What, do they bring all the Children with them too?

John Moody. Noa, noa, only the younk Squoire, and Miss *Jenny*. The other Foive are all out at board, at half a Crown a Head, a Week, with *Joan Growse*, at *Smoak-Dunghil* farm.

Man. Good again! a right *English* Academy for younger Children!

John Moody. Anon, Sir!   [*Not understanding him.*
[*Lady Grace.* Poor Souls! What will become of 'em?

John Moody. Nay, nay, for that Matter, Madam, they are in very good Hands: *Joan* loves 'um as thof' they were all her own: For she was Wet-Nurse to every mother's babe of 'um——Ay, ay, they'll ne'er want for a Belly-full there!

" *Lady Grace.* What Simplicity!]

Man. The Lud 'a Mercy on all good Folks! What Work will these People make!   [*Holding up his Hands.*"

Lord Town. And when do you expect them here, *John?*

John Moody. Why we were in hopes to ha' come Yesterday, an' it had no' been, that th' owld Wheaze-belly Horse tir'd: And then we were so cruelly Loaden, that the two Fore-Wheels came Crash! down at once, in *Waggon-Rut Lane*, and there we lost four Hours 'afore we could set things to rights again.

Man. So they bring all their Baggage with the Coach then?

John Moody. Ay! ay! and good Store on't there is——Why my lady's Geer alone were as much as fill'd four Portmantel Trunks, beside the great Deal Box, that heavy *Ralph* and the Monkey sit upon behind.

Lord Town. Lady *Grace*, and *Man.* Ha! ha! ha!

Lady Grace. Well, Mr. *Moody*, and pray how many are they within the Coach?

John Moody. Why there's my Lady and his Worship; and the younk Squoyre, and Miss *Jenny*, and the fat Lap-Dog, and my Lady's Maid, Mrs. *Handy*, and *Doll Tripe* the Cook, that's all——Only *Doll* puked a little with riding backwards, so they hoisted her into the Coach-Box— And then her Stomach was easy.

Lady Grace. Oh! I see 'em! I see 'em go by me.—Ah! ha! [*Laughing.*

John Moody. Then yow mun think, Measter, there was some Stowage for th' Belly, as well as th' Back too: Childer are apt to be famisht upo' th' Road; so we had such Cargoes of Plumb-Cake, and Baskets of Tongues, and Biscuits, and Cheese, and cold boil'd Beef——And then, in case of Sickness, Bottles of Cherry-Brandy, Plague-Water, Sack, Tent and Strong-Beer so plenty as made th' owld Coach crack again! Mercy upon them! and send 'em all well to Town, I say.

Man. Ay! And well out on't again, *John*.

John Moody. Ods bud! Measter, you're a wise Mon; and for that Matter, so am I——Whoam's, whoam, I say: I'm sure we ha' got but little good, e'er sin' we turn'd our Backs on't. Nothing but Mischief! Some Devil's Trick or other plagued us, awth' dey lung! Crack! goes one thing: Bawnce! goes another. Woa! says *Roger*——Then souse! we are all set fast in a Slough. Whaw! cries Miss! Scream go the maids! and bawl, just as thof' they were stuck! and so Mercy on us! this was the Trade from Morning to Night. But my Lady was in such a murrain haste to be here, that set out she would, thof' I told her, it was *Childermas* day.

Man. These Ladies, these Ladies, *John*——

John Moody. Ah, Measter, I ha' seen a little of em: and I find that the best——when she's mended, won't ha' much Goodness to spare.

Lord Town. Well said, *John*. Ha! ha!

[*Man.* I hope at least, you and your good Woman agree still.

John Moody. Ay! ay! much of a Muchness. *Bridget* sticks to me: Tho' as for her Goodness——why, she was willing to come to *London* too—— But hawld a Bit! Noa, noa, says I, there may be Mischief enough done, without you.

Man. Why that was bravely spoken, *John*, and like a Man.

John Moody. Ah, weast heart! were Measter but hawf the Mon that I am——Ods wookers! thof' he'll speak stawtly too sometimes—— But then he conno' hawld it——no! he conno' hawld it.

Lord Town. Lady Grace. Man. Ha! ha! ha!]

John Moody. Ods flesh! But I mun hye me whoam! th' Cooach will be coming every Hour naw——but Measter charg'd me to find your

Worship out; for he has hugey Business with you; and will certainly wait upon you, by that time he can put on a clean Neck-cloth.

Man. O *John!* I'll wait upon him.

John Moody. Why you wonno' be so kind, wull ye?

Man. If you'll tell me where you lodge.

John Moody. Juſt i'th' Street next to where your Worship dwells, the sign of the *Golden Ball*————It's Gold all over; where they sell Rib-bands, and Flappits, and other sort of Geer for Gentlewomen.

Man. A Milliner's?

John Moody. Ay, ay, one Mrs. *Motherly:* [Waunds! she has a couple of clever Girls there ſtitching i'th' Fore-room.

Man. Yes, yes, she is a Woman of good Business, no doubt on't—— Who recommended that house to you, *John?*

John Moody. The greateſt good Fortune in the World, sure! For as I was gaping about Streets, who should look out of the Window there, but the fine Gentleman, that was always riding by our Coach Side, at *York* Races————Count——Count *Basset;* ay, that's he.

Man. Basset? Oh, I remember! I know him by Sight.

John Moody. Well! to be sure, as civil a Gentleman, to see to————

Man. As any Sharper in Town. 　　　　　　　　　　　　　　*[Aside.*

John Moody. At *York,* he us'd to breakfaſt with my Lady every Morning.

Man. Yes, yes, and I suppose her Ladyship will return his Compliment here in Town.] 　　　　　　　　　　　　　　　　　　　*[Aside.]*

John Moody. Well, Meaſter————

Lord Town. My Service to Sir *Francis,* and my Lady, *John.*

Lady Grace. And mine, pray Mr. *Moody.*

John Moody. Ah, your Honors; they'll be proud on't, I dare say.

Man. I'll bring my Compliments my self: So honeſt *John.*————

John Moody. Dear Meaſter *Manly!* the Goodness of Goodness bless and preserve you. 　　　　　　　　　　　　　*[Exit* J. Moody.

Lord Town. What a natural creature 'tis.

Lady Grace. Well! I can't but think *John,* in a wet Afternoon in the Country, muſt be very good Company.

Lord Town. O! the *Tramontane!* If this were known at half the *Quadrille*-Tables in Town, they wou'd lay down their Cards to laugh at you.

Lady Grace. And the Minute they took them up again, they would do the same at the Losers————But to let you see, that I think good Com-pany may sometimes want Cards, to keep them together, what think you, if we three sat soberly down, to kill an Hour at *Ombre?*

Man. I shall be too hard for you, Madam.

Lady Grace. No Matter! I shall have as much Advantage of my Lord, as you have of me.

(198)

Lord Town. Say you so, Madam? Have at you then! Here! get the *Ombre*-table, and Cards.   *[Exit Lord* Townly.

Lady Grace. Come, Mr. *Manly*——I know you don't forgive me now!

Man. I don't know whether I ought to forgive your thinking so, Madam. Where do you imagine I could pass my Time so agreeably?

Lady Grace. I am sorry my Lord is not here to take Share of the Compliment——But he'll wonder what's become of us!

Man. I'll follow in a moment, Madam——   *[Exit* Lady Grace. It muſt be so——She sees I love her——Yet with what unoffending Decency she avoids an Explanation? How amiable is every Hour of her Conduct? What a vile Opinion have I had of the whole Sex, for these ten Years paſt, which this sensible Creature has recover'd in less than One? Such a Companion, sure, might compensate all the irksome Disappointments, that Pride, Folly, and Falshood ever gave me!

> Could women regulate, like her, their Lives,
> What *Halcyon* Days were in the Gift of Wives!
> Vain Rovers, then, might Envy, what they Hate;
> And only Fools would mock the Married State.   *[Exit.*

ACT II. SCENE I.

SCENE *Mrs.* Motherly's *House.*

Enter Count Basset *and Mrs.* Motherly.

Count Bas. **I** TELL you there is not such a family in *England*, for you! do you think I would have gone out of your lodgings for any Body, that was not sure to make you easy for the Winter?

Moth. Nay, I see nothing againſt it, Sir, but the Gentleman's being a Parliament-Man; and when People may, as it were, think one Impertinent, or be out of Humour, you know, when a Body comes to ask for one's Own——

Count Bas. Pshah! Pr'ythee never trouble thy Head—His Pay is as good as the Bank!——Why, he has above Two thousand Pound a Year!

Moth. Alas-a-day! that's Nothing: Your People of ten thousand a Year, have ten thousand Things to do with it.

Count Bas. Nay, if you are afraid of being out of your Money; what do you think of going a little with me, Mrs. *Motherly?*

Moth. As how?

Count Bas. Why I have a Game in my Hand, in which, if you'll croup me, that is, help me to play it, you shall go five hundred to nothing.

Moth. Say you so?——Why then, I go, Sir——and now pray let's see your Game.

Count Bas. Look you, in one Word my Cards lie thus—When I was down this Summer at *York*, I happened to lodge in the same House with this Knight's Lady, that's now coming to lodge with you.

Moth. Did you so, Sir?

Count Bas. And sometimes had the Honour to Breakfast, and pass an idle Hour with her——

Moth. Very good; and here I suppose you would have the Impudence to Sup, and be busy with her.

Count Bas. Pshah! pr'ythee hear me!

Moth. Is this your Game? I would not give Sixpence for it! What, you have a Passion for her Pin-Money——no, no, Country Ladies are not so flush of it!

Count Bas. Nay, if you won't have Patience——

Moth. One had need of a great deal, I am sure, to hear you talk at this Rate! Is this your way of making my poor Neice *Myrtilla* easy?

Count Bas. Death! I shall do it still, if the Woman will but let me speak——

Moth. Had not you a Letter from her this Morning?

Count Bas. I have it here in my Pocket——this is it.

> [*Shews it, and puts it up again.*

Moth. Ay, but I don't find you have made any Answer to it.

Count Bas. How the Devil can I, if you won't hear me?

Moth. What! hear you talk of another Woman?

Count Bas. O lud! O lud! I tell you, I'll make her Fortune—— 'Ounds! I'll marry her.

Moth. A likely matter! if you would not do it when she was a Maid, your Stomach is not so sharp set, now, I presume.

Count Bas. Hey-day! why your Head begins to turn, my dear! the Devil! you did not think I propos'd to marry her my self!

Moth. If you don't, who the Devil do you think will marry her?

Count Bas. Why, a Fool——

Moth. Humh! there may be Sense in that——

Count Bas. Very good——One for t'other then; if I can help her to a Husband, why should not you come into my Scheme of helping me to a Wife?

Moth. Your Pardon, Sir! ay! ay! in an honourable Affair, you know, you may command me——but pray where is this blessed Wife and Husband to be had?

Count Bas. Now have a little Patience——You must know then, this

Country Knight, and his Lady, bring up, in the Coach with them, their eldeſt Son, and a Daughter, to teach them to——wash their Faces, and turn their Toes out.

Moth. Good!

Count Bas. The Son is an unlick'd Whelp, about sixteen, juſt taken from School; and begins to hanker after every Wench in the Family: The Daughter, much of the same Age, a pert, forward Hussy, who having eight thousand Pound, left her by an old doating Grandmother, seems to have a devilish Mind to be doing, in her Way too.

Moth. And your Design is, to put her into Business for Life?

Count Bas. Look you, in short, Mrs. *Motherly*, we Gentlemen whose occasional Chariots roll, only, upon the four Aces, are liable sometimes you know, to have a Wheel out of Order: which, I confess, is so much my Case, at present, that my Dapple Greys are reduced to a Pair of Ambling Chair-men: Now if, with your Assiſtance, I can whip up this young Jade into a Hackney-Coach, I may chance, in a day or two after, to carry her in my own Chariot, *en famille*, to an Opera. Now what do you say to me?

Moth. Why, I shall not sleep—for thinking of it. But how will you prevent the Family's smoaking your design?

Count Bas. By renewing my Addresses to the Mother.

Moth. And how will the Daughter like that, think you?

Count Bas. Very well——whilſt it covers her own Affair.

Moth. That's true——it muſt do——but, as you say, one for t'other Sir——I ſtick to that—if you don't do my Neice's Business with the Son, I'll blow you with the Daughter, depend upon't.

Count Bas. It's a Bett—pay as we go, I tell you, and the five hundred shall be ſtak'd, in a third Hand.

Moth. That's honeſt——But here comes my Neice! shall we let her into the Secret?

Count Bas. Time enough! may be, I may touch upon it.

Enter Myrtilla.

Moth. So, Neice, are all the Rooms done out, and the Beds sheeted?

Myr. Yes, Madam, but Mr. *Moody* tells us the Lady always burns Wax, in her own Chamber, and we have none in the House.

Moth Odso! then I muſt beg your Pardon, Count; this is a busy Time, you know.   [*Exit Mrs.* Motherly.

Count Bas. Myrtilla! how doſt thou do, child?

Myr. As well as a losing Gameſter can.

Count Bas. Why, what have you loſt?

Myr. What I shall never recover; and what's worse, you that have won it, don't seem to be much the better for't.

Count Bas. Why Child, doſt thou ever see any body overjoy'd for winning a deep ſtake, six Months after it's over?

Myr. Would I had never play'd for it!

Count Bas. Pshah! Hang these melancholy Thoughts! we may be Friends ſtill.

Myr. Dull ones.

Count Bas. Useful ones, perhaps——suppose I should help thee to a good Husband?

Myr. I suppose you'll think any one good enough, that will take me off o' your hands.

Count Bas. What do you think of the young Country 'Squire, the Heir of the Family, that's coming to lodge here?

Myr. How should I know what to think of him?

Count Bas. Nay I only give you the hint, Child; it may be worth your while, at leaſt, to look about you——Hark! what buſtle's that without?

Enter Mrs. Motherly *in haſte.*

Moth. Sir! Sir! the Gentleman's Coach is at the Door! they are all come!

Count Bas. What, already?

Moth. They are juſt getting out!——won't you ſtep, and lead in my Lady? Do you be in the way, Neice! I muſt run and receive them.
                                                              [*Exit Mrs.* Motherly.

Count Bas. And think of what I told you.   [*Exit* Count.

Myr. Ay! ay! you have left me enough to think of, as long as I live ——a faithless Fellow! I am sure, I have been true to him; and for that only Reason, he wants to be rid of me, and yet 'tis not above six Months, since, like a merciless Highway-man, he made me deliver all I had in the World——I am sure, I begg'd piteously to save but one poor small Bawble! could I have kept that, I ſtill had kept him: but while Women are weak, Men will be Rogues! And for a Bane to both their Joys, and ours; when our Vanity indulges them, in such innocent Favours, as make them adore us; we can never be well, 'till we grant them the very one, that puts an end to their Devotion.—But here comes my Aunt, and the Company.

Mrs. Motherly *returns, shewing in Lady* Wronghead
led by Count Basset.

Moth. If your Ladyship pleases to walk into this Parlour, Madam, only for the present, 'till your Servants have got all your Things in.

Lady Wrong. Well! dear Sir, this is so infinitely obliging—I proteſt, it gives me Pain tho', to turn you out of your Lodging thus!

Count Bas. No Trouble in the leaſt, Madam; we single Fellows are soon mov'd: besides, Mrs. *Motherly*'s my old Acquaintance, and I could not be her Hindrance.

Moth. The Count is so well bred, Madam, I dare say he would do a great deal more, to accommodate your Ladyship.

Lady Wrong. O dear Madam!——A good well-bred sort of a Woman.
[*Apart to the* Count.

Count Bas. O Madam, she is very much among People of Quality, she is seldom without them, in her House.

Lady Wrong. Are there a good many People of Quality in this Street, Mrs. *Motherly?*

Moth. Now your Ladyship is here, Madam, I don't believe there is a House without them.

Lady Wrong. I am mighty glad of that! for really I think People of Quality should always live among one another.

Count Bas. 'Tis what one would chuse, indeed, Madam.

Lady Wrong. Bless me! but where are the Children all this while?

Moth. Sir *Francis*, Madam, I believe is taking Care of them.

Sir Fran. [*within*] *John Moody!* ſtay you by the Coach, and see all our Things out——Come, Children.

Moth. Here they are, Madam.

Enter *Sir* Francis, *Squire* Richard, *and Miss* Jenny.

Sir Fran. Well, Count! I mun say ıt, this was koynd, indeed!

Count Bas. Sir *Francis!* give me leave to bid you welcome to *London.*

Sir Fran. Pshah! how doſt do, Mon——Waunds, I'm glad to see thee! A good sort of a House this!

Count Bas. Is not that Maſter *Richard?*

Sir Fran. Ey! ey! that's young Hopeful——why doſt not Baw, *Dick?*

Squ. Rich. So I do, Feyther.

Count Bas. Sir, I am glad to see you———I proteſt Mrs. *Jane* is grown so, I should not have known her.

Sir Fran. Come forward, *Jenny.*

Jenny. Sure, Papa, do you think I don't know how to behave my self?

Count Bas. If I have permission to approach Her, Sir *Francis*——

Jenny. Lord, Sir! I'm in such a frightful Pickle——   [*Salute.*

Count Bas. Every Dress that's proper muſt become you, Madam,—— you have been a long Journey.

Jenny. I hope you will see me in a better, To-morrow, Sir.
[*Lady* Wrong. *whispers Mrs.* Moth. *pointing to* Myrtilla.

Moth. Only a Neice of mine, Madam, that lives with me; she will be proud to give your Ladyship any Assiſtance, in her Power.

Lady Wrong. A pretty sort of a young Woman.———*Jenny*, you two must be acquainted.

Jenny. O, Mamma! I am never ſtrange, in a ſtrange Place!

[*Salutes* Myrtilla.

Myr. You do me a great deal of Honour, Madam———Madam, your Ladyship's welcome to *London*.

Jenny. Mamma! I like her prodigiously! she call'd me, my Ladyship.

Squ. Rich. Pray mother, maun't I be acquainted with her too!

Lady Wrong. You! you clown! ſtay 'till you learn a little more Breeding firſt.

Sir Fran. Od's heart! my Lady *Wronghead!* why do you baulk the Lad? how should he ever learn Breeding, if he does not put himself forward?

Squ. Rich. Why ay, Feyther, does Mother think 'at I'd be uncivil to her?

Myr. Maſter has so much good Humour, Madam, he would soon gain upon any Body.

[*He kisses* Myr.

Squ. Rich. Lo' you theere, Moather: and yow would but be quiet she and I should do well enough.

Lady Wrong. Why how now, Sirrah! Boys muſt not be so familiar.

Squ. Rich. Why, an' I know nobody, haw the Murrain mun I pass my Time here, in a ſtrange Place? Naw you, and I, and Siſter, forsooth, sometimes, in an Afternoon moy play at One and thirty Bone-Ace, purely.

Jenny. Speak for your self, Sir! d'ye think I play at such Clownish Games?

Squ. Rich. Why and you woant, yo' ma' let it aloane; then she, and I, may hap, will have a bawt at All-fours, without you.

Sir Fran. Noa! Noa! *Dick*, that won't do neither; you mun learn to make one at Ombre, here, Child.

Myr. If Maſter pleases, I'll shew it him.

Squ. Rich. What! th' *Humber!* Hoy days! why does our River run to this Tawn, Feyther?

Sir Fran. Pooh! you silly Tony! Ombre is a Geam at Cards, that the better Sort of People play three together at.

Squ. Rich. Nay the moare the merrier, I say; but Siſter is always so cross-grain'd——

Jenny. Lord! this Boy is enough to deaf People——and one has really been ſtufft up in a Coach so long, that———Pray Madam———could not I get a little Powder for my hair?

Myr. If you please to come along with me, Madam.

[*Exeunt* Myr. *and* Jenny.

Squ. Rich. What, has Siſter ta'en her away naw! 'mess, I'll go, and have a little game with 'em.

[*Ex. after them.*

(204)

Lady Wrong. Well Count, I hope you won't so far change your Lodging, but you will come, and be at home here sometimes?

Sir Fran. Ay, ay! pr'ythee come and take a bit of Mutton with us, naw and tan, when thou'st nowght to do.

Count Bas. Well Sir *Francis*, you shall find I'll make but very little Ceremony.

Sir Fran. Why ay naw, that's hearty!

Moth. Will your Ladyship please to refresh your self, with a Dish of Tea, after your Fatigue? I think I have pretty good.

Lady Wrong. If you please, Mrs. *Motherly;* but I believe we had best have it above Stairs.

Moth. Very well, Madam; it shall be ready immediately.

[*Exit Mrs.* Motherly.

Lady Wrong. Won't you walk up, Sir?

Sir Fran. Moody!

Count Bas. Shan't we stay for Sir *Francis*, Madam?

Lady Wrong. Lard! don't mind him! he will come, if he likes it.

Sir Fran. Ay, ay! ne'er heed me——I ha' things to look after.

[*Exeunt Lady* Wrong. *and Count* Bas.

Enter John Moody.

John Moody. Did you Worship want muh?

Sir Fran. Ay, is the Coach clear'd? and all our Things in?

John Moody. Aw but a few Bandboxes, and the Nook that's left o'th' Goose Poy——But a plague on him, th' Monkey has gin us the slip, I think——I suppose he's goan to see his relations; for here looks to be a Power of 'um in this Tawn——but heavy *Ralph* is skawer'd after him.

Sir Fran. Why, let him go to the Devil! no matter, and the Hawnds had had him a Month agoe——but I wish the Coach and Horses were got safe to th' Inn! This is a sharp Tawn, we mun look about us here, *John*, therefore I would have you goa alung with *Roger*, and see that no Body runs away with them before they get to the Stable.

John Moody. Alas-a-day, Sir: I believe our awld Cattle woant heasily be run away with to-night——but howsomdever, we'st ta' the best care we can of um, poor sawls.

Sir Francis. Well, well! make hast then——

[Moody *goes out, and returns.*

John Moody. Ods flesh! here's Measter *Monly* come to wait upo' your Worship!

Sir Fran. Wheere is he?

John Moody. Just coming in, at threshold.

Sir Fran. Then goa about your Business.

[*Exit* Moody.

Enter Manly.

Cousin *Monly!* Sir, I am your very humble Servant.

Man. I heard you were come, Sir *Francis*—and——

Sir Fran. Odsheart! this was so kindly done of you, naw!

Man. I wish you may think it so, Cousin! for I confess, I should have been better pleas'd to have seen you in any other Place.

Sir Fran. How soa, Sir?

Man. Nay, 'tis for your own sake: I'm not concern'd.

Sir Fran. Look you, Cousin! thof' I know you wish me well; yet I don't question I shall give you such weighty Reasons for what I have done, that you will say, Sir, this is the wisest Journey that ever I made in my Life.

Man. I think it ought to be, Cousin; for I believe, you will find it the most expensive one—your Election did not cost you a Trifle, I suppose.

Sir Fran. Why ay! it's true! That—that did lick a little; but if a Man's wise, (and I han't fawn'd yet that I'm a Fool) there are ways, Cousin, to lick ones self whole again.

Man. Nay if you have that Secret——

Sir Fran. Don't you be fearful, Cousin——you'll find that I know something.

Man. If it be any thing for your good, I should be glad to know it too.

Sir Fran. In short then, I have a Friend in a Corner, that has let me a little into what's What, at *Westminster*——that's one Thing!

Man. Very well! but what Good is that to do you?

Sir Fran. Why not me, as much as it does other Folks?

Man. Other People, I doubt, have the Advantage of different Qualifications.

Sir Fran. Why ay! there's it naw! you'll say that I have liv'd all my Days i'the Country——what then——I'm o'th' *Quorum*——I have been at Sessions, and I have made Speeches theere! ay, and at Vestry too ——and mayhap they may find here,——that I have brought my Tongue up to Town with me! D'ye take me, naw?

Man. If I take your Case right, Cousin; I am afraid the first Occasion you will have for your Eloquence here, will be, to shew that you have any Right to make use of it at all.

Sir Fran. How d'ye mean?

Man. That Sir *John Worthland* has lodg'd a Petition against you.

Sir Fran. Petition! why ay! there let it lye——we'll find a way to deal with that, I warrant you!——why you forget, Cousin, Sir *John's* o'the Wrung side, Mon!

Man. I doubt, Sir *Francis*, that will do you but little service; for in Cases very notorious (which I take yours to be) there is such a Thing as a Short Day, and dispatching them immediately.

Sir Fran. With all my Heart! the sooner I send him home again, the better.

Man. And this is the Scheme you have laid down, to repair your Fortune?

Sir Fran. In one word, Cousin, I think it my Duty! the *Wrongheads* have been a considerable Family, ever since *England* was *England*; and since the World knows I have Talents wherewithall, they shan't say it's my Fault, if I don't make as good a Figure as any that ever were at the Head on't.

Man. Nay! this Project, as you have laid it, will come up to any thing your Ancestors have done these five hundred Years.

Sir Fran. And let me alone to work it! mayhap I hav'n't told you all, neither.——

Man. You astonish me! what! and is it full as practicable as what you have told me!

Sir Fran. Ay! thof' I say it——every whit, Cousin! you'll find that I have more Irons i'the Fire than one! I doan't come of a Fool's Errand!

Man. Very well.

Sir Fran. In a word, my Wife has got a Friend at Court, as well as my self, and her Dowghter *Jenny* is naw pretty well grown up——

Man. [*Aside.*] ——And what in the Devil's Name would he do with the Dowdy?

Sir Fran. Naw, if I doan't lay in for a Husband for her, mayhap i'this Tawn, she may be looking out for her self——

Man. Not unlikely.

Sir Fran. Therefore I have some Thoughts of getting her to be Maid of Honour.

Man. [*Aside.*] ——Oh! he has taken my breath away! but I must hear him out——Pray, Sir *Francis*, do you think her Education has yet qualified her for a Court?

Sir Fran. Why the Girl is a little too mettlesome, it's true! but she has Tongue enough: She woan't be dasht! Then she shall learn to daunce forthwith, and that will soon teach her haw to stond still, you know.

Man. Very well; but when she is thus accomplisht, you must still wait for a Vacancy.

Sir Fran. Why I hope one has a good Chance for that every Day, Cousin! For if I take it right, that's a Post, that Folks are not more willing to get into, than they are to get out of—it's like an Orange Tree, upon that accawnt——it will bear Blossoms, and Fruit that's ready to drop, at the same time.

Man. Well, Sir, you best know how to make good your Pretensions! But pray where is my Lady, and my young Cousins? I should be glad to see them too.

Sir Fran. She is but juſt taking a Dish of Tea with the Count, and my Landlady——I'll call her dawn.

Man. No, no, if she's engag'd, I shall call again.

Sir Fran. Ods-heart! but you mun see her naw, Cousin; what! the beſt Friend I have in the World!——Here! Sweetheart! [*To a Servant without.*] pr'ythee desire my Lady, and the Gentleman, to come dawn a bit; tell her, here's Cousin *Manly* come to wait upon her.

Man. Pray, Sir, who may the Gentleman be?

Sir Fran. You mun know him to be sure; why it's Count *Basset.*

Man. Oh! is it he?—Your Family will be infinitely happy in his Acquaintance.

Sir Fran. Troth! I think so too: He's the civileſt Man that ever I knew in my Life———why! here he would go out of his own Lodging, at an Hour's Warning, purely to oblige my Family. Was n't that kind, naw?

Man. Extreamly civil—the Family is in admirable hands already.

Sir Fran. Then my Lady likes him hugely—all the Time of *York* Races, she would never be withaut him.

Man. That was happy indeed! and a prudent Man, you know, should always take care that his Wife may have innocent Company.

Sir Fran. Why ay! that's it! and I think there could not be such another!

Man. Why, truly, for her Purpose, I think not.

Sir Fran. Only naw and tan, he—he ſtonds a leetle too much upon Ceremony; that's his fault.

Man. O never fear! he'll mend that every Day——Mercy on us! what a head he has!

Sir Fran. So! here they come!

Enter Lady Wronghead, *Count* Basset, *and Mrs.* Motherly.

Lady Wrong. Cousin *Manly!* this is infinitely obliging! I am extreamly glad to see you.

Man. Your moſt obedient Servant, Madam; I am glad to see your Ladyship look so well, after your Journey.

Lady Wrong. Why really! coming to *London* is apt to put a little more Life in one's Looks.

Man. Yet the way of living here, is very apt to deaden the Complexion ———and give me leave to tell you, as a Friend, Madam, you are come to the worſt Place in the World, for a good Woman to grow better in.

Lady Wrong. Lord Cousin! how should People ever make any Figure in Life, that are always moap'd up in the Country?

Count Bas. Your Ladyship certainly takes the Thing in a quite right Light, Madam: Mr. *Manly,* your humble Servant——a-hem.

Man. Familiar Puppy. [*Aside.*] Sir, your moſt obedient——I muſt be civil to the Rascal, to cover my Suspicion of him.   [*Aside.*

Count Bas. Was you at *White's* this morning, Sir?

Man. Yes, Sir, I juſt call'd in.

Count Bas. Pray——what——was there any thing done there?

Man. Much as usual, Sir, the same daily carcasses, and the same Crows about them.

Count Bas. The Demoivre Baronet had a bloody tumble yeſterday.

Man. I hope, Sir, you had your Share of him.

Count Bas. No, faith! I came in when it was all over——I think I juſt made a couple of Betts with him, took up a cool hundred and so went to the *King's Arms*.

Lady Wrong. What a genteel, easy Manner he has!   [*Aside.*

Man. A very hopeful Acquaintance I have made here.   [*Aside.*

Enter 'Squire Richard, *with a wet brown Paper on his Face.*

Sir Fran. How naw, *Dick!* what's the matter with thy Forehead, Lad?

Squ. Rich. I ha' getten a knuck upon't.

Lady Wrong. And how did you come by it, you heedless Creature?

Squ. Rich. Why I was but running after Siſter, and t'other young Woman, into a little Room juſt naw: and so with that, they slupt the Door full in my Feace, and gave me such a whurr here——I thowght they had beaten my Brains out! so I gut a dab of wet brown Paper here, to swage it a while.

Lady Wrong. They serv'd you right enough! will you never have done with your Horse-play?

Sir Fran. Pooh! never heed it, Lad! it will be well by to-morrow—— the Boy has a ſtrong Head!

Man. Yes truly, his Skull seems to be of a comfortable thickness.
                                                                    [*Aside.*

Sir Fran. Come, *Dick*, here's Cousin *Manly*——Sir, this is your God-son.

Lady Wrong. Oh! here's my daughter too.

Enter Miss Jenny.

Squ. Rich. Honour'd Gudfeyther! I crave leave to ask your Blessing.

Man. Thou haſt it, Child——and if it will do thee any good, may it be to make thee, at leaſt, as wise a Man as thy Father.

Lady Wrong. Miss *Jenny!* don't you see your Cousin, Child?

Man. And for Thee, my pretty Dear——[*Salutes her,*] may'ſt thou be, at leaſt, as good a Woman, as thy mother.

Jenny. I wish I may ever be so Handsome, Sir.

Man. Hah! Miss Pert! Now that's a Thought, that seems to have been hatcht in the Girl on this side *High-gate*.   [*Aside.*

Sir Fran. Her Tongue is a little nimble, Sir.

Lady Wrong. That's only from her Country Education, Sir *Francis*. You know she has been kept too long there——so I brought her to *London*, Sir, to learn a little more Reserve and Modesty.

Man. O, the best Place in the World for it—every Woman she meets will teach her something of it——There's the good Gentlewoman of the House, looks like a knowing Person; even she perhaps will be so good as to shew her a little *London* Behaviour.

Moth. Alas, Sir, Miss won't stand long in need of my Instructions.

Man. That I dare say: What thou can't teach her, she will soon be Mistress of.   [*Aside.*

Moth. If she does, Sir, they shall always be at her service.

Lady Wrong. Very obliging indeed, Mrs. *Motherly*.

Sir Fran. Very kind, and civil, truly——I think we are got into a mighty good Hawse here.

Man. O yes, and very friendly Company.

Count Bas. Humh! I'gad I don't like his Looks——he seems a little smoaky——I believe I had as good brush off——If I stay, I don't know but he may ask me some odd Questions.

Man. Well, Sir, I believe you and I do but hinder the Family——

Count Bas. It's very true, Sir—I was just thinking of going——He don't care to leave me, I see: But it's no matter, we have time enough. [*Aside.*] And so Ladies, without Ceremony, your humble Servant.
                              [*Exit Count* Basset, *and drops a Letter.*

Lady Wrong. Ha! what Paper's this? Some Billet-doux I'll lay my Life, but this is no Place to examine it.   [*Puts it in her Pocket.*

Sir Fran. Why in such haste, Cousin?

Man. O! my Lady must have a great many Affairs upon her Hands, after such a Journey.

Lady Wrong. I believe, Sir, I shall not have much less every Day, while I stay in this Town, of one sort or other.

Man. Why truly, Ladies seldom want Employment here, Madam.

Jenny. And Mamma did not come to it to be idle, Sir.

Man. Nor you neither, I dare say, my young Mistress.

Jenny. I hope not, Sir.

Man. Ha! Miss Mettle!——Where are you going, Sir?

Sir Fran. Only to see you to th' Door, Sir.

Man. Oh! Sir *Francis*, I love to come and go, without Ceremony.

Sir Fran. Nay, Sir, I must do as you will have me——Your humble Servant.   [*Exit* Manly.

Jenny. This Cousin *Manly*, Papa, seems to be but of an odd sort of a crusty Humour——I don't like him half so well as the Count.

Sir Fran. Pooh! that's another thing, Child——Cousin is a little proud indeed! but however you must always be civil to him, for he has a deal of Money; and no Body knows who he may give it to.

Lady Wrong. Pshah! a Fig for his Money! you have so many Projects of late about Money, since you are a Parliament-Man: What! we must make ourselves Slaves to his impertinent Humours, eight, or ten Years perhaps, in hopes to be his Heirs, and then he will be just old enough to marry his Maid.

Moth. Nay, for that Matter, Madam, the town says he is going to be married already.

Sir Fran. Who? Cousin *Manly?*

Lady Wrong. To whom, pray?

Moth. Why, is it possible your Ladyship should know nothing of it! ——to my Lord *Townly's* sister, Lady *Grace.*

Lady Wrong. Lady *Grace!*

Moth. Dear Madam, it has been in the News-Papers!

Lady Wrong. I don't like that neither.

Sir Fran. Naw, I do; for then it's likely it mayn't be true.

Lady Wrong. [*Aside.*] If it is not too far gone; at least it may be worth one's while to throw a Rub in his way.

Squ. Rich. Pray Feyther haw lung will it be to Supper?

Sir Fran. Odso! that's true! step to the Cook, Lad, and ask what she can get us?

Moth. If you please, Sir, I'll order one of my Maids to shew her where she may have any thing you have a mind to.

Sir Fran. Thank you kindly, Mrs. *Motherly.*

Squ. Rich. Ods-flesh! what, is not it i'th' Hawse yet——I shall be famisht——but howld! I'll go and ask *Doll,* an there's none o'th' Goose Poy left.

Sir Fran. Do so, and doest hear, *Dick*————see if there's e'er a Bottle o'th' strong Beer that came i'th' Coach with us——if there be, clap a Toast in it, and bring it up.

Squ. Rich. With a little Nutmeg, and Sugar, shawn't I, Feyther?

Sir Fran. Ay! ay! as thee and I always drink it for Breakfast——Go thy ways——and I'll fill a Pipe i'th' mean while. [*Takes one from a Pocket-Case, and fills it.*]   [*Exit Squ.* Rich.

Lady Wrong. This Boy is always thinking of his Belly!

Sir Fran. Why my Dear, you may allow him to be a little hungry after his Journey.

Lady Wrong. Nay, ev'n breed him your own way——He has been cramming in or out of the Coach all this Day, I am sure—I wish my poor Girl could eat a quarter as much.

Jenny. O for that I could eat a great deal more, Mamma; but then mayhap, I should grow coarse, like him, and spoil my Shape.

Lady Wrong. Ay so thou would'st, my Dear.

Enter Squire Richard *with a full Tankard.*

Squ. Rich. Here, Feyther, I ha' browght it——it's well I went as I did; for our *Doll* had just bak'd a Toast, and was going to drink it her self.

Sir Fran. Why then, here's to thee, *Dick!* [*Drinks.*

Squ. Rich. Thonk yow, Feyther.

Lady Wrong. Lord! Sir *Francis!* I wonder you can encourage the Boy to swill so much of that lubberly Liquor——it's enough to make him quite stupid.

Squ. Rich. Why it niver hurts me, Mother; and I sleep like a Hawnd after it. [*Drinks.*

Sir Fran. I am sure I ha' drunk it these thirty Years, and by your Leave, Madam, I don't know that I want Wit: Ha! ha!

Jenny. But you might have had a great deal more, Papa, if you would have been govern'd by my Mother.

Sir Fran. Daughter! he that is govern'd by his Wife, has no Wit at all.

Jenny. Then I hope I shall marry a Fool, Sir; for I love to govern dearly.

Sir Fran. You are too pert, Child; it don't do well, in a young woman.

Lady Wrong. Pray Sir *Francis,* don't snub her; she has a fine growing Spirit, and if you check her so, you will make her as dull as her Brother there.

Squ. Rich. [*After a long draught.*] Indeed Mother, I think my Sister is too forward!

Jenny. You! you think I'm too forward! sure! Brother Mud! your Head's too heavy to think of any thing but your Belly.

Lady Wrong. Well said, Miss; he's none of your Master, tho' he is your elder Brother.

Squ. Rich. No, nor she shawn't be my Mistress, while she's younger Sister!

Sir Fran. Well said *Dick!* shew 'em that stawt Liquor makes a stawt Heart, Lad!

Squ. Rich. So I wull! and I'll drink ageen, for all her! [*Drinks.*"

Enter John Moody.

Sir Fran. So *John!* how are the Horses!

John Moody. Troth, Sir, I ha' noa good Opinion o' this Tawn, it's made up o' mischief, I think!

Sir Fran. What's the Matter, naw?

John Moody. Why I'll tell your Worship——before we were gotten to th' Street End, with the Coach, here, a great Lugger-headed Cart, with Wheels as thick as a brick Wall, laid hawld on't, and has poo'd it aw to bits; Crack! went the Perch! Down goes the Coach! and Whang! says the Glasses, all to Shivers! Marcy upon us! and this be *London!* would we were aw weell i'the Country ageen!

Jenny. What have you to do, to wish us all in the Country again, Mr. Lubber? I hope we shall not go into the Country again these Seven Years, Mamma; let twenty Coaches be pull'd to Pieces.

Sir Fran. Hold your Tongue, *Jenny!*——Was *Roger* in no fault, in all this?

John Moody. Noa, Sir, nor I, noather——are not yow asheam'd, says *Roger*, to the Carter, to do such an unkind thing by Strangers? Noa, says he, you Bumkin. Sir, he did the thing on very Purpose! and so the Folks said that stood by—Very well, says *Roger*, yow shall see what our Measter will say to ye! Your Meyster? says he; your Meyster may kiss my— and so he clapt his Hand just there, and like your Worship. Flesh! I thowght they had better Breeding in this Tawn.

Sir Fran. I'll teach this Rascal some, I warrant him! Ods-bud! If I take him in hand, I'll play the Devil with him.

Squ. Rich. Ay do, Feyther, have him before the Parliament.

Sir Fran. Ods-bud! and so I will——I will make him know who I am! Where does he live?

John Moody. I believe, in *London*, Sir.

Sir Fran. What's the Rascal's Name!

John Moody. I think I heard somebody call him *Dick.*

Squ. Rich. What, my name!

Sir Fran. Where did he go?

John Moody. Sir, he went home.

Sir Fran. Where's that?

John Moody. By my Troth, Sir, I doan't know! I heard him say he would cross the same Street again to-morrow; and if we had a mind to stand in his way, he wou'd pool us over and over again.

Sir Fran. Will he so! Odszooks! get me a Constable.

Lady Wrong. Pooh! get you a good Supper. Come, Sir *Francis*, don't put yourself in a Heat for what can't be helpt. Accidents will happen to People that travel abroad to see the World———For my part, I think it's a Mercy it was not over-turn'd before we were all out on't.

Sir Fran. Why ay, that's true again, my Dear.

Lady Wrong. Therefore see to-morrow if we can buy one at Second-hand, for present Use; so bespeak a new one, and then all's easy.

John Moody. Why troth, Sir, I doan't think this could have held you above a Day longer.

Sir Fran. D'ye think so, *John?*

John Moody. Why you ha' had it, ever sen' your Worship were High-Sheriff.

Sir Fran. Why then go and see what *Doll* has got us for Supper——and come and get off my Boots. [*Exit Sir* Fran.

Lady Wrong. In the mean time, Miss, do you step to *Handy*, and bid her get me some fresh Night-cloaths. [*Exit Lady* Wrong.

Jenny. Yes, Mamma, and some for my self too. [*Exit* Jenny.

Squ. Rich. Ods flesh! and what mun I do all alone?

I'll e'en seek out where t'other pratty Miss is,
And she and I'll go play at Cards for Kisses. [*Exit.*

ACT III. SCENE I.

SCENE *the Lord* Townly's *House.*

Enter Lord Townly, *a Servant attending.*

Lord Town. WHO's there?

   Serv. My Lord!

Lord Town. Bid them get Dinner——Lady *Grace*, your Servant.

Enter Lady Grace.

Lady Grace. What, is the House up already? My Lady is not drest yet!

Lord Town. No matter—it's three a-clock—she may break my Rest, but she shall not alter my Hours.

Lady Grace. Nay, you need not fear that now, for she dines abroad.

Lord Town. That, I suppose, is only an Excuse for her not being ready yet.

Lady Grace. No, upon my Word, she is engaged to Company.

Lord Town. Where, pray?

Lady Grace. At my Lady *Revel*'s; and you know they never dine 'till Supper-time.

Lord Town. No truly——she is one of those orderly Ladies, who never let the Sun shine upon any of their Vices!——But pr'ythee, Sister, what Humour is she in To-day?

Lady Grace. O! in tip-top Spirits, I can assure you——she won a good deal, last Night.

Lord Town. I know no Difference between her Winning or Losing, while she continues her course of Life.

Lady Grace. However she is better in good Humour, than bad.

Lord Town. Much alike: When she is in good Humour, other People only are the better for it: When in a very ill Humour, then, indeed, I seldom fail to have my Share of her.

Lady Grace. Well, we won't talk of that now——Does any Body dine here?

Lord Town. *Manly* promis'd me—by the way, Madam, what do you think of his last Conversation?

Lady Grace. ——I am a little at a Stand about it.

Lord Town. How so?

Lady Grace. Why——I don't know how he can ever have any Thoughts of me, that could lay down such severe Rules upon Wives, in my hearing.

Lord Town. Did you think his Rules unreasonable?

Lady Grace. I can't say I did: But he might have had a little more Complaisance before me, at least.

Lord Town. Complaisance is only a Proof of good Breeding: But his Plainness was a certain Proof of his Honesty; nay, of his good Opinion of you: For he would never have open'd himself so freely, but in confidence that your good Sense could not be disoblig'd at it.

Lady Grace. My good Opinion of him, Brother, has hitherto been guided by yours: But I have receiv'd a Letter this Morning, that shews him a very different Man from what I thought him.

Lord Town. A letter! from whom?

Lady Grace. That I don't know, but there it is.   [*Gives a Letter.*

Lord Town. Pray let's see.   [*Reads.*

The Inclos'd, Madam, fell accidentally into my Hands; if it no way concerns you, you will only have the trouble of reading this, from your sincere Friend and humble Servant, Unknown, &c.

Lady Grace. And this was the inclos'd.   [*Giving another.*

Lord Town. [*Reads.*] *To* Charles Manly, *Esq.*

Your manner of living with me of late, convinces me, that I now grow as painful to you, as to my self: but however, though you can love me no longer, I hope, you will not let me live worse than I did, before I left an honest Income, for the vain Hopes of being ever Yours.

Myrtilla Dupe.

P.S. *'Tis above four Months since I receiv'd a Shilling from you.*

Lady Grace. What think you now?

Lord Town. I am considering——

Lady Grace. You see it's directed to him——

Lord Town. That's true! but the Postscript seems to be a Reproach, that I think he is not capable of deserving.

Lady Grace. But who could have Concern enough, to send it to me?

Lord Town. I have observ'd, that these sort of Letters from unknown Friends, generally come from secret Enemies.

Lady Grace. What would you have me do in it?

Lord Town. What I think you ought to do——fairly shew it him, and say I advis'd you to it.

Lady Grace. Will not that have a very odd Look, from me?

Lord Town. Not at all, if you use my Name in it: If he is Innocent, his Impatience to appear so, will discover his Regard to you: If he is guilty; it will be your best way of preventing his Addresses.

Lady Grace. But what Pretence have I to put him out of Countenance?

Lord Town. I can't think there's any fear of that.

Lady Grace. Pray what is't you do think then?

Lord Town. Why certainly, that it's much more probable, this Letter may be all an Artifice, than that he is in the least concern'd in it——

Enter a Servant.

Serv. Mr. *Manly,* my Lord.

Lord Town. Do you receive him; while I step a Minute in to my Lady.
                                        [*Exit Lord* Townly.

Enter Manly.

Man. Madam, your most Obedient; they told me, my Lord was here.

Lady Grace. He will be here presently: He is but just gone in to my Sister.

Man. So! then my Lady dines with us.

Lady Grace. No; she is engag'd.

Man. I hope you are not of her Party, Madam?

Lady Grace. Not 'till after Dinner.

Man. And pray how may she have dispos'd of the rest of the Day?

Lady Grace. Much as usual! she has Visits 'till about eight; after that 'till court-time, she is to be at Quadrille, at Mrs. *Idle*'s: After the Drawing-room, she takes a short supper with my Lady *Moon-light.* And from thence, they go together to my Lord *Noble*'s Assembly.

Man. And are you to do all this with her, Madam?

Lady Grace. Only a few of the Visits: I would indeed have drawn her to the Play; but I doubt we have so much upon our Hands, that it will not be practicable.

Man. But how can you forbear all the rest of it?

Lady Grace. There's no great Merit in forbearing, what one is not charm'd with.

Man. And yet I have found that very difficult, in my time.

Lady Grace. How do you mean?

Man. Why, I have pass'd a great deal of my Life, in the hurry of the Ladies, though I was generally better pleas'd, when I was at quiet without 'em.

Lady Grace. What induc'd you, then, to be with them?

Man. Idleness, and the Fashion.

Lady Grace. No Mistresses in the case?

Man. To speak honestly——Yes——being often in the Toyshop, there was no forbearing the Bawbles.

Lady Grace. And of course, I suppose, sometimes you were tempted to pay for them, twice as much as they were worth.

Man. Why really, where Fancy only makes the choice, Madam, no wonder if we are generally bubbled, in those sort of Bargains, which I confess has been often my Case: For I had constantly some Coquet, or other, upon my Hands, whom I could love perhaps just enough, to put it in her power to plague me.

Lady Grace. And that's a Power, I doubt, commonly made use of.

Man. The Amours of a Coquet, Madam, seldom have any other View. I look upon Them, and Prudes, to be Nusances, just a-like; tho' they seem very different: The first are always plaguing the Men; and the other are always abusing the Women.

Lady Grace. And yet both of them do it for the same vain Ends; to establish a false Character of being Virtuous.

Man. Of being Chaste, they mean; for they know no other Virtue: and, upon the Credit of that, they traffick in every thing else, that's Vicious: They (even against Nature) keep their Chastity, only because they find, they have more power to do Mischief with it, than they could possibly put in Practice without it.

Lady Grace. Hold! Mr. *Manly:* I am afraid this severe Opinion of the Sex, is owing to the ill Choice you have made of your Mistresses.

Man. In a great measure, it may be so: But, Madam, if both these Characters are so odious; how vastly valuable is that Woman, who has attain'd all they aim at without the Aid of the Folly, or Vice of either?

Lady Grace. I believe those sort of Women to be as scarce, Sir, as the men, that believe there are any such; or that allowing such have Virtue enough to deserve them.

Man. That *could* deserve them then——had been a more favourable Reflection!

Lady Grace. Nay, I speak only from my little Experience: For (I'll be free with you, Mr. *Manly*) I don't know a Man, in the World, that, in Appearance, might better pretend to a Woman of the first Merit, than your self: And yet I have a Reason, in my Hand, here, to think you have your Failings.

Man. I have infinite, Madam; but I am sure, the want of an implicit

Respect for you, is not among the Number——pray what is in your Hand, Madam?

Lady Grace. Nay, Sir, I have no title to it; for the Direction is to you.
[*Gives him a Letter.*

Man. To me! I don't remember the Hand——   [*Reads to himself.*

Lady Grace. I can't perceive any change of Guilt in him! and his surprize seems Natural! [*Aside*]——Give me leave to tell you one thing by the way, Mr. *Manly;* That I should never have shewn you this, but that my Brother enjoyn'd me to it.

Man. I take that to proceed from my Lord's good Opinion of me, Madam.

Lady Grace. I hope, at least, it will stand as an Excuse for my taking this Liberty.

Man. I never yet saw you do any thing, Madam, that wanted an Excuse; and, I hope, you will not give me an Instance to the contrary, by refusing the Favour I am going to ask you.

Lady Grace. I don't believe I shall refuse any, that you think proper to ask.

Man. Only this, Madam, to indulge me so far, as to let me know, how this Letter came into your Hands?

Lady Grace. Inclosed to me, in this, without a Name.

Man. If there be no Secret in the Contents, Madam——

Lady Grace. Why——there is an impertinent Insinuation in it: But as I know your good Sense will think it so too, I will venture to trust you.

Man. You oblige me, Madam.   [*He takes the other Letter and reads.*

Lady Grace. [*Aside.*] Now am I in the oddest Situation! methinks our Conversation grows terribly Critical! This must produce something :—— O lud! would it were over!

Man. Now, Madam, I begin to have some light into the poor Project, that is at the Bottom of all this.

Lady Grace. I have no Notion of what could be propos'd by it.

Man. A little Patience, Madam——First, as to the Insinuation you mention——

Lady Grace. O! what is he going to say now!   [*Aside.*

Man. Tho' my Intimacy with my Lord may have allow'd my Visits to have been very frequent here, of late: Yet, in such a talking Town, as this, you must not wonder, if a great many of those Visits are plac'd to your Account: And this taken for granted, I suppose has been told to my Lady *Wronghead,* as a piece of News, since her Arrival, not improbably without many more imaginary Circumstances.

Lady Grace. My Lady *Wronghead!*

Man. Ay, Madam, for I am positive this is her Hand!

Lady Grace. What View could she have in writing it?

Man. To interrupt any Treaty of Marriage, she may have heard I am engag'd in: Because if I die without Heirs, her Family expects that some part of my Estate may return to them again. But, I hope, she is so far mistaken, that if this Letter has given you the least Uneasiness,——I shall think that the happiest Moment of my Life.

Lady Grace. That does not carry your usual Complaisance, Mr. *Manly.*

Man. Yes, Madam, because I am sure I can convince you of my Innocence.

Lady Grace. I am sure, I have no right to enquire into it.

Man. Suppose you may not, Madam; yet you may very innocently have so much Curiosity.

Lady Grace. With what an artful Gentleness he steals into my Opinion? [*Aside.*] Well, Sir, I won't pretend to have so little of the Woman, in me, as to want Curiosity——But pray, do you suppose then, this *Myrtilla* is a real, or a fictitious Name?

Man. Now I recollect, Madam, there is a young Woman, in the House, where my Lady *Wronghead* lodges, that I heard somebody call *Myrtilla:* This Letter may be written by her——but how it came directed to me, I confess is a Mystery; that before I ever presume to see your Ladyship again, I think my self oblig'd, in Honour to find out. [*Going.*

Lady Grace. Mr. *Manly*——you are not going?

Man. 'Tis but to the next Street, Madam; I shall be back in ten Minutes.

Lady Grace. Nay! but Dinner's just coming up.

Man. Madam, I can neither eat, nor rest, 'till I see an end of this Affair!

Lady Grace. But this is so odd! why should any silly Curiosity of mine drive you away?

Man. Since you won't suffer it to be yours, Madam; then it shall be only to satisfie my own Curiosity—— [*Exit* Manly.

Lady Grace. Well——and now, what am I to think of all this? Or suppose an indifferent Person had heard every Word we have said to one another, what would They have thought on't? Would it have been very absurd to conclude, he is seriously inclin'd to pass the rest of his Life with me?——I hope not——for I am sure, the Case is terribly clear on my Side! and why may not I, without Vanity, suppose my——unaccountable somewhat——has done as much Execution upon him?——why—— because he never told me so——nay, he has not so much as mention'd the Word Love, or ever said one civil thing to my Person——well——but he has said a thousand to my good Opinion, and has certainly got it—— had he spoke first to my Person, he had paid a very ill Compliment to my Understanding——I should have thought him Impertinent, and never have troubled my Head about him; but as he has manag'd the matter, at least I am sure of one thing; that let his Thoughts be what they will, I shall never trouble my Head about any other Man, as long as I live.

Enter Mrs. Trusty.

Well, Mrs. *Trusty*, is my Sister dress'd yet?

Trusty. Yes, Madam; but my Lord has been courting her so, I think, 'till they are both out of Humour.

Lady Grace. How so?

Trusty. Why, it begun, Madam, with his Lordship's desiring her Lady-ship to dine at home To-day——upon which my Lady said she could not be ready; upon that, my Lord order'd them to stay the Dinner, and then my Lady order'd the Coach; then my Lord took her short, and said, he had order'd the Coachman to set up: Then my Lady made him a great Curt'sy, and said, she would wait 'till his Lordship's Horses had din'd, and was mighty pleasant: But for fear of the worst, Madam, she whisper'd me——to get her Chair ready.   [*Exit* Trusty.

Lady Grace. O! here they come; and, by their Looks, seem a little unfit for Company.   [*Exit Lady* Grace.

Enter Lady Townly, *Lord* Townly *following.*

Lady Town. Well! look you, my Lord; I can bear it no longer! nothing still but about my Faults, my Faults! an agreeable Subject truly!

Lord Town. Why, Madam, if you won't hear of them; how can I ever hope to see you mend them?

Lady Town. Why, I don't intend to mend them——I can't mend them ——you know I have try'd to do it an hundred times, and—it hurts me so—I can't bear it!

Lord Town. And I, Madam, can't bear this daily licentious Abuse of your Time and Character.

Lady Town. Abuse! Astonishing! when the Universe knows, I am never better Company, than when I am doing what I have a Mind to! But to see this World! that Men can never get over that silly Spirit of Contradiction———why but last *Thursday* now——there you wisely mended one of my Faults, as you call them——you insisted upon my not going to the Masquerade——and pray, what was the Consequence! was not I as cross as the Devil, all the Night after? was not I forc'd to get Company at home? and was not it almost three a-clock in the Morning, before, I was able to come to my self again? and then the Fault is not mended neither———for next time, I shall only have twice the Incli-nation to go: so that all this mending, and mending, you see, is but dearning an old Ruffle, to make it worse than it was before.

Lord Town. Well, the manner of Women's living, of late, is insupportable; and one way or other——

Lady Town. It's to be mended, I suppose! why so it may; but then, my dear Lord, you muſt give one Time——and when Things are at worſt, you know, they may mend themselves! ha! ha!

Lord Town. Madam, I am not in a Humour, now, to trifle.

Lady Town. Why then, my Lord, one Word of fair Argument—to talk with you, your own way now——You complain of my late Hours, and I of your early ones——so far are we even, you'll allow——but pray which gives us the beſt Figure, in the Eye of the Polite World? my active, spirited Three in the Morning, or your dull, drowsy Eleven at Night? Now, I think, One has the Air of a Woman of Quality, and t'Other of a plodding Mechanick, that goes to Bed betimes, that he may rise early, to open his Shop!——Faugh!

Lord Town. Fy, fy, Madam! is this your way of Reasoning? 'tis time to wake you then——'tis not your ill Hours alone, that diſturb me, but as often the ill Company, that occasion those ill Hours.

Lady Town. Sure I don't underſtand you now, my Lord; what ill Company do I keep?

Lord Town. Why, at beſt, Women that lose their Money, and Men that win it! Or, perhaps, Men that are voluntary Bubbles at one Game, in hopes a Lady will give them fair play at another. Then that unavoidable mixture with known Rakes, conceal'd Thieves, and Sharpers in Embroidery——or what, to me, is ſtill more shocking, that herd of familiar chattering crop-ear'd Coxcombs, who are so often like Monkeys, there would be no knowing them asunder, but that their Tails hang from their Head, and the Monkey's grows where it should do.

Lady Town. And a Husband muſt give eminent Proof of his Sense, that thinks their Powder-puffs dangerous.

Lord Town. Their being Fools, Madam, is not always the Husband's Security: Or if it were, Fortune, sometimes, gives them Advantages might make a thinking Woman tremble.

Lady Town. What do you mean!

Lord Town. That Women, sometimes, lose more than they are able to pay; and if a Creditor be a little pressing, the Lady may be reduc'd, to try if, inſtead of Gold, the Gentleman will accept of a Trinket?

Lady Town. My Lord, you grow scurrilous; you'll make me hate you. I'll have you to know, I keep Company with the politeſt People in Town, and the Assemblies I frequent are full of such.

Lord Town. So are the Churches——now and then.

Lady Town. My Friends frequent them too, as well as the Assemblies.

Lord Town. Yes, and would do it oftner, if a Groom of the Chambers there were allow'd to furnish cards to the Company.

Lady Town. I see what you drive at all this while; you would lay an Imputation on my Fame, to cover your own Avarice! I might take any Pleasures, I find, that were not expensive.

Lord Town. Have a Care, Madam; don't let me think you only value your Chastity, to make me reproachable for not indulging you in every thing else, that's vicious——I, Madam, have a Reputation too, to guard, that's dear to me, as yours——The Follies of an ungovern'd Wife may make the wisest Man uneasy; but 'tis his own fault, if ever they make him contemptible.

Lady Town. My Lord——you would make a Woman mad!

Lord Town. You'd mkae a Man a Fool.

Lady Town. If Heav'n has made you otherwise, that won't be in my Power.

Lord Town. Whatever may be in your Inclination, Madam; I'll prevent you making me a Beggar, at least.

Lady Town. A Beggar! *Cræsus!* I'm out of Patience! I won't come home, 'till four To-morrow Morning.

Lord Town. That may be, Madam; but I'll order the Doors to be lock'd at twelve.

Lady Town. Then I won't come home 'till To-morrow Night.

Lord Town. Then, Madam——You shall never come home again.

[*Exit Lord* Town.

Lady Town. What does he mean! I never heard such a Word from him in my Life before! the Man always us'd to have Manners, in his worst Humours! there's something, that I don't see, at the Bottom of all this——but his Head's always upon some impracticable Scheme or other, so I won't trouble mine any longer about him. Mr. *Manly*, your Servant.

Enter Manly.

Man. I ask pardon for my Intrusion, Madam; but I hope my Business with my Lord will excuse it.

Lady Town. I believe you'll find him in the next Room, Sir.

Man. Will you give me leave, Madam?

Lady Town. Sir———you have my leave, tho' you were a Lady.

Man. [*Aside.*] What a well-bred Age do we live in! [*Exit* Manly.

Enter Lady Grace.

Lady Town. O! my dear Lady *Grace!* how could you leave me so unmercifully alone, all this while?

Lady Grace. I thought my Lord had been with you.

Lady Town. Why yes——and therefore I wanted your Relief; for he has been in such a Fluster here——

Lady Grace. Bless me! for what?

Lady Town. Only our usual Breakfast; we have each of us had our Dish of Matrimonial Comfort, this Morning! we have been charming Company!

Lady Grace. I am mighty glad of it! sure it must be a vast Happiness, when a Man and a Wife can give themselves the same Turn of Conversation!

Lady Town. O! the prettiest thing in the World!

Lady Grace. Now I should be afraid, that where two People are every Day together so, they must often be in want of something to talk upon.

Lady Town. O my Dear, you are the most mistaken in the World! married People have Things to talk of, Child, that never enter into the Imagination of others————why, here's my Lord and I now, we have not been married above two short Years, you know, and we have already eight or ten Things constantly in Bank, that whenever we want Company, we can take up any one of them for two Hours together, and the Subject never the flatter; nay, if we have occasion for it, it will be as fresh next Day too, as it was the first Hour it entertain'd us.

Lady Grace. Certainly, that must be vastly pretty!

Lady Town. O! there's no Life like it! why t'other Day for Example, when you din'd abroad; my Lord and I, after a pretty cheerful *tête à tête* meal, sat us down by the Fire-side, in an easy indolent, pick-tooth Way, for about a Quarter of an Hour, as if we had not thought of any other's being in the Room————at last, stretching himself, and yawning————My Dear, says he,————aw————you came home very late, last Night————'Twas but just turn'd of Two, says I————I was in bed————aw————by Eleven, says he; so you are every Night, says I————Well, says he, I am amaz'd you can sit up so late————How can you be amaz'd, says I, at a Thing that happens so often?————upon which we enter'd into a Conversation———— and tho' this is a Point has entertain'd us above fifty times already, we always find so many pretty new Things to say upon it, that I believe, in my soul, it will last as long as we live!

Lady Grace. But pray! in such sort of Family Dialogues (tho' extreamly well for passing the Time) don't there, now and then, enter some little witty sort of Bitterness?

Lady Town. O yes! which does not do amiss at all! A smart Repartee, with a Zest of Recrimination at the Head of it, makes the prettiest Sherbet! Ay, ay! if we did not mix a little of the Acid with it, a matrimonial Society would be so luscious, that nothing but an old liquorish Prude would be able to bear it.

Lady Grace. Well————certainly you have the most elegant Taste————

Lady Town. Tho' to tell you the Truth, my Dear, I rather think we squeez'd a little too much Lemon into it, this Bout; for it grew so sour

(223)

at last, that——I think——I almost told him, he was a Fool——and he again——talk'd something oddly of——turning me out of Doors!

Lady Grace. O! have a care of that!

Lady Town. Nay, if he should, I may thank my own wise Father for that——

Lady Grace. How so?

Lady Town. Why——when my good Lord first open'd his honourable Trenches before me, my unaccountable Papa, in whose Hands I then was, gave me up at Discretion!

Lady Grace. How do you mean?

Lady Town. He said, the Wives of this Age were come to that pass, that he would not desire ev'n his own Daughter should be trusted with Pin-money; so that my whole Train of separate Inclinations are left entirely at the Mercy of an Husband's odd Humours.

Lady Grace. Why, that, indeed, is enough to make a woman of spirit look about her!

Lady Town. Nay, but to be serious, my Dear; what would you, really, have a Woman do in my Case?

Lady Grace. Why——If I had as sober a Husband as you have, I would make my self the happiest Wife in the World, by being as sober as he.

Lady Town. O! you wicked thing! how can you teize one, at this rate? when you know he is so very sober, that (except giving me Money) there is not one thing in the World he can do to please me! And I, at the same time, partly by Nature, and partly, perhaps, by keeping the best Company, do with my Soul love almost every thing he hates! I doat upon Assemblies! my Heart bounds, at a Ball; and at an Opera——I expire! then I love Play, to Distraction! Cards enchant me! and Dice—put me out of my little Wits! Dear! dear Hazard! oh! what a Flow of Spirits it gives one! do you never play at Hazard, Child?

Lady Grace. Oh! never! I don't think it sits well upon Women: there's something so Masculine, so much the air of a Rake, in it! you see how it makes the Men swear and curse! and when a Woman is thrown into the same Passion——why——

Lady Town. That's very true! one is a little put to it, sometimes, not to make use of the same Words to express it.

Lady Grace. Well——and, upon ill Luck, pray what Words are you really forc'd to make use of?

Lady Town. Why, upon a very hard case, indeed, when a sad wrong Word is rising just to one's Tongue's End, I give a great Gulp——and swallow it.

Lady Grace. Well——and is not that enough to make you forswear Play, as long as you live?

Lady Town. O yes! I have forsworn it.

Lady Grace. Seriously?

Lady Town. Solemnly! a thousand times; but then one is constantly forsworn.

Lady Grace. And how can you answer that?

Lady Town. My dear, what we say, when we are Losers, we look upon to be no more binding, than a Lover's Oath, or a great Man's Promise. But I beg Pardon, Child; I should not lead you so far into the World; you are a Prude, and design to live soberly.

Lady Grace. Why, I confess my Nature, and my Education do, in a good degree, incline me that way.

Lady Town. Well! how a Woman of Spirit, (for you don't want that, Child) can dream of living soberly, is to me inconceivable! for you will marry, I suppose!

Lady Grace. I can't tell but I may.

Lady Town. And won't you live in Town?

Lady Grace. Half the Year, I should like it very well.

Lady Town. My Stars! and you would really live in *London* half the Year, to be sober in it!

Lady Grace. Why not?

Lady Town. Why can't you as well go, and be sober, in the Country?

Lady Grace. So I would——t'other half Year.

Lady Town. And pray, what comfortable Scheme of Life would you form now, for your Summer and Winter sober Entertainments?

Lady Grace. A Scheme, that I think might very well content us.

Lady Town. O! of all things let's hear it.

Lady Grace. Why, in Summer, I cou'd pass my leisure Hours in Riding, in Reading, walking by a Canal, or sitting at the end of it under a great Tree, soberly! in dressing, dining, chatting with an agreeable Friend, perhaps hearing a little Musick, taking a Dish of Tea, or a Game at Cards, soberly! Managing my Family, looking into its Accounts, playing with my Children (if I had any,) or in a thousand other innocent Amusements ——soberly! And possibly, by these means, I might induce my Husband to be as sober as my self——

Lady Town. Well, my dear, thou art an astonishing Creature! for sure such primitive antediluvian Notions of Life have not been in any Head these thousand Years!——Under a great Tree! O' my soul!——But I beg we may have the sober Town-scheme too——for I am charm'd with the country one!——

Lady Grace. You shall, and I'll try to stick to my Sobriety there too.

Lady Town. Well, tho' I am sure it will give me the Vapours, I must hear it however.

Lady Grace. Why then, for fear of your fainting, Madam, I will first so far come into the Fashion, that I would never be dress'd out of it——

but still it should be soberly. For I can't think it any Disgrace, to a Woman of my private Fortune, not to wear her Lace as fine as the Wedding-suit of a first Dutchess. Tho' there is one Extravagance I would venture to come up to!

Lady Town. Ay now for it——

Lady Grace. I would every Day be as clean, as a Bride.

Lady Town. Why the Men say, that's a great Step to be made one—— Well now you are drest——pray let's see to what Purpose?

Lady Grace. I would visit—soberly—that is, my real Friends; but as little for Form as possible.——I would go to Court; sometimes to an Assembly, nay play at *Quadrille*——soberly: I would see all the good Plays; and, (because 'tis the Fashion) now and then an Opera——but I would not Expire there, for fear I should never go again: And lastly, I can't say, but for Curiosity, if I lik'd my Company, I might be drawn in once to a Masquerade! And this, I think, is as far as any Woman can go ——soberly.

Lady Town. Well! if it had not been for that last Piece of Sobriety, I was just going to call for some Surfeit-water.

Lady Grace. Why, don't you think, with the farther Aid of Break-fasting, Dining, taking the Air, Supping, Sleeping, not to say a word of Devotion, the four and twenty Hours might roll over in a tolerable Manner?

Lady Town. Tolerable? Deplorable! Why, Child, all you propose, is but to Endure Life, now I want to Enjoy it——

Enter Mrs. Trusty.

Trus. Madam, your Ladyship's Chair is ready.

Lady Town. Have the Footmen their white Flambeaux yet? for last Night I was poyson'd.

Trus. Yes, Madam; there were some come in this Morning.

[*Exit* Trusty.

Lady Town. My Dear, you will excuse me; but you know my Time is so precious——

Lady Grace. That I beg I may not hinder your least Enjoyment of it.

Lady Town. You will call on me at Lady *Revel*'s?

Lady Grace. Certainly.

Lady Town. But I am so afraid it will break into your Scheme, my Dear!

Lady Grace. When it does, I will——soberly break from you.

Lady Town. Why then, 'till we meet again, dear Sister, I wish you all tolerable Happiness. [*Exit Lady* Town.

Lady Grace. There she goes—Dash! into her stream of Pleasures! Poor Woman! she is really a fine Creature! and sometimes infinitely agreeable! nay take her out of the Madness of this Town, rational in her

Notions, and easy to live with; But she is so born down by this Torrent of Vanity in vogue, she thinks every hour of her Life is lost that she does not lead at the Head of it. What it will end in, I tremble to imagine!——Ha! my Brother, and *Manly* with him! I guess what they have been talking of——I shall hear it in my turn, I suppose, but it won't become me to be inquisitive. [*Exit Lady* Grace.

Enter Lord Townly, *and* Manly.

Lord Town. I did not think my Lady *Wronghead* had such a notable Brain: Tho' I can't say she was so very wise, in trusting this silly Girl you call *Myrtilla*, with the Secret.

Man. No my Lord, you mistake me; had the Girl been in the Secret, perhaps I had never come at it my self.

Lord Town. Why I thought you said the Girl writ this Letter, to you, and that my Lady *Wronghead* sent it inclos'd to my Sister?

Man. If you please to give me leave, my Lord——the Fact is thus.—— This inclos'd Letter to Lady *Grace* was a real Original one, written by this Girl, to the Count we have been talking of: the Count drops it, and my Lady *Wronghead* finds it: then only changing the Cover, she seals it up as a Letter of Business, just written by her self, to me: and pretending to be in a Hurry, gets this innocent Girl to write the Direction, for her.

Lord Town. Oh! then the Girl did not know she was superscribing a Billet-doux of her own, to you?

Man. No, my Lord; for when I first question'd her about the Direction, she own'd it immediately: but when I shew'd her, that her letter to the Count was within it, and told her how it came into my Hands, the poor Creature was amaz'd, and thought herself betray'd both by the Count and my Lady——in short, upon this Discovery, the girl and I grew so gracious, that she has let me into some Transactions, in my Lady *Wronghead*'s family, which, with my having a careful Eye over them, may prevent the Ruin of it.

Lord Town. You are very generous to be so sollicitous for a Lady, that has given you so much Uneasiness.

Man. But I will be most unmercifully reveng'd of her: for I will do her the greatest Friendship in the World——against her Will.

Lord Town. What an uncommon Philosophy art thou master of? to make even thy Malice a Virtue?

Man. Yet, my Lord, I assure you, there is no one Action of my Life gives me more Pleasure, than your Approbation of it.

Lord Town. Dear *Charles!* my Heart's impatient, 'till thou art nearer to me: And as a Proof that I have long wisht thee so: while your daily Conduct has chosen rather to deserve, than ask my Sister's Favour; I have been as secretly Industrious to make her sensible of your Merit: and since on this Occasion you have open'd your whole Heart to me, 'tis now with equal Pleasure, I assure you, we have both succeeded———she is as firmly Yours———

Man. Impossible! you flatter me!

Lord Town. I am glad you think it Flattery: but she her self shall prove it none: she dines with us alone: when the Servants are withdrawn, I'll open a Conversation, that shall excuse my leaving you together———O! *Charles!* had I, like thee, been cautious in my Choice, what melancholy Hours had this Heart avoided!

Man. No more of that, I beg, my Lord———

Lord Town. But 'twill, at least, be some Relief to my Anxiety (however barren of Content the State has been to me) to see so near a Friend and Sister happy, in it: Your Harmony of Life will be an Instance how much the Choice of Temper's preferable to Beauty.

> While your soft Hours in mutal Kindness move,
> You'll reach, by Virtue, what I lost by Love.   [*Exeunt.*

ACT IV. SCENE I.

SCENE *Mrs.* Motherly's *House.*

Enter Mrs. Motherly, *meeting* Myrtilla.

Moth. SO, neice! where is it possible you can have been these six hours?

Myr. O Madam! I have such a terrible Story to tell you!

Moth. A Story! Ods my Life! what have you done with the Count's Note of five hundred Pound, I sent you about? is it safe? is it good? is it Security?

Myr. Yes, yes, it is safe: But for its Goodness———Mercy on us! I have been in a fair way to be hang'd about it!

Moth. The dickens! has this Rogue of a Count play'd us another Trick then?

Myr. You shall hear, Madam; when I came to Mr. *Cash* the Banker's, and shew'd him his Note for five hundred Pounds, payable to the Count, or Order, in two Months,———he look'd earnestly upon it, and desir'd me to step into the Inner Room, while he examin'd his Books———after I had staid about ten Minutes, he came in to me———claps to the door, and charges me with a Constable for forgery.

Moth. Ah! poor soul! and how didst thou get off?

Myr. While I was ready to sink in this Condition, I beg'd him to have a little Patience, 'till I could send for Mr. *Manly*, whom he knew to be a Gentleman of Worth and Honour, and who, I was sure, would convince him, whatever Fraud might be in the Note, that I was myself an innocent abus'd Woman————and as good Luck would have it, in less than half an hour Mr. *Manly* came——so, without mincing the Matter, I fairly told him upon what Design the Count had lodg'd that Note in your Hands, and in short, laid open the whole Scheme he had drawn us into, to make our Fortune.

Moth. The Devil you did!

Myr. Why how do you think it was possible, I could any otherways make Mr. *Manly* my Friend, to help me out of the Scrape I was in? To conclude, he soon made Mr. *Cash* easy, and sent away the Constable; nay farther promis'd me, if I would trust the Note in his Hands, he would take care it should be fully paid before it was due, and at the same time would give me an ample Revenge upon the Count; so that all you have to consider now, Madam, is, whether you think yourself safer in the Count's Hands, or Mr. *Manly*'s?

Moth. Nay, nay, Child; there is no choice in the matter! Mr. *Manly* may be a Friend indeed, if any thing in our Power can make him so.

Myr. Well, Madam, and now pray, how stand Matters at home here? What has the Count done with the Ladies?

Moth. Why every thing he has a Mind to do, by this time, I suppose. He is in as high Favour with Miss, as he is with my Lady.

Myr. Pray, where are the Ladies?

Moth. Rattling abroad in their own Coach, and the well-bred Count along with them: They have been scouring all the Shops in Town over, buying fine things and new Cloaths, from Morning to Night: They have made one Voyage already, and have brought home such a cargo of Bawbles and Trumpery——Mercy on the poor Man that's to pay for them!

Myr. Did not the young Squire go with them!

Moth. No, no; Miss said, truly he would but disgrace their Party: so they even left him asleep by the Kitchen Fire.

Myr. Has he not ask'd after me all this while? for I had a sort of an Assignation with him.

Moth. O yes! he has been in a bitter Taking about it. At last his Disappointment grew so uneasy, that he fairly fell a crying; so to quiet him, I sent one of the Maids and *John Moody* abroad with him, to shew him——the lions and the Monument. Ods me! there he is, just come home again——you may have Business with him——so I'll even turn you together.

[*Exit Mrs.* Motherly.

[Enter Squire Richard.

Squ. Rich. Soah! soah! Mrs. *Myrtilla*, wheere han yow been aw this Day, forsooth?

Myr. Nay, if you go to that, Squire, where have you been, pray?

Squ. Rich. Why, when I fun' at yow were no loikly to come whoam, I were ready to hong my Sel——so *John Moody*, and I, and one o' your Lasses have been——Lord knows where—a seeing o' Soights.

Myr. Well, and pray what have you seen, Sir?

Squ. Rich. Flesh! I cawnt tell, not I——seen every thing I think. First there we went o' top o' the what d'ye call it? there, the great huge Stone Post, up the rawnd and rawnd Stairs, that twine and twine about, just an as thof it were a Cork-Scrue.

Myr. O, the Monument! well, and was it not a fine Sight, from the Top of it?

Squ. Rich. Sight, Miss! I know no'——I saw nowght but Smoak and brick Housen, and Steeple Tops——then there was such a mortal Ting-tang of Bells, and Rumbling of Carts and Coaches, and then the Folks under one look'd so small, and made such a Hum, and a Buz, it put me in mind of my Mother's great glass Bee-Hive, in our Garden in the Country.

Myr. I think, Master, you give a very good account of it.

Squ. Rich. Ay! but I did no like it: For my Head—my Head—begun to turn——so I trundled me dawn Stairs agen, like a round Trencher.

Myr. Well! but this was not all you saw, I suppose?

Squ. Rich. Noa! noa! we went after that, and saw the Lyons; and I lik'd them better by hawlf; they are pure grim Devils; hoh, hoh! I touke a Stick, and gave one of them such a Poke o' the Noase——I believe he would ha' snapt my Head off, an he could ha' got me. Hoh! hoh! hoh!

Myr. Well, Master, when you and I go abroad, I'll shew you prettier Sights than these——there's a Masquerade to-morrow.

Squ. Rich. O Laud! ay! they say that's a pure thing for *Merry Andrews*, and those sort of comical Mummers——and the Count tells me, that there Lads and Lasses may jig their Tails, and eat, and drink, without grudging, all Night lung.

Myr. What would you say now, if I should get you a Ticket and go along with you?

Squ. Rich. Ah dear!

Myr. But have a Care, Squire, the fine Ladies there are terribly tempt-ing; look well to your Heart, or Ads me! they'll whip it up, in the Trip of a Minute.

Squ. Rich. Ay, but they cawnt thoa——soa let 'um look to themselves, an' ony of 'um falls in love with me—mayhap they had as good be quiet.

Myr. Why sure you would not refuse a fine Lady, would you?

Squ. Rich. Ay, but I would tho' unless it were—one 'at I know of.

Myr. Oh! ho! then you have left your Heart in the Country, I find?

Squ. Rich. Noa, noa, my Heart——eh——my Heart e'ent awt o' this Room.

Myr. I am glad you have it about you, however.

Squ. Rich. Nay, mayhap not soa noather, somebody else may have it, 'at you little think of.

Myr. I can't imagine what you mean?

Squ. Rich. Noa! why doan't yow know how many Folks there is in this Room, naw?

Myr. Very fine, Master, I see you have learnt the Town Gallantry already.

Squ. Rich. Why doan't you believe 'at I have a Kindness for you, then?

Myr. Fy! fy! Master, how you talk! beside you are too young to think of a Wife.

Squ. Rich. Ay! but I caunt help thinking o' yow, for all that.

Myr. How! why sure, Sir, you don't pretend to think of me in a dishonourable way?

Squ. Rich. Nay, that's as yow see good——I did no' think 'at yow would ha' thowght of me for a Husband, mayhap; unless I had Means in my own Hands; and Feyther allows me but hawlf a Crown a Week, as yet a while.

Myr. Oh! when I like any Body, 'tis not want of Money will make me refuse them.

Squ. Rich. Well, that's just my Mind now; for 'an I like a Girl, Miss, I would take her in her Smuck.

Myr. Ay, Master, now you speak like a man of Honour: This shews something of a true Heart in you.

Squ. Rich. Ay, and a true Heart you'll find me; try me when you will.

Myr. Hush! hush! here's your Papa come home, and my Aunt with him.

Squ. Rich. A Devil rive 'em, what do they come naw for?

Myr. When you and I get to the Masquerade, you shall see what I'll say to you.

Squ. Rich. Well, Hands upon't then——

Myr. There——

Squ. Rich. One Buss and a Bargain.   [*Kisses her.*
Ads wauntlikins! as soft and plump as a Marrow-Pudding.

                                  [*Exeunt severally.*]]

Enter Sir Francis Wronghead *and Mrs.* Motherly.

Sir Fran. What! my Wife and Daughter abroad say you?

Moth. O dear Sir, they have been mighty busy all the Day long; they just came home to snap up a short Dinner, and so went out again.

Sir Fran. Well, well, I shan't stay Supper for 'em, I can tell 'em that: For Ods-heart! I have had nothing in me, but a Toast and a Tankard, since Morning.

Moth. I am afraid, Sir, these late Parliament Hours won't agree with you.

Sir Fran. Why, truly, Mrs. *Motherly*, they don't do right with us Country Gentlemen; to lose one Meal out of three, is a hard Tax upon a good Stomach.

Moth. It is so indeed, Sir.

Sir Fran. But, hawsomever, Mrs. *Motherly*, when we consider, that what we suffer is for the Good of our Country——

Moth. Why truly, Sir, that is something.

Sir Fran. Oh! there's a great deal to be said for't——the Good of ones Country is above all things——A true-hearted *Englishman* thinks nothing too much for it——I have heard of some honest Gentlemen so very zealous, that for the Good of their Country——they would sometimes go to Dinner at Midnight.

Moth. O! the Goodness of 'em! sure their Country must have vast Esteem for them?

Sir Fran. So they have Mrs. *Motherly;* they are so respected when they come home to their Boroughs, after a Session, and so belov'd——that their Country will come and Dine with them every Day in the Week.

Moth. Dear me! what a fine thing 'tis to be so populous!

Sir Fran. It is a great Comfort, indeed! and I can assure you, you are a good sensible Woman, Mrs. *Motherly*.

Moth. O dear Sir, your Honour's pleas'd to Compliment.

Sir Fran. No, no, I see you know how to value People of Consequence.

Moth. Good lack! here's Company, Sir; will you give me leave to get you a broil'd Bone, or so, 'till the ladies come home, Sir?

Sir Fran. Why troth, I don't think it would be amiss.

Moth. It shall be done in a Moment, Sir.　　　　　　　　　*[Exit.*

Enter Mr. Manly.

Man. Sir *Francis*, your Servant.

Sir Fran. Cousin *Manly!*

Man. I am come to see how the Family goes on here.

Sir Fran. Troth! all as busy as Bees; I have been upon the Wing ever since Eight a-Clock this Morning.

Man. By your early Hour, then, I suppose you have been making your Court to some of the Great Men.

Sir Fran. Why, Faith! you have hit it, Sir——I was advis'd to lose

no Time: So I e'en went ſtraight forward, to one great Man I had never
seen in my Life before.

Man. Right! that was doing Business: But who had you got to
introduce you?

Sir Fran. Why, no Body——I remember'd I had heard a wise Man
say—My son, be bold—so troth! I introduc'd myself.

Man. As how, pray?

Sir Fran. Why, thus——Look ye——Please your Lordship, says I,
I am Sir *Francis Wronghead* of *Bumper-Hall*, and Member of Parliament
for the Borough of *Guzzledown*——Sir, your humble servant, says my
Lord; thof I have not the Honour to know your Person, I have heard
you are a very honeſt Gentleman, and I am glad your Borough has made
choice of so worthy a Representative; and so, says he, Sir *Francis*, have
you any Service to command me? Naw, Cousin! those laſt Words, you
may be sure, gave me no small Encouragement. And thof I know, Sir,
you have no extraordinary Opinion of my Parts, yet I believe, you won't
say I miſt it naw!

Man. Well, I hope I shall have no Cause.

Sir Fran. So when I found him so courteous——My Lord, says I,
I did not think to ha' troubled your Lordship with Business upon my firſt
Visit; but since your Lordship is pleas'd not to ſtand upon Ceremony——
why truly, says I, I think naw is as good as another Time.

Man. Right! there you puſht him home.

Sir Fran. Ay, ay, I had a mind to let him see that I was none of your
mealy-mouth'd Ones.

Man. Very good!

Sir Fran. So in short, my Lord, says I, I have a good Eſtate——but
——a——it's a leettle awt at Elbows; and as I desire to serve my King,
as well as my Country, I shall be very willing to accept of a Place at
Court.

Man. So, this was making short Work on't.

Sir Fran. I'cod! I shot him flying, Cousin: some of your Hawf-witted
Ones naw, would ha' humm'd and haw'd, and dangled a Month or two
after him, before they durſt open their Mouths about a Place, and mayhap,
not ha' got it at laſt neither.

Man. Oh! I'm glad you're so sure on't——

Sir Fran. You shall hear, cousin——Sir *Francis*, says my Lord, pray
what sort of a Place may you ha' turn'd your Thowghts upon? My Lord,
says I, beggars muſt not be Chusers; but ony Place, says I, about a thousand a Year, will be well enough to be doing with 'till something better
falls in——for I thowght it would not look well to ſtond haggling with
him at firſt.

Man. No, no, your Business was to get Footing any way.

Sir Fran. Right! there's it! ah Cousin, I see you know the World!

Man. Yes, yes, one sees more of it every Day——well! but what said my Lord to all this?

Sir Fran. Sir *Francis*, says he, I shall be glad to serve you any way, that lies in my Power; so he gave me a Squeeze by the Hond, as much as to say, Give your self no Trouble——I'll do your Business; with that he turn'd him abawt to somebody with a colour'd Ribbon across here, that looked in my Thowghts, as if he came for a Place too.

Man. Ha! so, upon these Hopes, you are to make your Fortune!

Sir Fran. Why, do you think there's ony Doubt of it, Sir?

Man. Oh no, I have not the leaſt Doubt about it——for juſt as you have done, I made my Fortune ten Years ago.

Sir Fran. Why, I never knew you had a Place, Cousin.

Man. Nor I neither, upon my Faith, cousin. But you, perhaps, may have better Fortune: For I suppose my Lord has heard of what Import- ance you were in the Debate To-day——You have been since down at the House, I presume!

Sir Fran. O, yes! I would not negleĉt the House, for ever so much.

Man. Well! and pray what have they done there?

Sir Fran. Why, troth! I can't well tell you, what they have done, but I can tell you what I did: and I think pretty well in the main; only I happen'd to make a little Miſtake at laſt, indeed.

Man. How was that?

Sir Fran. Why, they were all got there, into a sort of a puzzling Debate, about the Good of the Nation——and I were always for that, you know ——but in short, the Arguments were so long-winded o' both sides, that, waunds! I did no well underſtand 'um: Hawsomever, I was convinc'd, and so resolv'd to vote right, according to my Conscience——so when they came to put the Queſtion, as they call it,——I don't know haw 'twas ———but I doubt I cry'd Ay! when I should ha' cry'd No!

Man. How came that about?

Sir Fran. Why, by a Miſtake, as I tell you——for there was a good- humour'd sort of a Gentleman, one Mr. *Totherside* I think they call him, that sat next me, as soon as I had cry'd Ay! gives me a hearty Shake by the Hand! Sir, says he, you are a Man of Honour, and a true *Englishman!* and I should be proud to be better acquainted with you——and so with that, he takes me by the Sleeve, along with the Crowd, into the Lobby—— so, I knew nowght——but Ods-flesh! I was got o'th' wrung side the Poſt ——for I were told, afterwards, I should have ſtaid where I was.

Man. And so, if you had not quite made your Fortune before, you have clinch'd it now!——Ah! thou Head of the *Wrongheads!*

Sir Fran. Odso! here's my Lady come home at laſt——I hope, Cousin, you will be so kind, as to take a Family Supper with us?

Man. Another time, Sir *Francis;* but to-night, I am engag'd.

Enter Lady Wronghead, *Miss* Jenny, *and Count* Basset.

Lady Wrong. Cousin! your Servant; I hope you will pardon my Rudeness: but we have really been in such a continual Hurry here, that we have not had a leisure Moment to return your laſt Visit.

Man. O Madam! I am a Man of no Ceremony; you see That has not hinder'd my coming again.

Lady Wrong. You are infinitely obliging: but I'll redeem my Credit with you.

Man. At your own time, Madam.

Count Bas. I muſt say that for Mr. *Manly,* Madam; if making People easy is the Rule of Good-Breeding, he is certainly the beſt-bred Man in the World.

Man. Soh! I am not to drop my Acquaintance, I find—[*Aside*] I am afraid, Sir, I shall grow vain upon your good Opinion.

Count Bas. I don't know that, Sir; but I am sure, what you are pleas'd to say, makes me so.

Man. The moſt impudent Modeſty that ever I met with.   [*Aside.*

Lady Wrong. Lard! how ready his wit is?   [*Aside.*

Sir Fran. Don't you think, Sir, the Count's a very fine ⎫
Gentleman?   ⎪
Man. O! among the Ladies, certainly.   ⎪
Sir Fran. And yet he's as ſtout as a Lion: Waund, he'll ⎬ *Apart.*
ſtorm any thing.   ⎪
Man. Will he so? Why then, Sir, take care of your Cittadel. ⎪
Sir Fran. Ah! you are Wag, Cousin.   ⎭

Man. I hope, Ladies, the Town Air continues to agree with you?

Jenny. O! perfeƈtly well, Sir! We have been abroad in our new Coach all Day long——and we have bought an Ocean of fine Things. And To-morrow we go to the Masquerade! and on *Friday* to the Play! and on *Saturday* to the Opera! and on *Sunday,* we are to be at what-d'ye-call it ——Assembly, and see the Ladies play at Quadrille, and Piquet, and Ombre, and Hazard, and Basset! And on *Monday,* we are to see the King! and so on *Tuesday*——

Lady Wrong. Hold, hold, Miss! you muſt not let your Tongue run so faſt, Child——you forget! you know I brought you hither to learn Modeſty.

Man. Yes, yes! and she is improv'd with a Vengeance——   [*Aside.*

Jenny. Lawrd! Mama, I am sure I did not say any Harm! and if one muſt not speak in ones Turn, one may be kept under as long as one lives, for ought I see.

Lady Wrong. O' my Conscience, this Girl grows so Head-ſtrong——

Sir Fran. Ay, ay, there's your fine growing Spirit for you! Now tack it dawn, an' you can.

Jenny. All I said, Papa, was only to entertain my Cousin *Manly.*

Man. My pretty Dear, I am mightily oblig'd to you.

Jenny. Look you there now, Madam.

Lady Wrong. Hold your tongue, I say.

Jenny [*Turning away and glowting.*] I declare it, I won't bear it: she is always snubbing me before you, Sir!——I know why she does it, well enough——   [*Aside to the Count.*

Count Bas. Hush! hush, my dear! don't be uneasy at that! she'll suspect us.   [*Aside.*

Jenny. Let her suspect, what do I care——I don't know, but I have as much Reason to suspect, as she——tho' perhaps I'm not so fraid of her.

Count Bas. [*Aside.*] I'gad, if I don't keep a tight Hand on my Tit, here, she'll run away with my Project before I can bring it to bear.

Lady Wrong. [*Aside.*] Perpetually hanging upon him! The young Harlot is certainly in love with him: but I must not let them see I think so——and yet I can't bear it. Upon my Life, Count, you'll spoil that forward Girl——you should not encourage her so.

Count Bas. Pardon me, Madam, I was only advising her to observe what your Ladyship said to her.

Man. Yes, truly her Observations have been something particular.   [*Aside.*

Count Bas. In one Word, Madam, she has a Jealousy of your Ladyship, and I am forc'd to encourage her, to blind it; 'Twill be better to take no notice of her Behaviour to me.

Lady Wrong. You are right, I will be more cautious.

Count Bas. To-morrow at the Masquerade, we may lose her.

Lady Wrong. We shall be observ'd. I'll send you a Note, and settle that Affair——go on with the Girl, and don't mind me.   } *Apart.*

Count Bas. I have been taking your Part, my little Angel.

Lady Wrong. *Jenny!* come hither Child———you must not be so hasty, my Dear——I only advise you for your good.

Jenny. Yes, Mama; but when I am told of a thing before Company, it always makes me worse, you know.

Man. If I have any Skill in the fair sex; Miss, and her Mama, have only quarrell'd, because they are both of a Mind. This facetious Count seems to have made a very genteel Step into the family.   [*Aside.*

Enter Myrtilla. [*Manly talks apart with her.*]

Lady Wrong. Well, Sir *Francis,* and what news have you brought us, from *Westminster,* to-day?

Sir Fran. News, Madam? I'cod! I have some——and such as does not come every day, I can tell you——a word in your Ear——I have got a promise of a Place at Court of a thousand Pawnd a Year, already.

Lady Wrong. Have you so Sir? And pray who may you thank for it? Now! who is in the Right? Is not this better, than throwing so much away, after a ſtinking Pack of Fox-hounds, in the Country? Now your Family may be the better for it!

Sir Fran. Nay! that's what persuaded me to come up, my Dove.

Lady Wrong. Mighty well——come——let me have another hundred Pound then.

Sir Fran. Another! Child? Waunds! you have had one hundred this Morning, pray what's become of that, my Dear?

Lady Wrong. What's become of it? why I'll ſhew you, my Love! *Jenny!* have you the Bills about you?

Jenny. Yes, Mama.

Lady Wrong. What's become of it? Why laid out, my Dear, with fifty more to it, that I was forc'd to borrow of the Count here.

Jenny. Yes, indeed, Papa, and that would hardly do neither——There's th' Account.

Sir Fran. [*Turning over the bills.*] Let's see! let's see! what the Devil have we got here?

Man. Then you have sounded your Aunt you say, and she readily comes into all I propos'd to you?

Myr. Sir, I'll answer, with my Life, she is moſt thankfully yours in every Article: she mightily desires to see you, Sir.

Man. I am going home, directly: bring her to my House in half an hour; and if she makes good what you tell me, you shall both find your Account in it.

Myr. Sir, she shall not fail you.

> *Apart.*

Sir Fran. Ods-life! Madam, here's nothing but Toys and Trinkets, and Fanns, and Clock-Stockings, by wholesale.

Lady Wrong. There's nothing but what's proper, and for your Credit, Sir *Francis*——Nay you see, I am so good a Housewife, that in Necessaries for my self, I have scarce laid out a Shilling.

Sir Fran. No, by my troth, so it seems; for the devil o' one thing's here, that I can see you have any occasion for!

Lady Wrong. My Dear! do you think I came hither to live out of the Fashion? why, the greateſt Diſtinction of a fine Lady in this Town is in the variety of pretty Things she has no Occasion for.

Jenny. Sure Papa, could you imagine, that Women of Quality wanted nothing but Stays and Petticoats?

Lady Wrong. Now, that is so like him!

Man. So! the Family comes on finely.   [*Aside.*

Lady Wrong. Lard! if Men were always to govern, what Dowdys would they reduce their Wives to?

Sir Fran. An hundred Pound in the Morning, and want another afore Night! Waunds and Fire! the Lord Mayor of *London* could not hold it, at this rate!

Man. O! do you feel it, Sir?   [*Aside.*

Lady Wrong. My Dear, you seem uneasy; let me have the hundred Pound, and compose your self.

Sir Fran. Compose the Devil, Madam! why do you consider what a hundred Pound a Day comes to in a Year?

Lady Wrong. My Life, if I account with you from one day to another, that's really all that my Head is able to bear at a time——But I'll tell you what I consider——I consider, that my Advice has got you a thousand Pound a Year this Morning————That, now, methinks you might consider, Sir.

Sir Fran. A thousand a Year? Waunds, Madam, but I have not touch'd a Penny of it yet!

Man. Nor ever will, I'll answer for him.   [*Aside.*

Enter Squire Richard.

Squ. Rich. Feyther, an yow doan't come quickly, the Meat will be coal'd; and I'd fain pick a bit with you.

Lady Wrong. Bless me, Sir *Francis!* you are not going to sup by your self!

Sir Fran. No, but I am going to dine by my self, and that's pretty near the matter, Madam.

Lady Wrong. Had not you as good ſtay a little, my Dear? we shall all eat in half an hour; and I was thinking to ask my cousin *Manly* to take a family Morsel, with us.

Sir Fran. Nay, for my Cousin's good Company, I don't care if I ride a day's Journey, without Baiting.

Man. By no means, Sir *Francis.* I am going upon a little business.

Sir Fran. Well, Sir, I know you don't love Compliments.

Man. You'll excuse me, Madam——

Lady Wrong. Since you have Business, Sir——   [*Exit* Manly.

Enter Mrs. Motherly.

O, Mrs. *Motherly!* you were saying this Morning, you had some very fine Lace to show me——can't I see it now?   [*Sir* Francis ſtares.

Moth. Why really, Madam, I had made a sort of a promise, to let the Countess of *Nicely* have the firſt Sight of it, for the Birth-day: But your Ladyship——

Lady Wrong. O! I die, if I don't see it before her.

Squ. Rich. Woan't you goa, Feyther?

Sir Fran. Waunds! Lad, I shall ha' noa Stomach, at this rate! } *Apart.*

Moth. Well, Madam, though I say it, 'tis the sweeteſt Pattern that ever came over——and for Fineness——no Cobweb comes up to it!

Sir Fran. Ods Gutts and Gizard, Madam! Lace as fine as a Cobweb! why, what the Devil's that to coſt now?

Moth. Nay, if Sir *Francis* does not like of it, Madam——

Lady Wrong. He like it! dear Mrs. *Motherly*, he is not to wear it.

Sir Fran. Flesh, Madam, but I suppose I am to pay for it!

Lady Wrong. No doubt on't! Think of your thousand a Year, and who got it you, go! eat your Dinner, and be thankful, go. [*Driving him to the door.*] Come, Mrs. *Motherly*. [*Exit Lady* Wronghead *with Mrs.* Motherly.

Sir Fran. Very fine! so here I mun faſt, 'till I am almoſt famish'd for the Good of my Country; while Madam is laying me out an hundred Pound a-day in Lace, as fine as a Cobweb, for the Honour of my Family! Ods flesh! things had need go well, at this rate!

Squ. Rich. Nay, nay——come Feyther. [*Exit Sir* Francis.

Enter Mrs. Motherly.

Moth. Madam, my Lady desires you and the Count will please to come, and assiſt her fancy, in some of the new Laces.

Count Bas. We'll wait upon her—— [*Exit Mrs.* Motherly.

Jenny. So! I told you how it was! you see she can't bear to leave us together.

Count Bas. No matter, my Dear: You know she has ask'd me to ſtay Supper: so, when your Papa and she are a-bed, Mrs. *Myrtilla* will let me into the House again; then you may ſteal into her Chamber, and we'll have a pretty Sneaker of Punch together.

Myr. Ay, ay, Madam, you may command me any thing.

Jenny. Well! that will be pure!

Count Bas. But you had beſt go to her alone, my Life: it will look better if I come after you.

Jenny. Ay, so it will: and to-morrow, you know at the Masquerade. And then!——hey! *O! I'll have a Husband. Ay, Marry.* [*Exit singing.*

Myr. So Sir! am not I very commode to you?

Count Bas. Well, Child, and don't you find your account in it? Did not I tell you we might ſtill be of use to one another?

Myr. Well, but how ſtands your Affair with Miss, in the main?

Count Bas. O she's mad for the Masquerade! it drives like a Nail, we want nothing now but a Parson, to clinch it. Did not your Aunt say she could get one at a short Warning?

Myr. Yes, yes, my Lord *Townly*'s Chaplain is her Cousin, you know; he'll do your Business and mine, at the same time.

(239)

Count Bas. O! it's true! but where shall we appoint him?

Myr. Why you know my Lady *Townly*'s House is always open to the Masques upon a Ball-night, before they go to the *Hay-market*.

Count Bas. Good!

Myr. Now the Doctor proposes, we should all come thither in our Habits, and when the Rooms are full, we may steal up into his Chamber, he says, and there——crack——he'll give us all Canonical Commission to go to bed together.

Count Bas. Admirable! Well, the Devil fetch me, if I shall not be heartily glad to see thee well settled, Child.

Myr. And may the Black Gentleman tuck me under his Arm at the same time, if I shall not think my self oblig'd to you, as long as I live.

Count Bas. One Kiss, for old Acquaintance sake——I'gad I shall want to be busy again!

Myr. O you'll have one shortly will find you Employment: But I must run to my Squire.

Count Bas. And I to the Ladies——so your humble servant, sweet Mrs. *Wronghead*.

Myr. Yours, as in Duty bound, most noble Count *Basset*.   [*Exit* Myr.

Count Bas. Why ay! Count! That Title has been of some use to me indeed! not that I have any more Pretence to it, than I have to a blue Riband. Yet, I have made a pretty considerable Figure in life with it: I have loll'd in my own Chariot, dealt at Assemblies, din'd with Ambassadours, and made one at Quadrille, with the first Women of Quality—— But——*Tempora mutantur*——since that damn'd squadron at *White*'s have left me out of their last Secret, I am reduc'd to trade upon my own Stock of Industry, and make my last Push upon a Wife: if my Card comes up right (which I think can't fail) I shall once more cut a Figure, and cock my Hat in the Face of the best of them! For since our modern Men of Quality are grown wise enough to be Sharpers; I think Sharpers are Fools that don't take up the Airs of Men of Quality.   [*Exit.*

ACT V. SCENE I.

SCENE *Lord* Townly's *House.*

Enter Manly *and Lady* Grace.

Man. THERE's something, Madam, hangs upon your Mind, To day. Is it unfit to trust me with it?

Lady Grace. Since you will know it————my Sister then——unhappy Woman!

Man. What of her?

Lady Grace. I fear, is on the Brink of Ruin!

Man. I am sorry for it——what has happen'd?

Lady Grace. Nothing so very New! but the continual Repetition of it, has at last rous'd my Brother to an Intemperance, that I tremble at.

Man. Have they had any Words upon it?

Lady Grace. He has not seen her since Yesterday.

Man. What! not at home all Night!

Lady Grace. About five this Morning, in she came! but with such Looks, and such an Equipage of Misfortunes, at her Heels——what can become of her?

Man. Has not my Lord seen her, say you?

Lady Grace. No! he chang'd his Bed last Night——I sat with him alone 'till twelve, in Expectation of her: But when the Clock struck, he started from his Chair, and grew incens'd to that degree, that had I not, almost on my Knees, disswaded him, he had ordered the Doors, that Instant, to have been locked against her.

Man. How terrible is his Situation? when the most justifiable Severities he can use against her, are liable to be the Mirth of all the dissolute Card-Tables in Town!

Lady Grace. 'Tis that, I know, has made him bear so long: but you, that feel for him, Mr. *Manly*, will assist him to support his Honour, and if possible, preserve his Quiet! therefore, I beg you don't leave the House, 'till One, or Both of them can be wrought to better Temper.

Man. How amiable is this concern, in you?

Lady Grace. For Heaven's sake don't mind me, but think of something to preserve us all.

Man. I shall not take the Merit of obeying your Commands, Madam, to serve my Lord——but pray Madam, let me into all that has past, since yester Night.

Lady Grace. When my Intreaties had prevail'd upon my Lord, not to make a Story for the Town, by so publick a Violence, as shutting her at once out of his Doors; he order'd the next Apartment to my Lady's to be made ready for him——while that was doing——I try'd, by all the little Arts I was Mistress of, to amuse him into Temper; in short, a silent Grief was all I could reduce him to——on this, we took our Leaves, and parted to our Repose: What his was, I imagine by my own: For I ne'er clos'd my Eyes. About five, as I told you, I heard my Lady at the Door; so I slipt on a Gown, and sat almost an Hour with her, in her own Chamber.

Man. What said she, when she did not find my Lord there?

Lady Grace. O! so far from being shock'd, or alarm'd at it; that she blest the Occasion! and said, that in her Condition, the Chat of a Female Friend was far preferable to the best Husband's company in the World.

Man. Where has she Spirits to support so much Insensibility?

Lady Grace. Nay! 'tis incredible! for though she had loſt every Shilling she had in the World, and ſtretch'd her Credit ev'n to breaking; she rallied her own Follies with such Vivacity, and painted the Penance, she knows she muſt undergo for them, in such ridiculous Lights, that had not my Concern for a Brother been too ſtrong for her Wit, she had almoſt disarm'd my Anger.

Man. Her Mind may have another Caſt by this time: the moſt flagrant Dispositions have their Hours of Anguish; which their Pride conceals from Company: But pray, Madam; how could she avoid coming down to dine?

Lady Grace. O! she took care of that, before she went to bed; by ordering her woman, whenever she was ask'd for, to say, she was not well.

Man. You have seen her since she was up, I presume?

Lady Grace. Up! I queſtion whether she be awake yet.

Man. Terrible! What a Figure does she make now! That Nature should throw away so much Beauty upon a Creature, to make such a slatternly Use of it!

Lady Grace. O fy! there is not a more elegant Beauty in Town, when she's dreſt.

Man. In my Eye, Madam, she that's early dreſt, has ten times her Elegance.

Lady Grace. But she won't be long now, I believe: for I think I see her Chocolate going up——Mrs. *Truſty*,——a hem!

Mrs. Truſty *comes to the Door.*

Man. [*Aside.*] Five a Clock in the Afternoon, for a Lady of Quality's Breakfaſt, is an elegant Hour, indeed! which to shew her more polite way of living too, I presume she eats in her Bed.

Lady Grace [*To Mrs.* Truſty.] And when she is up, I would be glad she would let me come to her Toilet—That's all, Mrs. *Truſty*.

Truſty. I will be sure to let her Ladyship know, Madam.

[*Exit Mrs.* Truſty.

Enter a Servant.

Serv. Sir *Francis Wronghead*, Sir, desires to speak with you.

Man. He comes unseasonably——what shall I do with him?

Lady Grace. O see him by all means, we shall have time enough; in the mean while I'll ſtep in, and have an Eye upon my Brother. Nay, nay, don't mind me——have business.——

Man. You muſt be obey'd—— [*Retreating while Lady* Grace *goes out.*
Desire Sir *Francis* to walk in—— [*Exit servant.*

I suppose by this time his wise Worship begins to find, that the Ballance of his Journey to *London* is on the wrong side.

Enter Sir Francis.

Sir *Francis*, your servant; how came I by the Favour of this extraordinary Visit?

Sir Fran. Ah! cousin!

Man. Why that sorrowful Face, man?

Sir Fran. I have no Friend alive but you——

Man. I am sorry for that——but what's the Matter?

Sir Fran. I have plaid the Fool by this Journey. I see now——for my bitter Wife——

Man. What of her?

Sir Fran. Is playing the Devil!

Man. Why truly, that's a Part that most of your fine Ladies begin with, as soon as they get to *London*.

Sir Fran. If I am a living Man, Cousin, she has made away with above two hundred and fifty Pound, since yesterday morning!

Man. Hah! I see a good House-wife will do a great deal of work in a little time.

Sir Fran. Work do they call it? Fine work indeed!

Man. Well! but how do you mean, made away with it? What, she has laid it out, may be——but I suppose you have an Account of it.

Sir Fran. Yes, yes, I have had the Account, indeed; but I mun needs say, it's a very sorry one.

Man. Pray, let's hear.

Sir Fran. Why, first, I let her have an hundred and fifty, to get things handsome about her, to let the World see that I was Some-body! and I thought that Sum very genteel.

Man. Indeed I think so; and, in the Country, might have serv'd her a Twelvemonth.

Sir Fran. Why so it might——but here in this fine Tawn, forsooth! it could not get through four and twenty hours——for, in half that time, it was all squandered away in Bawbles, and new-fashion'd Trumpery.

Man. O! for Ladies in *London*, Sir *Francis*, all this might be necessary.

Sir Fran. Noa! theere's the Plague on't! the Devil o' one usefull Thing do I see for it, but two pair of lac'd Shoes; and those stond me in three Paund three Shillings a Pair too.

Man. Dear Sir! this is nothing! Why we have City Wives here, that while their good Man is selling three Penny-worth of Sugar, will give you twenty Pound for a short Apron.

Sir Fran. Mercy on us! what a mortal poor Devil is a Husband!

Man. Well, but I hope, you have nothing else to complain of?

Sir Fran. Ah! would I could say so too—but there's another hundred behind yet, that goes more to my Heart, than all that went before it.

Man. And how might that be disposed of?

Sir Fran. Troth, I am almost asham'd to tell you.

Man. Out with it.

Sir Fran. Why she has been at an Assembly.

Man. What, since I saw you! I thought you had all Supt at home last Night?

Sir Fran. Why, so we did——and all as merry as Grigs——I'cod! my Heart was so open, that I toss'd another hundred into her Apron, to go out early this Morning with——But the Cloth was no sooner taken away, than in comes my Lady *Townly* here (——who between you and I—— mum! has had the Devil to pay yonder——) with another rantipol Dame of Quality, and out they must have her, they said, to introduce her at my Lady *Noble*'s Assembly forsooth——a few Words, you may be sure, made the Bargain——so, bawnce! and away they drive as if the Devil had got into the Coach-box—so about four or five in the Morning——home again comes Madam, with her Eyes a Foot deep in her Head——and my poor hundred Pound left behind her at the Hazard-Table.

Man. All lost at dice!

Sir Fran. Every Shilling———among a Parcel of Pig-tail Puppies, and Pale-fac'd Women of Quality.

Man. But pray, Sir *Francis*, how came you, after you found her so ill an House-wife of one Sum, so soon to trust her with another?

Sir Fran. Why, truly, I mun say that was partly my own fault: for if I had not been a Blab of my Tongue, I believe that last hundred might have been sav'd.

Man. How so?

Sir Fran. Why, like an Owl, as I was, out of good-will, forsooth, partly to keep her in Humour, I must needs tell her of the thousand Pound a year, I had just got the Promise of——I'cod! she lays her Claws upon it that moment——said it was all owing to her Advice, and truly she would have her share on't.

Man. What, before you had it yourself?

Sir Fran. Why ay! that's what I told her——My Dear, said I, mayhap I mayn't receive the first Quarter on't this half year.

Man. Sir *Francis*, I have heard you with a great deal of Patience, and I really feel Compassion for you.

Sir Fran. Truly, and well you may, Cousin, for I don't see that my Wife's Goodness is a bit the better, for bringing to *London*.

Man. If you remember, I gave you a Hint of it.

Sir Fran. Why ay, it's true you did so: but the Devil himself could not have believ'd she would have rid post to him.

Man. Sir, if you stay but a fortnight in this Town, you will every Day see hundreds as fast upon the gallop, as she is.

Sir Fran. Ah! this *London* is a base place indeed——waunds, if things should happen to go wrong with me at *Westminster*, at this rate, how the Devil shall I keep out of a Jayl?

Man. Why truly, there seems to me but one way to avoid it.

Sir Fran. Ah! would you could tell me that, Cousin.

Man. The way lies plain before you, Sir; the same Road that brought you hither will carry you safe home again.

Sir Fran. Ods-flesh! cousin, what! and leave a thousand Pound a Year behind me?

Man. Pooh! pooh! leave any thing behind you, but your Family, and you are a Saver by it.

Sir Fran. Ay, but consider, Cousin, what a scurvy Figure I shall make in the Country, if I come dawn withawt it!

Man. You will make a much more lamentable Figure in a Jayl, without it.

Sir Fran. May hap 'at yow have no great Opinion of it then, Cousin?

Man. Sir *Francis*, to do you the Service of a real Friend, I must speak very plainly to you: you don't yet see half the Ruin that's before you!

Sir Fran. Good-lack! how may yow mean, Cousin?

Man. In one Word, your whole Affairs stand thus——In a Week, you will lose your Seat, at *Westminster*: In a Fortnight, my lady will run you into a Jayl, by keeping the best Company————In four and twenty Hours, your Daughter will run away with a Sharper, because she han't been used to better Company: And your Son will steal into Marriage with a cast Mistress, because he has not been used to any Company at all.

Sir Fran. I'th' name of goodness why should you think all this?

Man. Because I have proof of it; in short, I know so much of their Secrets, that if all this is not prevented to-night, it will be out of your Power to do it, to-morrow morning.

Sir Fran. Mercy upon us! you frighten me————Well, Sir, I will be govern'd by yow: But what am I to do in this Case?

Man. I have not time here to give you proper Instructions: but about eight this Ev'ning, I'll call at your Lodgings: and there you shall have full Conviction, how much I have it at Heart, to serve you.

Enter a Servant.

Serv. Sir, my Lord desires to speak with you.

Man. I'll wait upon him.

Sir Fran. Well then, I'll go straight home, naw.

Man. At eight depend upon me.

Sir Fran. Ah dear Cousin! I shall be bound to you as long as I live. Mercy deliver us! what a terrible Journey have I made on't!

[*Exeunt severally.*

The SCENE *opens to a Dressing room. Lady* Townly, *as juſt up, walks to her Toilet, leaning on Mrs.* Truſty.

Truſty. Dear Madam, what should make your Ladyship so out of order?

Lady Town. How is it possible to be well, where one is kill'd for want of Sleep?

Truſty. Dear me! it was so long before you rung, Madam, I was in hopes your Ladyship had been finely compos'd.

Lady Town. Compos'd! why I have layn in an Inn here! this House is worse than an Inn with ten Stage-coaches! What between my Lord's impertinent People of Business in a Morning, and the intollerable thick Shoes of Footmen at Noon, one has not a wink all Night.

Truſty. Indeed, Madam, it's a great pity, my Lord can't be persuaded into the Hours of People of Quality——Though I muſt say that, Madam, your Ladyship is certainly the beſt Matrimonial Menager, in Town.

Lady Town. Oh! you are quite miſtaken, *Truſty!* I menage very ill! for, notwithſtanding all the Power I have, by never being over-fond of my Lord——yet I want Money infinitely oftner than he is willing to give it me.

Truſty. Ah! if his Lordship could but be brought to play himself, Madam, then he might feel what it is to want Money.

Lady Town. Oh! don't talk of it! do you know that I am undone, *Truſty?*

Truſty. Mercy forbid, Madam!

Lady Town. Broke! ruin'd! plunder'd!——ſtripp'd, even to a Confiscation of my laſt Guinea.

Truſty. You don't tell me so, Madam!

Lady Townly. And where to raise ten Pound in the World——What is to be done, *Truſty?*

Truſty. Truly, I wish I was wise enough to tell you, Madam: but may be your Ladyship may have a run of better Fortune, upon some of the good Company that comes here to-night.

Lady Town. But I have not a single Guinea, to try my Fortune!

Truſty. Hah! that's a bad Business indeed, Madam——Adad! I have a Thought in my Head Madam, if it is not too late——

Lady Town. Out with it quickly then, I beseech thee!

Truſty. Has not the Steward something of fifty Pound Madam, that you left in his hands, to pay somebody about this time?

Lady Town. O! ay! I had forgot——'twas to—a—what's his filthy Name?

Trusty. Now I remember, Madam, 'twas to Mr. *Lutestring*, your old Mercer, that your Ladyship turn'd off, about a Year ago, because he would trust you no longer.

Lady Town. The very Wretch! if he has not paid it, run quickly, Dear *Trusty*, and bid him bring it hither immediately——[*Exit* Trusty.] Well! sure mortal Woman never had such Fortune! Five! Five, and Nine, against poor Seven for ever!——No! after that horrid Bar of my Chance, that Lady *Wronghead's* fatal red Fist upon the Table, I saw it was impossible, ever, to win another Stake——Sit up all Night! lose all one's Money! dream of winning Thousands! wake without a Shilling! and Then——how like a Hag I look! In short——the Pleasures of Life, are not worth this Disorder! If it were not for Shame now, I could almost think, Lady *Grace's* sober Scheme not quite so ridiculous——If my wise Lord could but hold his Tongue for a Week, 'tis odds, but I should hate the Town in a Fortnight——But I will not be driven out of it, that's positive! [Trusty *returns.*

Trusty. O Madam! there is no bearing it! Mr. *Lutestring* was just let in at the Door, as I came to the Stair Foot; and the Steward is now actually paying him the Money in the Hall.

Lady Town. Run to the Stair-case Head, again——and scream to him, that I must speak with him this Instant. [Trusty *runs out, and speaks.*

Trusty. Mr. *Poundage*——a hem! Mr. *Poundage*, a word ⎫
with you quickly!   ⎪
Pound. [*within.*] I'll come to you presently.   ⎪
Trusty. Presently won't do, Man, you must come this ⎬ *without.*
minute.   ⎪
Pound. I am but just paying a little Money, here.   ⎪
Trusty. Cods my life! paying Money? is the man distracted? ⎪
Come here I tell you, to my Lady, this Moment, quick! ⎭
                                    [Trusty *returns.*

Lady Town. Will the Monster come, or no?——

Trusty. Yes, I hear him now, Madam, he is hobling up, as fast as he can.

Lady Town. Don't let him come in—for he will keep such a babbling about his Accounts,——my Brain is not able to bear him.

[Poundage *comes to the Door with a Money-bag in his hand.*

Trusty. O! it's well you are come, Sir! where's the fifty Pound?

Pound. Why here it is; if you had not been in such haste, I should have paid it by this time——the Man's now writing a Receipt, below, for it.

Trusty. No matter! my Lady says, you must not pay him with that Money, there is not enough, it seems; there's a Pistole, and a Guinea, that is not good, in it——besides there is a Mistake in the Account too

———[*Twitching the bag from him.*] But she is not at leisure to examine it now; so you must bid Mr. What-d'ye-call-um call another time.

Lady Town. What is all that Noise there?

Pound. Why and it please your Ladyship———

Lady Town. Pr'ythee! don't plague me now, but do as you were order'd.

Pound. Nay what your Ladyship pleases, Madam———

[*Exit* Poundage.

Trusty. There they are Madam———[*Pours the money out of the Bag.*] The pretty Things———were so near falling into a nasty Tradesman's hands, I protest it made me tremble for them———I fancy your Ladyship had as good give me that bad Guinea, for luck's sake———thank you Madam.

[*Takes a Guinea.*

Lady Town. Why, I did not bid you take it.

Trusty. No, but your Ladyship look'd as if you were just going to bid me, and so I was willing to save you the trouble of speaking, Madam.

Lady Town. Well! thou hast deserv'd it, and so, for once———but hark! don't I hear the Man making a noise yonder? Though I think now we may compound for a little of his ill humour———

Trusty. I'll listen.

Lady Town. Pry'thee do.   [*Trusty goes to the door.*

Trusty. Ay! they are at it, Madam———he is in a bitter Passion, with poor *Poundage*———bless me! I believe he'll beat him———mercy on us! how the wretch swears!

Lady Town. And a sober Citizen too! that's a shame!

Trusty. Hah! I think all's silent, of a sudden———may be the Porter has knock'd him down—I'll step and see———   [*Exit* Trusty.

Lady Town. Those Trades-people are the troublesomest Creatures! no Words will satisfy them!   [*Trusty returns.*

Trusty. O Madam! undone! undone! my Lord has just bolted out upon the Man, and is hearing all his pitiful Story over———if your Ladyship pleases to come hither, you may hear him yourself!

Lady Town. No matter: it will come round presently: I shall have it all from my Lord; without losing a word by the way, I'll warrant you.

Trusty. O lud! Madam! here's my Lord just coming in.

Lady Town. Do you get out of the way then. [*Exit* Trusty.] I am afraid I want Spirits! but he will soon give 'em me.

Enter Lord Townly.

Lord Town. How comes it, Madam, that a Tradesman dares be clamorous, in my House, for Money due to him, from you?

Lady Town. You don't expect, my Lord, that I should answer for other Peoples Impertinence!

Lord Town. I expect, Madam, you should answer for your own Extravagances, that are the Occasion of it——I thought I had given you Money three months ago, to satisfy all these sort of People!

Lady Town. Yes, but you see they Are never to be satisfied.

Lord Town. Nor am I, Madam, longer to be abus'd thus! what's become of the last five hundred, I gave you?

Lady Town. Gone.

Lord Town. Gone! what way, Madam?

Lady Town. Half the Town over, I believe by this time.

Lord Town. 'Tis well! I see Ruin will make no Impression, 'till it falls upon You.

Lady Town. In short, my Lord, if Money is always the Subject of our Conversation, I shall make you no Answer.

Lord Town. Madam, Madam! I will be heard, and Make you answer.

Lady Town. Make me! then I must tell you, my Lord, this is a Language I have not been us'd to, and I won't bear it.

Lord Town. Come! come, Madam, you shall bear a great deal more, before I part with you.

Lady Town. My Lord, if you insult me, you will have as much to bear, on your side, I can assure you.

Lord Town. Pooh! your Spirit grows ridiculous——you have neither Honour, Worth, or Innocence, to support it!

Lady Town. You'll find, at least, I have Resentment! and do you look well to the Provocation!

Lord Town. After those you have given me, Madam, 'tis almost Infamous to talk with you.

Lady Town. I scorn your Imputation and your Menaces! The Narrowness of your Heart's your Monitor! 'tis there! there my lord, you are wounded; you have less to complain of than many Husbands of an equal Rank to you.

Lord Town. Death, Madam! do you presume upon your Corporal Merit! that your Person's less tainted, than your Mind! is it there! there alone an honest Husband can be injur'd? Have you not every other Vice that can debase your Birth, or stain the Heart of Woman? Is not your Health, your Beauty, Husband, Fortune, Family disclaim'd, for Nights consum'd in Riot and Extravagance? The Wanton does no more; if she conceals her Shame, does less: And sure the Dissolute avow'd, as sorely wrongs my Honour, and my Quiet.

Lady Town. I see, my Lord, what sort of Wife might please you.

Lord Town. Ungrateful Woman! could you have seen yourself, you in yourself had seen her——I am amaz'd our Legislature has left no Precedent of a Divorce for this more visible Injury, this Adultery of the Mind, as well as that of the Person! when a Woman's whole Heart is alienated to Pleasures I have no Share in, what is't to me whether a Black Ace, or a powder'd Coxcomb has Possession of it?

Lady Town. If you have not found it yet, my Lord; this is not the way to get possession of mine, depend upon it.

Lord Town. That, Madam, I have long despair'd of; and since our Happiness cannot be mutual, 'tis fit, that with our Hearts, our Persons too should separate.——This House you sleep no more in! Tho' your Content might grosly feed upon the Dishonour of a Husband, yet my Desires would starve upon the Features of a Wife.

Lady Town. Your Style, my Lord, is much of the same Delicacy with your Sentiments of Honour.

Lord Town. Madam, Madam! this is no time for Compliments——I have done with you.

Lady Town. If we had never met, my Lord, I had not broke my Heart for it! but have a Care! I may not, perhaps, be so easily recall'd as you imagine.

Lord Town. Recall'd—Who's there!

Enter a Servant.

Desire my Sister and Mr. *Manly* to walk up.

Lady Town. My Lord, you may proceed as you please, but pray what Indiscretions have I committed, that are not daily practis'd by a hundred other Women of Quality?

Lord Town. 'Tis not the Number of ill Wives, Madam, that makes the Patience of a Husband less contemptible: and tho' a bad one may be the best Man's Lot, yet he'll make a better figure in the World, that keeps his Misfortunes Out of Doors, than he that tamely keeps her Within.

Lady Town. I don't know what Figure you may make, my Lord, but I shall have no Reason to be asham'd of mine, in whatever company I may meet you.

Lord Town. Be sparing of your Spirit, Madam, you'll need it to support you.

Enter Lady Grace *and* Manly.

Mr. *Manly*, I have an Act of Friendship to beg of you, which wants more Apologies, than Words can make for it.

Man. Then pray make none, my Lord, that I may have the greater Merit in obliging you.

Lord Town. Sister, I have the same Excuse to intreat of you too.

Lady Grace. To your Request, I beg, my Lord.

Lord Town. Thus then——as you both were present at my ill-consider'd Marriage, I now desire you each will be a Witness of my determin'd Separation——I know, Sir, your Good-nature, and my Sister's, must be shock'd at the Office I impose on you! But, as I don't ask your Justification of my Cause; so I hope you are conscious——that an ill Woman can't reproach you, if you are silent, upon her side.

Man. My lord, I never thought, 'till now, it could be difficult to oblige you.

Lady Grace. [*Aside.*] Heavens! how I tremble!

Lord Town. For you, my lady *Townly*, I need not here repeat the Provocations of my parting with you—the World, I fear, is too well inform'd of them.——For the good Lord, your dead Father's sake, I will still support you, as his Daughter——As the lord *Townly*'s Wife, you have had every thing a fond Husband could bestow, and (to our mutual Shame I speak it) more than happy Wives desire——But those Indulgences must end! State, Equipage and Splendor but ill become the Vices that misuse 'em——The decent Necessaries of Life shall be supply'd——but not one Article to Luxury! Not even the Coach, that waits to carry you from hence, shall you ever use again! Your tender Aunt, my Lady *Lovemore*, with Tears, this Morning has consented to receive you; where if Time, and your Condition brings you to a due Reflection, your Allowance shall be increas'd——But, if you still are lavish of your little, or pine for past licentious Pleasures, that little shall be less! nor will I call that Soul my Friend, that names you in my Hearing!

Lady Grace. My Heart Bleeds for her! [*Aside.*

Lord Town. O *Manly!* look there! turn back thy Thoughts with me, and witness to my growing Love! there was a time when I believ'd that Form incapable of Vice, or of Decay! There I propos'd the Partner of an easy Home! There! I, for ever, hop'd to find a chearful Companion, an agreeable Intimate, a faithful Friend, a useful Help-mate, and a tender Mother——But oh! how bitter now the Disappointment!

Man. The World is different in its Sense of Happiness: Offended as you are, I know you still will be just.

Lord Town. Fear me not.

Man. This last Reproach, I see, has struck her. [*Aside.*

Lord Town. No, let me not (though I this Moment cast her from my Heart for ever) let me not urge her Punishment beyond her Crimes—— I know the World is fond of any Tale that feeds its appetite of Scandal: And as I am conscious, Severities of this kind seldom fail of Imputations too gross to mention, I here, before you both, acquit her of the least Suspicion rais'd against the Honour of my Bed. Therefore, when abroad her Conduct may be question'd, do her Fame that Justice.

Lady Town. O sister! [*Turns to Lady* Grace *weeping.*

Lord Town. When I am spoken of, where without Favour this Action may be canvass'd, relate but half my Provocations, and give me up to Censure. *Going.*

Lady Town. Support me! save me! hide me from the World!

                                     [Falls on Lady Grace's *neck.*

Lord Town. [*Returning.*]——I had forgot me——You have no Share in my Resentment, therefore, as you have liv'd in Friendship with her, Your Parting may admit of gentler Terms, than suit the Honour of an injur'd Husband.   *[Offers to go out.*

Man. [*Interposing.*] My Lord, you must not, shall not leave her, thus! One Moment's Stay can do your Cause no wrong! If Looks can speak the Anguish of the Heart, I'll answer with my Life, there's something labouring in her Mind, that would you bear the hearing, might deserve it.

Lord Town. Consider! since we no more can meet; press not my Staying, to insult her.

Lady Town. Yet stay, my Lord——the little I would say, will not deserve an Insult; and Undeserv'd, I know your Nature gives it not. But as you've call'd in Friends, to witness your Resentment, let them be equal Hearers of my last reply.

Lord Town. I shan't refuse you that, Madam——be it so.

Lady Town. My Lord, you ever have complain'd, I wanted Love; but as you kindly have allow'd I never gave it to another; so when you hear the Story of my Heart, though you may still complain, you will not wonder at my Coldness.

Lady Grace. This promises a Reverse of Temper.   *[Apart.*

Man. This, my Lord, you are concern'd to hear!

Lord Town. Proceed, I am attentive.

Lady Town. Before I was your Bride, my Lord, the flattering World had talk'd me into Beauty; which, at my Glass, my youthful Vanity confirm'd: Wild with that Fame, I thought Mankind my Slaves, I triumph'd over Hearts, while all my Pleasure was their Pain: Yet was my own so equally insensible to all, that when a Father's firm Commands enjoyn'd me to make choice of One; I even there declin'd the Liberty he gave, and to his own Election yielded up my Youth——His tender Care, my Lord, directed him to You——Our Hands were join'd! But still my Heart was wedded to its Folly! My only Joy was Power, Command, Society, Profuseness, and to lead in Pleasures! The Husband's Right to Rule, I thought a vulgar Law, which only the Deform'd, or Meanly-spirited obey'd! I knew no Directors, but my Passions, no Master but my Will! Even you, my Lord, some time o'ercome by Love, were pleas'd with my Delights; nor, then, foresaw this mad Misuse of your Indulgence——And, though I call myself Ungrateful, while I own it, yet, as a Truth, it cannot be deny'd ——That kind Indulgence has undone me! it added Strength to my habitual Failings, and in a Heart thus warm, in wild unthinking Life, no wonder if the gentler Sense of Love was lost.

Lord Town. O *Manly!* where has this Creature's Heart been buried? } *Apart.*

Man. If yet recoverable——How vaſt a Treasure? }

Lady Town. What I have said, my Lord, is not my Excuse, but my Confession! My Errors (give 'em if you please, a harder Name) cannot be defended! No! What's in its Nature Wrong, no Words can Palliate, no Plea can Alter! What then remains in my Condition, but Resignation to your Pleasure? Time only can convince you of my Future Conduct: Therefore, 'till I have liv'd an Object of Forgiveness, I dare not hope for Pardon——The Penance of a lonely contrite Life were little to the Innocent; but to have deserv'd this Separation, will ſtrow perpetual Thorns upon my Pillow.

Lady Grace. O happy, heavenly Hearing!

Lady Town. Siſter, farewell! [*Kissing her.*] Your Virtue needs no warning from the Shame that falls on me: But when you think I have atton'd my Follies paſt,——persuade your injur'd Brother to forgive them.

Lord Town. No Madam! Your Errors thus renounc'd, this Inſtant are forgotten! So deep, so due a Sense of them, has made you, what my utmoſt Wishes form'd, and all my Heart has sigh'd for.

Lady Town. [*Turning to Lady* Grace.] How odious does this Goodness make me!

Lady Grace. How amiable your thinking so?

Lord Town. Long-parted Friends, that pass through easy Voyages of Life, receive but common Gladness in their Meeting: But from a Ship-wreck sav'd, we mingle Tears with our Embraces.

[*Embracing Lady* Townly.

Lady Town. What Words! what Love! what Duty can repay such Obligations!

Lord Town. Preserve but this Desire to please, your Power is endless.

Lady Town. Oh!——'till this Moment, never did I know, my Lord, I had a Heart to give you!

Lord Town. By Heav'n! this yielding Hand, when firſt ıt gave you to my Wishes, presented not a Treasure more desirable! O *Manly!* Siſter! as you have often shar'd in my Disquiet, partake of my Felicity! my new-born Joy! see here the Bride of my Desires! this may be called my Wedding-day!

Lady Grace. Siſter! (for now methinks that Name is dearer to my Heart than ever) let me congratulate the Happiness that opens to you.

Man. Long, long, and mutual may it flow——

Lord Town. To make our Happiness compleat, my Dear, join here with me to give a Hand, that amply will repay the Obligation.

Lady Town. Siſter! a Day like this——

Lady Grace. Admits of no Excuse against the general Joy.

> [*Gives her hand to* Manly.

Man. A Joy like mine——despairs of Words to speak it.

Lord Town. O *Manly!* how the Name of Friend endears the Brother!

> [*Embracing him.*

Man. Your Words, my Lord, will warn me, to deserve them.

Enter a Servant.

Serv. My Lord, the Apartments are full of Masqueraders——And some People of Quality there desire to see your Lordship and my Lady.

Lady Town. I thought, my Lord, your Orders had forbid this Revelling?

Lord Town. No, my Dear, *Manly* has desir'd their Admittance to-night, it seems, upon a particular Occasion———Say we will wait upon them instantly. [*Exit Servant.*

Lady Town. I shall be but ill Company to them.

Lord Town. No matter: not to see them, would on a sudden to be too particular. Lady *Grace* will assist you to entertain them.

Lady Town. With her, my Lord, I shall be always easy——Sister, to your unerring Virtue, I commit the Guidance of my future Days.

> Never the Paths of Pleasure more to tread,
> But where your guarded Innocence shall lead.
> For in the married State the World must own,
> Divided Happiness was never known.
> To make it mutual, Nature points the Way:
> Let Husbands govern: Gentle Wives obey.

> [*Exeunt.*

The SCENE *opening to another Apartment discovers a great Number of People in Masquerade, talking all together, and playing one upon another:* Lady Wronghead *as a Shepherdess;* Jenny, *as a nun; the Squire as a running Footman; and the Count in a Domino. After some time, Lord and Lady* Townly, *with Lady* Grace, *enter to them unmask'd.*

Lord Town. So! here's a great deal of Company.

Lady Grace. A great many People, my Lord, but no Company——as you'll find——for here's one now, that seems to have a mind to entertain us.

> [*A Mask, after some affected Gesture, makes up to Lady* Townly.

Mask. Well, dear Lady *Townly,* shan't we see you by-and-by?

Lady Town. I don't know you, Madam.

Mask. Don't you, seriously? [*In a squeaking Tone.*

Lady Town. Not I, indeed.

Mask. Well, that's charming! but can't you guess?

Lady Town. Yes, I could guess wrong, I believe.

Mask. That's what I'd have you do.

Lady Town. But, Madam, if I don't know you at all, is not that as well?

Mask. Ay, but you do know me.

Lady Town. Dear Sister, take her off o' my Hands; there's no bearing this.   [*Apart.*

Lady Grace. I fancy I know you, Madam.

Mask. I fancy you don't: What makes you think you do?

Lady Grace. Because I have heard you talk.

Mask. Ay, but you don't know my Voice, I'm sure.

Lady Grace. There is something in your Wit and Humour, Madam, so very much your own, it is impossible you can be any Body but my Lady *Trifle.*

Mask. [*Unmasking.*] Dear Lady *Grace!* thou art a charming Creature.

Lady Grace. Is there no Body else we know here?

Mask. O dear, yes! I have found out fifty already.

Lady Grace. Pray, who are they?

Mask. O charming Company! there's Lady *Ramble*———Lady *Riot* ———Lady *Kill-Care*———Lady *Squander*———Lady *Strip*———Lady *Pawn*———and the Dutchess of *Single-Guinea.*

Lord Town. Is it not hard, my Dear! that people of Sense and Probity, are sometimes forc'd to seem fond of such Company?

Lady Town. My Lord, it will always give me Pain to remember their Acquaintance, but none to drop it immediately.

} *Apart.*

Lady Grace. But you have given us no Account of the Men, Madam. Are they good for any thing?

Mask. O yes! you must know, I always find out them, by their Endeavours to find out me.

Lady Grace. Pray, who are they?

Mask. Why, for your Men of Tip-top Wit and Pleasure, about Town, there's———my Lord *Bite*———Lord *Arch-wag*———Young *Brazen-Wit* ———Lord *Timberdown*———Lord *Joint-Life*———and———Lord *Mortgage.*

Then for your pretty Fellows only———there's Sir *Powder Peacock*——— Lord *Lapwing,*———*Billy Magpye*———Beau *Frightful*———Sir *Paul Plaister-crown*, and the Marquis of *Monkeyman.*

Lady Grace. Right! and these are the fine Gentlemen that never want Elbow-room at an Assembly.

Mask. The rest, I suppose, by their tawdry, hired Habits, are Tradesmens Wives, Inns-of-Court Beaux, *Jews*, and kept Mistresses.

Lord Town. An admirable Collection!

Lady Grace. Well, of all our Public Diversions, I am amaz'd how this that is so very expensive, and has so little to shew for it, can draw so much Company together.

Lord Town. O! if it were not Expensive, the better sort would not come into it: And because Money can purchase a Ticket, the Common People scorn to be kept out of it.

Mask. Right, my Lord. Poor Lady *Grace!* I suppose you are under the same Aſtonishment, that an Opera should draw so much good Company.

Lady Grace. Not at all, Madam; it is an easier matter sure to gratifie the ear, than the Underſtanding. But have you no Notion, Madam, of receiving Pleasure and Profit at the same time?

Mask. Oh! quite none! unless it be sometimes winning a great Stake; laying down a *Vole, sans prendre* may come up, to the profitable Pleasure you were speaking of.

Lord Town. You seem attentive, my Dear?

Lady Town. I am, my Lord; and amaz'd at my own Follies, so ſtrongly painted in another Woman. } *Apart.*

Lady Grace. But see, my Lord, we had beſt adjourn our Debate, I believe, for here are some Masks that seem to have a mind to divert other People as well as themselves.

Lord Town. The leaſt we can do is to give them a clear Stage then.

[*A dance of Masks here, in various Charaſters.*
This was a Favour extraordinary.

Enter Manly.

O *Manly!* I thought we had loſt you.

Man. I ask Pardon, my Lord; but I have been oblig'd to look a little after my Country Family.

Lord Town. Well, pray, what have you done with them?

Man. They are all in the House here, among the Masks, my Lord; if your Lordship has Curiosity enough, to ſtep into a lower Apartment, in three Minutes I'll give you an ample Account of them.

Lord Town. O! by all means: We will wait upon you.

[*The Scene shuts upon the Masks to a smaller Apartment.*

Manly *re-enters, with Sir* Francis Wronghead.

Sir Fran. Well, Cousin, you have made my very Hair ſtand on an End! Waunds! if what you tell me be true, I'll ſtuff my whole Family into a Stage-Coach, and trundle them into the Country on *Monday* morning.

Man. Stick to that, Sir, and we may yet find a way to redeem all: In the mean time, place yourself behind this Screen, and for the Truth of what I have told you, take the Evidence of your own Senses: But be sure you keep close 'till I give you the Signal.

Sir Fran. Sir, I'll warrant you——Ah! my Lady! my Lady *Wrong-head!* What a bitter Business have you drawn me into?

Man. Hush! to your Post; here comes one Couple already.

[*Sir* Francis *retires behind the screen. Exit* Manly.

Enter Myrtilla *with Squire* Richard.

Squ. Rich. What! is this the Doctor's Chamber?

Myr. Yes, yes, speak softly.

Squ. Rich. Well, but where is he?

Myr. He'll be ready for us presently, but he says he can't do us the good Turn, without Witnesses: So, when the Count and your Sister come, you know, he and you may be Fathers for one another.

Squ. Rich. Well, well, Tit for Tat! ay, ay, that will be friendly.

Myr. And see! here they come.

Enter Count Basset, *and Miss* Jenny.

Count Bas. So, so, here's your Brother, and his Bride, before us, my Dear.

Jenny. Well, I vow, my Heart's at my Mouth still! I thought I should never have got rid of Mama! but while she stood gaping upon the Dance, I gave her the Slip! Lawd! do but feel how it beats here.

Count Bas. O the pretty Flutterer! I protest, my Dear, you have put mine into the same Palpitation!

Jenny. Ah! you say so——but let's see now——O Lud! I vow it thumps purely—well, well, I see it will do, and so where's the Parson?

Count Bas. Mrs. *Myrtilla,* will you be so good as to see if the Doctor's ready for us?

Myr. He only staid for you, Sir: I'll fetch him immediately.

[*Exit* Myrtilla.

Jenny. Pray, Sir, am not I to take Place of Mama, when I'am a Countess?

Count Bas. No doubt on't, my Dear.

Jenny. O Lud! how her Back will be up then, when she meets me at an Assembly? or You and I in our Coach and Six, at *Hyde-Park* together?

Count Bas. Ay, or when she hears the Box-keepers, at an Opera, call out—*The Countess of* Basset's *Servants!*

Jenny. Well, I say it, that will be delicious! And then, mayhap, to have a fine Gentleman with a Star and What-d'ye-callum Ribbon, lead me to my Chair, with his Hat under his Arm all the way! Hold up, says the Chairman, and so, says I, my Lord, your Humble Servant. I suppose, Madam, says he, we shall see you at my Lady *Quadrille's!* Ay, ay, to be sure, my Lord, says I———So in troops I, with my Hoop stuff'd up to my Forehead! and away they trot; swing! swang! with my Tassils

(257)

dangling, and my Flambeaux blazing, and————Oh! it's a charming Thing to be a Woman of Quality!

Count Bas. Well! I see that plainly, my Dear, there's ne'er a Dutchess of 'em will become an Equipage like you.

Jenny. Well, well, do you find Equipage, and I'll find Airs, I warrant you.   [*Sings.*

Squ. Rich. Troth! I think this Masquerading's the merriest Game that ever I saw in my Life! Thof, in my mind, and there were but a little Wrestling, or Cudgel-playing naw, it would help it hugely. But what a-Rope makes the Parson stay so?

Count Bas. Oh! here he comes, I believe.

Enter Myrtilla *with a Constable.*

Const. Well, Madam, pray which is the Party that wants a Spice of my Office here?

Myr. That's the Gentleman.   [*Pointing to the Count.*

Count Bas. Hey-day! what, in Masquerade, Doctor?

Const. Doctor! Sir, I believe you have mistaken your Man: But if you are called Count *Basset,* I have a *Billet-doux* in my Hand for you, that will set you right presently.

Count Bas. What the Devil's the meaning of all this?

Const. Only my Lord Chief-Justice's warrant against you for Forgery, Sir.

Count Bas. Blood and Thunder!

Const. And so, Sir, if you please to pull off your Fool's Frock there, I'll wait upon you to the next Justice of Peace immediately.

Jenny. O dear me! what's the matter?   [*Trembling.*

Count Bas. O! nothing, only a Masquerading Frolick, my Dear.

Squ. Rich. Oh oh! is that all?

Sir Fran. No Sirrah! that is not all.
    [*Sir* Francis *coming softly behind the Squire, knocks him down with his Cane.*

Enter Manly.

Squ. Rich. O Lawd! O Lawd! he has beaten my Brains out!

Man. Hold, hold, Sir *Francis,* have a little Mercy upon my poor Godson, pray Sir.

Sir Fran. Waunds, Cozen, I han't Patience.

Count Bas. Manly! nay, then I am Blown to the Devil.   [*Aside.*

Squ. Rich. O my Head! my Head!

Enter Lady Wronghead.

Lady Wrong. What's the Matter here, Gentlemen? for Heavens sake! What, are you murdering my Children?

(258)

Con. No, no, Madam! no murther! only a little Suspicion of Felony, that's all.

Sir Fran. [*to* Jenny.] And for you, Mrs. *Hot-upon't,* I could find in my Heart to make you wear that Habit, as long as you live, you Jade you. Do you know, Hussy, that you were within two Minutes of marrying a Pick-Pocket?

Count Bas. So, so, all's out, I find.   [*Aside.*

Jenny. O the mercy! why, pray, Papa, is not the Count a Man of Quality then?

Sir Fran. O yes! one of the unhang'd ones, it seems.

Lady Wrong. Aside.] Married! O the confident Thing! There was his urgent Business then——slighted for her! I han't Patience!—and for ought I know, I have been all this while making a Friendship with a Highway-man!

Man. Mr. Constable! secure that Door there.

Sir Fran. Ah my Lady! my Lady! this comes of your Journey to *London!* but now I have a Frolick of my own, Madam; therefore pack up your Trumpery this very Night, for the Moment my Horses are able to crawl, you and your Brats shall make a Journey into the Country again.

Lady Wrong. Indeed, you are mistaken, Sir *Francis*——I shall not stir out of Town yet, I promise you.

Sir Fran. Not stir! Waunds! Madam——

Man. Hold, Sir,—if you'll give me leave a little—I fancy I shall prevail with my Lady to think better on't.

Sir Fran. Ah! Cousin, you are a Friend indeed!

Man. [*Apart to my Lady.*] Look you, Madam, as to the Favour you design'd me, in sending this spurious Letter inclosed to my Lady *Grace*, all the Revenge I have taken, is to have sav'd your Son and Daughter from Ruin——Now if you will take them fairly and quietly into the Country again, I will save your Ladyship from Ruin.

Lady Wrong. What do you mean, Sir?

Man. Why, Sir *Francis*——shall never know what is in this Letter; look upon it. How it came into my Hands you shall know at leisure.

Lady Wrong. Ha! my *Billet-Doux* to the Count! and an Appointment in it! I shall sink with Confusion!

Man. What shall I say to Sir *Francis*, Madam?

Lady Wrong. Dear Sir! I am in such a Trembling! preserve my Honour, and I am all Obedience!   [*Apart to* Manly.

Man. Sir *Francis*——my Lady is ready to receive your Commands for her Journey, whenever you please to appoint it.

Sir Fran. Ah Cousin! I doubt I am oblig'd to you for it.

Man. Come, come, Sir *Francis!* take it as you find it. Obedience in a

Wife is a good thing, though it were never so wonderful!——And now, Sir, we have nothing to do but dispose of this Gentleman.

Count Bas. Mr. *Manly!* Sir! I hope you won't ruin me.

Man. Did not you forge this Note for five hundred Pound, Sir?

Count Bas. Sir——I see you know the World, and therefore I shall not pretend to prevaricate——But it has hurt no Body yet, Sir! I beg you will not stigmatize me! since you have spoil'd my Fortune in One Family, I hope you won't be so cruel to a young Fellow, as to put it out of my Power, Sir, to make it in Another, Sir!

Man. Look you, Sir, I have not much Time to waste with you: But if you expect Mercy yourself, you must shew it to one, you have been cruel to.

Count Bas. Cruel, Sir!

Man. Have not you ruin'd this young Woman?

Count Bas. I Sir!

Man. I know you have——therefore you can't blame her, if, in the Fact you are charg'd with, she is a principal Witness against you. However, you have one, and one only Chance to get off with. Marry her this Instant——and you take off her Evidence.

Count Bas. Dear Sir!

Man. No words, Sir; a wife, or a *Mittimus*.

Count Bas. Lord, Sir! this is the most unmerciful Mercy!

Man. A private Penance, or a publick one——Constable!

Count Bas. Hold, Sir, since you are pleas'd to give me my Choice; I will not make so ill a Compliment to the Lady, as not to give her the Preference.

Man. It must be done this Minute, Sir: the Chaplain you expected is still within call.

Count Bas. Well, Sir,——since it must be so——Come, Spouse—— I am not the First of the Fraternity that has run his Head into one Noose, to keep it out of another.

Myr. Come, Sir, don't repine: Marriage is, at worst, but playing upon the Square.

Count Bas. Ay, but the worst of the Match too, is the Devil.

Man. Well, Sir, to let you see it is not so bad as you think it. As a Reward for her Honesty, in detecting your Practices, instead of the forg'd Bill, you would have put upon her, there's a Real One of five hundred Pound, to begin a new Honey-Moon with.   [*Gives it to* Myrtilla.

Count Bas. Sir, this is so generous an Act——

Man. No Compliments, dear Sir,——I am not at leisure now to receive them: Mr. *Constable*, will you be so good as to wait upon this Gentleman into the next Room, and give this Lady in Marriage to him?

Const. Sir, I'll do it faithfully.

Count Bas. Well! five hundred will serve to make a handsome push with, however.   [*Exeunt Count,* Myr. *and Constable.*

Sir Fran. And that I may be sure my family's rid of him for ever———come, my Lady, let's even take our Children along with us, and be all Witness of the Ceremony.

[*Exeunt Sir* Fran. *Lady* Wrong. *Miss and Squire.*

Man. Now, my Lord, you may enter.

Enter Lord and Lady Townly, *and Lady* Grace.

Lord Town. So, Sir, I give you Joy of your Negociation.

Man. You overheard it all, I presume?

Lady Grace. From first to last, Sir.

Lord Town. Never were Knaves and Fools better dispos'd of.

Man. A sort of Poetical Justice, my Lord, not much above the Judgment of a Modern Comedy.

Lord Town. To heighten that Resemblance, I think, Sister, there only wants your rewarding the Hero of the Fable, by naming the Day of his Happiness.

Lady Grace. This day, To-morrow, every Hour, I hope, of Life to come, will shew I want not Inclination to compleat it.

Man. Whatever I may want, Madam, you will always find Endeavours to deserve you.

Lord Town. Then all are happy.

Lady Town. Sister! I give you Joy! consummate as the happiest Pair can boast.

> In you, methinks, as in a Glass, I see
> The Happiness, that once advanc'd to me.
> So visible the Bliss, so plain the Way,
> How was it possible my Sense could stray?
> But, now, a Convert, to this Truth, I come,
> That Married Happiness is never found from Home.

EPILOGUE

M ETHINKS *I hear some Powder'd Criticks say,*
    " *Damn it! this Wife Reform'd has spoil'd the Play!*
" *The Coxcomb should have drawn her more in Fashion,*
" *Have gratify'd her Softer Inclination,*
" *Have tipt her a Gallant, and clinch'd the Provocation.*
But there our Bard stopt short: For 'twere uncivil
T' have made a modern Belle, *all o'er a Devil!*
He hop'd, in honour of the Sex, the Age
Would bear one mended Woman——on the Stage.

    From whence, you see by Common Sense's Rules,
Wives might be govern'd, were not Husbands Fools.
What-e'er by Nature Dames are prone to do,
They seldom stray, but when they govern you.
When the wild Wife perceives her Deary tame,
No Wonder then she plays him all the Game.
But Men of Sense meet rarely that Disaster;
Women take Pride, where Merit is their Master:
Nay, she that with a Weak Man wisely lives,
Will seem t' obey the due Commands she gives!
Happy Obedience is no more a Wonder,
When Men are Men, and keep them kindly under.
But modern Consorts are such High-bred Creatures,
They think a Husband's Power degrades their Features;
That nothing more Proclaims a Reigning Beauty,
Than that she never was reproach'd with Duty:
And that the greatest Blessing Heav'n e'er sent,
Is in a Spouse Incurious, and Content.

    To give such Dames a diff'rent Cast of Thought,
By calling home the Mind, these Scenes were wrought.
If, with a Hand too rude, the Task is done,
We hope the Scheme, by Lady Grace *laid down,*
Will all such Freedom with the Sex attone:
That Virtue there unsoil'd, by modish Art,
Throws out Attractions for a Manly's *Heart.*

EPILOGUE

You, You, then Ladies, whose unquestion'd Lives,
Give you the foremost Fame of Happy Wives,
Protect, for its Attempt, this helpless Play;
Nor leave it to the vulgar Taste, a Prey;
Appear the frequent Champions of its Cause,
Direct the Crowd, and give yourselves Applause.

FINIS.

The Words and Musick by Mr. CAREY.

OH, I'll have a Husband! ay, marry;
For why should I longer tarry,
For why should I longer tarry
Than other brisk girls have done?
For if I ſtay, 'till I grow Grey,
They'll call me old Maid, and fuſty old Jade;
So I'll no longer tarry;
But I'll have a Husband, ay, marry,
If Money can buy me One.

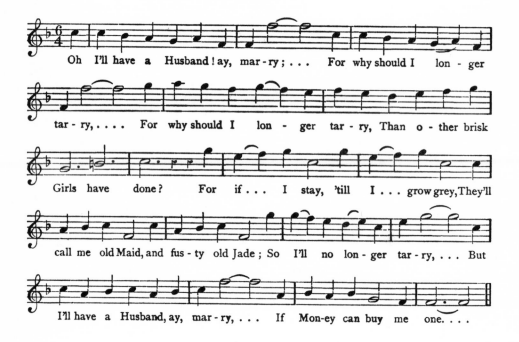

Oh I'll have a Husband! ay, mar-ry; . . . For why should I lon - ger tar - ry, ... For why should I lon - ger tar - ry, Than o - ther brisk Girls have done? For if . . . I stay, 'till I . . . grow grey, They'll call me old Maid, and fus - ty old Jade; So I'll no lon - ger tar - ry, . . . But I'll have a Husband, ay, mar - ry, . . . If Mon-ey can buy me one. . . .

My Mother she says I'm too coming;
And still in my Ears she is drumming,
And still in my Ears she is drumming,
      That I such vain Thoughts shou'd shun.
My Sisters they cry, Oh fye! and Oh fye!
But yet I can see, They're as coming as me;
      So let me have Husbands in Plenty:
I'd rather have twenty times twenty,
      Than die an Old Maid undone.

Sung by Mrs. CIBBER *in the Fourth Act.*

The Words and Musick by Mr. CAREY.

I.

WHAT tho' they call me Country Lass,
    I read it plainly in my Glass,
That for a Dutchess I might pass:
    Oh, cou'd I see the Day!
Wou'd fortune but attend my Call,
At Park, at Play, at Ring and Ball,
I'd brave the proudest of them all,
    With a *Stand by*——*Clear the Way*.

II.

Surrounded by a Crowd of Beaux,
With smart Toupees, and powder'd Cloaths,
At Rivals I'll turn up my Nose;
    Oh, cou'd I see the Day!
I'll dart such Glances from these Eyes,
Shall make some Lord or Duke my Prize;
And then, Oh! how I'll tyrannize,
    With a *Stand by*——*Clear the Way*.

III.

Oh! then for ev'ry new Delight,
For Equipage and Diamonds bright,
Quadrille, and Plays, and Balls, all Night;
    Oh! cou'd I see the Day!
Of Love and Joy I'd take my Fill,
The tedious Hours of Life to kill,
In ev'ry thing I'd have my Will,
    With a *Stand by*——*Clear the Way*.

FINIS.

What tho' they call me Coun - try Lass, I read it plain - ly in . . . my glass, That for a Dut - chess I . . . might pass : Oh, cou'd I see the Day ! . . . Wou'd For - tune but at - tend my call, At Park, at Play, at Ring and Ball, I'd brave the proud - est of them all, With a *Stand by—Clear the Way !* . .

For the FLUTE.

TEXTUAL
NOTES

The Confederacy

Dram. Pers.	*Moneytrap.* Q has " Monytrap " here but " Moneytrap " in the text of the play. Q prints " Mony " in Act I, but " Money " in the rest of the play. Since 1719 etc. print " Money " consistently, this spelling has been adopted throughout.
p. 15, l. 9.	*Enter Dick.* This is where *Les Bourgeoises de Qualité* begins.
p. 15, l. 36.	*in's Bed?* 1719 etc. Q, " in's Bed."
p. 16, l. 29.	*Whos's that? Brass!* 1719 etc. Q, " Who's that, *Brass?* "
p. 19, l. 3.	*Fey:* so Q consistently. 1719 etc., " Fy: "
p. 19, l. 6.	*splenatick* Q. 1719 etc., " splenetick." It may be deliberate.
p. 19, l. 39.	*to make love to me;* 1719 etc. Q, " to love me; " The later text appears to have the right meaning. There is no similar remark in the French to act as guide.
p. 21, l. 3.	*Me?* Q. 1719 etc., " Me! "
p. 21, l. 33.	*But Six and Fifty Pound?* Q. Subsequent editions " Pound! " or " Pounds! "
p. 21, l. 40.	*go fetch it* Q. Subsequent editions and Ward, " go and fetch it "
p. 22, l. 5.	*make great losses,* Q. Subsequent editions, except Ward, " have great losses,"
p. 22, l. 32.	*hags* Q and early editions, " haggs; " but hag in Act II.
p. 22, l. 33.	*ay* Q. 1719 etc., " ah "
p. 22, l. 42.	*me blessing,* 1776 and 1779, " my blessing,"
p. 23, l. 34.	*now how* Q. Subsequent editions, " now, how "
p. 24, l. 30.	*Cashkeeper!* Q only, " Cashkeeper? "
p. 26, l. 2.	*goes ill.* Q only, " goes ill,"
p. 27, l. 17.	*Quality . . . come at last.* Omitted in 1779.
p. 27, l. 24.	*expect you,* Q. Later editions " expect you! "
p. 27, l. 25.	*to-day?* Q only, " to-day."
p. 27, l. 39.	*ruine* Q only; but as the older spelling is consistently used throughout, it is here preserved.
p. 28, l. 13.	*Why, can* first in 1730. Q and 1719, " Why can "
p. 28, l. 15.	*Sweat?* 1719 etc. Q " Sweat."
p. 29, l. 2.	*Company;* 1719 etc. Q " Company,"
p. 29, l. 9.	*babbled* 1719 etc. Q " babled "
p. 29, l. 12.	*ach* Q only. Subsequent editions " ache "
p. 29, l. 29.	*supream* Q. 1719 " supreme," but the older spelling was still common.
p. 29, l. 33.	*Portion; do* 1719 etc. Q " Portion, Do "
p. 30, l. 1.	*devilish* 1719 etc. Q " devellish "
p. 32, l. 2.	*sower* Q only. Subsequent editions " sour "
p. 35, l. 1.	*Neighbour's* 1730 etc. Q and 1719 " Neighbours "
p. 36, l. 16.	*borne* 1719 etc. Q " born "
p. 36, l. 24.	*you'll* Q " you'l " By 1705 this was becoming archaic.
p. 37, l. 3.	*that, Trapes.* Q only, " that Trapes."

p. 37, l. 14.	*Their Wives . . . his own peace.* Omitted in 1779.
p. 38, l. 2.	*Mother,* Q " Mother "
p. 38, l. 9.	*Blessing,* Q only. 1719 etc., " Blessing? "
p. 38, l. 10.	*Parents?* 1719 etc. Q " Parents."
p. 38, l. 17.	*sure?* Q only, " sure! "
p. 38, l. 26.	*chaſt* Q only, but the spelling was still in use.
p. 39, l. 24.	*hark* Q " heark," but " hark " lower down.
p. 40, l. 7.	*confess—but* Q " confess.—but "
p. 40, l. 36.	*Desarts* Q only; but it seems in conformity with Vartue higher up.
p. 41, l. 24.	*agen* Q only; but although " again " is used in Q, the difference in spelling seems to mark a class distinction, as " agen " is also used later.
p. 42, l. 1.	*beholding* Q only, but Vanbrugh seems always to use it. 1719 etc. have " beholden "
p. 42, l. 18.	*Pique and Repique* Q " Picque and Repique "
p. 42, l. 28.	*have kept* Q only, " has kept." This seems a misprint from the previous " has," for Brass speaks correct, if low English.
p. 43, l. 21.	*won't* Q misprints " won't not "
p. 43, l. 41.	*indeed.* 1719 etc. Q " indeed,"
p. 44, l. 7.	*à propos;* Q, 1709, 1730 " a propo "; 1751 " à propo "; 1762 " apropos "; 1776 " a propos "; 1779, in despair of finding another false variant, " à propos."
p. 44, l. 35.	*sola* italics: Q " sola " romans.
p. 44, l. 39.	*pritty* Q only; but so frequently that it seems deliberate.
p. 44, l. 39.	*Mistriss* similarly.
p. 45, l. 3.	*Sir;* Q " Sir,"
p. 45, l. 10.	*And how?——And how d'you think? you would have me do't, and . . .* Q " And how?——And how d'you think? you would have me do't. And . . ." All other editions punctuate, " And how!—— And how d'you think you would have me do't. And . . ."
p. 45, l. 28.	*Giving him a slap* There is, of course, none of this in Dancourt.
p. 47, l. 27.	*Sum* Q " Summ," but " Sum " lower down.
p. 47, l. 31.	*Pounds too, look* 1719. Q " Pounds too look " 1751 " Pounds, too, look "
p. 48, l. 3.	*manage* Q only, " mannage "
p. 48, l. 22.	*Quarrel* Q and 1719 " Quarrel." Later editions " Quarrel,"
p. 48, l. 22.	*to——with* 1719 etc. Q " to be with " The French has " se préparer à une querelle que je lui ai conseillé."
p. 48, l. 40.	*Terror* Q only, " Terrour "
p. 49, l. 8.	*hobbling* Q only, " hobling "
p. 49, l. 21.	*rowl* Q only. 1719 etc. " roll." Vanbrugh seems to prefer " rowl."
p. 49, l. 29.	*confess;* Q " confess," 1719 " confess: "
p. 49, l. 34.	*under;* 1719 Q " under,"
p. 50, l. 18.	*rob'd* Q only, remainder " robb'd." But the earlier spelling is consistent with others in the text.
p. 50, l. 33.	*Linnen* 1719 " Linen," but the older spelling was still in use.
p. 52, l. 16.	*acquainted?* 1719. Q " acquainted."
p. 52, l. 32.	*over him?* 1719 and most others. Q " over him,"

p. 53, l. 2.   *safe*, 1719.   Q " safe "

p. 53, l. 6.   *sower*   Q " sowre "   1719 " sour."   It is here made to agree with
 Act II.

p. 53, l. 16.   *Rogue!*   Q " Rogue? "

p. 54, l. 29.   *my Life.* 1730, 1759.   Q and 1719 " my Life,"

p. 56, l. 8.   *Cousin* 1719.   Q has " Cozen," but Vanbrugh had used " cousin "
 earlier in *The Country House*, supposing the 1715 edition of that
 play to be from a manuscript of about 1703.

p. 56, l. 37.   *Pox!*———— 1719.   Q, " Pox? "————

p. 57, l. 9.   *advantagious* Q.   1719 etc. " advantageous ", but the " i " may well
 be deliberate.

p. 58, l. 43.   *that's the Rule.* 1719.   Q, " that's the Rule? "

p. 60, l. 27.   *it*———— 1719 etc.   Q " it."

p. 60, l. 29.   *Why what,* 1719 etc.   Q " Why, what "

p. 61, l. 21.   *Penny*   Q " Peny "

p. 62, l. 25.   *good a Humour* 1719 etc.   Q " good Humour "

p. 64, l. 3.   *complement* Q.   1719 " compliment."   The older spelling was becoming
 out of date, but Vanbrugh seems to have been partial to it.

p. 64, l. 21.   *on't;* 1719   Q " on't,"

p. 64, l. 23.   *War Horse,*   Q " Ware, Horse."   1719 etc. which makes the
 meaning clearer; but the phrasing is clearly that of Q and of Ward,
 who has " War horse! "

p. 65, l. 18.   SCENE *Opens.*   From here to the entry of Mr. Clip is Vanbrugh's
 interpolation.   This necessitated the deletion of small, purely
 mechanical scenes (v to viii) of the original, and a slight alteration
 in dovetailing.

p. 65, l. 30.   *home;* 1719.   Q " home,"

p. 66, l. 10.   *dispense* 1719.   Q " dispence "

p. 66, l. 20.   *seldom* Q and 1719.   1730 " never," but 1751 restores.

p. 67, l. 11.   *Victoria!* 1730   Q " *Victoria* " 1719 " *Victoria,*"

p. 67, l. 31.   *Penniworth* Q   1719 etc " Pennyworth "   But if " penniless," why
 not " penniworth? "

p. 69, l. 8.   *Immotion* Q   1719 etc. " Emotion."   See explanatory notes.

p. 69, l. 22.   *coolly* 1719.   Q " cooly "

p. 69, l. 31.   *Flippanta.*   Q " Flippanta." in romans 1719 " *Flippanta!* "

p. 71, l. 30.   *B'ye*   Q " Buy "   1719 " B'y "

p. 72, l. 8.   *What, the Colonel* 1730, 1751 etc.   Q and 1719 " What the Colonel "

p. 72, l. 15.   *done't* 1719 etc.   Q " don't "

p. 72, l. 24.   *Hang'd* 1719.   Q " hang'd "

p. 72, l. 26.   *neither: If* 1719.   Q " neither, If "

p. 72, l. 43.   *the pretty pair, the pretty Pair,* Q.   1719 has " Pair " in each case;
 but Q may indicate a change of emphasis.

p. 73, l. 35.   *for any thing that belongs to him* 1762, 1776.   " for any thing belongs
 to him." Q, 1719, 1730, 1759, 1779, and Ward.

p. 73, l. 12.   *Broil* 1719.   Q " Broyl."   Vanbrugh uses the more modern spelling
 in the earlier *The Mistake*.

Ep., l. 22.   *Feats.*   Q misprints " Feasts."

The Mistake

p. 87, l. 25.   *from her,* 1719. Q " from her "

p. 88, l. 31.   *Generosity.* Q and 1719 " Generosity,"

p. 90, l. 6.   *Good by* 1719. Q " God by "

p. 90, l. 29.   *return you——?* 1719. Q " return you?—— "

p. 91, l. 29.   *yielded* 1719. Q " yeilded," but " yielded " later.

p. 92, l. 40.   *Rack.* 1719. Q " Wrack," but " Rack " elsewhere

p. 93, l. 22.   *borne* 1719. Q " born." This alteration has been made throughout this play.

p. 94, l. 34.   *tell him?* 1719. Q " tell him."

p. 95, l. 7.   *pierce* 1719. Q " peirce "

p. 95, l. 29.   *my own:* 1719. Q " my own,"

p. 96, l. 26.   *inclin'd* 1719. Q " enclin'd "

p. 97, l. 22.   *Farewel.* This has usually been modernised, but is used in this form consistently throughout this play, and is followed by 1719.

p. 99, l. 32.   *Racks* 1719. Q " Wracks "

p. 100, l. 9.   *Filio* 1719 Q misspells " Fillio ", and " Fillius ".

p. 101, l. 10.   *Quintilian* Q spells as in the French, " *Quintilien* "

p. 102, l. 13.   *O Tempora! O Mores!* The end is slightly different in the French. Albert goes out to get a bell, while Métaphraste soliloquises. He comes back with the bell, and it is that, and not blows, which makes the pedant fly. He cries " *Miséricorde! à l'aide!* " his Latin deserting him at so critical a moment. Q misprints " *Tempore.* "

p. 103, l. 26.   *Councils.* Q. 1719 " Counsels," but the former seems to be Vanbrugh's usual spelling.

p. 103, l. 29.   *Villainy* Q " Villany," but " villainous " later.

p. 104, l. 6.   *looks upon me!* 1776 and Ward. Q and 1719 " looks upon me? "

p. 105, l. 36.   *oddly* 1719. Q " odly "

p. 105, l. 37.   *thorough* Q. 1719 " through."

p. 106, l. 20.   *Hony-Moon* so Q consistently. 1719 " Honey-Moon."

p. 106, l. 32.   *my Marriage?* This question mark is also printed in 1719. It seems to imply a question to Lopez; the remark must be made enquiringly, not as a statement. Later editions print a full stop.

p. 109, l. 8.   *recall* 1719. Q " recal "

p. 110, l. 1.   *Who's there?* Q " Who's there; "

p. 111, l. 10.   *villainy.* Q " villany." See note *ante.*

p. 111, l. 24.   *comers* Q " commers "

p. 112, l. 5.   *Downfall* Q and 1719 " Downfal "

p. 113, l. 23.   *There possibly may be another.* Vanbrugh fails to reproduce a typical Molièrism.

> *Ascagne.* Si rien ne peut m'aider, il faut donc que je meure.
> *Frosine.* Ah! pour cela, toujours il est assez bonne heure.

p. 113, l. 34. *begone* Q " begon " 1719 " be gone "
p. 114, l. 3. *Ha, a, a,* Q. 1719 " Ha, ha, ha."
p. 114, l. 6. *arraign* Q " arrain "
p. 114, l. 21. *fleas* archaic for flays, but 1719 follows.
p. 114, l. 25. *wield* 1719. Q " weild "
p. 115, l. 1. *Salamancha* 1719. Q " Salamancho "
p. 115, l. 16. *Mariners* 1719. Q " Marriners "
p. 115, l. 27. *wash their dirty Faces.* A Vanbrughism.
p. 118, l. 36. *foolish Woman!* Ward gives this line to Jacinta, since Marinette says, " *Oh, la làche personne!* " But it is like Vanbrugh to have given it to Leonora.
p. 120, l. 11. *Hearing;)* Q " Hearing) "
p. 120, l. 20. *Cloth* 1719. Q " Cloath."
p. 122, l. 41. *rowl* Q " roul " 1719 " roll " Q has " rowl " elsewhere, and this is Vanbrugh's usual spelling.
p. 124, l. 5. *pitiful* 1719. Q " pittiful," but " Pity " later.
p. 124, l. 39. *Horrendum* Q mispells " *Horendum* "
p. 127, l. 31. *Mysteries* Q " Misteries," but " Mysteries " earlier.

A Journey to London

p. 137, l. 38. *by which they will see,* 1776. Early editions have " by which, they will see,"
p. 139, l. 29. *in duty bound to do* 1776. The three early editions read " in duty bound, to do " which makes nonsense.
p. 144, l. 19. *smoke* This curiously modern spelling is probably a misprint for " smoake," which both the 1730 editions read.
p. 144, l. 25. *Enter Col Courtly.* Leigh Hunt and Ward make a new scene here, but it scarcely seems necessary.
p. 149, l. 6. *at all;* 1776. 1728, 1730 and 1730 " at all,"
p. 151, l. 41. *Coquet.* 1728 " Coquett " the first time
p. 157, l. 42. *are you in love with her?* Early editions omit ?
p. 158, l. 3. *Martilla* 1728 " *Martylla* "
p. 165, l. 5. *ready;* Early editions " ready,"
p. 166, l. 5. *Captain* Toupee Early editions " Capt *Toupee* "

The Provok'd Husband

Preface. *Paraphernalia* 1728 " *Paraphenalia* "
p. 186, l. 7. *some men have!* 1728 " some men have? "
p. 188, l. 1. *'Tis* 1728 " 'tis "
p. 188, l. 29. *Prepossession* 1728 misprints " Possession "

p. 190, l. 42. *you are!* 1728 " you are? "

p. 197, l. 18. *Meaſter* 1728 " Master " here and elsewhere in John Moody's mouth ; once " Mester " ; but more often " Measter," which is adopted here.

p. 202, l. 26. *and yet . . . kept him* Omitted in 1729 et seq.

p. 204, l. 14. *feyther.* 1728 " feather," and a little lower; otherwise " feyther."

p. 211, l. 27. *howld* 1728 " howl'd "

p. 215, l. 25. *if it in no way* 1728 omits the " *if,*" but prints it as a catchword in mistake for " *trouble.*"

p. 222, l. 35. *do we live in!* Early editions " do we live in? " The correction is ventured on here.

p. 228, l. 34. *claps to* 1728 " claps too "

p. 229, l. 43. *Exit Mrs Motherly.* This direction is not printed in the eighteenth-century editions. It is clearly necessary with the addition of the passage in brackets.

p. 231, l. 42. *say you.* In 1728, without the interpolated scene, the " say you " is replaced by " *Mrs Motherly,*" for obvious reasons.

p. 234, l. 30. *cry'd ay!* 1728 misprints " cry'd no! "

p. 239, l. 33. *Exit singing.* This is where the second song comes, according to the edition of 1804, where it is marked to be omitted, though printed in full.

p. 239, l. 33. *ay Marry* 1729 misprints " *and Marry* "

The Confederacy

Prologue. *a Brother.* Brother Van, of course.

nick'd it. See the note on Hazard in the notes to *A Journey to London.* He means that when he gave away his profits and wrote for praise he was successful; but now that he wants the money . . .

their House about his Ears. Namely the Bishop of Gloucester's attack. See Introduction.

p. 13. *Conscience.* The City being largely dissenting, and freedom of conscience a particular point with it, to associate the word conscience with the City in this way would be a good topical joke.

p. 14. *pays his club.* This passage is quoted by the N.E.D. The phrase is still in use with us: to club expenses. It means that Dick could pay his share when he dined or wined with the fine company he kept. Cf. Swift, *Imitation of Horace* I, Ep. vii:

> Yet, when he's not so rich as I,
> I pay my club, and so good-bye.

p. 18. *it's dated in Rhime.* There is nothing about this in the French. It is a robbery from Congreve, *The Way of the World* (1700), Act II:

"Pray Madam, do you pin up your hair with all your Letters; I find I must keep copies."

"Only with those in verse, Mr. *Witwoud.* I never pin up my Hair with Prose."

p. 19. *possession of it is intolerable.* There is no such thought in the French, but we may again remind ourselves of Congreve's Angelica in *Love for Love* (1695): "Would any thing but a madman complain of Uncertainty? Uncertainty and Expectation are the Joys of Life. Security is an insipid thing, and the overtaking and possessing of a wish discovers the Folly of the Chace."

p. 20. *the Rising of the Lights.* Clarissa seems to refer to the discomfort of having to repress eructation, or some similar digestive trouble. In the modern vulgar phrase, she could not spit it out. Lights, of course, is the familiar butcher's word, "lights and liver."

p. 20. *Iron-Bodice.* Stays. Cf. *Tatler,* 262: "for that she, the said Rebecca Shapely, did always wear a pair of steel bodice, and a *false rump.*" (1710.) (Addison and Steele.)

p. 21. *Commode.* A tall head-dress, consisting of wire covered with lace. Cf. Granville:

> She like some pensive statesman walks demure,
> And smiles, and hugs, to make destruction sure;
> Or under high commodes, with looks erect,
> Barefac'd devours, in gaudy colours deck'd.

p. 22. *gim.* "Neat, spruce, well-dressed." Johnson. The N.E.D. quotes this passage.

p. 23.　*Gin of all Trades.*　According to the N.E.D., which quotes this passage but no other in illustration, Gin is the feminine of Jack.　The word also means a female ferret, so the phrase may be doubly insulting.

p. 27.　*one Rubbers.*　We now say one rubber, e.g. a rubber of bridge.　The old form was in the plural, especially at bowls.

p. 27.　*take it for a favour.*　The whole of this crude passage is Vanbrugh's interpolation.　It seems to be borrowed from the terrible Nicky-Nacky scene (III, i) of Otway's *Venice Preserv'd* (1682): " Ah, toad, toad, toad, toad! spit in my face a little, Nacky—spit in my face, prythee spit in my face, never so little, etc."

p. 32.　*Cotquean.*　A man who busies himself with women's affairs or meddles in the household.　" They fell upon him with opprobrious words of Coward Cotquean, Milksop."　J. Smyth, *c.* 1640, *Lives.*　(N.E.D.)

p. 33.　*peeking.*　A variant of peeping, peering.

p. 33.　*good stomachs,* to a certain kind of feast understood.　Cf. Halifax's *Character of Charles* II (*c.* 1685): " He had more properly, at least in the beginning of his Time, a good Stomach to his Mistresses, than any great Passion for them."

p. 34.　*I shift,* i.e. change my linen.　It was the old expression.　Cf. *The White Devil:*

> You shift your shirt there
> When you retire from tennis?

and *Hudibras,* III, ii, 1299 (1678):

> And nastier, in an *old opinion*
> Than those who never shift their Linnen.

p. 37.　*curs'd;* ill-tempered.　We still use it as slang, cusséd.　Cf. Shaftesbury's *Characteristics* (1711): " Any Nature, thorowly savage, curst, and inveterate."　See also *Æsop,* Part II, Scene i.

p. 37.　*a crooked Stick;* i.e. an Exchequer tally, which was " a crooked stick, about two feet long, cut into a peculiar shape, with certain notches cut in it, to denote the amount paid in pounds, shillings and pence, the same being given as a receipt for money paid into the Exchequer."　The writer adds, " I believe it has been disused for some fifty years."　*Notes and Queries,* III, x, 197.　8 September, 1866.

p. 37.　*Zest.*　Apparently hist, zut.　The N.E.D. quotes this sentence, applying the meaning of " haste! " to the word—quick action.　The only other instance it gives is 1602, *Contention between Lib. and Prod.* Bar, lady, zonne, zest true.

p. 39.　*of the Pudding;* of the affair, fraud.　This appears to be a nonce word, as the N.E.D. gives no example of it in this sense.　As a verb it exists.　To " pudden " a dog was to quiet it by giving it a narcotic ball.

p. 41.　*capitolade.*　See notes to *The False Friend.*　Vanbrugh evidently liked the word, as Dancourt has *galimatias.*

p. 42.　*a Rowland, for her Oliver.*　(Dancourt has *à bon chat bon rat.*) a quid pro quo, a tit for tat.　Oliver and Roland, equal among Charlemagne's

EXPLANATORY NOTES

paladins, fought together for five days on an island in the Rhine, without either gaining the least advantage over the other. For early use in Vanbrugh's sense cf. Edward Hall, *Henry VI* (c. 1500): "But to have a Roland to resist an Oliver, he sent solempne ambassadors to the King of England, offeryng hym hys doughter in marriage."

p. 42. *Pique and Repique*—at Piquet. Pique is when the player scores 30 in his hand and play before his opponent scores a point: he then counts 61 instead of 31. If on the cards alone, it is repique, and he counts 91.

p. 47. *smoak*, suspect. See notes to *The Provok'd Husband*.

p. 50. *I learnt it at Algier*. Algiers was then a famous pirate stronghold, which harassed Mediterranean shipping, enslaving the sailors and treating them cruelly. Cf. Bishop King's *Elegy on Sir Charles Lucas and Sir George Lisle*, with reference to the enslavement of Welshmen, and the events at Colchester:

> Though luckless *Colchester* in this outvies
> *Argiers* or *Tunis* shameful Merchandise;

etc.

p. 50. *Turkish*. Not strictly correct, but will serve. In 1669 the Corsairs drove out the Pashas, who were sent as governors from Turkey, and elected Deys to rule over them.

p. 51. *Prince Eugene's march into Italy*. This being the year after the battle of Blenheim, Prince Eugene was in high favour. His march into Italy was in 1705, against Vendôme, to relieve Turin. This, however, he did not do until 1706, for the battle of Cassano, 16 August, where Eugene was severely wounded, was indecisive. The subject would be immediately topical, thus this does probably not refer to Eugene's Italian campaign of 1701.

p. 51. *Jackadandy*. A little, pert, conceited fellow. The earliest reference in the N.E.D. is to Brome's *Northern Lass* (1632): "Ile throw him into the Dock rather than he shall succeed Iack O'Dandy."

p. 51. *with a Witness*. We would now say, with a vengeance. Cf. Collier's *Short View*, the passage quoted in notes to *A Short Vindication*.

p. 52. *purely*; splendidly. See notes to *A Journey to London*.

p. 53. *Gar there*. This is a Gallicism, *gare à*. Cf. the recent Edinburghian *Garaloo* (Gare à l'eau) before emptying a pail of slops from a window. N.E.D quotes Vanbrugh under Gare.

p. 53. *temperance*: moderation. See notes to *The Provok'd Husband*.

p. 55. *in the fund*: at bottom. One expects to find *au fond* in the French, but one does not.

p. 60. *Come away*: make haste. Cf. Dowland's *First Booke of Ayres* (1597):

> Come away, sweet love,
> The golden morning breakes . . .
>
> Come away, come sweet love,
> Do not in vain adorne. . . .
> Haste then, sweet love, our wishes' flight.

The phrase is still used by the Scotch in this sense.

p. 62.   *Tester:* a slang word for a sixpence, used as late as Praed in 1862:

> Well! it was worth a silver tester,
> To see how she frown'd when the abbess blest her. (N.E.D.)

p. 64.   *War Horse.* War means be ware of, look out. (Cf. Gar!) Though usually spelt Ware nowadays, it is still pronounced War.

p. 69.   *Immotion.* The N.E.D. refers to this as an obsolete nonce word, for impulse (?), illustrating it from Vanbrugh's *The Mistake* (IV). It is therefore not a nonce word, but seems to be Vanbrugh's peculiar property. In this instance, but not in the other, 1719 has emotion; but it would seem that is a definite attempt to coin a word, and not carelessness in spelling.

p. 69.   *presently:* at once, though used in the modern sense ante.

p. 71.   *Tintamar:* fuss, noise; from Dancourt's *tintamarre.*

p. 72.   *Pumpt,* that is, soused under a pump by way of summary punishment. Cf. Shadwell's *Virtuoso* (1676), II: " Pump him soundly, impudent fellow."

The Mistake

Prologue.   *Ruel* and *Desbarques* were two French dancers, Ruel belonging to Drury Lane and Desbarques to the Haymarket.

p. 88.   *Jackadandy,*   See notes to *The Confederacy.*

p. 91.   *a Scotch Pair of Boots.* The boots were a form of torture used in Edinburgh, much to the delight of the Duke of York when he resided there prior to becoming James II. The boots were put on, and the knee-cap was battered.

p. 93.   *add with the Poet.* Does this couplet exist anywhere in an English play? At any rate it seems a tolerable translation of:

> Nous ne sommes plus sots, ni mon maître ni moi,
> Et désormais qu'elle aille au diable avecque toi.

p. 101.   *Quintilian's own Precept. Quintilien en fait le précepte.* . . This phrase does not occur in Quintilian's work; nor, being a hexameter, is it likely that it should. It was one of Molière's little jokes. It is a verse by Despautère, according to the French commentators, but the allusion is to Book X of the *Institutiones Oratoriæ.* Despautère (*c.* 1460–1520) was the author of *Commentarii Grammatici,* and his Latin verses were long taught in the schools.

p. 109.   *Pistole.* See notes to *The Provok'd Husband.*

p. 109. *I am in a Wood;* viz. I am puzzled. This was a common phrase. As Mr. Montague Summers notes, this was the point of the title of Wycherley's play, *Love in a Wood, or St. James' Park.*

p. 111. *snubbing;* reprimanding, chastizing. See Wright's *Dialect Dictionary.*

p. 112. *Pot-gun:* we say pop-gun. A common form. Cf. Congreve, *The Old Batchelour,* III, i (1693): "That Pot-gun charg'd with wind."

p. 115. *Immotions.* N.E.D. quotes this as a nonce word. See notes to *The Confederacy.*

p. 121. *keep your back Hand:* Toledo's meaning is clear as a duelling phrase, which Lopez twists to its meaning at tennis in the next speech.

p. 122. *making Jack-pudding of a Blunderbuss:* a Jack-pudding is a buffoon, or clown, especially an attendant one. Cf. Etherege, *The Comical Revenge,* III, iv (1664): "Sir, in a word, he was Jack-pudding to a mountebank."

p. 126. *stoter'd;* hit hard, felled. The N.E.D. quotes this passage; also D'Urfey, *Collins Walk,* 1690:

> He . . . knew by wisdom outward
> What Ox must fall, and Sheep be stoter'd.

Epilogue. This was spoken by Mrs. Porter, as Isabella.

Mr. Motteux. Peter Antony Motteux (1660–1718), well known as the completer of Urquhart's *Rabelais.* He was a tea merchant, a Frenchman who settled in England after the Revocation of the Edict of Nantes. He also wrote plays, e.g. *Love's a Jest* (1696); *Europe's Revels,* an Interlude (1697); *The Island Princess* (1699); *Love's Triumph* (1708). He edited the *Gentleman's Journal* (1692), and translated *Don Quixote* (1712).

Whites. See notes to *The Provok'd Husband.*

A Journey to London

p. 137. *Dutch-Gingerbread.* Gingerbread contained almonds, aniseed, treacle, lemon-peel, rosewater and perhaps liquorice. Dutch possibly, because it was a spice cake, and the South Sea Islands were largely in Dutch hands, though ginger, which was the main flavouring, came mostly from Calicut, which was never Dutch.

p. 137. *Naples Biscuits.* Mentioned by Chambers as a common delicacy, but not described.

p. 137. *Neats-Tongues.* Neat, the now obsolete word for ox.

> The steer, the heifer and the calf
> Are all called neat.—*Winter's Tale.*

Smoak preserveth flesh; as we see in bacon, neat's tongues, and martlemas beef. Bacon's *Natural History.*

p. 137. *Usquebaugh.* Infuse a quart of brandy with Spanish raisins, dates, currants, the tops of thyme, bawm, savory, mint and rosemary. Add cinnamon, mace, aniseed, nutmeg, coriander and orange- or lemon-peel. Stand in a warm place for forty-eight hours. Add a quart of white port and a pint of canary, and you have usquebaugh. Chambers, 1738.

p. 137. *Black-cherry Brandy.* Cherry brandy, made simply by half filling a bottle with cherries, and adding brandy, was usually made of black cherries.

p. 137. *Cinnamon-water,* was obtained by boiling cinnamon in water and adding sugar: or it was made of cinnamon and rosewater mixed with white wine. Chambers's *Dictionary,* 1738.

p. 137. *Sack.* A general name for a class of white wines formerly imported from Spain and the Canaries. It was at this date rather a country squire's wine. Probably not *vino secco.*

p. 137. *Tent, vino tinto,* a Spanish wine, deep red, chiefly from Galicia; much used as Sacramental wine.

p. 137. *Perspective-Glass.* See notes to *The Relapse.*

p. 138. *Griggs.* To be merry as a grig (a grig being either a cricket or a Greek according to etymological taste) is an old proverbial expression. N.E.D. gives 1556, Drant, *Horace Satires,* I, iii: " A merry grigge, a jocande frende." The N.E.D. quotes the parallel passage in *The Provok'd Husband.*

p. 140. *errant* i.e. "arrant." This spelling was not uncommon in those days. Cf. Etherege, *Letterbook, c.* 1687 (B.M. Add. MSS.): " Sir George, intending to forestall the rest of the ministers in paying the honour due to her character (that of an errant whore), was civilly pleased to send his steward to make her a compliment." In either case a pun might be intended, as in *The Way of the World* (1700), end of Act IV:

> *Wait.* E'er long you shall substantial Proof receive
> That I'm an arrant Knight——
> *Frib.* Or arrant Knave.

p. 141. *seven Years.* The Septennial Act was passed in 1716.

p. 141. *presently* at once. This sense was obsolescent at this time, but is found as late as Scott, in recorded conversations. At this time it was sometimes used in its modern meaning, as later in this play.

p. 141. *skawar'd* i.e. scoured, run fast, sprinted.

p. 142. *Tunbridge Sugar-box.* Tunbridge was famous for its inlaid marquetry boxes; cf.:

> To Noddles cram'd with Dighton's musty Snuff,
> Whose nicer Tasts think Wit consists alone
> In Tunbridge Wooden Box with Wooden Spoon.
> Prologue to *Hampstead Heath.*

That play is by Thomas Baker, acted 1705, printed 1706.

p. 142. *pure,* that is, delightful, good, nice, fine, capital. The N.E.D. quotes this passage. It was a favourite word with Miss Prue in *Love for Love* (1695), e.g. in her scene with Tattle at the end of Act II: " O Lord, I swear this is pure! "

p. 143. *Norfolk-nog*: strong ale. N.E.D. quotes Prideaux, *Lett Camden:* " A bottle of old strong beer, wch in this countrey (Norfolk) they call ' nog.' " 1693.

> Walpole laid a quart of nog on't
> He'd either make a hog or dog on't.

p. 145. *danger in that:* since by Privilege of Parliament members could not be sued for debt.

p. 146. *Window's broke.* The mob sometimes make themselves guardians of national virtue, and in these days would break the windows of houses they considered to be of ill-fame. Pepys gives an extreme instance. On March 24, 1668, he records the 'prentices being taken in charge for storming the brothels. " They do give out that they are for pulling down the bawdy-houses which is one of the greatest grievances of the nation. To which the King made a very poor insipid answer: ' Why, why do they go to them then? ' " And on the 25th: " These idle fellows have had the confidence to say that they did ill in contenting themselves in pulling down the little bawdy-houses, and did not go and pull down the great bawdy-house at White Hall." Lady Herford's windows were broken when the tumultuary opinion favoured Queen Caroline.

p. 147. *mechanick*, that is, given to manual rather than intellectual toil. Cf. the " rude mechanichals " in the *Midsummer Night's Dream.*

p. 147. *go to Bed early and rise so.* The proverb is evidently of a date prior to this. The familiar jingle appeared in *Poor Richard's Almanac*, 1757. In *A Health to the Gentle Profession of Serving Men* we read: " My hour is eight o'clock, though it is an infallible rule "—" Sanat, sanctificat, et ditat, surgere mane." (That he may be healthy, happy, and wise, let him rise early.) Clarke's *Parœmiolgia*, 1639. See Bartlett, *Fam. Quot.*, 10th Ed., p. 360.

p. 150. *Surfeit-water* was distilled from poppies and other herbs as a cure for indigestion.

p. 156. *feggings*—a variant of fackins, diminutive of i'fac, in faith.

p. 161. *Channel*, that is gutter, often a dangerous river of mud.

> For thee the scavenger bids kennels glide
> Within their bounds, and heaps of dirt subside.
> > *Trivia* (1716), I, 15.

Gay gives an account of a similar accident:

> I've seen a beau, in some ill-fated hour
> When o'er the stones choaked kennels swell the show'r
> In gilded chariot loll; he with disdain
> Views spatter'd passengers all drench'd in rain;
> With mud fill'd high, the rumbling cart draws near,
> Now rule thy prancing steeds, lac'd charioteer;
> The dustman lashes on with spiteful rage,
> His ponderous spokes thy painted wheel engage,

Crush'd is thy pride, down falls the shrieking beau,
The slabby pavement crystal fragments show,
Black floods of mire th' embroidered coat disgrace,
And mud enwraps the honour of his face.

Trivia, II, 524.

p. 166. *Seven's the Main*, at Hazard. "This game of Hazard has been very fatal to many a good Gentleman, of which it will not be amiss to give one Example, for the better Information of them who are so bewitch'd as to venture their Fortunes on the Turn of the Dice. Suppose 7 is the Main, the Caster throws 5, and that's his Chance, and so has 5 to 7; if the Caster throws his Chance, he wins all the Money was set him, but if he throws 7, which was the Main, he must pay as much Money as is on the Board: If again, 7 be the Main, and the Caster throws 11, that is a Nick, and sweeps away all the Mony on the Table; but if he throws a Chance, he must wait which will come first: Lastly, if 7 be the Main and the Caster throws *Ames-Ace, Deuce-Ace* or 12, he is out; but if he throws from 4 to 10 he has a Chance, though they two are accounted the worst Chances on the Dice, as 7 is reputed the best and easiest Main to be flung:"

Memoirs | of the Lives, Intrigues | and | Comical Adventures | Of the most Famous | Gamesters | and | Celebrated Sharpers | In the Reigns of |

Charles II	William III
	and
James II	Queen Anne.

By Theophilus Lucas Esq: 2nd Edition 1714.

See the game played later in the scene. Lady Arabella first plays with the dice. Then, when seven is the main, she throws out with twelve. Lady Headpiece, when eight is the main, throws a chance of seven, but throws the main next time, and loses. Miss Betty also throws out. Sir Francis was right, these dice are loaded: they are always throwing "at all," namely two sixes.

The Provok'd Husband

Dedication. *To the Queen*, namely Queen Caroline, who certainly deserved the compliments addressed to her, even if George II was unworthy of those aimed at him.

so gloriously Refus'd. This refers to the fact that at one time Princess Caroline had been designed to marry the Archduke Charles of Spain, who afterwards became the Emperor Charles VI. For this she would have had to change her religion, but appears to have been dissuaded by the old Electress and Leibniz.

Preface. *corrupt it.* This no doubt refers to the opera, which hit the actors of the old patentee companies severely. It was long considered as a comparatively degrading performance, the " silly diversion of the nobility," for was it not obviously easier to satisfy the senses than to satisfy the mind? Or it might refer to the pantomimes and similar shows introduced by the younger Rich.

p. 197. *Plague-water.* "*Aqua epidemica*, is prepared from the roots of masterwort, angelica, pyony and butter-bur; viper grass, Virginia snake-root, rue, rosemary, bawm, carduus, water-germander, marigold, dragon, goats' rue, and mint; the whole infused in spirit of wine, and distilled. It is of frequent use as an alexipharmic: it revives the spirits and promotes diaphoresis. It is the basis of most juleps now prescribed, especially in feverish cases." Chambers, 1738.

For the other stimulants and potations mentioned, see notes to *A Journey to London.*

p. 197. *Childermas day.* The Festival of the Holy Innocents, 28 December.

p. 201. *smoaking.* Suspecting, finding out. The word is common in the literature of the period. N.E.D. gives examples but no derivation. Mr. David Garnett has suggested to me that the word means literally to smell out, to scent. Keepers still sometimes call their dogs " Smoker."

p. 201. *Wax.* Wax candles were still something of a refinement. Tallow was the usual material for candles. Cf. Sir Fopling Flutter, *The Man of Mode* (1776), Act IV, snuffing a tallow candle. " How can you breathe in a Room where there's Grease frying? *Dorimant*, thou art intimate with my Lady, advise her for her own sake, and the good Company that comes hither, to burn Wax Lights."

p. 204. *bone-ace*, that is dice. Dice were commonly known as the bones. Cf. Dryden:

> But then my study was to cog the dice,
> And dext'rously to throw the lucky sice:
> To shun ames ace that swept my stakes away;
> And watch the box, for fear they should convey
> False bones, and put upon me in the play. *Johnson.*

p. 204. *All-fours.* " A low game at cards, played by two; so named from the four particulars by which it is reckoned, and which, joined in the hand of either of the parties, are said to make *all-fours*." *Johnson.*

p. 204. *Ombre.* The fashionable game of the time; the one played in *The Rape of the Lock*. As Squire Richard suggests, it was pronounced " umber." Cf. Etherege, *Epistle to Dryden:*

> Such ropes of pearls her hands encumber
> She scarce can deal the cards at ombre.

It was played with forty cards, the eight, nine and ten of the ordinary pack being thrown out.

p. 209. *White's.* The famous Chocolate House at the lower end and the western side of St. James's Street. It was founded in about 1698, but being burned down in 1733 was moved to its present side of the street, but lower down than where it now stands. It was a favourite meeting-place for the fashionable, or, as Swift puts it, " the common Rendez-vous of famous Sharpers and noble Cullies." It is not to be confused with White's Coffee House, which stood near the Royal Exchange.

p. 209. *The Demoivre Baronet.* This is a mysterious reference. White's was, of course, famous for its fantastic bets, and in 1709 Sir Scipio Hill had gone so far as to bet on the chances of his life. The Baronet here mentioned was evidently a gambler with a system, for Demoivre, or de Moivre (1667–1754) was a famous mathematician, who was the first to produce a life-probability table, used by the insurance companies. His *Doctrine of Chances* was published in 1718.

p. 209. *The King's Arms.* There was the King's Arms Inn, on the north-west side of Crutched Friars (Hatton, 1708), and The King's Arms Tavern, on the south side of Newgate Street (Strype, 1720). The Count may have meant King's Coffee House, a very low place. " What rake is ignorant of King's Coffee House " (Fielding, Prologue to *The Great Covent Garden Tragedy,* 1732). But this was the resort " of all gentlemen to whom beds are unknown." There was also the King's Head in Fenchurch Street, where Queen Elizabeth is said to have spent a night. There was again the King's Arms stairs, opposite Whitehall and Whitehall stairs. Most likely, however, is the King's Head at Chancery-Lane-End, the tavern owned by Ned Ward himself, " The best of all *Vintners* that ever God made."

p. 210. *smoaky,* suspicious. See note *ante.*

p. 211. *a toast,* actually a piece of toast in our sense of the word: defined as " bread dried and put into liquor," by Johnson. Cf. Pope:

> Some squire, perhaps, you may delight to rack,
> Whose game is whisk, whose treat a toast in sack.

Whist in those days did not hold its own with ombre and quadrille.

p. 211. *Pipe.* See notes to *The Provok'd Wife.*

p. 213. *Perch.* This word was sometimes used for the pole, but usually as now for the narrow platform to which the swingle-trees are attached, on which the driver can put his feet, and which bears on the axle: " Just at Holborne-conduit the bolt broke that holds the fore-wheels to the perch " (*Pepys,* 6 February, 1689). Cf. Dryden:

> For the narrow perch I cannot ride.

p. 214. *at Cards for Kisses.* Perhaps a reminiscence of Lyly's

> Cupid and my Campaspe played
> At cards for kisses

though it is doubtful if the sport has gone out even now. " Kisses " were also small cakes.

p. 221. *their Tails hang from their Head.* About this time the full-bottomed wigs began to disappear, to make way for the queue. Usually, however, the bottom was carried in a bag. The real pig-tail did not come in till the '70's, in spite of Sir Francis's remark in Act V.

p. 221. *Powder-Puffs.* See notes to *The Relapse.*

p. 226. *Quadrille,* a game of cards, and thus a refinement upon Lady Wronghead's hazard. It was ousting ombre as a fashionable game. Cf. Swift:

> My Lady Club will take it ill
> If he should fail her at quadrille.
>
> *Elegy on the Death of Dr. Swift.*

p. 226. *white Flambeaux,* that is, wax as opposed to pitch links.

p. 228. *dickens!* This apparent modernism appears as early as 1598. Perhaps a contraction of devilkins, but perhaps from Dickon, Richard. Congreve uses it, as well as Vanbrugh in other plays.

p. 229. *the lions,* at the Tower, which contained lions, tigers, hyenas, etc.: being, in fact, the Zoological Gardens of the time. "There is that *Royal Palace* where the King of Beasts keeps his Court, and may every day, at a proper distance, be seen at Dinner without danger; tho', like the Czar of Muscovy, if you stare at him too near, he'll be apt to do you mischief." *The London Spy,* XIII.

The Moors first presented Charles II with lions in connection with Tangier.

p. 235. *Basset.* A card game imported from Venice.

p. 239. *sneaker,* "a small vessel of drink" (Johnson). He quotes a passage from the *Spectator* about "a sneaker of five gallons."

p. 240. *blue Riband,* namely, the Garter.

p. 241. *temper:* temperance, moderation. Cf. *Pepys,* 26 February, 1666: "... My wife and I fell out. But with much ado to sleep again, I beginning to practice more temper, and to give her her way." And *The Way of the World* (1700) V, iv, Ed. 1710: "More Temper would look more like Innocence."

p. 246. *menager;* a vague Gallicism.

p. 247. *Pistole.* This was a Spanish gold coin in common use in the early seventeenth century. It was becoming scarce, because in 1686 Charles II of Spain raised its value by 25 per cent to try to prevent the exportation of gold. The guinea was shortly afterwards introduced, but had only been recently standardised at 21 shillings under Newton's regime at the Mint. Pistole was also used as a name for the French *louis d'or,* value about 17 shillings.

p. 249. *this Adultery of the Mind.* The question of divorce for incompatibility of temper had of course been raised by Milton in his essay on the subject, and mentioned by Halifax in *Advice to a Daughter* (1686); but on the stage it had already been treated by Farquhar in *The Beaux's Stratagem* (1707): "What law can search into the abyss of nature? What evidence can prove the unaccountable disaffections of wedlock? Can a jury sum up the endless aversions that are rooted in our souls, or can a bench give judgment upon antipathies?"

p. 251. *censure*, that is opinion, not necessarily adverse. Its use in this sense is common in the literature of the period. Cf. Congreve's *The Old Batchelour*, IV, v, Ed. 1710: I only beg a favourable censure of this and your *Araminta*.

p. 252. *all my Pleasure was their Pain.* The idea is from Congreve; see the song in *The Way of the World* (1700), III:

> Love's but a Frailty of the Mind
> When 'tis not with Ambition join'd. . . .

> If there's Delight in Love, 'tis when I see
> The Heart which others bleed for, bleed for me.

p. 260. *Mittimus;* a warrant committing a person to prison. To judge from the literature of the period, the public was quite familiar with legal terms. Cf. Congreve: I'll firk *him with a certiorari. The Double Dealer*, II, i (1693). The Widow Blackacre in Wycherley's *The Plain Dealer* (1676) is naturally full of such phrases, and the audience was expected to know what covert-baron meant.

p. 260. *Noose.* The penalty for forgery was hanging.

p. 264. *The Words and Musick by Mr. Carey.* Henry Carey (*c.* 1690–1743), who liked to be thought the illegitimate son of George Savile, Marquis of Halifax, was a member of Addison's " little senate." Poet and musician, he wrote *The Contrivances* (1715); *Amelia* (1732); *The Tragedy of Chrononhotonthologos:* Being the most Tragical Tragedy, that ever was Tragediz'd by any Company of Tragedians (1734); and several other plays and burlesques. He coined the word namby-pamby at the expense of Ambrose Philips, and was long credited with the music of *God Save the King.* He was supposed to have committed suicide, but not before having issue, by whom he became great-grandfather to Edmund Kean.